ABSTRACTS

of

BLACK CAB LORE

A History of the London Cab Driver

Sean Farrell

Cover artwork – Paul Osborne

Driver – Dave Curnick

Dedicated to the memory of Jim Farrell and Billy Osborne

they both said this would happen one day.

CONTENTS

ACKNOWLEDGMENTS

Whilst this work is primarily my own, and I alone take responsibility for any errors within, I would like to give my grateful thanks to two taxi drivers, Malcolm Linskey and Alan Fisher. Between them they have nearly a century of experience – and much of that experience they have shared with me, whether as oral knowledge or in their generosity with their trade related ephemera I was fortunate to receive from each. I thank them sincerely.

Also, thanks should be extended to my wife, Kay, and children Dan & Jess, not only for putting up with me, but for being there.

Sean Farrell

.

Introduction

"Who is it that hunts in a pack but is unseen by all?" A riddle poised by Benedict Cumberbatch's Sherlock Holmes, in BBC TV's *Sherlock*, *A Study in Pink*. The answer was of course a taxi driver. He drives around London all day searching for fares, surrounded by hundreds of other taxi drivers doing likewise; his vehicle is iconic, known throughout the world but the man behind the steering wheel is something of a mystery. In one form or another, cab drivers have been hunting for work on the streets of London for over four hundred years but remain elusive to historians. We know the names of thirteen of the first Master Hackney Coachmen who were licensed in 1654, these were owners of hackney coaches. We also know the names of "The 400", also Master Hackney Coachmen, this time from 1662. Many would today be described as owner-drivers but the names of any of their "servants", today's journeymen, who drove for them, are lost in time. Even that great chronicler of the time, Samuel Pepys, who rode in hundreds of hackney coaches during the period he kept a diary, only records the names of three hackney coachmen, and then only because he knew them from a time they were not driving a coach.

The Hackney Coach Office burnt down in 1770 and many of its records were destroyed. Even then, there would not have been records of the drivers, they were not licensed at the time, just the proprietors. From 1800, the drivers had to undergo a form of registration but the system itself was never rigorously enforced. It is not until 1838 that the first drivers were licensed but even these names are lost to history. No list of drivers from any period has ever been published, or even known to exist. Many records were destroyed during the Blitz and the authorities, whether in the guise of the Metropolitan Police's Public Carriage Office (PCO), or Taxi & Private Hire at Transport for London (TfL), systematically destroy all documents that are no longer relevant. Even the drivers of today, despite the wealth of information supplied by the internet and social media, will be an unknown entity. All records are computerised and the Data Protection Act ensures that all such entries remain confidential.

Cab drivers are like shooting stars. They may burn bright in the filament, whether famously or infamously, and are then forgotten, lost in time. There are exceptions, but not many. Ask someone today to name a London cab driver that is not related to them, they may come up with Fred Housego - Fred won BBC TV's *Mastermind* competition back in 1982 and has remained in the public eye ever since. Though his appearances on TV and radio have diminished, so too has the memory of him. But he's had a good run. How many know the name of Fred Borders? He also received nationwide acclaim after winning Hughie Green's *Double Your Money* television show in 1958. His skill as a mathematical genius brought him overnight fame (or to be precise, over two nights) but he too returned to the mists of obscurity and it was only his death after swallowing cyanide in 1960, that his name was pushed once more into the public arena.

When Frederick Hitch died in January 1913 (and it should be said that not all cab drivers were called Fred), several hundred people followed his coffin as it was slowly conveyed through the streets of Chiswick. Thousands more lined those streets to pay their respect, not to a king or a major statesman but a taxicab driver. It was his life before he entered the trade that won the heart of the public, when, in 1879, he fought at the Battle of Rorke's Drift and was awarded a Victoria Cross. Hitch, the 'cab driver VC', was immortalised in Cy Enfield's 1963 classic film, *Zulu*, but the film does nothing towards showing the valour he played in his part of the defence. His portrayal in that film, like that of cab drivers in history, is all but written out.

Even taxi drivers themselves appear to want to forget about their colleagues. In the opening chapter of *Cab Sir?* (1939), Herbert Hodge warns the reader that there will be no names, other than the occasional nickname, mentioned in his book. Hodge has been described as the "Philosophical Cabby" following his talks on the radio before and after the war. He remains, to date, the only London taxi driver to have been a castaway on BBC Radio's *Desert Island Discs*, but like the other cab drivers he cares not to mention in his books, he is all but forgotten, except by a few.

When Maurice Levinson wrote *Taxi!* in 1963, an angst-ridden autobiographical account of his life as a taxi driver, he does not identify a single fellow cabbie by name, not even his brother. He fairs slightly better in *The Taxi Game*, written ten years later. Now resigned to being a taxi driver, he gives a much better account of the trade and names a number of individuals prominent in the trade at the time – as well as his own brother who talked him into becoming a taxi driver in the first place.

Philip Warren's *History of the London Cab Trade*, Trevor May's *Gondola's and Growlers* and Bill Munro's *London Taxis: A Full History*, have all covered the trade in depth but in each of these, the driver himself is largely a peripheral figure.

This history attempts to redress the balance. Using newspaper archives as my main source of reference I have compiled a large number of these for the present history. I make no apologies for the heavy emphasis placed on the Victorian cabbie, after all, most of the laws that a driver has to abide by today were formulated in the nineteenth century. That, and the almost unlimited supply of court reports that seemed to keep the Victorian newspaper reader happy, but which went into rapid decline after the First World War, is a veritable feast for the trade historian.

As a framework for this history I have utilised the *Abstract of Laws* that every cab driver has been issued with since 1838. The *Abstract of Laws relating to Cab Drivers within the Metropolitan Police District and City of London*, hereinafter called the *Abstract of Laws*, or, more familiarly, the *Abstract*, may seem dull and boring to the cab driver who is about to enter the world for the first time but within its pages is a reminder, which TfL call a 'general guidance', of the laws in place. Having spent several years on the Knowledge learning thousands of streets and thousands of points of interest, the butterboy/girl now has to be aware of at least twenty-five Acts of Parliament, which, unreassuringly from TfL, is "not an exhaustive or definitive statement of the laws governing the use of taxis." In other words, there is a lot more out there that the cab driver has to know. If a cab driver falls foul of the law and is before a magistrate or judge, with badge and licence with him (as required by the Hackney Carriages Act 1843) they cannot cite ignorance of the law as a defence, as the publication of the *Abstract* negates any such response, no matter if the infringement is covered by the Hackney Carriage Act of 1831 (the oldest legislation cited in the *Abstract*) or the Equality Act 2010 (the most recent). A cab driver also has to be aware of such legislation as the Vehicle Excise Act 1971, and the Public Health (Control of Diseases) Act 1984, and the Disability Discrimination Act 1995. After spending several years on the knowledge, a taxi driver might ponder if their time would have been better spent at law school.

Not wishing to burden the reader with a book twice the size as the present one, I have removed several chapters and ignored several of the regulations within the chapters I do include. The chapters appear in the same order as they do within the *Abstract*, except for those regarding "Taximeters" and "Fares" which I have reversed in the interests of chronology. Whilst on the subject of chronology – to all those who like their history linear and chronological (like I myself do) then I offer apologies now. What follows is a series of thematic histories which, in combination, cover much of the history of the London taxi trade. Each of the chapters may be chronological within that chapter but could well have a different timeline when compared to the chapters before and after it. There are also a large number of footnotes within this book. These are merely references for anybody wishing to look up the article quoted; for the casual reader, all the footnotes can be ignored. All chapter headings (excluding chapter numbers, sub-headings and italicised entries are, unless otherwise stated, taken from the 2013 *Abstract of Law* issued by Transport for London.

For the uninitiated, a word might be expressed on the evolution of the taxi and of the old style of money.

Hackney coaches were the earliest form of hackney carriage (itself a generic term that has survived 400 years), which had four wheels and was pulled by at least two, sometimes four horses. Hackney chariots appeared around 1820. They were a smaller version of the coach, again with four wheels but could be pulled by one horse (usually) or two (very rarely). Cabs started off around the same time and at first were very unpopular with the drivers, because they charged less per mile than the coaches or chariots. Originally called cabriolets, after their collapsible roof, the shortened form of 'cab' soon became prominent – in terms of both numbers and the vernacular. There were originally several types of cab, with the Hansom cab becoming the most popular. Perhaps for reasons that the Hansom cab had very little to do with its original designer, Joseph Hansom, it began to lose its eponymy and for a while was downgraded to being just a hansom cab, and then just a cab. Whilst it is most likely true that a driver of a four-wheeler, or a Growler as they were more popularly known, would not describe himself as a cab driver, and vice versa, the press had no problem describing every hackney carriage as a cab, so synonymous had the term become. I have made it clear in several episodes that although the vehicle is described as a 'cab' (two wheels), it is in fact a four-wheeled hackney coach. To avoid repetition I've have only done this a few times and left the others as they were. It makes little difference to the story.

The first motor cabs were called just that – motor cabs. The term still survives on a cab drivers' licence, his Bill, which is his Motor Cab Licence. Once the motor cabs were fitted with taximeters they were described as "taximeter motor cabs", which eventually was abridged to 'taxi'. Perhaps the evolution is still continuing as many members of the public, and less so the drivers, refer to a London taxi as a "black cab" - no matter what their colour.

In 1971 Britain went decimal and many a schoolchild was thankful that calculations were now based on the number of fingers we had and not on the imperial system of a dozen pennies to the shilling. Not wishing to bore the reader with futile conversions within the text, the following should suffice:

1d =   one penny

12d =   one shilling (1s)   =   5p

20s =   one pound (£1)   =   a sovereign

21s =   one guinea (1gn)

1 Taxi Drivers' Licences and Badges

Taxi drivers to be licensed, wear badge and display identifiers

Every taxi driver in the Metropolitan Police District and the City of London must hold a licence issued to him by TfL, and he must at all times when working as a taxi driver wear a numbered badge issued by TfL and have in his possession a copy of his licence.

Whether you take as your starting point, c.1600 when the first fare paying passengers began using hackney coaches, or 1634 when Captain Baily ranked up his four coaches in the Strand, or 1654 when Oliver Cromwell first "legitimised" hackney coaches by licensing the owners, the fact remains that for most of the history of the licensed cab trade, the drivers themselves have been unlicensed. For at least two centuries, the various powers considered that there was no need for such a system.

From 1662 every hackney carriage had at least a unique number, sometimes even the name and address of the proprietor, upon it. Any dispute, whether it be between the driver and the passenger, or the driver and a pedestrian or even another road user, all one had to do was take the number of the coach and report it to whatever body was in charge. From 1687 it would have been the Hackney Coach Office and from 1832 the Stamp Office, a defunct adjunct of the Treasury. If a summons was to be issued it would be issued in the name of the proprietor, a master hackney coachman. If the owner was a master, then, by definition, whoever worked for him was a servant. If the driver had infringed the law in any way, it was up to the master either to stand before a magistrate himself or produce the driver. In many ways it made sense. Drivers lived from day to day, they had no assets and, for a large number of them, the only roof they had over their head was usually never permanent. The Master had assets. A hackney coach and at least two horses, usually more for the more conscientious master. The coach, horses, harness and stable had material worth with which loans could be secured. If a driver was sued for damage done to another vehicle, it was the master who would have to pay, and then he in turn could sue his driver - albeit a pointless exercise given that he would know his servant had no money. Many masters did exactly that, especially those who had more than one driver

And so the situation persisted for the next two centuries. There was never any apparent need to change anything, as, for the most part, the system worked. There was no compulsion on the part of the master to name his driver, though not to do so could see the master standing trial and being found guilty for an offence committed by his driver. Even so, the only people who were not happy with the situation were the masters themselves. In many cases they were levied with a fine, to which they in turn would summons the driver. Invariably the driver could not pay the fine so he would be locked up in default – leaving the master out of pocket and possibly with a cab in the yard without a driver. Even up to and including the first few years when the drivers were licensed, driving a hackney coach or cab was never an occupation for most men. It was a way of getting ready money, which in most cases was spent in an ale house whilst the horse and cab were sitting on a nearby rank.

Although not licensed, from about 1800 drivers had at least to be registered with a central office,[1] at, of all places, the Sewers Office. The Sewers Office was responsible for the pipes and gulleys, as well as the paving of the streets, and was paid for from licence fees of public vehicles as well as carts and drays. Proprietors could be fined for each driver they failed to register. Given the transient nature of driving a hackney coach at the time, many proprietors never bothered. In 1826 a master produced his driver at the Hackney Coach Office in Essex Street to answer a charge of theft. The driver was later found guilty at the Old Bailey and sentenced to transportation for seven years. The master however was fined £2 for not having registered him in the first place.

August 1828 saw a large meeting of hackney coach proprietors held at the Hercules Pillars tavern in Great Queen Street. Though their main grievance at the time was the rise in cabriolets, two wheeled cabs pulled by one horse, with a tariff that was two-thirds that of a coach, they called for the dismissal of the Hackney Coach Commissioners and the introduction of licensing of the drivers. They complained that under the present system they had no control over their drivers, "therefore the public must expect to be plundered...By their all being licensed, a sufficient check would be obtained over their character."[2] Despite their continuing calls and petitions to Parliament to bring about change, nothing happened.

In 1829 when a particular driver overcharged, the number of the hackney coach was taken and a summons was duly issued. In court was the driver's master, a proprietor by the name of Jacobs. He explained that whilst he was "excessively sorry" but when he gave his driver the first summons, he simply disappeared and had not been seen since. As the original summons had not been answered, a second one was taken out and the master now had to appear in place of the driver. The magistrate ordered that the master be fined 10s for the overcharging, plus 7s 6d costs. Jacobs explained that the driver had only brought him in 9s for that day's work "and he thought it very hard that he should have to pay 17s 6d out of it." The magistrate, Conant, replied that if the "delinquent had been before him, he should not have escaped so easily." It was a lesson to all proprietors to employ steady men as their drivers. Jacobs "paid the fine, and retired much dissatisfied with the issue of the day's work."[3]

Francis Roe owned ten cabs in 1830; in 1834, with presumably a similar size fleet, he informed an inquest jury that as many as 1000 drivers might pass through his stable every year, such was the nature of being a hackneyman. He would dismiss a driver for "coming home short", not having earned enough money to pay for the daily rental of the horse and cab; and that driver would go and take another cab out the following day from another proprietor and so on. The men used false names, false addresses and false characters; there was no way of checking each of them. Eventually the same driver, having done the rounds would end up back at Roe's, usually with a different name but looking for another chance of a day's casual labour at his expense.

Roe is an important, albeit fleeting, figure within the cab trade in the nineteenth century and was an early advocate of driver licensing. In 1832 he called for a minimum age of drivers and for them to be licensed following the death of Lady Barham - the driver responsible for her death was just 15 years old. At another inquest hearing in 1834, Roe admitted to the jury that he could not find the driver of the cab who, whilst driving furiously, upset the cab enough for the passenger to be thrown out into the street and fatally injured. Such accidents were none too rare given the condition of the roads, the speed of the cabs and, in many instances, the inebriation of the driver. In this instance, the passenger was thrown out but the driver, of whom it was believed must have been aware of the accident, did not stop but drove his horse on with the whip. The number of the cab was taken, hence Roe's appearance. Despite the disappearance of the driver, Roe informed the jury that it was not one of his men, whom he could not rate low enough, "because if it had been, the fellow would probably have left the cab in the street and made off." According to the court reporter "[Roe] informed them that no man could have a worse opinion of these men than he had, and if the Jury could only witness one half of their conduct which he did, they would be fully convinced they were the worst set of scoundrels God Almighty ever created and, worst of all, the Government would do nothing to get rid of the public nuisance."[4]

A court case in September 1833 highlighted how one master, named Stevens, did produce his driver "after considerable difficulty." The driver, J Gambler, had charged a man 2s 6d for a journey from Temple Bar to the Saracen's Head in Snow Hill, when the legal fare was only 1s 6d. The Saracen's Head was a famous coaching inn, and he may have hoped, that rather than miss the departure of a coach, or a seat inside the coach, the passenger would not have time to argue the matter. He was wrong to assume this. The number of the coach was taken and a summons was issued, and promptly ignored, as was a second one. The usual practice after two summons had been ignored was to issue a warrant, and it was the search for Gambler at this stage in the proceedings that caused the arresting officer "considerable difficulty" in detaining him, but he was taken that morning and now appeared in court. Gambler admitted to the overcharge and gave no mitigating circumstances which led him to do it. Minshull, the magistrate, called it a "gross case" and fined Gambler 30s plus 16s 6d in costs, which his master, Stevens, had to pay. Gambler was not home and dry. Stevens then immediately sued him for 46s 6d, which of course Gambler could not pay. He was locked up in default for three weeks in the House of Correction.[5] To those who wished to maintain the status quo of the proprietor being responsible for the actions of the driver, it was a perfect example of how the system worked and there was no need to go down the path of licensing drivers.

In 1836 Colonel Charles De Laet Waldo Sibthorpe, member of Parliament for Lincoln proposed to the House of Commons that all drivers of cabriolets should wear a badge "to distinguish them". Presumably Sibthorpe had in mind all hackney carriage drivers but the rise in the use of the cab in London had been so tremendous that a high proportion of drivers were now cabmen and not coachmen. Sibthorpe was no stranger to the cab trade of London. Three years previously, in 1833, he brought a charge of obstruction against cab driver William England. "The Gallant Colonel", as the newspaper and fellow members of the Commons called him, told Dyer the magistrate, that William England had jumped down from his cab, grabbed hold of his horse's head and refused to let him go. Not being given any reason for the actions of the driver by Sibthorpe, the magistrate asked England to explain himself. England stated that he was coming out of Haymarket and turned into Pall Mall at a rate of about three miles an hour. He was then overtaken by Sibthorpe's cabriolet and, as he passed, England said he was struck across the face by Sibthorpe's whip and "Not wishing to be horsewhipped tamely, especially as [I] was on the right side of the road, [I] jumped down and stopped the complainant's horse." England demanded the name and address of the person who whipped him, but instead, Sibthorpe called over a policeman. The constable had no problem in deciding between a 'Gallant Colonel' who was a member of Parliament, and a common cabman. He came down on the side of principle and arrested the cabman for obstruction. Fortunately for William England, Dyer, who once stated in court that he would not shirk from his duty of coming down hard on transgressing cabmen, actually sided with the cabman and dismissed the charge against him.[6]

Having said that the conduct of hackney coach and cabmen was generally of the most insolent description, Sibthorpe was now on the attack by his proposal for cabmen to wear a badge. The idea of wearing a badge was not universally approved of. Thames watermen had to wear one, as did the porters in Smithfield Market. The Act of 1831 brought in badges for the watermen and their assistants at cab stands. The wearing of a badge carried with it opprobrium that the wearer was nothing short of a criminal. Many believed that cab drivers already were of the criminal class but Alderman Wood, whose bill for regulating hackney carriages in London was under discussion in Parliament had already looked into the matter. Wood informed the 'Gallant Colonel' that the idea of badges for cab drivers had been proposed in his bill the previous year but was generally disapproved of by the House. For many MP's, the idea of a badge was becoming more acceptable but there were still those that believed that making a cab driver pay 5s a year for the ignominy of wearing one was going too far.

The Standard newspaper described Alderman Wood's proposed bill (he was also MP for the City of London) as being highly advantageous to "those most abominable of all nuisances, omnibuses" whilst being completely vexatious towards hackney coaches and cabs. The editor, somewhat surprising given the number of court cases his paper reported on, stated that with the cabmen of London, "we can say with perfect truth, that we have never met, in any rank of life, a class of men more uniformly contented with their hire, and more respectful, when treated with the consideration due from every man to every other man in the intercourse of life."[7] Such praise does not come along often from the press. Alderman Wood came in for heavy criticism and the idea of the cabmen having to wear a badge and pay a 5s fee every year for the privilege, raised the question whether England was still a free country or under the rule of a despot.

Emblin was another proprietor who wished for a better class of driver, and one that was licensed. In May 1838, a three-year old girl was hit by a cab in Gray's Inn Road, the horse was seen to kick her head and one of the wheels went over her. Emblin admitted that he was the owner of the cabriolet, number 1302, but he had since found out that the man he had hired it to, had let another man drive the cab for a few hours (these bucks, as they were called, will be discussed later in this chapter). Neither of the two men could subsequently be located. The mother, in reply to the magistrate, said that her daughter was in great pain, and she was afraid that she might not survive. Emblin reiterated that he had used every effort to locate the driver, but could not find him. "You," said Rogers the magistrate, "are responsible for his conduct." Having then conveyed to Emblin that he could be punished for the action of his driver, he turned on the parents of the girl; "I must say that it is highly improper for parents to suffer such children to stroll about the streets to run such risks, as it is well known that cabriolet drivers were quite reckless as to the lives of men or children." To emphasise his point, it later transpired that the father of the girl had been knocked down in similar circumstances and had only just been released from hospital. He appeared in court on crutches. Rogers informed Emblin that unless he came to some arrangement with the parents, he would be fined 40s and costs. Emblin was not exactly overly generous in his compensation offer. Knowing he was to be fined £2 he offered this to the parents and agreed to pay the doctor's bills as well. The compensation was accepted and the summons was dismissed.[8]

Although Alderman Wood was the prime mover of the 1838 Hackney Carriages (Metropolitan) Act, credit for establishing the licences, badges and *Abstract* not only for the hackney coach and cabmen but omnibus drivers and their conductors should go to Daniel Whittle Harvey. In 1838 Harvey, already the MP for Southwark, was also appointed the first Commissioner of Metropolitan Carriages, with an office in Adam Street, off the Strand. He turned down the offer of the salary that went with the position, having made a fortune from establishing, and selling on, *The Sunday Times,* and marrying a wife who brought with her a dowry of £30,000, he was not leaving himself short. Harvey took to the role assiduously. During the summer of 1838 (his entry in the *Dictionary of National Biography* wrongly states that he took up the post in 1839) Harvey gave out over six thousand applications for licences as hackneymen, metropolitan stage-men (bus drivers) and their conductors, as well as to the previously licensed watermen on the cab stands. All applicants had to have a character reference signed by at least two rate payers who had known the applicant for at least a year. As the number of applications exceeded the number of licences issued by more than 2000, Harvey saw this as a successful method of weeding out undesirables. Although he had been given access to the criminal records of the applicants, Harvey would not have it on his conscience that he denied a man and his family an income for a previous misdemeanour. If a previous miscreant had fallen foul of the law it was not for him to say that that person was more prudent having once been punished. There were a few applicants who had only recently been up before a magistrate and were punished. Harvey personally interviewed each one of these before allowing their application to continue. He informed them that any such recurrence of bad behaviour would see the badge and licence forfeited. On the rear of every licence he entered the admonition, so that any magistrate could see the man's character, if need be, in the near future. These were the first endorsements to appear on cab licences.

When the Act passed into law on Sunday 7th October 1838, Harvey and his team of clerks began the momentous task of issuing the licences and badges. Harvey began working 14-hour shifts from Wednesday 3rd through to Saturday 6th October, followed by a seven-hour working day on the Sunday. During the whole of that period he, allegedly, personally interviewed every applicant and filled in details of their licence. Every driver had to attend in person as Harvey would record their name, height, age, eye colour, hair colour, complexion and the name and address of the applicants last employer. All these details were entered on the 'certificate', the licence. By Saturday, over 2000 applications had been processed and a further 1,500 were awaiting delivery to the successful applicants. No doubt mistakes were made.

In what was to the first case of a licensed driver in court, though as a complainant and not a defendant, Thomas Jackson, who was described by the court reporter as a "droll-looking fellow of diminutive stature" had his description of himself on the licence questioned by the magistrate, Hoskins.

Mr Hoskins: (inspecting [the licence]) "You do not mean to say that you are five feet ten, the height put down here?"

Jackson: "No, your vership; that's a mistake of Sir Wittol Harvey's; I never measured more than four feet ten in my purfessional wooden clogs."

Mr Hoskins: "It's a mistake of one foot then?"

Jackson: "Purcisely so."

Mr Phillips (the clerk): "And that's not the only error. You are described as having a prominent nose and light grey eyes, whereas your nose is very small, and your eyes apparently black."

Jackson (stroking his chin): "Wot signifies that 'ere. I'm the hindividual meant and no mistake; and if Sir Wittol has drawd it wrong on the paper, vy, he must halter me, and that's all about it, or return the five bob I paid him for doing it."

Although Jackson was the complainant, the magistrate informed him that his licence would be retained so as to be amended. Jackson took the badge from his neck, which according to the newly issued *Abstract of Laws*, every driver has to wear when in court, and exclaimed, "Here, take this too; it's no use without the licence".[9]

The difference may not have been due to a mistake on the part of Harvey. There is no guarantee that Jackson actually went up before the Registrar, he may have had a friend to impersonate him especially if Jackson, whose master said he liked a drink, felt he was too intoxicated to undergo an interview.

Despite successfully organising the biggest upheaval in hackney carriage history, Daniel Whittle Harvey was forced to relinquish his post the following January. Though he had took on the role of Registrar as unpaid, his political enemies, and he had a few, were gunning for him. In order to preserve his seat as MP for Southwark he had to relinquish his position. He did eventually give up his Southwark seat in 1840 when he became the first Commissioner of the City of London Police, a position he maintained until his death at his home in Old Jewry, in 1863. Harvey is a forgotten figure within the hackney cab trade. He set the bar high for those that followed and although it was a painfully slow process at times he managed to rid the trade of the large criminal element that had infested it for the previous two centuries. The reputation of the modern London taxi trade, regularly voted as the best in the world, owes not a little to Daniel Whittle Harvey.

Along with the licence, came the badge. The first badges were made from bronze and therefore quite a weight to suspend from one's neck for a whole day. The most prominent feature on them was not the number but the letters VR, denoting the badge was issued during the reign of Queen Victoria. The watermen on the cab stands, who had first been badged back in 1831, had a similar designed badge but with WR upon them. Following the death of William IV and the accession of Victoria, these badges had to be recalled and new ones issued. Despite the costs involved whenever the monarchy changed, the practice of the epigram continued for some time, though with a young queen on the throne it was perhaps wise to believe she would have a long reign. The number itself was situated under the epigram and could only be inspected from close quarters but it was the weight of the badge that caused the biggest problems, and not just for the drivers.

In August 1842, Edward Lowrie, badge number 5577, parked his cab on a stand in Baker Street by Madame Tussaud's (then situated in Baker Street before moving to Marylebone Road in 1884). He later stated that a previous passenger had treated him to some brandy and he went into the cab to sleep off the intoxicating effects. Sometime later, PC Berry was doing his rounds and seeing the slumbering cabman tried to arouse him and get him to move on. He was unsuccessful but at that moment Inspector Black and police sergeant Burke happened to chance upon the scene. They too were unsuccessful in awaking Lowrie, no doubt much to the amusement of the other drivers on the stand. Black told Berry to climb upon the box and drive the cab to the station house, where, no doubt, Lowrie would be placed in a cell and charged with drunkenness and his cab would be taken to a green yard (the equivalent of a car pound). As PC Berry climbed up, one of the cabmen on the rank shouted out to Lowrie to wake up. This had the desired effect, Lowrie rose from his slumber, no doubt thinking that the shout was for a job, but was faced with one person on the box about to drive his cab, and two others by the side of his cab. Lowrie jumped out of the cab and immediately struck the inspector, sending him crashing against some railings. Lowrie then turned his attention to sergeant Burke and knocked him to the ground. As the two struggled, Burke was heard to cry out "Oh God, he's biting my leg". Inspector Black picked himself up and went to Burke's assistance but he was struck in the face by a stick that Lowrie was suddenly wielding. As he lay down on the street, Lowrie kicked him in the head.

By this time constable Berry joined in the affray, after getting a bystander to hold the horse, but he too was smashed over the head with the heavy stick brandished by Lowrie. A passing pedestrian joined in and managed to grab hold of Lowrie from behind and managed to get him down on the ground, at the cost of Lowrie nearly biting one of his fingers completely off. It transpired that Lowrie had not armed himself with a stick. He had taken the heavy bronze badge from his neck and with the leather strap had wielded it with frenzy.

In Marylebone police court the following morning constable Berry appeared in the witness box with his head covered in plaster, sergeant Burke could only walk to the witness box with great difficulty and inspector Black testified that the police surgeon had informed him that if Lowrie's boot had been an inch lower, his jaw would have been broken. Lowrie pleaded with the magistrate, Rawlinson, for a lenient sentence as he had a wife and family to support. For the attack on the pedestrian Lowrie was fined 50s which was defaulted on being unable to pay to two month's imprisonment. For the combined attack on the police officers, no fine was imposed but the apparently 'lighter' sentence of one month's imprisonment was handed down. The sentencing was however consecutive. No mention is made of his licence but it is unlikely he would ever legally drive a cab again.[10]

After just six years, from June 1st (the day in the calendar when all driver's licences were renewed) 1844, new badges were issued to the drivers. The new ones were, much to the delight of policemen as well as cabmen, lighter than the originals, the badge number was much larger and the initials VR were dropped in favour of a Crown. It was alleged that the new design was prompted by reports of the large number of unfit people who held a badge illegally. The drivers were given the new badge when they handed in their old one and the police were informed that they could seize the badge of any driver wearing an old style one. It is doubtful if the issue of new badges had the desired effect; six years later it was stated at a meeting of the trade in the Temperance Hall in Westminster, that there were 800 badges "working foul…by the lowest and most degraded characters."[11] It was seen as an aim of the foundling Protective Association, the formation of which prompted the mass meeting, to detect and punish such offenders. Not for the first, nor last, time, did the trade have little belief that the authorities could actually police the trade.

One driver who very much resented wearing a badge was Thomas Whetton. In February 1846 he was summoned by Captain Gay of the telegraph office at the Admiralty in Whitehall. Gay testified that Whetton was "lounging on the box and reading a book" with his cab blocking the entrance to the Telegraph Office. An argument between the cabman and the Captain ensued when the naval officer grabbed the cab horse's head and backed it up a little. "Damn you," shouted Whetton, "What business have you to touch my horse's head? Do you know that that horse is worth more than you and all your breed, seed, and generation, put together? Who the Devil let you out?" Gay tried to obtain Whetton's badge number but the cabman manoeuvred his cab to prevent divesting the information. When Gay threatened to get a policeman to get the badge number, Whetton apparently lifted up the skirt of his coat and pointing to his backside and cried out "Here it is." Eventually a policeman came upon the scene and Whetton was forced to give up his number to the captain. In his defence, Whetton refused to ask Captain Gay any questions over his version of events, but he did address the magistrate. "Has not a cabman a right to enjoy his book whilst sitting on his dickey, without being roused and disturbed by people who call themselves gentlemen...I am a man who am [sic] fitted for better things than driving cabs; I have had a first rate education, and I know that because I wear a badge, I am not considered worthy of belief, either here or elsewhere, the sin of my badge is upon me; and I know it is of no use my saying anything here." He was right. The magistrate had no doubt that the captain's version of events was a true account and fined Whetton twenty shillings or fourteen day's hard labour in the House of Correction. Whetton counted out the money in the dock and marched off, according to the court reporter "a martyr to the cause of the cabmen."[12]

In 1862 a large meeting of cabmen from across London met to discuss several grievances that faced the trade. One of which was the law requiring them to wear a metal badge, which they wanted replaced with a certificate. Whether the certificate had to be worn round the neck or affixed to the cab was not reported. That the motion was carried shows that after nearly a quarter of a century following the introduction of the metal badge, it was still seen as a slur upon the character of the cabmen of London. Two months later the same body of men were still calling for the badge to be abolished "it being no proof that the driver wearing it is the person duly licensed, and that in its place a certificate containing the description of the person licensed… which he shall produce when called upon."[13] In 1865 *The Standard* was reporting that "…while the badge is a great annoyance to those who are compelled to wear it, it really affords no protection to the public, but rather favours personation. The men would carry a sort of "passport" or certificate, to be produced when required, and which should contain a personal description of the licensed driver, so as to guard against temporary transfer of the privilege."[14] What was being asked for was basically the "copy licence" which, as will be seen, was still over forty years away. Even as late as 1871 in a pamphlet written by an "ex-cabman", who wrote that "cabmen are compelled to wear a badge like a Smithfield drover"[15] showed that there was continual resentment over the metal ticket. It was no wonder the compulsion of having to wear a badge to earn a living was resented by the trade.

Offences

(a) Acting as a taxi driver without a licence and badge.

(b) Transferring or lending a licence to another person.

(c) Permitting any other person to use or wear a badge.

(d) Plying for hire without a licence.

(e) Failing to display badge number and licensed area identifier

In one of the first cases brought under the 1838 Act, Edward Aymer, badge number 5, was before the magistrates charged with allowing another person to drive a hackney cab whilst wearing his badge. A policeman stated that he stopped a cab on Sunday morning and realising that the badge did not belong to the driver seized both. At that moment Aymer appeared and explained to the constable that the young man driving the cab was out of work and wanted a job. In court, Aymer did not deny the charge but told the magistrate that as he himself had been taken ill he was obliged to engage a friend to drive the cab for him. The policeman replied that Aymer had made no mention of being ill, just that his friend was out of work.

Twyford, the magistrate, then correctly asserted that the law had been placed within the new Act to precisely prevent this kind of offence. "bucks" as these part-time drivers were known, were responsible for many of the outrages forced upon passengers and they were completely untraceable. An innocent cabman, though not so innocent if he lent his cab to a buck, would be before a magistrate, charged with an offence he knew nothing about. Aymer was fined 20 shillings, a fine he could not pay so instead found himself locked up for 14 days within the House of Correction. The first licensed driver to be jailed for a hackney carriage offence. Although locked up for a fortnight, Aymer would have been able to find employment when he left prison easily enough as the magistrate, on the grounds that it was a first offence, refused to endorse the licence.[16]

On the same day that Aymer was before a magistrate at Bow Street, William Clarke, a "buck" was in the dock at Worship Street. The police had been warned to be on the lookout for bucks illegally driving cabs and as the transfer between driver and buck usually took place at a stand outside a tavern, then all a policeman had to do was wait and observe, which was probably how Aymer was caught. PC Davies explained to the court that he had stopped cab number 840 outside Shoreditch Church at 6pm. As the badge was by law supposed to be worn in a prominent position and PC Davies could not see one, he felt justified in asking the driver to pull over. On being told that the real driver was at tea, and that he had been given permission to drive the cab, Davies arrested the buck and had the cab taken to a green yard. The cab was later released after the licensed driver paid the fees. To have not done so would have meant going back to his master, not only with short money but minus the horse and cab. Once having paid the fees, that was not the end of the problem for the un-named driver. If he felt the whole episode would not come to the attention of his master, Isaac Nathan, then he was mistaken. The magistrate at Worship Street ordered that Clarke be detained pending bail and Nathan be brought to the court to explain why "he suffered a person other than the one licensed to drive his cabriolet."[17]

As with the relationship between master and driver, the relationship between a driver and a buck was again based on trust and understanding. A driver would allow a buck to 'borrow' the cab for a couple of hours for an agreed price. Within that timeframe the buck would do all he could to raise as much money as he could. If this meant furious driving and overcharging, then so be it. If he had gone back to the driver short, then that driver would not use him again. Drivers had to be choosy who they employed in this illegal activity, they did not want a buck who would drive recklessly and damage the coach, neither would they want a buck being too liberal with the whip, which many were accused of. The buck had to be reliable and agree to return the cab to the driver within a few hours of picking it up. Some drivers asked for a specific sum, others, who knew the buck, would go for a cut, usually around two thirds or even three quarters. There was no outlay for the buck and as harsh as the rates might seem, it did give them at least a chance to earn some money and a good buck could end up working for several drivers in one day and take a few shillings home.

As has been seen, the practice of using a buck was brought to a sudden stop, at least in the eyes of the law, by the Act of 1838. That same Act created a new type of buck that would be harder for the police to catch. These were ex-hackneymen who could not gain regular employment because of drink or continually coming home short etc. John Morgan was one such person who for one reason or another found himself without regular employment. He earned his money as a buck but unlike his fellow bucks, Morgan had a legal badge and licence to drive a hackney carriage, he just could not find an employer to take him on.

The advantage Morgan had to being a buck was that if he was ever pulled up by a policeman, he would only have to show his badge and hope that the policeman was none the wiser. On October 18th 1838 Mrs Sarah Holden, having arrived in London by coach from Orpington, where she stayed for her health, hired Morgan's coach from the stand in Blackman Street (now Borough High Street). She had a reticule (a large purse or small handbag), which contained four sovereigns, 4s 6d in cash and several bottles of medicine. When she arrived at her home in Shoreditch, Morgan and her passenger's brother assisted her in taking all the luggage from the coach. She was charged 2s 6d for the fare, nearly double the actual legal fare but it seems to have been paid without any demurring. It was shortly after Morgan drove off that it was found that the reticule Mrs Holden had placed on a seat in the coach was not with the rest of her belongings.

Having told her husband, Mr Holden went straight to the Worship Street office to report the loss, fortunately for him, his wife had taken the number of the coach, 348. Having reported the loss at Worship Street, Mr Holden then proceeded, along with an officer of the court, James Tilt, to the coach stand in Blackman Street. There, Morgan, badge number 1775, was identified as the driver of the coach but a quick search inside revealed nothing. The hackney coach was owned by a Mr Edmonds whose stables were in the nearby Borough Road. On enquiring there, he found that as far as Edmonds was concerned, the licensed driver of his coach was badge number 3089. Morgan was then arrested to a chorus of cat-calls from his colleagues on the stand who called out "What about the medicine?" which Tilt took to show they all knew about the theft.

In court, Morgan admitted to being a 'buck with a licence', he was doing nothing more than jobbing around. His licence was produced which contained a "reasonably tolerant description of him". The magistrate, Groves, read from the 1838 Act on how heavy penalties could be imposed for allowing an unauthorised person to drive a cab. The Act even specified that the driver or the proprietor would be liable to a heavy fine. To emphasise his point, he noted an article in that morning's paper where a proprietor was fined £10 because the driver had not handed in lost property. Edmonds, the proprietor, fearing that he might himself be fined for the actions of his driver pleaded ignorance of the whole affair until Tilt had informed him of it. Fortunately for him, Tilt had summoned the real driver of the coach to attend court.

James Thomas Watts, badge number 3089, "a smart looking young man" entered the witness box. He denied allowing Morgan to take a fare, just authorising him to attend to his coach whilst he returned some lost property he had found in his cab. He then produced a letter from E. E.

Cope, naming him, as well as his badge number and thanking him for returning the valuables that had been left in his coach the previous night. Mrs Cope hoped that the fact that he had left his coach on a stand whilst he was elsewhere may be forgiven due to the honesty of the driver. Watts may have felt the epistle would be accepted by the magistrate, he himself thought it seemed cast iron and beyond reproach. Groves felt it "...was a rather curious coincidence, that while the driver was honestly returning a bag of valuables which had been left by one lady in his coach the night before, another lady should have lost her bag and money in the same coach." Groves was not so easily duped and held Morgan on remand for further investigation though nothing further appears to have occurred with the case.[18]

Despite the severe penalties being handed out to proprietors and drivers for allowing a buck to use their vehicle, the practice continued and led to problems with identifying drivers, which was exactly why the introduction of the badge was introduced. In November 1838, two summons were granted to two different people for alleged overcharging. In each case the badge number was taken but all to no avail as neither driver could be traced. The public had been told that recording the badge number was sufficient to bring a driver who had broken the law to justice. They were now being told that they should take not only the badge number, but the number of the cab or coach as well. A year later in 1839, a police inspector at Marlborough Street informed the magistrate that tracing drivers was becoming very difficult as they appear to be transferring their badges with one another in order to avoid detection. He further complained that the problem was compounded by the proprietors who were transferring their plates from one vehicle to another, a practice that was allowed should a vehicle become damaged. In October 1841 a pedestrian was seen to keel over and fall to the ground in Holborn. He died shortly after as a policeman was trying to help him. Other than a knife and 3d there was nothing else on the body to identify him except for a cab driver's badge, number 4002, around his neck. Despite this, it was still several days before the body could be identified and even then it was through his description being circulated in the press.

When Everett, a cab proprietor, heard that one of his cabs was being worked by a buck and that the horse was being badly treated, he went off in search of his cab. Given the smaller (by modern standards) size of London in 1841, it was still a formidable task but after having visited several stands he finally found his cab, with the buck driving it, in Pall Mall East. He followed, and as soon as he saw a policeman he had the driver arrested. In court, the buck, John Burches, stated that he was a licensed driver and that he had been asked to look after the cab whilst the real driver took refreshment. This gave the magistrate a problem, there was no provision in the Act of 1838 that forbad a licensed driver to drive a hackney carriage without the owner's consent. Such discrepancies were why the Act of 1838 was repealed and succeeded by the Act of 1843. The driver was licensed and had been handed the cab by the legitimate driver. The magistrate could do no more than inform Everett he should take the prosecution to the County Court where the matter could be addressed satisfactorily. Everett said he would, but does not appear to have pursued the matter.[19]

A few months later another cab proprietor who went in search of a buck who was driving a cab without the proper permission was one of the Isaacs brothers, of Little Warner St, who will feature in several cases in this chapter. Isaacs found his cab, plate number 1917, and questioned the driver as to what right he had to drive it. The buck replied that the real driver had entrusted him with the cab "in order to sort out his own affairs" and that he could be found in Farringdon Street, a short distance from Isaacs's yard. When he located the real driver, he first stated that he left the cab in the care of the buck for just a few minutes but soon after admitted that he allowed the buck to have the cab for several hours. The real driver was probably dismissed from Isaacs's employ and word would have been circulated to other cab proprietors that he was the sort of man who would resort to using a buck. The buck himself appeared at Bow Street and was charged with being in possession of a hackney cabriolet. Isaacs explained to the magistrate, Jardine, that the practice of "bucking" was a major nuisance to him and along with other proprietors he was determined to put a stop to it any way he could. Jardine was in agreement with Isaacs and informed the prisoner that he was to be released on bail to answer the charge at the next Sessions. The buck however could not raise the £10 bail or find the sureties and he was locked up in order to appear at his next sessions.[20]

On Boxing Day 1842, a driver named Fletcher took out a cab at eight in the morning and was to return it at three in the afternoon. When Fletcher failed to return, the foreman of the yard went out in search of him. After several hours, the cab was found on a rank at ten o'clock in the evening. On the box was not Fletcher, but James Neal, a licensed driver with badge number 6311. The foreman hailed him and directed him to go to a specific street. A short distance later, on seeing a policeman, Neal was arrested. In court the following morning it was explained how Neal had been detained, and the court was informed that the horse, which had been worked for fourteen hours, was in a terrible state. It had been whipped so badly that strips of its flesh were hanging off. The foreman reiterated how it was the practice of bucks to earn as much money as they could in the time allotted and this meant driving at speed and recklessly endangering the lives of pedestrians and other road users. The owner of the cab informed Maltby, the magistrate, that only last week a cab of his had been driven by a buck and had ran over a woman who was still in hospital. "It was almost impossible to get hold of the offender, owing to the system." Police Inspector Beresford informed the magistrate that the prisoner was one of a class of men who gave much trouble to the police. They operated outside of the law and were rarely prosecuted. He cited the Haymarket rank (see Chapter 5) as being "in the hands of these bucks, most of whom openly stated that they would not take a situation with a master, as their occupation as bucks was far more profitable."

Maltby was in complete agreement with the witnesses. The use of bucks defeated the purpose of the legislation and that only "men of good character should be permitted to exercise the calling of a hackney carriage driver."[21] There was however a "but" coming. Once again it was noted that whilst the Act of 1838 allows for any person unlawfully driving a hackney carriage to be apprehended, there was no provision of fines or punishment. James Neal would be released on bail, again to be brought before a judge in a county court, but as there had been no conviction thus far, his hackney carriage licence would be returned to him without any endorsement. Though no reason was given, Neal would remain in police custody for a further 24 hours, after which he was free to leave.

The London Hackney Carriages Act of 1843 finally closed the loophole that allowed bucks to escape punishment. Now they could be fined a maximum £5, though perversely, a driver who allowed a buck to use his cab was not covered by the act at all, whilst the proprietors, who as a body were all determined to stamp out the practice, could be fined £10 if they employed an unlicensed driver, however unwittingly.

With the driver only having to suffer the wrath of his master if he was caught employing a buck, the bucks themselves took the risk of arrest and carried on in earnest. In 1847 John Yeoman, a cab proprietor, prosecuted one of his drivers, John Dutch, for allowing a buck to drive his cab. He informed the magistrate at Marlborough Street, Bingham, that he, along with many other cab proprietors were determined to end the practice of "bucking". Yeoman wrongly believed that his driver could be punished with a fine or imprisonment but in this he was in error. The 1843 Act could only fine a driver if he allowed his badge to be used by a buck, there was, as already stated, no provision for lending a cab to a buck. Yeoman did not want his driver fined however. He knew his drivers subscribed to a fund on a daily basis. "Box money", as it was called, was collected in many yards. Some drivers saw it as a further tax, like yard money, which they were enforced to pay on a daily basis. If a driver was fined, then the box money would pay the required amount. Such insurance schemes were frowned upon, particularly by those not involved with them. Yeoman stated that threats and intimidation were used against the men to ensure they subscribed to the scheme. Bingham was hesitant to imprison the cabman, he would have been acting illegally had he done so, he did however suspend John Dutch's cab licence for one month, but he issued a warning to other drivers that in future, he may revoke a cabman's licence indefinitely.[22]

Six weeks later John Yeoman was back at Marlborough Street, this time bringing charges against a buck and calling for the maximum fine of £5 to be levied. Yeoman's solicitor informed the court that "The evils arising to the public and to cab proprietors from the proceeding of men of the description of the prisoner were greater than could be conceived. The bucks were persons of the lowest class, who hang about the different cab-stands for the purpose of taking the licensed driver's place, and by this means of taking every opportunity to commit depredations and break the laws by furious driving. Extortionate charges, foul language and often in addition injuring both horse and cab. The buck was also the principal agent in the removal of stolen property. The cab proprietors were, however, determined to suppress the system of employing bucks, and they hoped to have the assistance of the magistrates in effecting this object." Hardwick, the magistrate at Marlborough Street, fined the defendant £3 which in all probability was defaulted to one month's imprisonment with the proviso that any subsequent offence of a similar nature would see the highest penalty imposed.[23]

In 1850, cab proprietor George Jennings, brought a prosecution against his driver for non-payment of 11s, the daily rental for a cab that the driver, James Bond, had hired. The solicitor acting on behalf of Jennings said the case against the defendant was abundantly clear, but on behalf of his client he wished to bring the attention of the court to a practice, now prevalent, that greatly damaged not only cab proprietors but the general public as well. He continued, "...there were at the present time at least two drivers licensed to every cab, and therefore nearly double the number of drivers that were required. The consequence of this state of things was, that at every watering and night house there were batches of the unemployed in constant attendance, and these fellows exercised such a control over those actually in employment that, with very few exceptions, they were obliged to give them a turn with their cab by day or night, to enable them to support themselves and get drink at the expense of the cab masters." The prosecution against Bond may have been nothing more than a put-up case for Jennings to publicise what he knew to be happening. Jennings did not wish to press for a conviction and the summons was allowed to stand over for a few days as Bond promised to pay back the money he owed.[24]

The following year, 1851, saw Henry Mayhew publish his survey of the working class of London. he believed there were at least "800 to 1000 bucks hanging about the cab stands, and these are mostly regular thieves. If they catch any person asleep or drunk in a cab, they are sure to have a dive into his pockets...they steal from one another while dozing in cabs or tap rooms." Mayhew believed that all the bucks were unlicensed, though they had been cabmen at one time but had been deprived of their licence "through bad conduct". "They are mostly of intemperate habits, being generally 'confirmed sots'. Very few of them are married men…They seldom sleep in a bed. Some few have a bedroom in some obscure part of the town, but the most of them loll about and doze in the tap rooms by day, and sleep in the cabs by night. When the watering-houses shut they resort to the night coffee-shops, and pass the time there until they are wanted as bucks."[25]

Sometimes there were serious consequences of allowing a buck to drive a cab. John Pettitt, licensed cab driver number 13737, picked up a young lady on December 3rd 1859, who having missed the omnibus, wanted to take a cab to her home in Hammersmith. At some point during the journey Pettitt chanced upon a coachman he knew, Charles Taylor. Pettitt invited Taylor up on to the box whilst he climbed into the cab with the young lady. Instead of going to Hammersmith as planned, the destination was changed to Amelia Street, Bermondsey, the home of her mother, where she had spent the previous day. It was only when the suspicions of a policeman were raised that Pettitt and Taylor were arrested. It is difficult to determine what happened to the young lady inside the cab. The newspapers called it a "gross outrage" a euphemism for rape but her own counsel stated that according to the woman, and the medical evidence, she was not actually raped. Her injuries from "Pettitt's violence" was so great she could not attend the original hearing of the case. Pettitt's defence solicitor could show the young woman was not as virtuous as she would like people to believe – she had got off an omnibus earlier that evening arm in arm with a man she had just met. The magistrate, Combe, actually took this into consideration, adding that were it not for the girl's conduct, he would have sent the case for trial. "His conduct as a cab driver was very bad. He had a young woman for a fare, and, instead of driving her as he ought, he engages another man called a 'buck' to drive, and then he got inside and drove about with her, according to his own account, more than two hours." Pettitt had pleaded guilty earlier to indecent assault but Combe said it was not desirable to hear any further evidence "as it would not improve the morals of the public." The heaviest sentence as a magistrate he could lay down was three month's hard labour in the House of Correction.

Before he sentenced Taylor, the defence solicitor argued that Taylor was not a 'buck' as the magistrate had described him, "but a respectable coachman" who was asked to drive a cab by a man he knew. Combe replied that "that made him a 'buck' in every sense of cab phraseology. He had neither licence nor badge." Taylor was perhaps fortunate that he was only suffered to be released on his own recognisances for six months.[26]

William Lodwick was described as "a rough-looking fellow" when he appeared in court in September 1860. A policeman had found him asleep on a cab in Coventry Street and upon waking him found him to be drunk and he was arrested. Although he was wearing a badge, it transpired that Lodwick was actually a buck and that he admitted to taking a cab from a stand and taking a fare for which he was paid 2s 6d. The owner of the cab, James May stated that as soon as the regular driver had earned his money, he allowed the prisoner to take his turn. The horse, he said, had been greatly distressed and the cab had probably collided with something as the axletree was bent. Mr Beadon the magistrate, said "...it was monstrous. He [Lodwick] was driving with a badge, but not his own. He was liable to a fine of £2 for driving without the consent of the owner; £5 for driving without a licence; and to two months' imprisonment for being a driver and for being drunk, and for all these offences he should commit him for two months."[27]

John Henry Gordon was using his brother's licence when he was charged with reckless driving and assaulting two police officers. Witnesses to the arrest however said the police were heavy handed and Gordon was only trying to defend himself. It transpired that Gordon had been a cab driver himself but following a term of imprisonment for two months for being drunk and assaulting a police officer his licence was taken away. It was noted by Gordon's defence counsel that when a cabman is convicted of assault, his livelihood is taken away from him, but what happens when a policeman is convicted of assault? "Generally speaking, the W Division [Brixton & Clapham] was the usual one appointed for that system of penal servitude."[28] Gordon was remanded but lack of further reporting on the case would suggest the charges against him were dropped.

In the latter days of the horse cab, "Darkey" Cooper was the "cabman's terror" of the ranks. An ex-cabman himself - it is not clear if his nickname refers to the colour of his skin or his nefarious activities - would hang around cab ranks waiting for an opportunity to strike. When it availed itself, he would drive off with the cab. He worked the cab for a day or two, overworking the horse, before abandoning it somewhere in London. He would take from the cab whatever was portable, the whip, cape and rug and these he would pawn. His reign of terror was finally ended when he was sentenced to twenty-one month's hard labour – to "much rejoicing among London Jehus."[29]

A policeman stopped a cab in Piccadilly in July 1891 which had a passenger as well as a man on the springs. The PC soon found out that the man driving the cab was originally the passenger and that the passenger was in reality the driver. It's unclear who the man on the springs was. "It's all right, Bobby," said Charles Lowther the pseudo-cabby, "it's only a lark. I asked the cabby to let me drive for a little while." Quite unusually for cases like this, all three men were sober. In court the following morning, Lowther admitted to Hannay the magistrate, "It's all my fault, your worship; but I was totally unaware that I was committing any breach of the law. I really cannot see so far into the intricacies of the law as to understand why I should not drive a cab as much as any other vehicle." Hannay looked up from the bench and informed him, "You can if you get yourself a licence and badge." He then fined Lowther 20s."[30]

Such antics were not restricted to gentlemen of independent means; Charles Steadman, the Consul of Liberia, was found to be drunk when he was stopped whilst not only driving the cab but wearing the cabman's badge as well. The cabman was also drunk and "was inside impersonating the fare". Steadman was fined 20s and a summons was issued to the cabman for allowing an unlicensed person to drive his cab.[31]

Where independent gentleman and Consuls travelled, the nobility were not far behind. When Sir Capel Fitzgerald Bt. decided to drive a cab he had ordered from his home in Half Moon Street, Piccadilly, to the nearby Arlington Club, he allegedly threatened to run over a policeman who ordered him to stop. The baronet denied shouting any threats to the policeman and said he had only driven the cab a short distance. The magistrate, Newton, admonished the knight and that "on his own showing he had driven a cab without a licence and persons, particularly those calling themselves gentlemen, should not do such things. The magistrate fined Sir Capel 40s, and warned him "not to act so foolishly again."[32] The driver, who had been riding on the springs as Sir Capel drove appears to have escaped punishment.

It may seem strange but there was one class of person who could not drive a hackney, and should have been able to, and that was the person who owned it. A proprietor was just that, a proprietor. His license indicated that he was the owner, but if he wanted to drive the cab, not even if he necessarily wanted to work it, he had to have a cab driver's licence as well. It was stated that Joseph Swain did indeed hold a cab driver's licence at least until the Great Exhibition of 1851, but the police could find no record of him doing so, but by 1867 he was the owner of six cabs. After one of his drivers failed to turn up for work, Swain decided to take a cab out himself – trouble was, he had had a bit too much to drink. He was charged with being drunk and taken into custody and it was then that it was ascertained that he did not have a cab driver's licence. For the next three days, Swain remained in jail whilst the police checked their records. When he did appear before Alderman Lusk MP at the Mansion House, it was hoped that the three days would be deemed sufficient punishment for driving your own cab. For being drunk, Lusk fined Swain 5s; for driving his own cab without a licence, which carried a maximum penalty of £10, he was fined £5. "It was no use inflicting a fine of a sovereign, as on a common cabman, because that would be no punishment at all," was Lusk's closing comment on the case[33]

When George Phillips, alias Cook, was charged with fraudulently obtaining a horse and cab in September 1857 he cited the London Hackney Carriages Act 1843 as his defence. The Act stated that an unlicensed driver could drive and ply for hire for a maximum of 24 hours, this could even be extended if there was "unavoidable Necessity"[34] and was sanctioned by a JP. Phillips however had failed to get the permission of the owner of the horse and cab, R. Kennett, of Broadway, Westminster, having tricked the horse keeper that such permission had been granted. Phillips was fined £5 for driving without a licence, a sum which in all likelihood he was unable to pay.

One cab proprietor who did fall foul of the 24-hour rule was Prudame. He had been found guilty of using an unlicensed driver for one of his cabs on three consecutive days. In mitigation, he explained to the magistrate that his regular man left all of a sudden, and not wishing to send out any ruffian with his cab "who might insult and impose on the fares" he chose to send out a man who was unlicensed but one who was known for his good conduct. The magistrate, Knox, said that "It was well known that cab proprietors generally had been making a great deal of money out of their cabs during the present season [1862] for they had raised the daily charge to the cabmen very largely." Knox went onto suggest that if he lowered his daily rental, he would have no trouble finding drivers. After being warned of the seriousness of the offence, Prudame was perhaps fortunate only to be fined 20s and costs.[35]

Birch Brothers have been associated with the London cab trade for well over a century. William Birch began with a horse drawn cab in 1837 and soon built up a large fleet that would not only include hackney carriages but also stage coaches and omnibuses. Up until the late 20th century "Birch Brothers" were synonymous with the coach industry. William died in 1846 and his widow, Elizabeth, took over before handing over the business to her two sons, John and William. Elizabeth Birch had been infamous for her non-compromising attitude when it came to charging the men for the daily rental to take out a cab. In 1854, she was charging her men 17 shillings a day, a rate which was given as the main reason why one of her driver's was overcharging by 6d – it was the only way he could make up the daily rental. After John and William Birch took over the cab side of the family business in 1874, the drivers at the cab yard in Horseferry Road were not expecting any change for the better. Relations between the drivers and the Birch brothers became so untenable in 1876 that the drivers went on strike, in consequence of which the siblings dismissed all their drivers – an action that they would often repeat. No drivers usually meant no income but the Birch brothers were aware of the 1843 Act, which had still not yet been repealed, and offered work as cabdrivers to unlicensed men, principally those employed as conductors and drivers on their fleet of buses.

Both John & William were summoned by Richard Boyle, a cabman who had formerly worked for them and was backed in his action by the Amalgamated Society of London Cabdrivers, a trade union which represented a little over 20% of all drivers. In court Boyle informed the magistrate, Arnold (who was not a great friend of the cab trade), that he knew that a Birch cab was being driven by an unlicensed driver. He informed a policeman who questioned the driver, Edward Waller, who readily informed the officer that he was not a licensed cabman, but was a licensed conductor. Waller was arrested and for a brief time held in a police cell. The lawyers for the union now contended that according to the 1869 Metropolitan Public Carriages Act, the most recent act of Parliament that affected the cab trade, it was illegal for an unlicensed man to drive a cab. The lawyers for the Birch's contested this with the 1843 Act which allowed for an unlicensed man to drive a cab for up to 24 hours. The two statutes were in direct contradiction to each other. Kisch, the lawyer for the union, pointed out that Birch had dismissed his men, he was not protected by "unavoidable necessity." Any other magistrate may have cited the spirit of the 1869 law as one that ends the practice of allowing unlicensed drivers, but not Arnold. Having looked at both statutes he came down on the side of John and William Birch and would dismiss the summons against them and their unlicensed driver, Edward Waller.

The matter did not end there. Arnold stated that he was agreeable for the case to go before a higher court. The summons had been withdrawn and the legal question was now allowed to be put forward that Edward Waller had acted illegally by being an unlicensed driver of a hackney carriage, with the full consent of the proprietors, John and William Birch.

One of the Birch brothers, the court reporter does not say which, was then placed in the witness stand and asked if Waller was driving one of his cabs on the day in question. Birch refused to reply – Arnold did it for him: That is "the most extraordinary thing [I] ever heard of for an advocate to ask such a question. It was asking a man to incriminate himself." Kisch informed Arnold that if he could not continue with that line of questioning then he could not pursue the matter any further. To add insult to injury, Arnold awarded Mr Birch, one guinea (£1 1s) costs. Next, Edward Waller was put in the witness box and Kisch asked him directly whether or not he had a cab drivers licence. Arnold once again came to aid of the defendants and informed Waller not to answer the question, again on the grounds of self-incrimination. Kisch tried another line of questioning: Did he know for a fact that other men drove a Birch cab on the same day with a licence. Arnold once again interjected and informed Kisch that questions such as that one could not be put to the defendant. Kisch informed Arnold that he could not carry the case any further. He asked for an adjournment on the basis that Waller had informed the policeman that he was not licensed. Arnold had heard enough. He dismissed the summons (again) and once more awarded costs to the defendant of one guinea.[36]

Just before midnight on August 2nd 1852, a policeman on patrol in Grays Inn Road saw a cabriolet driving towards him with three people on the box. All three were smoking cigars, one of whom was a woman and it was she who had the reins. "Halloa," cried out the policeman, "That won't do." But the "lady" replied that everything was all right, and whipped the horse to speed off. Unfortunately for them, PC Fisher was nimble enough to give chase and stop the horse. After ascertaining who was the cabman, the policeman asked for his badge. John White, replied that he had left it at home. Whilst the policeman was questioning White, the third person that was on the box made their escape, as did some of their companions inside the cab. PC Fisher arrested both John White and the "lady"; he placed them in the cab and then walked the cab to the nearest station house. Whilst doing this however, White and the "lady" made their escape from the cab. Fisher took the horse and cab to the green yard then went looking for the two fugitives. It perhaps says something of his detective skills that within a couple of hours he found the pair of them travelling in a cab in Bagnigge Wells Road (now Kings Cross Road). This time they did not get away.

The court reporter perfunctorily described White as the "driver of a cabriolet, badge number 5230", and the second prisoner, "Emma Smallbone, a well-dressed, portly looking woman, 30 years of age, who was described in the police-sheet as a married woman, residing at No. 103 Holborn Hill..." Both were charged with being drunk and disorderly. Having given a presumably accurate description of her, as well as her name and address, Emma Smallbone perhaps had no option but to deny that she had charge of the reins or that she was smoking a cigar. PC Fisher stuck with his original statement, and added for good measure that at the station house Smallbone insisted that "she was a respectable woman and that the landlord of the Old Bell Inn, Holborn, was her brother."

"Under the circumstances," stated Corrie the magistrate, "he should discharge the "lady"." No doubt feeling that she had brought a certain amount of ignominy upon herself. White was initially fined 5s but later this was rescinded and instead, as a warning to his future conduct, his licence was endorsed. "Mrs Smallbone then left the court (with her brother) an object of attraction and curiosity, and [John White] repaired with a host of his fraternity to a neighbouring public-house, who appeared delighted at his "spree"."[37]

A generation later, in 1878, another "married woman" – supposedly an indication or respectability – was charged with being drunk, furiously driving a horse and cab and unlawfully acting as a cab driver, again in Grays Inn Road. Caroline Sooby, of 3 Wakefield Mews, Regent's Square, admitted being the driver of the cab (although not stated in court, she was the wife of a cab proprietor) but denied being drunk. Even the wife of a cab proprietor has to think about the neighbours. Sooby was fined 10s or seven day's hard labour. The real cab driver, 20 year-old William Messenger, of Drummond Street was fined 40s, or one month's hard labour if he should default on the payment of the fine.[38] There were no reports of a celebratory drink but the pair did share the infamy of being national news and having their little adventure depicted on the front page of the *Illustrated Police News*, the 19th century equivalent to a tabloid newspaper

The novelty of a female cab driver appeared to be on the wane when, shortly after Caroline Sooby's exploit, Isabella Graham and Alfred Sinfield, were both charged with being drunk and recklessly driving a horse and cab. According to the evidence, Isabella Graham was wearing

Sinfield's hat and badge, and he was wearing her bonnet. They were taking turns between themselves at driving the cab. Graham, unlike her predecessors, was not described as a married woman, was fined 20s plus costs. Sinfield, who had previously been warned as to his future conduct with regard to being drunk on duty was fined 40s and had his licence revoked.[39]

One of the more curious cases came to light in 1875 following the arrest for theft, of cabman William Seymour in Liverpool. Seymour had been arrested on suspicion of stealing 25s of meat from a butcher. He was arrested and charged and remanded in Walton Gaol. It was whilst undergoing a medical examination at the prison that it was revealed that William Seymour was a woman named Mary Hanniwell. For the previous six years' Hanniwell had been working as a cabman in Liverpool and, according to press reports, three years prior to that, she had been driving a cab in London. According to her brief history, she was married to an army-surgeon before she was 15 years old before leaving him and running away to London. There, "… she procured a suit of men's clothes, cut off her hair, and turned cab-driver."[40] It is somewhat difficult, given the period of time whether it can be stated that the claims she was a London cab driver can be substantiated. There is little doubt she worked as a cabman in Liverpool, but no proof it was for the six years stated. By keeping herself to herself, a woman could pass as a cabman, given the numerous layers of clothing they were compelled to wear, her femininity could easily be disguised. A speech defect allegedly deflected any attention away from her voice. Not having been properly licensed by the Metropolitan Police in London she, if she did drive a cab, was no more than a buck, but one who may have had some assistance from a licensed driver. She used several different names; it is believed she was born Mary Seymour and even her existence in London between 1866 and 1869 is subject to a certain amount of speculation.

Hanniwell was sentenced to two months with hard labour for the theft of the meat – despite allegedly having saved a sum of money in the bank. On the day of her release from Walton Gaol the Liverpool cabmen blocked the surrounding roads, all wanting to pay tribute to the "Boadicean cabby". It had even been asserted that a collection had been raised to start her off legitimately as a cab driver. The hordes of cabmen waited all day outside the prison but after hearing from an official that "Mary had eloped by a side door" the "cabbies returned from their generous mission "crestfallen and sadly disappointed."[41]

As the nineteenth century drew to a close there was much debate concerning the ability of women to drive a cab – usually from the women themselves. A correspondent to the *Pall Mall Gazette* in 1895 asked "Why should not a gentlewoman drive a hansom cab?" The anonymous author described herself as having once been a lady of society that now, through one reason or another, she had fallen on hard times and was in desperate need of regular income. Having dismissed other forms of female employment, that was acceptable to society, she ponders on driving a cab. She tells us that she is well trained in driving carriages and "has learned the London streets". "When she was rich she drove for pleasure and was not considered unrefined or unladylike then.... A gentlewoman can be refined even when driving a hansom." The focus of still maintaining an air of dignity is telling. It is not the misogynistic world of the cabman but it is society, her old society, that that is the biggest hurdle to cross for her becoming a cab driver. She even has qualms about mentioning the idea to her family for fears they might lock her up as a lunatic.[42]

Somewhat less worthy of being dubbed "London's First Woman Taxicab Driver" was a Mrs Moule from Portsmouth. Moule and her husband, who had been invalided out of the Army during the early years of the Great War, had tried to start up a fleet of taxis in Portsmouth. This had not proved financially viable so Mrs Moule, like several women up and down the country, (with the exception of London), applied and received a licence to drive a taxicab. Her licence only allowed her to work within the realm of the local borough council, but once armed with a licence she drove up to London and began working there. By December 1916 she had held a licence for eighteen months and how much of that period was spend illegally working in London is not known. Her license was worthless in London and the "taxicab" she drove was not plated. After being fined at Bow Street for driving an unlicensed taxicab, Mrs Moule said she "could not understand why Scotland Yard will not grant licences to women." Though as she later admitted to carrying eleven people in her car at one time, it may have been just the sort of excuse Scotland Yard needed. There was another consideration; "I get a lot of work from the Cecil and Savoy hotels," she told a reporter. "The porters ask me to come back, but the other taximen swear when they see me, and try to hustle me."[43] Even with large numbers of men being called up for King and Country, the taxi drivers of London were not about to let women drive taxis, even if Scotland Yard were about to licence them. A number of women, as we shall see in the next section, were about to put that to the test.

Application for a taxi driver's licence

Applicants will be required, before a licence is granted, to pass examinations as to their Knowledge of London and their ability to drive a taxi.

Only Transport for London (as well, it has to be said, the Public Carriage Office before them), can reduce the hardest entry test for a taxi driver anywhere in the world to a single sentence. Until recently, they even sent the badge through the post, thus reducing its status to a mere formality. At least in the days of the Metropolitan Police's Public Carriage Office, you received a handshake as well as the badge, as some form of recognition of the arduous journey the applicant has just completed.

"What exactly is the Knowledge?" was the rhetorical question asked by the fictional examiner Mr Burgess in Jack Rosenthal's *The Knowledge* (1979) "All the Knowledge means" he explains to the ten applicants before him, "is that you commit to memory, every street within a six-mile radius, of Charing Cross. Every street and what's on every street, every hotel, every club, every hospital, every department store, every shop, government building, theatre, cinema, restaurant; park, art gallery; church, synagogue, mosque etc, etc, etc. Every building or amenity in public use, you name it, you've got to know it."

It was not always so, and it seems somewhat remarkable that a topographical examination of any kind, did not appear until the 1860's, two hundred years after the first hackney coaches were licensed and twenty-two years after the drivers were first licensed. Even if the hackney coachman could read, and very few could, there were very few street signs for a coachman to go by. Drivers were more reliant on familiar buildings, such as churches or, with more than a passing familiarity, taverns and ale houses. Pepys' hackney coachman could perhaps be forgiven for getting lost when, seventeen months after the Great Fire, they were taken around the ruins from Hercules Pillars in Holborn, via London Wall. An indication of how London was changed by the fire can be found that the driver then drove down Coleman Street, in Moorfields, a good mile from where Pepys lived by the Tower. Pepys himself thought it was all a contrived plan by the driver and the linkman to rob him and his fellow passengers. There was, he thought, no better place to attack them as any cries for help could not be heard. He was somewhat relieved that it was nothing more than a mistake by the coachman.[44]

Local knowledge was essential and there was probably a reliance on the passenger's knowledge of the area rather than the experience of the driver. As we have seen earlier in this chapter, prior to 1838 there was no bar to becoming a hackney coachman. An owner could rent his vehicle out to anybody who was willing to pay. It is not until the reforms of Daniel Whittle Harvey, already touched upon, that the applicants for a licence to drive a hackney carriage had to declare that they were "well acquainted with the streets, in and about London". Though as the next proviso was that the applicant had to be at least 16 years old, it is a wonder how such a young person could have gained sufficient knowledge of London and its environs.[45]

Edward Surman was just 16 years old when he was engaged by a passenger in Paddington Station to take him to Manchester Street, Surman stated that he did not know the way there. When he was asked how long he had been a cabman, Surman replied that it was "Only a fortnight." His passenger then volunteered to show him the way, he was by this time sitting in the vehicle. But Surman, betraying a wealth of experience unbefitting his 16 years, threatened the passenger that he would be pulled from the cab unless he got out. "Had you any luggage?" asked Rawlinson the magistrate.

"No, nothing more than one parcel."

"Aye, a short fare and little luggage is what these cab drivers do not approve."

Rawlinson was right. As will be seen elsewhere, drivers benefitted financially when there were more passengers with a large amount of luggage. It's hard to tell if Surman really did not know where Manchester Street was. It was, and still remains, a fashionable part of town and any cab driver with experience behind him would have known it. Once he realised that it was a short fare, with just one passenger without any luggage, he tried, to use a cab trade expression, "to broom the job off", whilst he could then look for a more profitable ride. Surman was a "privileged" cabman, a select few who could work from railway stations, as opposed to working on the streets, so when the passenger complained about Surman's conduct to a railway company official, the cabbie was told to leave the station (it being private property). Angry that he was to be deprived, for the time being, of his livelihood, he struck the railway officer with his whip. For the misbehaviour towards the passenger and the assault on the officer, Surman was fined the maximum 40s in each case. Unable to pay he was imprisoned for one month.[46]

Like Surman, William Eaton was also new to the trade – "a butterboy" in cab trade lexicography – but unlike him, he was an owner driver. Many drivers aspired to becoming an owner driver, their own master. For Eaton to enter the trade owning his own cab would imply that he had savings before he took to cab driving. Eaton, badge 5580, was summoned, in July 1853, for overcharging – 4s for a fare that should not have been more than 2s 6d. His passenger informed the magistrate that he initially engaged Eaton in Bond Street and asked him to take up some ladies, waiting in nearby Hanover Square. Eaton did not know how to get from Bond Street to Hanover Square, even though the two are virtually next to each other.

There are many who cite the Great Exhibition of 1851, with its influx of foreign visitors to London, as the point when the topographical examination of London began. There were more complaints from visitors regarding being overcharged, and of the condition of the horses, than questions over the actual knowledge of London held by the cab drivers. After all, everyone knew where the Crystal Palace was, and the drivers, those so inclined, would find it more beneficial to get the passengers to the Great Exhibition as quickly as possible, then try to extract as much money from them as possible. As the Great Exhibition may not be responsible for the Knowledge, we shall see in Chapter 6 that it was responsible for the introduction of the official book of fares, which every cabman was legally bound to carry. The Great Exhibition was in 1851, Eaton not knowing the way to Hanover Square was in 1853, if a topographical examination had been in place, he would have known.[47] Eaton was later fined 20s for demanding 4s for a 2s fare after carrying five people in his two-seater cab.

Exactly when what is now called "The Knowledge" began, is still shrouded in mystery. In his *History of the Knowledge of London*, Philip Warren admits that trying to prove when the examinations actually initiated have proven "to be very elusive".[48] Trevor May, is more precise, he states that the "legendary test of 'The Knowledge' was started in May 1866 on the express orders of Sir Richard Mayne (Commissioner of the Metropolitan Police).[49] The examination of candidates was entrusted to Lieutenant Colonel Paschal, a former officer of the King's German Legion and a veteran of the Battle of Waterloo,[50] who "subjects [the applicants] to a searching examination in the topography of London, selecting various points of "taking up" and "setting down."[51] Little has changed over the years. When Fred Simmons was elected President of the Cab Drivers Union in in 1897, he was asked about the "stiff examination" at Scotland Yard. "You sit down, and he sits down – then he says he wants you to drive him from the Yard to the Bank."[52] Even today, the test remains oral. When, during the Great War there was a shortage of drivers due to many enlisting, the Home Secretary was asked in the Commons if the oral test should be replaced with a written one. McKenna replied that the test was purposely made oral "as many of the candidates would be unable to do themselves justice if set a written paper."[53] The only thing that has changed regarding the Knowledge is its degree of difficulty in passing.

Successive generations of cab drivers all believe that their predecessors had a much easier time on the Knowledge, and they may have a point. An "Ex-Cabby" described it as a "slight examination" in 1871[54] In 1888 the editor of the *Morning Post* stated that in order to get a badge, all a candidate has to do is "prove he possesses an elementary knowledge of the topography of London, the licence is granted as a matter of course..."[55] During a debate on the London Streets (Removal of Gates) Bill, two years later, Alfred Mills, secretary of the Cab Proprietor's Protection Association complained that the gates were a great nuisance for the cabmen of London. Mills explained that whilst the cabmen had to pass an examination of their knowledge of London, he did not think they would know when such gates, prolific in the Bloomsbury area and preventing through traffic, were opened or closed. "What an ignorant set of men they must be," exclaimed Balfour Browne, chairman of the committee, and the debate then left the subject of gates and highlighted each of the panel's experiences of cabmen taking them to the wrong addresses.[56] The mistakes probably had more to do with the drivers mis-hearing the destination than from the inadequacy of the Knowledge. W J Gordon, writing about the horses of London believes that the elementary knowledge required is "not very great" but 34% of the 1500 candidates each year fail or "ploughed" as he puts it.[57]

When before a Select Committee of the House of Commons, Alfred Mills, believed that the examination "was much too severe."[58] This was a familiar refrain from the proprietors who were always calling for a softer examination, especially when they had cabs idling in the yard for want of a driver.

In 1938 it was stated that, "It takes the average intelligent man ten months of very hard study and plodding the streets of London to pass his first test..."[59] By 1966 it took about 18 months and by the mid 1980's Knowledge boys, and now girls, were taking two to three years. Despite the number of road closures and with a much greater emphasis on points today, 2018, it can take as long as four years to get the coveted green badge.

Thirty years after the introduction of the knowledge, the would-be cab driver had to prove he could actually drive a horse and cab, there was no requirement of such proof prior until June 1896.[60] Applicants were required to drive a horse and chaise, supplied by Scotland Yard, before they were licensed. It was perhaps prudent of Scotland Yard to introduce a driving test at this stage. The motor car was already making an impact and there was little doubt the cab would soon become horseless – a fear that was proven correct the following year with the introduction of the Bersey Electric cab.

Passing the topographical exams has always preceded the driving test. As the trade made the transition from horse cab to motor cab from 1907, many, especially older drivers, had difficulty in passing the new driving test. Initially, a cabman had just three attempts to pass the driving test before he was permanently excluded. Reluctantly, many of the older cabmen were faced with either retiring, which, without savings usually meant the workhouse, or try to embrace the new technology. Frederick Hitch VC had a fleet of thirteen cabs before the arrival of the motor cab had all but ruined him. He managed to pass the driving test, despite having a weakened arm as a result of being shot in the shoulder at the Battle of Rorke's Drift. Hitch's attitude was definitely akin to the "if you can't beat them, join them" philosophy and his reluctance in holding a steering wheel as compared to a set of reins was palpable when he explained that the "motor taxi trade, now owed him."[61]

Due to the high failure rate, Scotland Yard removed the maximum limit of driving tests a candidate could apply for. Replacing it with four free tests, then a charge of 2s 6d for each subsequent test. The Union were helping their members adapt to the changing needs of the profession, but their boast, in 1904, that they could "instil the necessary knowledge in the short space of two hours" appears to be somewhat fanciful.[62] The large cab firms also saw the benefit of training drivers, not only for the driving test but running their own knowledge schools. The British Motor Cab Company was one such company. Anybody who became licensed through their schools was tied to the company for a year, or pay a forfeit of £5 to break the contract. The General Cab Company, later part of the same group as the British Motor Cab Co also trained their drivers, using an instructor from the RAC.[63] It took 63 year old, Henry Ellerington three months from signing up with the General before he could actually take a cab out.[64] Whilst George Vardy, on trial for causing bodily harm to Charles Lott, a horse cabman, and Lott's passenger, when he crashed his taxi into them, said he "...had six months' tuition with these Fiat cabs and the last month I was doing the taxi test with the police."[65] Vardy was found not guilty of the charges against him but, if the Fiat Motor Cab Company had fired him for damaging one of their cabs, he could not just walk into another company such as the General. Even though he had passed a driving test, he had passed it in a Fiat cab, The General's fleet was entirely made up of Renault cabs; if he wanted to drive one of them, he would have to take a test in a Renault – another stipulation which kept drivers tied to a particular yard.

Despite the hardships of the driving test, it was the topographical examination that was holding back many drivers. One "well-known cab proprietor" mulled that the "knowledge of London examination is very strict, but, in the event of a strike, the standard might be lowered to meet the situation... for there are hundreds of men who are qualified to drive if they could pass the test." In the strike of the drivers in 1894 (over paying too much rental), various cab proprietors were taking advantage of an unofficial laxity in the knowledge examination by applying for their horse keepers and cab washers to become drivers. Such people, who were temporarily dismissed whenever the drivers went on strike, had no problem being labelled strike-breakers or blacklegs. When Sir Edward Bradford, the Commissioner of Scotland Yard, heard what was happening, he immediately put a block on any more licences being issued.[66] During the 1896 strike against the privilege system, where it was claimed the railway companies were flooding Scotland Yard with applicants from their employees, Bradford said he knew of no law that prevented the issuing of cab driving licences to such people. He did however report that since the strike had begun, there had been 124 applications for a licence. Of these only 48 had passed the examinations, and of these, only 14 had actually been licensed.[67]

When in 1911, a Mr Du Cros, (it was not stated which of the eponymous brothers of W & G Du Cros Cab Company of Acton they were referring to), was asked before a House of Commons Committee why there was a shortage of taxis, he put the blame squarely on the severity of the knowledge examination. A departmental Committee of the Home Office looking into a potential increase of cab fares recommended that the "standard of qualification for a licence [was] to be strictly maintained." [68]

The call for women to be licensed took on added impetus during the Great War. A large number of drivers had initially volunteered to fight, and many others would be conscripted. Women had shown their worth in many industries but driving a London taxi was still a male domain. The principle argument against female taxi drivers was the fear of the men of post-war unemployment. It had been stated that one of the reasons so many taxi drivers had signed up voluntarily in the first months of the war was the promise that there would be no change to their licensing conditions whilst they were away. It was a facile argument. All the licensing conditions prevailed upon were based on the applicant passing the Knowledge of London examinations and the subsequent driving test. There was nothing regarding gender in the legislation. It was a point raised by Sir Henry Norman MP in a letter to the Home Secretary, he wanted to know if refusal to licence women was based on a "statutory disqualification of a woman or on a decision of the Home Office."[69] McKenna, the Home Secretary, sidestepped the issue by placing the decision wholly with the Commissioner of Police, "who informs me that he cannot in the present circumstances recommend the grant of a licence to a woman."[70] With thousands of men dying in the trenches on an almost daily basis, and women filling the manpower gap up and down the country, it's hard to imagine just what extra circumstances Sir Edward Henry, the Commissioner of Police, envisaged.

Circumstances did change. The war got bloodier and there appeared little hope of an early victory. Many men, such as bus and tram drivers, were exempted from being enlisted as a reserved occupation but in February 1917 the Army Council was forced to revoke the dispensation and many of the drivers would now be called up. In response, Sir Edward Henry was forced to concede that women could now be licensed as drivers of public carriages – buses, trams, and finally, taxis. It appears that the British Motor Cab Company had anticipated the decision and had a "list of suitable women" already lined up. Unlike the London General Omnibus Company which was completely caught out by the decision and had made no plans for the eventuality of women bus drivers.[71]

There was the inevitable divide of opinion within the trade, split between the drivers and the main proprietors. A Union official said driving a taxi was "not a moral occupation for a woman to follow." A spokesman for the Motor Cab Owner Drivers Association thought it was all a storm in a teacup as it would take a woman six months to pass the examinations and that as there were more drivers than taxis, she would be denying a man over military age of his living. The manager of a "well known taxicab company" – most likely the British Motor Cab Company – said they were quite prepared to take on women. "Women taxi drivers are answering so well in the country that we see no reason to doubt that they will in London."[72]

Sir George Cave pointed out that if any women were to be licensed, then the Commissioner of Police was under no obligation to indefinitely renew their licences. There is no doubt that the decision was part of the war effort and that many women in other trades and industries were well aware that their job would be given to a man at the end of hostilities. It shows the arbitrary power of the Commissioner of Police that he can just refuse to renew a woman's licence, without having had any complaints about her, just on the basis of her gender. If women were to become taxi drivers, they were not going to be given any concessions; Scotland Yard announced that standards would not be lowered for women taking the Knowledge of London examinations, they also added, perhaps as a scare tactic, that some men had failed the topography test six times.[73]

The rise of the suffragette and the Women's Social and Political Union in the post-Victorian era saw women venture into many male-dominated professions, though the take up for those applying to be cab or taxi drivers was slow. Sheila O'Neill is sometimes cited, wrongly, as the first female taxi driver of London. Little is known of her background other than she had served in South Africa during the Boer War as a nurse and was now said to be "practising daily" for a licence to drive a taximeter cab.[74] She never received one. Several historians cite the fact that having failed to obtain a badge she was employed as a female chauffeur to a businessman. There are reports that she had a figure of a policeman, hand raised as if to be stopping traffic, mounted on the bonnet of her car, symbolising the impenetrable barrier at Scotland Yard that prevented her from being badged.[75]

Given the action and views of the suffragette movement prior to the war, the taxi drivers were under no illusion that a number of women would take up the call. This view was emphasised the day after the Home Secretary's announcement with the *Daily Mirror* displaying a photograph of three women "who called for their licences at Scotland Yard". That the women had only applied for a licence, and were not picking their licences up, may have caused many drivers to believe the flood gates were about to open.[76] *The Times* was slightly more stoic, saying that the number of women who applied for licences "was not very great". The drivers responded by saying that ten men would walk out of any garage for every woman employed. This prompted one proprietor, who had a quarter of his fleet standing idle in the yard, to promise he would not hesitate to replace all his men with female drivers if need be.[77]

The London & Provincial Union of Licensed Vehicle Workers, which included not just cab and taxi drivers, but bus and tram men, called a strike in protest against the introduction of women into their workspace, for March 18th 1917. A circular proclaiming the action stated, "A grave crisis has arisen. In consequence of the Home Secretary's refusal to cancel his order licensing woman drivers, our livelihood, and that of our brothers in the trenches is in peril. These men look to us to keep their jobs open for them when they return."[78] The circular was penned by Ben Smith, the organising secretary of the Union. Smith would later become a Labour MP and would eventually serve in Churchill's wartime coalition cabinet. Smith, unknowingly, has also added to the burden of the knowledge boy/girl by having a street named in his honour – Ben Smith Way SE16, in Bermondsey

There was a climb down by the Home Office. They agreed that no woman would be licensed to drive an omnibus or a tram – but there was nothing, other than the examinations, to stop them becoming a taxi driver. Despite this intervention, the strike was still planned to go ahead.

In the event, the strike was called off. Ostensibly it was due to the intervention of the Minister of Labour who said he would ask the Home Secretary to cancel his order. On the strength of this, the Union apparently called off the strike. In reality, a notice was posted on the gates at Scotland Yard informing the workers than any such stoppage of transport would be a breach of regulation 42 of the Defence of the Realm Act. Any stoppage of public transport could hinder workers of the munition factories. The notice was aimed primarily at the bus and tram workers, munition workers could ill afford taxis, but a strike by the taxi drivers alone would only end in defeat.

"The first woman taxicab driver in London" announced the *Daily Express* in June 1917, "will probably be a slight, graceful girl, with clear grey eyes, hair worn á la Gaby Desiys, lovely white teeth, and a string of pearls."[79] The last part of the description, the "string of pearls" shows that the "graceful girl" was not your average working-class girl. She was in fact Susan Dudley Ryder, cousin to the Earl of Harrowby, and sister of champion woman's golfer, Mrs Gavin.[80] Ryder had passed the Knowledge at her eighth attempt and now only needed to pass her driving test at Scotland Yard.

In replying to a question from Earl Russell, the Lord Chamberlain, Lord Sandhurst informed the upper house that to date "only one woman" had qualified as a taxi driver.[81] According to Phil Warren, Susan Dudley Ryder, badge number 1366, obtained her licence in August 1917 and held it until May 1920. Was she the first female taxi driver? In the same PRO file, Warren states that a Miss Denning (badge 2380) was licensed in May 1917, a Miss Bowen (662) was licensed in August 1917, and a Miss Perry (748) was licensed in November 1917.[82] The Lord Chamberlain's statement was issued in October, by which time, according to Warren, three women were licensed. It is difficult to determine where the discrepancy lies, but according to the press, who are not always the arbiter of solid facts, the first female taxi driver in London was Miss Susan Dudley Ryder.

These four were the only women to be licensed and each of them, with the exception of Perry, never had their licences renewed after the three-year expiry date. Perry's licence expired in November 1920 and she was granted a second licence in November 1922, which was not subsequently renewed.[83]

After the Great War, the government set up a select committee to look into transport problems within London which included a lack of taxis and of taxi drivers. The traffic manager of the British Motor Cab Company, F.W.C. Ashwood, was asked, given the role of women during the war if he was in favour of women taxicab drivers. He replied with a blunt "No." When asked to elaborate, he replied that "I think taxi-cab driving is essentially a man's occupation. Sometimes very undesirable types of people are encountered by taxi-drivers." Ben Smith was asked a similar question – and replied with a similar answer. He acknowledged that "Many of them are expert drivers," though blotted his copybook by adding, "but after 6 o'clock I do not think they are." He was asked to explain why such a change should come over the women at a particular time. The future Labour MP replied that it was not the women but the "immorality of the London streets after that hour." Cabs were used, he explained for "driving passengers from one place to another."[84] Which is a taxi driver's job in a nutshell. He didn't elaborate but if he would have done it would have needed him to explain what the passengers were doing in the back of the cab. Not that the Select Committee were unaware of such goings on. The following day, Herbert Bundy of the Motor Cab Owners Association was asked if he was aware that there were "...owner drivers who prowled the West End with their flags down in order to find women of a certain class accompanied by men, and refused to take other fares." Bundy at first replied that he was unaware of such activity as the risk to the owner driver was too great. He then not only contradicted himself by saying such fares was the reason he was against women driving taxis but he himself had picked up such fares before.[85] In his memoirs, Maurice Levinson described such jobs as a "Bob a nob"[86] whilst Walter Geake stated that the business was usually done as one drove up the Mall, round Queen Victoria's Memorial and back down the Mall to Trafalgar Square, and was called "a short one."[87]

The issue of women taxi drivers was swept under the carpet and only made a fleeting appearance during the Second World War. The Sex Disqualification (Removal) Act of 1919 had removed any legal barrier to women becoming taxi drivers and if they had insisted on their right, the inspectors at the Public Carriage Office would hold them up. As Assistant Commissioner 'B' noted in March 1942, "...she [an un-named woman] should be discouraged as much as possible from applying for a license [sic]. If she insists she could be held up for a long time in the Knowledge of London examinations, but if she still persists she should be allowed to continue."[88] Outside of London, there does not appear to be any apprehension about licensing women, though five ladies in Bridlington were prevented from working as taxi drivers during the hours of darkness.

Mrs Shirley Preston is credited with being the first female taxi driver, at least of modern times. Little is known of her except that she was married to a cab driver who owned three cabs and she drove one of them. In 1965 the boroughs of Romford and Hornchurch were incorporated into the Greater London area. Up until then, each of these boroughs licensed their own taxis, with nothing to do with the Public Carriage Office in London. Once incorporation had taken place, then the taxis, which then were saloon cars, were licensed to ply as if they were a yellow badge, which was what the drivers were now required to wear. The cars were examined as to their conditions of fitness by the Carriage Office, with 16 being rejected. The drivers were given three years before they would have to conform to the regular conditions of fitness and drive a purpose built "London taxi".[89] One of these drivers, there were 115 in all, was Shirley Preston. The local drivers had no problem with her whilst she was driving a saloon car, but once she began driving a London taxi she says she faced hostility from other taxi drivers who felt they were now the laughing stock of London.[90]

The first woman to obtain a badge, albeit a yellow one, by doing the Knowledge, was Romford-based, mother of four, Sheila Anker. She obtained her badge in May 1972. Sheila also has another footnote in cab trade history by becoming the first owner of a Metrocab in 1986.

The first woman of modern times to have completed the Knowledge and become a fully-fledged green badge taxi driver was Marie White. Marie, the wife of a London taxi driver, passed the Knowledge in 1977 and was given badge 25292. Unlike her male contemporaries, Marie did her blue book runs in a mini as she did not like to use a moped. She was a frequent user of the St Pancras Station rank up until shortly before her death from cancer in 1993 and could frequently be seen with her small dog which she took to work every day, sitting in the luggage compartment.

Offences in relation to application for a taxi driver's licence

(1) A person applying for/or attempting to procure a taxi driver's licence commits an offence if he:

(a) makes or causes to be made any false representation in regard to any particulars, or

(b) does not truly answer all questions demanded of him.

Walter Samuel Skinner felt he was doing a friend a favour when he applied for a cab driver licence in March 1894. The friend, Edward Doe, a whip maker, had recently lost his wife and was struggling to find the money to feed his three children. Skinner himself was a licensed driver already but on receiving the application form at New Scotland Yard he entered his name as Thomas Allen. The form also asked whether the applicant had ever held a cab licence previously, to which he entered that he had not; it also asked him if he had any previous convictions, again he answered in the negative, a statement he actually believed to be true of his friend but one he subsequently found out was wrong.

Over the previous months the cabmen of London had been finding it more and more difficult to earn enough to pay their masters and earn enough to feed themselves and their family. At such periodic times, there was the usual complaint about too many cab drivers with not enough work to go around between them. These were also coupled against long standing grievances such as the "privilege system" (they could set down at a railway terminus but were prevented from picking a fare up), and how difficult it was to be paid after being bilked, even when the culprit was in court (see chapter 8). It was addressing a supposed superfluous number of licences that caused Inspector Andrews of New Scotland Yard to look more assiduously into the cab applications before him, particularly that of Thomas Allen.

Each application form to become a cab driver was accompanied by a reference from a rate payer who had known the applicant for at least two years. In the bogus application of Thomas Allen, the referee was none other than Edward Doe himself, who was ultimately the intended recipient of the cab licence. Doe had signed the form to the effect that he had known Thomas Allen for more than two years and that to the best of his ability, he was not aware of any convictions against him. Both these statements were in error; there was no Thomas Allen and Doe himself was a convicted felon, a fact Skinner had not known at the time. Doe informed the police that he had filled out hundreds of such forms for cabmen in the past, his job as a whip maker brought him into contact with many of them. Inspector Andrews stuck to his task and eventually Doe and Skinner were arrested. In court both men pleaded guilty, but neither thought they were doing any harm, they had attempted to get Doe a job as a cabman so he could feed his starving children. The magistrate was not in a sympathetic mode, he fined Walter Skinner £3 and Edward Doe, £2. Neither could pay so both were sent to prison for one month.[91]

Minimum age for drivers

Taxi driver's licences shall not be granted to persons under 21 years of age. A licence, if granted to a person under 21, is void.

Ever since hackney coaches begun proliferating from the beginning of the 17th century, there had never been any attempt by all the subsequent laws to establish a minimum age, at least not until a member of the nobility was killed by a hackney coach in 1832. Back in the days when the hackney coaches were pulled by two horses it would seem obvious that a strong person would be needed to hold the reins and control the animals. Many an accident was caused, whether in a two-horse coach or a single horse cab where a mature and physically strong driver could not control his horse or horses and an accident ensued. It seems perverse then that the owners of a hackney carriage should entrust their property to a young child, an event that probably occurred more often than the records show.

In 1810, driving coach 999, 12-year old Thomas Harrison was fined for exaction from a Mr Joseph Orme of 10s 6d from the Vauxhall Leisure Gardens to his house in Charles Street (now Mortimer Street, W1). Whether Harrison overcharged through sheer bravado or ignorance is not recorded but one has to consider the likelihood of a fare paying adult passenger being intimidated enough by a boy that they would hand over more money than they expected. In all events Mr Orme was having none of it and summoned the owner of hackney coach 999, who was probably all too willing to produce the boy. Harrison was fined 20s, which is doubtful that he could pay, but whether the fine was rescinded for a custodial sentence is not recorded. There was no mention by the magistrate or by the court reporter that a hackney coach driven by a 12-year old boy was anything other than unusual.[92]

Seven years later the *Morning Chronicle* reported the case of another 12-year old driving a hackney coach. No offence was stipulated but this time "...the court expressed their decided opinion of the gross impropriety of permitting the public safety to be entrusted to such children, and trusted the Commissioners for Hackney Coaches would feel it their duty to take care such was not the case again."[93]

The 63-year-old, and recently widowed, Lady Caroline Barham was struck by a cab as she crossed Margaret Street, just north of Oxford Circus on October 31st 1832. The cab driver refused to stop even though a fishmonger alerted him to the accident. Lady Barham was placed in a coach and taken to her residence, 26 Queen Anne St. She was sitting in a chair when her physician arrived but he sent her straight to bed and diagnosed a broken wrist, several broken ribs and possibly internal bleeding.

The fishmonger did manage to read the plate on the back of the cab, 897, and this was handed to the police. The fishmonger would later receive 5s for this information which he felt was a small amount in carrying out his civic duty. His reward was later increased to 20s.

Furnished with the plate number a plain clothes police officer, from the fledgling Metropolitan Police waited outside Bartholomew's cab yard in Kepple Mews North, Bloomsbury (later rebuilt as part of Malet Street). It was not long before cab number 897 pulled into the yard. The cab was driven by 15-year-old Henry Bartholomew, son of the proprietor. Henry readily admitted to causing the accident but admitted to being to afraid to return to the scene. Henry was taken into police custody. Matters soon took a turn for the worse for him, when, after three days, Lady Barham died from her injuries.

The subsequent inquest found Henry Bartholomew guilty of manslaughter, and the jury expressed their disgust that a father should allow his young son to drive a cab on the streets of London. To show their dismay, they levied a deodand of £50 against Henry's father. This ancient right, it survived till about the 1860's, allowed the victim's family to receive money forfeited from the sale of the weapon used to kill the victim, whether it be a knife, sword, gun, or in this case, a hackney cabriolet and the horse. So, Bartholomew senior was deprived of one of his cabs (but kept the licence - he owned two plates) and Bartholomew junior was deprived of his liberty – bail was refused and he was incarcerated in Newgate Gaol.

A couple of weeks later, a tearful Henry Bartholomew appeared in the dock at the Old Bailey. Many testified to his safe driving skills and others stated that it was impossible for that particular horse to ride at a gallop (after all, the fishmonger had chased and caught up with it). Henry was found not guilty of manslaughter by the jury who felt that his father had acted irresponsibly in sending out a cab driven by one so young. They recommended that both licences held by Bartholomew should be revoked. After some heavy petitioning by Lady Barham's relatives, this eventually occurred, though as Trevor May suggests it may have been the only instance of this ever happening.[94]

The case did not stop other proprietors sending out youngsters. Whilst Henry was imprisoned in Newgate awaiting trial, Thomas Horne "a mere lad" was found guilty of furious driving. His master was fined 40s (£2).

The following year, 1833, a proprietor was fined the maximum amount of £5 following a collision between a cab, plate number 1217 and a private carriage with three people on board. The cab was driven by the proprietor's son, Thomas Price, described as a boy. The phaeton was badly damaged in the collision, which was said to have occurred when Price tried to drive between it and a hackney coach at speed. Two women in Price's cab were thrown out into the street such was the force of the collision. The magistrate stated that "…it was abominable such youths as the defendant should be allowed to take the place of men". Price's father could not pay the £5 fine so he was committed to prison for six weeks.[95]

A similar fate befell the father of 12-year old John Robert Amos in 1834. He crashed his father's cab into a phaeton, turning it over and injuring the four passengers, one of which was an 18-month old baby. Amos senior could not pay the £5 1s damages and the 40s fine, so was sentenced to hard labour for one month in default.[96]

If licences and the law were designed to eliminate children acting as cab drivers then the message was not getting through to some people. At Hammersmith police court in March 1849, a cab proprietor, S Colley, was charged with allowing a fifteen-year old boy to work a cab belonging to him. Colley was fined £5 and costs which he was unable to pay so was imprisoned for one month. The lad who drove the cab was fined ten shillings plus costs for "acting as a driver without being licensed."[97]

Surprisingly, there was no impetus from either the public or the legislature to increase the minimum age to which a licence could be granted to cab driver. Notwithstanding Daniel Whittle Harvey's comprehensive reforms, the minimum age was set at 16 years and enshrined in the Hackney Carriage Act of 1838. Despite the outcry over the age of Henry Bartholomew in the Lady Barham case, Harvey was allowing boys just a year older than Bartholomew, to legally drive a cab or coach. Five years later the minimum age of 16 years was reinforced by the 1843 Act, and would remain as such until 1907, when, mainly due to the introduction of the motorcab, it was raised to 21 years of age. The Act of 1831 allowed for proprietors to be at least 21 years old; the irony being that the position as a cab proprietor, in effect a small business, could not be entrusted to a boy of 16 years of age, but the same boy could drive a horse and cab, or a two-horse hackney coach, at speed through the streets of London.

We have already seen how 16-year old Edward Surman had acted beyond his years when he refused a fare and assaulted a railway official. A less belligerent youngster was John Cockram, who later became a strong advocate of six day working, especially if the seventh day was a

Sunday – he would later win £20 for a 19,000 essay on the virtues of not working on a Sunday. In his book, *Omnibuses and Cabs – Their Origin and History*, Henry Charles Moore includes a biography of Cockram, but even Moore was under the impression that a cab driver had to be twenty-one. Moore alleges that as Cockram was willing to accept 6d fares, when the rest of the cabmen were charging 8d, they put in a complaint about him to Scotland Yard that he was driving a cab under age. "But when Sir Richard Mayne discovered that Cockram was the sole support of his mother, and moreover, thoroughly qualified for a cab-driver in every respect, except age, he declined to prohibit him from driving."[98] Such was the historiography surrounding one of the more well-known Victorian cab drivers. But it wasn't true. According to Moore's own history, Cockram was born in 1833 and became a cab driver in 1851, which would make him 17 years old and thus legally old enough to drive a cab. But, in the census of 1851, he is employed as a carman, a delivery driver, not as a cab driver. His mother had taken over the proprietorship of the licence(s) held by Cockram's father following his death.

Just how big a problem of what were perceived to be underage drivers is difficult to determine. In 1878 at a speech given at the Cabmen's Benevolent Association, in which the Commissioner of the Metropolitan Police, Sir Edmund Henderson was chairman, Moses Smith, a cab proprietor, "thought that licences ought not to be granted to drivers under 21 years of age, nor without their being shown to be capable of driving in the streets."[99]

In the census of 1881, four drivers are aged 16; nine are aged 17, thirty-five are 18; fifty-six are nineteen and seventy-six are 20 years' old. Forty-nine of those under the age of 21 have a father who is either a driver or a proprietor. One in ten of the drivers are supporting a widowed mother. There are no doubt enumerator and transcription errors in these numbers (there are four 15-year old cab drivers) but a conservative estimate would put the number of drivers aged below twenty-one to at least 150, out of a workforce of 12,000.[100]

"They pretend only to licence men of twenty-one years of age" complained one anonymous driver in 1888. "But that is all nonsense. Why, there are boys of only sixteen who are driving gents about London today."[101] The 1891 census reveals, with the same margins of error, three sixteen-year olds driving cabs, all of whom were sons of cabmen, and eleven who were seventeen years' old.[102] In 1893 a deputation of the cab trade met with the Home Secretary, Herbert Asquith, and reported a number of grievances the cabmen had; but the first item on the agenda was the issuing of licences "to boys". Asquith replied that, "No licence is ever given to anyone under seventeen years of age, and that it is only under special circumstances that the requisite permission is granted to a youth under the age of twenty-one." He would, however, make enquiries and, if necessary, would attempt to find a remedy.[103] It was the contention of the men that drivers who had families to support were forced to work longer hours, partly due to "boys" given licences and flooding the ranks, partly due to lack of work and partly due to the high rental charged by the masters. It was this last grievance that would precipitate the trade into a strike in 1894, which only ended when Asquith, acting as mediator and moderator, devised the "Asquith Awards", a rental charging system which all proprietors eventually signed up to. *The Spectator* thought the complaint against boy drivers "was wide of the mark". If there were any such driver out there, presumably none of the editorial staff of the magazine had encountered one, "then he was conspicuous by his absence... The cab driver of tender years is very rarely seen; when he is met with, we are by no means sure that, in spite of his inexperience, we do not prefer him to the ancient and grumpy driver of the old school who sometimes growls abuse from the box of the four-wheeler."[104]

The number of boy drivers may well have diminished through the interaction of Asquith. When a trade delegation met his successor, Herbert Gladstone, to discuss more trade grievances in 1907, the Home Office argued for a *reduction* in the age of drivers to 18 years of age, in order to increase the pool of drivers, especially younger men. It was felt, younger men might be more adaptable to driving a motorcab than some of the more aged cabmen. It was agreed however that there would be no public approval of a reduction in the minimum age – which *de facto* was now accepted as 21 but *de jure* was still 16 years. The Hackney Carriage Act of 1907 settled the matter by stating that no applications for a licence would be given to anybody under the age of twenty-one. Which is still in force today – much to the chagrin of Kevin MacLaren. The son of a taxi driver, MacLaren passed the Knowledge, after two years in 2008. The fact that he was still just 19 years old precluded him from receiving his badge for at least another two years.[105]

Grounds for refusal and appeal options

TfL may refuse to grant a taxi driver's licence if the applicant fails to satisfy the Licensing Authority that he is of good character and fit to act as a taxi driver...

Anyone who is refused a taxi licence today has the right of appeal, but it was not always so. Prior to the takeover of London's taxis by TfL, the decision to refuse a licence was taken by the Commissioner of the Metropolitan Police. When Albert Bowes was refused a taxi driver's licence in 1912, by order of Sir Edward Henry, he took a gun and shot him.

Born in 1850, Edward Henry had been Commissioner of the Metropolitan Police since 1903. It was he who had established that fingerprints could be catalogued and recorded, and be used to capture villains. He was knighted in 1911 for the security he provided for the coronation of George V, though his own security was much less robust.

Albert George Bowes (erroneously called Alfred in some reports) was the youngest of four children born to George & Julie Bowes in 1887. His father, a house painter, had died when Albert was thirteen, and whilst his mother was living with a daughter, and Albert with another sister in the census of 1911, it appears that as youngest child, it was Albert's responsibility to care for his mother. He was working as a porter when he applied to do the Knowledge of London examinations, which he apparently passed. It is not clear if he had taken the driving test but before he was actually issued with a badge, a police check on his character revealed a conviction for drunkenness against him. His application to become a taxi driver was refused. Bowes tried to appeal against the decision and wrote several times to Sir Edward at Scotland Yard, and once to his home at Campden House Court, just off Kensington Church Street. He never received any replies so, armed with a "Webley No. 2, five-chambered revolver" he set out to avenge himself against the man who, as he saw it, had ruined all his plans.

Until recently, Sir Edward use to walk to and from his home to work, but now in his early sixties, the chauffeur-driven car was more practical. After leaving Scotland Yard at six pm on 27th November 1911, he would have arrived outside his home, fifteen or twenty minutes later. After having dismissed his driver, telling him he would not be needed that night, Sir Edward turned towards the door of the communal block of apartments. It was his usual time of arrival. From an upstairs window one of his two daughters watched as he got out the car and made his way to the entrance. He had partially opened the door when he was confronted by Bowes. "I want to speak to you."

"I am too busy." Sir Edward replied, "Call at the office." With that Bowes aimed his gun and fired three shots at close range, only one of which found its target. Sir Edward staggered through the entrance of the house where he collapsed in the hallway, he had been shot in the abdominal area.

Bowes was seized almost immediately by Sir Edward's driver, Albert English, and a passing decorator. As the three struggled on the street, a porter from a neighbouring block of apartments blew a police whistle he owned and also helped secure Bowes. As he was being held, Bowes called out, "Let me go! He has done me an injury."[106]

Despite his age, Sir Edward's wound was not considered to be serious, though he did suffer for some time from shock. Whilst Bowes' family would later claim that "his brain was not properly balanced,"[107] the late Gordon Honeycombe thought that "…Bowes had developed distorted feelings of injustice and humiliation which focused for some reason on the Commissioner. Bowes imagined that the Commissioner was personally responsible for his failure to get a licence."[108] As far as Bowes was concerned, the Commissioner was the man who was responsible for him not getting a licence. He would have received a letter signed by Sir Edward stating that he was not thought to be a "fit and proper person", or words to that effect. Having had a conviction for drunkenness, and now trying to assassinate the Commissioner of Police, it was obvious to any sane person that Bowes was not "fit and proper".

To the surprise of many, Sir Edward appeared in court and spoke up in mitigation for Bowes. Sir Edward had heard that Bowes had ambitions to become a taxi-driver so he could support his widowed mother who was now forced to do washing and sewing for others. Mr Justice Darling informed Bowes that had it not been for the Commissioner's plea for mercy, he would be spending the rest of his life behind bars. In the event, Bowes was sentenced to fifteen years. But why the sudden change of heart by Sir Edward? According to Honeycombe, "After Bowes was imprisoned, Sir Edward periodically drove to Acton, where he dismissed his chauffeur-driven car before calling on Mrs Bowes. He gave her enough money to satisfy her needs and keep herself comfortable and warm. After each visit – and they continued for several years – he returned to Kensington by public transport. For a long time, no one, not even his wife, knew about these visits." When Bowes was released from prison in 1922, Sir Edward paid for his passage to Canada to start a new life.[109]

Limitations on taxi driver's licence

A licence may be limited as to the types of taxis the holder may drive and as to the area in which the holder may ply for hire. It is an offence to fail to observe these conditions.

The limitations regarding a cab driver's licence appertain to what type of vehicle he can drive and where he can work. A cab driver's licence, his bill, originally his "bill of health" to denote he was a fit and proper person, is entitled a "Motor Cab Licence"; this limits the driver into only driving motor cabs and not horse cabs. The last horse cab plied for hire in 1947 but the Public Carriage Office, and latterly Transport for London, have not yet acknowledged the changes enforced on them by seventy years of progress.

A restriction on many licences, particularly those drivers who obtained their badge from about 1990 onwards, limits them to automatic transmission taxis. As with the DVLA driving test, if you pass the driving test in a manual gear shift, then you are permitted to drive any car; pass in an automatic, then you can only drive automatics. The same applies to the taxi driver. Driving a manually geared taxi through the streets of London with its continuous stop-start traffic played havoc with the driver's left knee, which was continually pressing on the clutch. Modern advancements in taxi design, not only with the gears, but also with power steering, allowed a driver more freedom as he was not so tired at the end of his working day. Many drivers persisted with manual gears, such taxis were cheaper to purchase and could sell for more as provincial drivers preferred manuals to automatics. Slowly, automatics won the day in London and from about 1990 the only type of taxi available rent from the garages were automatics.

Up until just before the second world war, a driver would have to take a test for every different type of taxi he drove. Some drivers managed to master the differences between one taxi and another, with some having floor-based gear shifts, some were on the dashboard whilst others were on the steering column. The fleet owners were quite happy with such a situation; men were unwilling to leave their employ if they had to lose a few weeks' wages to learn to drive a different type of taxi. The Commissioner of Police eventually dropped this requirement in a bid to boost the dwindling number of taxi drivers. They had already made concessions to make the Knowledge of London examinations easier, but as there were fewer manufacturers of taxis and more standardisation within those that remained, it was perhaps a sensible move.

The second limitation of a licence is readily denoted by the colour of the badge. A taxi driver who has completed the full Knowledge of London examinations, which includes an intimate knowledge of everywhere within six miles of Charing Cross, and a working knowledge of the suburbs, is rewarded with a green badge. This entitles the wearer to ply for hire anywhere within the Metropolitan Police District. For those not wishing to subject themselves to the full rigour of a green badge, they can opt for the yellow, or suburban badge. Applicants only had to have an intimate knowledge of one of several regions scattered around central London and a working knowledge of central London – the opposite to a green badge.

In 1911, a Departmental Committee appointed by the Home Secretary to look into taxi cab fares proposed several recommendations. In fact, the only item remaining unchanged was the tariff; the committee, accused by the proprietors of exceeding their brief, suggested that drivers keep the extras, petrol should be supplied at discount rate and that special licences should be granted for "distant suburbs". Sir Archibald Williamson's committee noted the "bad service" given by the trade to suburban areas. They recommended that "a special licence might be granted to cabs to ply locally in those special districts at 1s a mile. The driver would be allowed to carry a fare outside his own area ... but not to ply outside his own locality."[110] The committee believed that if such licences were granted it would encourage small proprietors to set up business there, catering for the local trade.

Lord St Aldwyn's Court of Arbitration, which presided over another trade dispute in 1912, endorsed the previous committee's recommendation for a suburban licence. With two such high powered recommendations behind the idea, as well as the apparent lack of service to the suburban areas, it should come as no surprise that nothing was done about the situation until 1934. The London Cab Order of that year allowed for a limited knowledge in specific areas. The first take up was in Haven Green, Ealing, by three green badge drivers: A.A. Baker, E.J. Clinch and J. Warner. Although they would have been allowed to ply anywhere within the Metropolitan Police District, Phil Warren states that they still had to undergo a series of examinations at Ealing Police Station to prove their knowledge of the local area.[111]

There was sufficient work generated at Haven Green to warrant 35 drivers working from the rank although it was not until 1937 when these, and other suburban drivers, could be differentiated when the yellow badge system was adopted and 107 men passed a suburban knowledge in that year.[112]

The introduction of the yellow badge and the associated "quickie knowledge" created another problem, one that exacerbated the drivers nearly as much as the minicab problem. A man would apply and go onto the knowledge of a suburban area, taking about three months to complete it. Once he got his badge there was nothing to stop him working outside his area as if he had done the full, green badge knowledge. It was always a risky business to do so. If a driver was caught plying outside his area, he not only infringed hackney carriage laws but his hire and reward insurance was null and void. Up until the mid-1990's it was hardly worth the chance. A yellow badge might "nick an opportunistic job" but the frequent "badge and bill" checks by Carriage Officers and the police, would make it a very nervous method of working.

The problem existed, particularly at night when the Carriage Officers had gone home and the police had more important things to do than check to see if a taxi driver was complying with the hackney carriage laws. In 1970 Maxwell Stamp acknowledged the "serious abuse" of the system, with "...many drivers with only limited knowledge habitually offering themselves for hire in places well outside their area of qualification, without much fear of detection." The police were all for abolishing the yellow badge system as they found it difficult to prevent the abuse. Maxwell Stamp was against this suggestion as he felt that the yellow badges provided a useful role in the suburbs. His committee recommended that a disc bearing the badge number of the driver should be placed in the windscreen of the taxi and it should be made an offence to either carry the wrong disc or no disc at all.[113] It was a sensible suggestion and it only took forty years to implement.

From the mid-1990's the problem took on epidemic proportions. A Carriage Officer was never to be seen and the police lost interest in getting an "easy nick" by pulling over taxi drivers. Even several of the radio circuits were complicit in the illegal activity by allowing yellow badges to pick up in green badge areas with Dial-a-Cab, the Owner-Drivers circuit, being the only exception. A driver on that circuit, Tom Reynolds, wrote to the Public Carriage Office informing them that certain radio circuits were letting yellow badges pick up outside of their area. Reynolds suggested that drivers should display a green or yellow card in their windscreen, to show what type of badge they possessed. The PCO sympathised and stated that they were looking into an electronic method where a driver would swipe a card. Nothing ever came of it.

Call Sign magazine, the in-house newsletter of Dial-a-Cab carried a rare anonymous letter in its mailshot section in October 2008. The writer was the wife of a Dial-a-Cab driver, she later identified herself as Michelle

Haslam, and had written to the London Development Agency giving her concerns of yellow badge drivers working in London. In a second letter she actually gave the registration number of the yellow badge taxi that was working in central London but this was redacted by the editor of the magazine, Alan Fisher.[114]

Finally, in 2011, Transport for London decided to do something about it. Drivers were to display an "identifier" in the windscreen, with their badge number clearly visible and the colour of the identifier, green or yellow, corresponding with the type of badge held by the driver. Green badge drivers welcomed the move, but with fears that it would not work. A complaint was made by the London Suburban Taxi Association, an organisation that up until then, nobody in the trade had heard of. Melvyn Stanley of the association, highlighted the number of Jewish taxi drivers who would now be made to wear yellow identifiers, which he likened to the wearing of the yellow star forced on Jews by the Nazis during the second world war.[115] Presumably Mr Stanley had no problem wearing a yellow badge upon his chest, or he would have done the green badge knowledge instead.

The introduction of the green & yellow identifiers, made compulsory from March 1st, 2012, was not without a few problems. TfL wanted to make the complaint process easier so any member of the public could go to the TfL website, punch in the number on the identifier, and find the name and address of the taxi driver. It was only when the trade organisations pointed out to Transport for London that they could be held complicit, not only in computer fraud, by giving away such details, but with a taxi driver working in London, it was a good bet that his home was empty and thus liable to be burgled. TfL quickly withdrew this facility. The first issue of the identifiers lasted a little over two years. They were so easily reproducible that they nullified any effectiveness that was intended. On November 17th 2014, new identifiers, complete with hologram and bar code became compulsory, and remain so for the present.

Copy Licence, abstract of laws and badge

At the time of granting a licence the Licensing Authority shall deliver to the licence holder... an abstract of the laws in force relating to taxi drivers and of the penalties to which they are liable for any misconduct.

It was with the reforms of Daniel Whittle Harvey in 1838 that the first *Abstract of Laws*, "a very useful little book", was published. Its aim was to prevent cabmen and coachmen pleading ignorance of the law, though how many could read the contents is a matter of debate. Originally it was issued to drivers of hackney carriages and omnibuses, as well as the conductors and also the watermen on the cab stands – all of whom wore a badge and came under Harvey's remit. The book was issued free to those thus employed but members of the public could also purchase a copy should they so wish.

Unlike the badge (and much later the copy licence), there was no compulsion to carry *the Abstract* and a driver could not be fined for not doing so. They only had to be aware of its wide-ranging contents, though some drivers did give their own interpretation to its contents: A driver named Wells summoned Reverend Henry Christmas for non-payment of his fare from the Plough at Clapham to Tooting during the summer of 1862. When asked how he made up his fare, which included back fare as it went past the radius, Wells said he charged according to *the Abstract*. The magistrate, Dayman, was well aware of this construction; "*The Abstract* did not state that a fare should be divided into two parts. When the Act first came out a book was published, which contained that opinion, and many of the cabmen were misled by it. They could not adopt that view unless it was specified in the act." What Wells was guilty of, as will be seen in Chapter 6, was charging for a full mile up to the radius, then double fare after. This split the fare into two halves, which was not allowed by subsequent acts, though Wells did state that two other magistrates, Elliott and Norton, were of the same opinion as him. Dayman felt they may have at one time believed that interpretation but a recent meeting of the magistrates had discussed the issue and now they were all of the same opinion. Dayman informed Wells that his fare was 3s, not the 3s 6d he had demanded. As was the norm in such cases, Wells was denied costs as he had made an overcharge. The Reverend Christmas was none too charitable and only reluctantly paid over the 3s as he felt

Wells had greatly exaggerated the distances involved, but rather than delay the outcome by having the ground measured, he paid over the money.[116]

John Riches likewise cited *the Abstract* after he summoned his passenger for not paying the full fare. He had picked his passenger up at Hammersmith, just outside the radius, and set him down in Cork St, Mayfair. Riches stated that according to "the book of regulations which every cabman received it was stated that 1s per mile was the legal fare if hired outside the radius. The magistrate, Newton, told Riches that it was "absurd to suppose that a cabman was entitled to charge a shilling per mile if hired a few yards or so outside the radius to take a fare inside the radius. Newton perfunctorily dismissed the summons.[117] He should not have done. *The abstract*, and indeed the law, did specify that Riches interpreted the law correctly. It was an anomaly, and one that would soon be corrected.

In truth, the powers that be are very slow to amend *the Abstract*, even though it is regularly republished. There are still references to "marks" (see Chapter 2) and to the "box", and of course, the cab driver's licence still refers to him as a motor cab driver – to distinguish him from a horse cab driver.

One person who was perplexed by the contradictions within *the Abstract* was taxi driver Maurice Levinson, who vented his spleen on a whole chapter on the subject of taxis and the law in his best-selling book *Taxi!* One inconsistency he noted was concerned with the subject of carrying a person suffering from a contagious disease; *the Abstract* states that it is an offence for a taxi driver to knowingly convey a person suffering from one of a number of certifiable diseases, but in the next paragraph, *the Abstract* states that the driver is allowed to carry such a person if he is compensated to cover loss and expense in having the vehicle disinfected.[118]

The debate even went to the House of Commons, where, on more than one occasion, Sir Barnet Janner, Labour MP for Leicester North-west, (and father of disgraced MP/Lord, Greville Janner), cited Levinson's book and the several contradictory statements and anachronisms contained within *the Abstract of Laws*. Eventually the ruling was changed; it is illegal for a person suffering from a notifiable disease, or a person in charge of them, to allow a person to enter a taxi, without informing the driver. The driver can refuse to carry such a person but if he does, he is allowed to charge extra for the cost of disinfection etc. Whether such a minimal correction satisfied Maurice Levinson is not recorded.

Custody of taxi driver's licence

The taxi owner must demand delivery of the licence to him and on receipt of such demand the licence holder must hand over the licence to the owner.

The very first offence to come before a magistrate with regards to the Act of 1838 was brought by a cabman against his proprietor for illegally retaining his licence. According to the Act any driver renting a vehicle from a proprietor must give to that proprietor his licence. The proprietor must then enter the start date of employment and when the driver leaves his employ he must insert the last date of employment – then return the licence to the driver. If the driver cannot get his licence back from the proprietor, then he is virtually unemployable as no proprietor would be allowed to employ him without retaining that licence – it was their only proof of who they rented the cab to. Thomas Jackson, we met him earlier in the case where his profile was nothing like his description on his licence, summoned his proprietor, George Walter, for illegally retaining his licence and preventing him from working.

Jackson explained that he had been employed by Walter for some time but on the previous Saturday he was dismissed by him for 'coming home short' – he had not earned enough to cover the daily rental of the hackney coach he had been driving. There had to be an element of trust between the proprietor and the driver when it came to paying their daily rental. The proprietor had no idea how much money their drivers took during the working day, though some, like Francis Roe, actually worked their cabs to give them an awareness of the earnings of a driver. The proprietor knew that usually a driver would earn the first few shillings for himself, which would be spent on food and ale. Reliable drivers would often have the rental money for the proprietor on a regular basis but owing to fluctuations in the work even these drivers could not make enough money, not only to pay the proprietor but to take sufficient money home to buy food for their family. Most masters were understandable and had to take the word of their driver on trust, usually with the outstanding balance added to the next day's rental. But if a driver kept 'coming home short' when other drivers in his employ were not, then the proprietor knew he was being fleeced by that driver.

George Walter probably felt the same way when he dismissed Thomas Jackson, enough had been enough. When asked by Hoskins the magistrate why he retained the licence, Walter replied that as he had lent the cost of the licence, five shillings, to Jackson in the first place, and had not been repaid, he felt he was justified in keeping hold of it. The magistrate agreed and it was then that Jackson, who had been demanding the return of his licence, threw down his badge upon the table and exclaimed that the badge was no good without the document, which, according to the Act of 1838 was perfectly true.[119]

Perhaps the most notorious of proprietors were the Isaacs brothers, Moses and Solomon, who each ran their own cab business from separate Clerkenwell addresses, Moses was based in Bowling Green Lane and Solomon in Great Ormond Yard. Both the Isaacs were wise to the fact that the only security they had, other than retaining a driver's licence, was to get the driver to sign a contract agreeing to conditions such as bringing home the horse and cab undamaged, to work to prescribed hours, and, more importantly, to guarantee the proprietor a fixed sum every day. As previously stated, driving a cab is, and always has been, a precarious occupation with no two days being similar and never have passengers been a guarantee for any working day. When driver George Simmons signed the contract that Moses Isaacs offered him in 1844, he must have felt the 12s bounty was achievable. Some proprietors were at this time charging drivers as little as 6s a day for the hire of a horse and cab, but there were others, like the Isaacs' who were charging double this. The hire of the horse and cab was open to fluctuation throughout the year, with Epsom Derby week, being the busiest week of the year (remaining so until the 1960's) and as the drivers were earning more when it was busy, so their master's increased the daily rental of their stock.

Simmons found it hard on the streets and within three days he was already 12s behind. Moses Isaacs was very much the type of master that did not trust his drivers, he had an agreement, the contract, with the driver, that ensured he would be paid. All told, Simmons was soon in Isaacs' debt to 36s. The two soon parted company, though it is not clear if Simmons was sacked, whilst still in debt to Moses, or if Simmons felt he could find work with another proprietor and pay Moses off with instalments. Simmons had no control over the latter option as he owed his master money and Moses was well within his rights to retain Simmons bill until he was paid. Legally, Moses was not allowed to retain the licence indefinitely but to bring the case before a magistrate who would decide on the case and this is what should have occurred. Instead, Moses summoned Simmons for the outstanding balance.

In Clerkenwell magistrates court, Simmons was described as, "a cabman, but whose appearance and manner were much superior to most of his class...". By the time the case had come to court Simmons had managed to reduce the debt from 36s to 12s - a day's rental. On the stand, Simmons told Combe, the magistrate, that he paid his employer "every farthing he had received" and pleaded with Combe not to punish him as he had a large family who would be thrown into distress. It was often said that bachelor cabmen would suddenly become 'married with large families' when they were before a magistrate, often paying stooges to appear in court as so, but in Simmons case it appeared to be a true statement of the facts. Combe asked him if he could pay anything off the debt to which Simmons replied that he had pawned a few little things that morning and could pay Moses a further 4s which he would gladly hand over to him now. Moses wanted all his money, every penny, plus the costs, or Simmons would go to jail. Both the magistrate and the clerk of the court implored Moses to change his mind. Whether he wanted to set an example with Simmons or not, Moses was determined that he should be paid in full, or that Simmons be incarcerated.

The law stated only a maximum penalty for such cases and faced with such intransigence from Moses, Combe announced that he had no option but to send Simmons to jail. If he was reluctant to incarcerate a man who was down on his luck, then his sentence did not reflect it. Simmons was sent to one of the most notorious jails in London, the Clerkenwell House of Correction for fourteen days. On entering the prison, Simmons would be given a bath (whether he needed one or not), he would have his head shaved and be de-loused. He would then be forced to wear a mask at all times to ensure the no-talking policy. Then, for the duration of his imprisonment he would be on the infamous treadmill, nicknamed the cock-chafer, for twelve hours of each of those days. And all this for owing just 12s; what to any right-minded person was a matter of debt, saw cabmen treated as felons. If ever there was a case to highlight the injustice of the law against cab drivers, then it was this. The previous year a law had been passed that prohibited debtors being imprisoned if the sum owed was less than £20; now a cab driver was jailed for owing just twelve shillings.

Just how long George Simmons was in Clerkenwell is not recorded, suffice to say it was not very. He was soon released, not by any judicial process or a change of heart by Isaacs, but by the generosity of the public. A total of £14 was soon received by the court, more than enough for Simmons to pay Isaacs, fetch all his property out of pawn and treat his family. Simmons was not to be the only driver Isaacs upset that year.

On Boxing day of the same year, 1844, Moses Isaacs was assaulted by Richard Davis, badge number 52. The cause of the assault is not reported but if Davis had signed a contract similar to Simmons, then that contract would have stipulated that the proprietor was entitled to his 'pound of flesh' every day. Every day including Christmas Day. Isaacs' faith may have precluded him in joining in with the festivities but both he and his brother expected their drivers to work on that day or at least pay their rental and keep the horses stabled. The result of the disagreement ended up with Davis, who had had a drink, assaulting Isaacs, with such severity that the proprietor could not come to the court himself to press the charges. If he had done he would have seen his old friend, Combe, presiding over the case. Combe said he would not deal with the charge of assault, that would be left to a later date when Isaacs could appear, for now he was happy to proceed with the charge of drunkenness. If Davis was expecting a small fine for being drunk, then he was to be disappointed. Combe, with what was appearing to be a one-man crusade against cabmen, told Davis that unless he could produce someone to give him a good character by five o'clock that day, when the court closed, he would have no hesitation in fining him £5, which, if it could not be paid, would be defaulted to two months imprisonment. On top of this, his cab driver's licence would be suspended for three months. Unfortunately for Davis, he could not get anybody to give him a good character reference, which may say something about him, and he was duly locked up.

Combe was not always so vexatious against the trade, just those whom Moses Isaacs preferred charges against. In court the following day was another cab driver, named Vaughan, who was before Combe on a charge of drunkenness – it became a long running joke in the Victorian press of the numbers of cabmen who appeared before a magistrate for being drunk over the Christmas period. Vaughan pleaded with Combe that in his twelve years of being a cabman he had never once been up on a charge and produced his licence, "which, was perhaps, what no other cabman could show, without a speck." Combe, showing that he could indulge in goodwill during the holiday period "generously forgave... poor cabby [who] left the court with flying colours".[120] For the same offence of drunkenness, which saw Davis incarcerated for two months, Combe was happy to let Vaughan escape with what amounted to something much less than a slap on the wrist.

In August 1845, cab driver George Logan was up before the magistrates under similar circumstances to George Simmons. He too had signed a contract with the proprietor, this time it was Moses' brother, Solomon Isaacs. Logan had agreed to pay Isaacs 13s a day, and the proprietor produced, what he called the 'bond', to prove so, and which in effect rendered Logan as his servant who was duty bound to honour the conditions laid down in the 'bond'. Solomon informed Greenwood the magistrate that despite agreeing to pay a rate of 13s a day, Logan had defaulted on the first day, and that all he had received from him was just a shilling. From the dock, Logan responded that he had paid him 1s 9d, to which Isaacs replied that 9d of which went to the yard keeper. This was yard money and was to be a long running grudge with the drivers well into the twentieth century, even though the practice had been banned from around 1896. A driver paid the proprietor, his master, for a cab for the day, the condition of which was usually unspecified. Drivers could not take out a dirty cab as they ran the risk of being stopped and fined by a policeman. To ensure that the horse was groomed and the carriage cleaned, a driver had to pay the foreman of the yard "yard money" on top of the daily rental. A driver reluctant to pay, would often find his cab put at the back of the queue, whilst those drivers who were willing and able to pay, could go straight out to work.

Logan informed the magistrate that all he had earned that day was 3s. he gave Isaacs 1s 9d out of that and with the remaining 1s 3d he kept to provide food for his family. He asked if the debt could be rolled over for eight or nine days but Solomon was just as intransigent as his brother. Logan then appealed to the judge for leniency with the sentencing, he would have been only too aware of the fate of George Simmons. He stated that he had two small children and that his wife was confined to bed. Greenwood refused Logan's offer of allowing for more time, and hiding behind the old refrain of the law must be upheld, sent Logan to prison, but in this case it was for seven days and without the hard labour.

For all the rights and wrongs of compelling drivers to sign a contract, most drivers were able to comply with its terms. The drivers had a horse (two horses on a long shift) and cab they could take out every day and thus earn a living. For the proprietor he had as close a guarantee as he could wish for, even if it needed the threat of imprisonment to enforce it.

The next driver to fall foul of the Isaacs was Richard Homer. He had defaulted on his contract to pay Solomon Isaacs 14s a day and on Saturday 29th July 1846 he appeared before Combe at Clerkenwell. As before, Isaacs would not take part payment or give his driver time to pay the debt. As before, Combe had 'no option' as he put it, than to send Homer to jail. He was sent to the House of Correction at Cold Bath Fields for 15 days. Unlike the George Simmons case there was no public subscription to pay off his debt, there was no public indignation at how the Constitution, which stated a man could not go to prison for debts of less than £20, was suspended in the case of a cab driver. Not at first anyway. Fourteen days into his fifteen-day sentence, Richard Homer had a choking fit and died within the walls of the House of Correction. He was 23 years old.

The inquest into Homer's death was held within the walls of the same prison. After obtaining a brief outline of the case, the coroner Thomas Wakley MP adjourned until the following day for more information to be gathered. On August 14th Wakley questioned Richard Homer's brother, John, also a cabman who also worked for Isaacs, on the contract that the men signed. John told Wakley, "We pay when we come home at night. If we do not pay, we are liable to be imprisoned, should there be an agreement in writing, not else."[121] It was clear therefore that not all the men who worked for Isaacs worked under the contract system, for those who had a verbal agreement between them, Isaacs could not resort to the threat of imprisonment. Wakley commented that the law states that no man could be imprisoned for a debt of less than £20 but "Cabmen, according to this account of the law, are treated much worse than any other species of debtor." Wakley also noted that the warrant for Homer's imprisonment had been produced, with a scribble that was barely recognisable as Combe's. He also mentioned that there was no sign of the contract signed between Homer and Isaacs. As a warning for all concerned, he informed the jury that if it is proved that the "deceased died from the effects of confinement, some may be guilty of murder, for I do not know if the confinement is legal or not."

A lawyer had been despatched by the family of Homer to the nearby Clerkenwell police court, in order to try and release papers relating to the case. He found Combe very unco-operative and the magistrate scorned the lawyer, "I suppose you are come for food for an action. Bring your action if you like." The lawyer reported the conversation to Wakley and the jury at the inquest, which after hearing from several witnesses, both doctors and fellow prisoners, it was found that Richard Homer died of 'naturally caused suffocation' and could have died anywhere. The jury accepted the testimony and following advice from Wakley, appended the following to the verdict; "In passing their verdict the jury express their regret that the law should afford to any magistrate reason that he could send drivers of cabriolets to prison and hard labour for under £20, when the almost universal public opinion exists that imprisonment for debts under that sum is abolished; and at the same time they express their regret that Mr Combe, one of the magistrates of the Clerkenwell police-court, should know better what is the courtesy due from one gentleman to another, and from one judge of the law to another, than to send such a reply as he had done this day to an application from the coroner's court by John Hutton Esq., solicitor, and they agree in considering the answer of Mr Combe to have been in every respect improper, rude, and undignified."[122]

The Standard described Combe as acting like the "…sharpest of sharp-practising attorneys caught in some illegal act…"[123] in his reaction to the officer sent to his court by the coroner. *The Standard* pondered whether the remarks of the jury regarding Combe were just or not, but *The Era* stated that the jury's statement should be "written in gold and Mr Combe should be made to repeat it on every cab-stand in the kingdom."[124]

Whilst the debate on the treatment of Richard Homer was still raging, Solomon Isaacs took out another summons, this time against driver Henry Clifford. Isaacs informed the magistrate, and once again it was Combe - the two must have been on first name terms by now - that Clifford had reneged on his contract to pay him 12s a day. The action he brought was for the outstanding balance of 10s plus the 2s costs in bringing the summons. Clifford informed Combe that he had only worked for Isaacs for just one day but failed to earn enough to pay for the rental of the horse and cab. If he was given time, then he was sure he would be able to pay off the debt by instalments. Once again Combe went through the motions of asking Isaacs to be reasonable and allow time for the debt to be paid. Once again, Isaacs insisted that the driver should go to jail. The criticism Combe had suffered over the previous fortnight had had an effect on him – he allowed Clifford to pay off the debt over time.

If relations between the Isaacs' and Combe had appeared frosty, it did not last for long. In 1849 an un-named cab driver was summoned by Isaacs, the report does not state which one, to Clerkenwell Court on a charge of being drunk and damaging the cab. Combe was once more the magistrate and after hearing the evidence, he adjudged the cabman guilty and was about to lay down a fine when Isaacs interposed. The proprietor informed the magistrate that a fine would have no effect on the driver.

Isaacs believed that the drivers paid a weekly amount into a society, an anonymous one in this instance, and any fines imposed would be immediately paid. This form of insurance, box money, was frowned upon by many as it meant the guilty were back on the streets and the public were once again at their mercy. There are reports that such societies existed around this time and that some drivers were forced into contributing, but as some drivers were still being jailed for being unable to pay their fines the practise was by no means universal. Coombe seems to have agreed with the pleadings of Isaacs and despatched the unfortunate cabman to one month's hard labour in the Clerkenwell House of Correction.[125]

The approbation heaped on Combe did not travel very far. Cab driver John Robins had signed a written contract to pay his master, John Norris, 11s a day. Soon he was found to be 22s in debt and Norris issued a summons against his driver. Robins did not deny that he had taken out a cab on the two days in question, but he had, at least he thought he had, a legitimate case for not paying his master. "The agreement is to pay day by day," said Robins, "and as he allowed me to go out on the last day he can't recover for the first, because he ought to have had payment for the first before he let me go out again." The magistrate informed Robins that his knowledge of the law was very limited and he had to convince him of the errors of his argument. When Burrell the magistrate asked Robins if he was willing to pay the outstanding 22s, Robins replied that he was not. Having given the option of paying, Burrell had himself no option but to send Robins to jail for 21 days.[126]

At Westminster police court, a number of drivers were summoned by a variety of proprietors over the non-payment of the cab rental as per their contract. One, un-named proprietor, who had given his driver several more days to pay off his debt, asked the magistrate if hard labour could be added to any jail sentence he handed out. He argued that the drivers cared little about being incarcerated in Tothill Fields Prison, as friends and family could bring in food "of any description". The drivers "treated the matter as a sort of respite from labour", which, if the phrase had been around at the time, would have described the prison as a 'holiday camp'. Given such a lackadaisical report on the conditions of prison, the magistrate, Broderip, felt obliged to state that he would indeed add hard labour to any future sentences.[127]

The year 1858 was infamous for being the year of the Great Stink. The long hot summer combined with a lack of adequate sewage disposal caused many who could afford it to pack up and leave London earlier than they usually planned. The upper and middle classes were apt to spend the "season" in London where they would congregate at balls and dinners and other such extravaganzas, each one creating work for the cabs. But when the season ended and they left *en bloc* for their country retreat, London was all but deserted except for the poorer classes and those who, because of commitments, could not leave. Unfortunately for the cab trade once "the season" ended, the work became scarce. Those that could, invariably resorted to different employment during the next few months. For those that remained, they just had to endure the long period between jobs and earn what they could.

One such cab driver was William Ransom who hired a cab, under contract from a Mr Gard of Notting Hill. Gard had summoned Ransom as he was now in debt to him for £3. The contract had originally been for 13s a day but as the work began to dry up, Gard had been willing to accept 10s a day from the driver, but even this proved hard to earn. Ingham the magistrate looked through Gard's accounts and saw that the driver had kept up his payments to about mid-August. Gard acknowledged that "…it had been a very bad time for cabs. The season this year terminated about mid-July…" but as Ransom "had not "behaved well to him", he wanted the matter dealt with by the magistrate.

Ingham asked Ransom what he was willing to pay to his master. Ransom replied that he "…had not a farthing and could not pay anything." Ingham said he had no alternative but to order the defendant to pay the £3 and 2s costs. Already having declared he had no money, Ransom was imprisoned for 21 days in default of payment.[128]

The lack of co-ordination among magistrates had long been a bone of contention within the cab trade. Certain magistrates would fine a drunk cabman ten shillings or have him serve a week in prison in default of payment; another magistrate would, for exactly the same offence, fine a driver a pound or send him to prison, invariably with hard labour, for a month. Such was the discrepancies within the magistracy. The differences had been highlighted in 1857 by the defence barrister for a driver named Wright who had defaulted on his contract and owed his master, West, the princely sum of ten shillings. What made this case different was that it was being held at Lambeth police court, on the Surrey side of the river. Wright's advocate informed the magistrate that his client would be pleading guilty to owing the money and that he was unable to pay. It was therefore an inevitability that his client would be sent to prison. Wontner, the barrister, pleaded with the magistrate that his client should be sent to Horsemonger Lane Gaol as a common debtor and not to the Wandsworth House of Correction where he would be shaved and forced to wear a mask and treated like a common felon – all for being ten shillings in debt. Whenever cabmen were sentenced at this court for failing to honour their contract they were routinely sent to Wandsworth. For the same offence on the Middlesex side of the river, the cabmen were imprisoned for debt, such was the discrepancy within the magistracy separated by the width of the river Thames.

Elliott the magistrate had much sympathy with Mr Wontner's view but denied the magistrates were in error. The problem as he saw it was with the opening of the jail at Wandsworth, which saw the closure of the prisons at Guildford and Kingston, and it would have been to the latter that his client would have been sent at one time. As for the Horsemonger Lane Gaol they only admitted prisoners committed to trial, prisoners under remand, bail defaulters and deserters; every other type of prisoner was therefore sent to the only other prison in the county, Wandsworth House of Correction. Elliott stated however that he could not believe that the people who framed the Hackney Carriage Act ever envisaged drivers having their hair cut off and subjected to wearing a mask just on account of being in arrears. He therefore would seek time to confer with other magistrates and take their opinion. A few days later all the concerned parties were back in court and Elliott surprised them all when he said that having looked at the agreement between Wright and West "…it appeared to be a contract for the hire of a carriage from day to day, and nothing about earnings, so that it amounted merely to a matter of debt, with which he [Elliott] had nothing to[with]."[129] The charge against Wright was dismissed, the magistrate having washed his hands of the conundrum was quite content for the master to take his driver to the county court where it would be the judge's problem. It was exactly what the cab drivers had been saying for years but precedents are not made at magistrate's courts and as far as other defaulting cab drivers were about to find out, the proprietors had other tricks up their sleeves

Defacement or loss of taxi driver's licence

The licence becomes void if any of the particulars on it are erased or defaced. The taxi owner must preserve it undamaged and undefaced and make no unauthorised mark on it.

Only a magistrate or a judge has the power to place an endorsement on a cabman's licence; the only entries a proprietor can make is the date the driver began working for him and the date he left. This however did not stop masters penning their thoughts upon the cabman's licence, as some found out to their costs.

When a cabman named Sutton left the service of his master, Ruscoe, a proprietor in Bishopsgate, there appears to have been a discrepancy between the amount the driver could pay in on his daily rental, and the amount the master was expecting. Ruscoe handed back the licence to Sutton – he could have deposited it in a police court if he wanted redress over the money owed – but on the reverse side of the licence, Ruscoe added that Sutton "could not be depended upon". Sutton had subsequently applied at three different cab yards for employment but was refused at each of them. In desperation he sought advice from a magistrate who told him his only redress was to take the matter to the county court. This he did and the jury found for the cabman and set the damages at £10.[130]

To avoid being fined by the courts and at the same time protecting their interests by warning other cab masters of problematic drivers they had to devise a way to beat the system in such a way that the masters could be forewarned on the conduct of a cabman, but the driver himself would be unaware that he had been blacklisted. "The proprietors," stated one anonymous driver, "who are, by the way, in the closest combination – have a secret system of marks; and if a driver is so unlucky as not to earn during the day, the amount of the hire of his cab, or, as the slang of the profession is, "brings home short money," his license is straightway branded by a mysterious damning sign, understood by all masters."[131] The system of using 'damning signs' was called "chairmarking" and at various times throughout the nineteenth century, a variety of codes were used.

In the same year that cab proprietor Ruscoe was fined, 1858, one of the more prominent cab proprietors, Richard Case of Gough Street, Grays Inn Road, was also charged with defacing a cabman's licence. In this instance the driver, Ireson, informed the court that after working "on and off" over a period of 14 years for Case, he had been given a kicking horse which he could not control. As Case would not allow him to take another horse out, Ireson asked for his bill (his licence), which was not immediately forthcoming. Ireson had to return the following day to see if Case would give up the licence, but even then, the proprietor was determined to have the last say in the matter. He threw the licence to the ground and as Ireson went to pick it up, Case lunged at him with a pitchfork he was holding. Instead of stabbing him, he struck him with the flat of the prongs upon the shoulder "which did not hurt him". When Ireson asked to be allowed to clear up his possessions from the stable, Case chased him out into the street with the pitchfork. The assault did not form the basis of the court case. Instead, Ireson alleged that Case had entered several initial letters onto the reverse, and it was these initial letters that had prevented him from getting work with other cab proprietors. Case denied the charge, or even that he had written the initial letters on the licence. He knew he was charged with defacing a cabman's licence but it was not until he saw the actual licence in court that he was aware of what exactly the defacement consisted of. A member of the jury asked if it was possible that they could be told what the initial letters stood for. The question was objected to by Case's lawyers and the question was deemed by the judge to be inadmissible. The jury conferred and then informed the Judge it was of no matter. One of the members of the jury was aware of the code and they would be informed when they came to reach a verdict. It was bad news for Richard Case, the jury found for the plaintiff, Ireson, and awarded him damages of £20.[132]

Cabman Allen had worked for William Denyer from May 1859 until he was dismissed for "coming home short" in August of that year. After filling in the required dates, Denyer also added "a mark like the letter O". In court, two cab proprietors who had turned down Allen's application for work, both stated that the "O" on the back of a licence signified that the driver had "brought home nothing". Another witness, a cabman, said he had asked Denyer why he had marked Allen's licence, Denyer's reply was "Because the _____ owes me a day's work.". There was further debate on whether the "O" was larger than the one Denyer admitted writing, he said his one was small and he himself had employed drivers with an "O" on the licence. A cab proprietor named Howard informed the court that he had tried to act as an arbitrator between the plaintiff and defendant. He had promised Allen £5 plus employment, plus he would endeavour to get his licence replaced if he would drop the charges against Denyer. Allen had informed him that it was in the hands of his lawyers and he could not pull out. The jury deliberated for over an hour before finding for the cabman and Denyer was told he would have to pay Allen £2 10s damages. Perhaps the last laugh in this case should go to the final witness who informed the court that; "It is strange that Denyer should mark your licence, for he never marked mine, and I have shown him as bad tricks as anybody could."[133]

Hyam Hart took his master, Alfred Paine, who was also a publican, to court for chairmarking his licence in 1877, "by filling out the date of dismissal in words instead of figures" Hart had once been a proprietor, so "was aware of the secret understanding of the trade". To strengthen his case, Hart was allowed to produce a witness, George Totman, a cab proprietor, who had refused to employ Hart. Instead of bolstering Hart's case, Totman said he knew nothing about any secret understanding within the trade, and that he had refused to employ Hart for a totally different reason. Hannay said he had no option than to dismiss the charge against Paine.[134]

When Thomas Posgate was charged with passing off a worthless coin as a half sovereign, the horse keeper of the yard from where he was employed, said Posgate "had a very bad character. I only know it by his license, on which the date is endorsed in writing instead of figures, and that means a bad character... the date in writing, also means getting drunk and all like that."[135] The horse keeper, generally the enforcer of the yard, informed the Old Bailey that he himself was teetotal and he denied the accusation from Posgate that, "he was generally about three sheets to the wind between 1 and 2 o'clock in the night." Fortunately for Posgate, his version of events was believed and he was acquitted by the jury. It does show however, that if the writing of the date was in written form, there were still proprietors who were willing to employ a man with such a licence.

One cabman complained to a magistrate that the date had been "written large... and in a peculiar way. We call them 'chair' marks" he explained. Partridge the magistrate, could see nothing wrong with the entry and told the driver he should take his claim to the County Court if he was that aggrieved – an option the driver could not take as he was now unemployed and could not afford to do so.[136] William Hempstead believed he had been chairmarked when his employer filled in the entries on the licence in red ink. The case came up before Hannay, who adjourned so that fellow magistrate Paget could decide the case. Paget said the proprietor, William Rogers, had done all that was required by law and the act did not specify the colour of the writing and dismissed the summons.[137] Another driver, whose licensed had been marked in red ink had a similar outcome when the magistrate said he saw nothing wrong. "You can't?" replied the cabman, "It prevents me from getting a livelihood. It is a fair 'chair' mark." The magistrate advised the driver that he should take the licence to Scotland Yard where a replacement may be issued, which he immediately left the court for.[138]

A driver who had been refused employment by three different proprietors showed his licence to Shiel, the Westminster magistrate. "What is the matter with it?" enquired Shiel on examining the licence.

"The particulars of my last service look as if they were written with a stick. The writing is large and beastly – that is understood in the trade."

"If a man chooses to write large," replied the magistrate, "I have no power to make him write small." The application for a summons was dismissed.[139]

Despite the recent lack of convictions, the practice was all too real for the drivers. Many who were chairmarked had come home short on the last day. "Chairmarking is generally the result of spite." So Frederick Edmunds, secretary of the Cabdriver's Mutual Aid and Protection Society informed the *Pall Mall Gazette*. The society could report on a rare success against a proprietor, whose mark on the back of a member's licence had prevented the driver from being employed for three or four weeks. In court, the proprietor was asked for a specimen signature, and when this was compared with the scrawl on the back of the licence, the magistrate had come down in favour of the driver who was awarded £5 plus costs. Such actions showed the advantages of belonging to a Union or a protection society and CMAPS had several other successes against proprietors. As an indication of the strength they wielded, they forced several proprietors to seek a replacement licence for the driver in order to avoid a heavy fine in court. If the driver was out of work whilst this process was going on, the society would summon the proprietor for illegally retaining the licence.[140]

One method of avoiding prosecution, as far as the proprietors were concerned originated with a group of owners in Westminster "...by far the lowest in the trade"[141] in the 1850's. What became known as The Westminster Red Book contained the names and addresses of those drivers who had failed to pay their master the full amount of rental, or were continually drunk or any other misdemeanour. Any driver whose name was entered within the book would find it hard to gain employment from a subscribing proprietor. As its popularity among proprietors grew it became known just as the 'Red Book' and was infamous within the trade, the proprietors who subscribed to it formed an ad hoc Red Book Association. A Red Book started up in Clerkenwell in 1890 had, by 1894, 1785 names, mostly from drivers refusing to pay their last day's rental – which usually occurred as a the drivers went on strike.

Copy of licence to be available

A taxi driver must have the copy of his licence with him at all times during his employment or when appearing before a court, and must produce it for inspection on demand to a police constable or authorised officer or any officer of a Court.

Since the introduction of badges and licences in 1838, a policeman pulling up a cab driver for whatever reason could only rely on the badge as proof of identification. He would not know if the man driving the cab was the legal holder of the badge – at least not until he checked the records at Scotland Yard. One way of circumventing this was to have the drivers carry a duplicate, or copy, licence. In every way it was similar to the original licence held by the owner of the cab; it would contain a description, which would later be a photo, his name and address, as well as, at one time, the name and address of the owner of the cab.

For the proprietors, the issue of the copy licence was a godsend. The only security they had against a driver was the licence they held whilst the driver was in their employ. No proprietor would take on a new driver without being handed a driver's licence which was tantamount to a character reference – a "bill of health, hence to this day it is described by a driver as his "bill". Filled in correctly it would give the length of service with past employers and from this, future employers could judge the character of the driver they were about to employ. However, if the driver were to attend a court, in any capacity, he was required by law to have his badge and licence with him. The proprietor was compelled by law to hand the licence over to the driver without any guarantee that the driver would return with it, or use the opportunity to seek employment elsewhere, especially if he was in debt to the proprietor. The copy licence nullified this fear of the proprietor; he held onto the cabman's licence throughout the tenure of employment. If the cab driver were to appear in court then his copy licence, and badge, would suffice.

For the drivers however, it was another cudgel to beat them with. They now had to wear a badge, conspicuously upon their left breast, as well as carry a paper document with them that they must look after, no matter how inclement the weather. The copy licence became law with the 1907 Act, the same act that legalised taximeters and pushed the London cabmen into the modern world. A large demonstration against the Act, which marched from the north side of Waterloo Bridge to Hyde Park, voiced their anger over the copy licence but all to no avail. The law remained and continues to do so.

Badge to be worn

Every licensed taxi driver must at all times during his employment and when required to attend before any justice, wear his badge conspicuously upon his breast, in such manner that the whole of the writing on it is distinctly legible, and must when required, produce it for inspection, and permit any person to note the writing on it.

The above ruling relates not only to cab drivers having to always wear a badge when working, but also when "required to attend before any justice". Most drivers are aware that if they appear in court defending a charge under the hackney carriage laws they must wear a badge, but the ruling states that a badge must be worn before any justice, whether a magistrate or a high court judge, an inquest or family court, as prosecutor, defendant or witness. In 1844 an inquest jury heard that a cabman who had testified at an inquest of a man who died in prison was imprisoned for one month for not wearing his badge. Both the Coroner and the inquest jury spoke out against the "monstrous severity of such a sentence" before resuming their examination of the dead man.[142]

In 1855 an un-named cabman charged a carman with assault but before he could give his evidence the magistrate noticed he was without a badge. The magistrate informed the cabman that that he was guilty of an offence by standing there without his badge and as such the magistrate could not hear his evidence. After the cabman pleaded his ignorance of such a law, which as has already been stated is no defence, the magistrate relented and heard the case. The carman was fined 20s for the assault but the magistrate then turned to the cabman and informed him that he could be fined 40s for not wearing his badge in court. To the cab drivers of London this summed up their lot. A drunk man who drags a cab driver from his box, by grabbing hold of the badge, assaults him and tears his clothes to shreds is only fined 20s; but the penalty for the victim of the assault for not wearing a badge was deemed to be twice as severe. Fortunately in this case, after admonishing the cabman, no further action was taken.[143]

That a cab driver must wear the badge "conspicuously on his chest" can be a matter of interpretation between a driver and a policeman.

A driver who had charged a woman 5s for a 2s 8d fare was summoned before a magistrate for the alleged overcharge and not wearing his badge in a conspicuous place. As the female passenger did not turn up for the hearing, the overcharge summons was dismissed. As to the badge it had "slipped into his pocket inadvertently." He was fined 10s.[144] The driver who held badge number 3612 was fined 10s for wearing his badge on his back, where it had "shifted accidently".[145] In 1865 the police at Notting Hill had a purge on cabmen, and omnibus drivers, for not wearing their badge 'conspicuously'. John Emery was one of the cabmen summoned and he was wearing his badge in court, hanging by a strap from a button hole of his coat. He informed Dayman, the magistrate, that he always wore his badge in such a manner but he did concede that his arm could have covered the badge whilst he was driving. Dayman reiterated the importance of wearing the badge upon the breast, where it could be seen by a policeman. By Emery's own admission he was not wearing the badge as required as it hung down by his trouser pockets. Emery disagreed; the badge was on his breast. "Your knowledge of anatomy them," replied Dayman, "is very imperfect." Emery was fined 2s 6d plus 2s costs. Dayman also dealt with another cabman, even more leniently. He had been wearing the badge upon his breast, but wore two coats over it. He dismissed the summons against that driver but advised him in future to wear the badge on the outermost coat.[146] Bizarrely, all that could be said about the body of cabman George Swain when it was pulled out of the Regent's canal, after being submerged for three weeks, was that the driver's badge "was in its proper place."[147] Richard John Cope was stopped by a policeman whilst driving his taxicab in the City of London. When asked for the badge, Cope pulled it out of his pocket. He told the Lord Mayor, sitting as a magistrate, that he did not have to wear a badge as he was not working, the people in the taxi were his wife and brother-in-law. The Chief Clerk of the court informed the Lord Mayor of the fact that whenever a taxicab was in a public street it was deemed to be plying for hire. The Lord Mayor agreed and whilst he thought the police constable was perfectly correct in bringing the case to the attention of the court, he would dismiss the charge against Cope on payment of the costs.[148] The Chief Clerk's remarks will be looked at again in Chapter 3.

Licence and badge to be surrendered on expiry

Upon the expiration of his licence every driver must within three days deliver his licence and badge to the Licensing Authority.

John Morgan Stannard had been one of the original receivers of a badge, 4168, when first issued in 1838. Having driven a hackney coach for the best part of a year he realised the profession was not for him. When, on the following June 1st 1839 he had not applied for a renewal, he had three days to hand his badge and licence back to the Metropolitan Carriage office. It was explained to the court that "It was very material to the public that these [metal] tickets should be returned, otherwise they got into the hands of "cads" [bucks] at coach ranks, who had been refused licences and who, possessing the badges, set up as drivers without being licensed at all, and who, of course, could not be found if they committed any offence." Stannard, who had admitted to losing the badge, now informed the magistrate that he had lied when he said he handed it in within the prescribed period, he was perhaps fortunate to be fined only 20s plus costs.[149]

Stannard was more fortunate than fellow hackney coachman, Wolfe Israel. He too neglected either to renew his licence or return the badge within three days. The magistrate, Burrell, saw no reason why the penalties of the 1838 act "should not be rigorously enforced" and fined Israel 40s or hard labour for one week if he couldn't pay.[150]

Prohibition against using unauthorised badge

No person may use or wear or retain any badge without a licence in force relating to it or, for the purpose of deception, use or wear or have any badge resembling or intended to resemble any badge granted under lawful authority.

Those people who obtained a badge without being licensed and illegally worked with it are dealt elsewhere. In this section we deal with those who had another driver's badge but had no intention, at least at the outset, of working illegally with it. John William's highlighted the uselessness of a badge when he appeared in court in 1856. He was not up on any charge but disagreed with a letter published in the *Morning Advertiser* from Daniel Whittle Harvey, the Commissioner of Police, on remedying the congestion on the streets of London. Williams stated to the Alderman the 'real' reasons why traffic was so bad and that reform of the hackney carriage trade would alleviate the problem. Alderman Lawrence supposed that Williams would like to propose a new Act of Parliament, which Williams said he would. Williams argued that the badge was useless for identifying the driver. He had been an owner driver for fifteen years and had evaded the law. Williams' assertion that he evaded the regulations is open to interpretation. He was known as 'The Cabmen's Attorney-general' but, as will be noted at various places throughout this book, he had a singular lack of winning any cases. He believed, wrongly, that as the law allowed an unlicensed driver to take a cab out for 24 hours, he could legally, roll over each 24-hour period, which he apparently did for 15 years before being fined – for being unlicensed. He now informed the Alderman that "about sixteen months ago he took to wearing the badge, and he sometimes wore his own number [2819] and sometimes a 'foul' one." He also admitted to owning ten badges with 'foul' numbers. He did not elaborate if the badges had been legitimate badges at one time and not handed back, thus putting a "stop" on the number, or if they were fraudulently made badges that he had come across. In either case, he was legally bound to hand them over, but Alderman Lawrence, probably fully aware of Williams' sobriquet, interrupted him and told him to put all his thoughts down on paper, and, taking the hint, Williams left the court.[151]

The importance of a badge to a driver was so important that it took on its own intrinsic value, and could even be left, albeit illegally, as security for a loan, or, as George Levy found out, security for a fine. Levy had been fined 5s for being drunk but as he could not afford to pay the fine he was allowed to leave his badge with the court as security. This allowed Levy to try and raise the money, which he could not do by driving a cab as it was illegal to work without a badge. A couple of days later he was arrested once more for being drunk in charge of his cab. He had ignored the warnings of not taking a cab out until he redeemed his badge, and in place of his badge, he had a card with his badge number written upon it. The magistrate was not impressed. For being drunk and for working without a badge, he was fined £3. The term of imprisonment he would most likely serve for not paying the fine was not mentioned.[152]

After being accused of aiding a prostitute to rob a gentleman of his gold watch and chain and £6 in gold, Stephen Owens was asked by a policeman for his badge. He first replied that he did not have one, then admitted that he had left it behind the bar of the New Barn tavern in the Strand as security on a loan of a couple of shillings. When he went there, the policeman found that the publican had two other badges which he held as security for loans of 1s, 2s and four shillings. It was for the latter amount that Owens had pledged his badge, 16757. Flowers, the Bow Street magistrate, felt that advancing money to cabmen, which in all certainty would be spent in drink was too great a temptation. "In his opinion it was as bad as the offence the prisoners were charged with." Other than advising the carriage office, no further action appears to have been taken against the publican.[153]

When a driver named Morton did not return his badge after its expiry date a policeman from the carriage department at Scotland Yard was despatched to Morton's home in Caledonian Crescent, King's Cross. Once there, he soon found out that the badge was in possession of the Morton's landlord, and was being held by him as security for the 18s 6d rent that he was owed. The policeman demanded the badge back, stating that it was not Morton's property to hand over in the first place. The landlord said the policeman could have the badge – as long as he was willing to pay 18s 6d for it. The landlord became "greatly excited" and eventually pushed the constable out of the front door and down the steps of the house. The landlord was then arrested for assaulting a police officer. "The defendant said that [Morton] had tricked him into accepting the badge by representing that he was bound to redeem it before he could get another licence, and he thought the police were helping the man." The magistrate, Roe, sympathised and only fined him 5s plus costs for the assault on the constable, and ordered him to surrender the badge, paying the 2s costs of that summons.[154]

2 Taxi Licences, Plates, Notices and Marks

Driver not to use taxi with unauthorised or counterfeit plate or mark

On every taxi licensed by TfL a plate is fixed on the outside at the rear of the vehicle bearing the following particulars:

Taxi No...

Licensed to carry .... persons

On the rear of every licensed taxi in London is a white rectangular plate. It bears the name of the licensing authority, today that is Transport for London, it informs the public of the maximum number of passengers the vehicle can carry. The largest piece of information is the plate number, a unique number for that particular cab which it would hold for one year.

In 1654 the Fellowship of Master Hackney Coachmen was created with thirteen of their number being appointed as overseers to the other 187 members. Each of the members was a master hackney coachman in that he owned the coach and horses and could employ a man, a servant, as he was a master, to work the hackney coach for him. The Act of 1654 clearly stated that the maximum number of hackney coaches allowed on the streets of London, Westminster, Southwark and its environs was to be a maximum of 200, but allowing the hackney coachmen to police themselves was to be a big mistake. Every member of the Fellowship had to pay an initial fee of forty shillings followed by an annual fee, or a "fine" as it was called, of twenty shillings. Once the 200 vacancies (allowing for a reserve body of 13) were filled, the overseers still found men wanting to be licensed and willing to pay a little bit more.

Despite the maximum of 200 coaches permitted under the Act, the overseers themselves thought that 250 hackney coaches was a more acceptable number, and were quite open about the flagrant breach of the law at a hearing before the Court of Aldermen. The Aldermen believed that the actual number of hackney coaches was nearer 300 than 200. The Act of 1654 clearly stated that the maximum number of drivers was to be 200; rather confusingly it then stated that the number of coaches should not exceed 300, nor the horses to exceed 600. The extra number of carriages would be necessary to cover breakdowns, which were all too frequent. But who owned these 100 surplus carriages is not made clear. Each member of the Fellowship was only allowed one licence, there were no plates at the time so there was no way of enforcing compliance. If every master hackney coachman had three horses, two at work and one resting, then this would be sufficient for a maximum of 200 coaches. There was clearly ample opportunity for misinterpretation of the law, which no doubt proved to be of financial benefit to the overseers. All thirteen of them were replaced but the corruption remained and after just three short years of licensed control the Fellowship was dissolved.

Dissolution of the Fellowship did not mean an end of the hackney coaches, they were now unlicensed hackney coaches and anyone with a coach and horses could now operate in a free-for-all system which saw the numbers profligate. All of this was a bit hard on the original 200 members of the Fellowship, who formed themselves into a body called, appropriately enough, "The 200". They had obeyed the original law and paid the requisite sums of money, now all and sundry could drive around London and steal the work they thought was rightfully theirs.

Following the restoration of the monarchy in 1660 they appealed to Charles II for legislation to regulate the trade. Charles was more affable to licensing hackney coaches than his father who saw them as a nuisance. Not only had Charles I licensed sedan chairs as direct competition against the hackney coaches but an Act of Parliament in 1636, which allowed up to fifty coaches, was designed to make it uneconomical to run a hackney coach at all. In 1662 a more substantial Act than its 1654 predecessor was passed. Parliament, seeing the mistake of letting hackney coachmen govern themselves appointed commissioners to regulate the trade, and these commissioners could be fined for any breaches of the Act such as excessive numbers. The Act brought in the first "condition of fitness" a phrase not used at the time but today denotes a requirement that has to be fulfilled in order for a taxi to obtain the white rectangular plate. In 1662, the condition of fitness referred only to the horses and that they had to be at least 14 hands high. Just as important, the Act allowed for a "marke of distinction by figure or otherwise as the Commissioners shall thinke fitt..." This mark of distinction was the forerunner of the white plate. It would not only allow for easy identification of the hackney coach following a complaint, but by each coach having a unique number, up to the maximum of 400 allowed by the Act, that figure could not be exceeded. The Act of 1662 allowed for the 'mark of distinction' to be in force for the duration of the Act, seventeen years. There was no provision within the Act that the coach should be inspected prior to licensing. Given the condition of the roads at the time any particular coach had a short shelf life but the Act allowed for the 'mark' to be transferred between coaches as long as it was only on one coach at any one time.

The Act of 1662 did run its full course of seventeen years but as Charles II had prorogued Parliament in 1679 there was no renewal or replacement and once again the streets of London became a free-for-all for anyone with a coach and a pair of horses. In 1688 James II increased the number of hackney coaches to 600, but the Court of Alderman in the City of London saw this as an infringement of their right to license hackney coaches within their own jurisdiction and would not recognise the legality of these newly licensed coaches. The drivers of the extra 200 could take a fare into the City of London, or Southwark but they could not sit on a stand for a return fare or pick anyone up of the streets – the very fact that their 'mark of distinction' was over the number of 400 would cause them to be readily identified. They were in effect, the first suburban drivers, similar restrictions are placed on today's yellow badge drivers with their yellow identifiers providing the same role. This situation remained until 1694 when Parliament once more addressed the situation of having regulated licensed hackney coaches on the streets, and since that date, the licensing of hackney coaches in London has been continuous. The Act stipulated that "...every Coach soe lycensed shall have a Marke of distinction by Figure or otherwise as the said Commissioners shall thinke fitt And the said Marke shall be placed on each side of every such Coach in the most convenient to be taken Notice of to the end they may be knowne if any Complainte shall be made of them."

These 'marks' need only be painted on at this stage and the number could be transferred from one coach to another, again, as long as no two coaches held the same number.

From 1713 the 'mark of distinction' could rightly be called a 'plate' as all hackney coaches, 800 at the time, were compelled to carry a tin plate with their number stamped upon it. The design of these tin plates would go through a variety of changes but would remain with the cab trade until the last years of the Public Carriage Office in the 1990's.

In 1844, cab proprietor, James Standen, described as a very respectable man, pleaded guilty to the offence of not having the words "to carry two persons" inscribed legibly on his plate. Standen informed the magistrate, Burrell, that the neglect was due to the repairs effected by the coachmaker who, following an accident, had omitted to replace the plate. What rankled Standen most was that he was in court not because he had been arrested by a policeman or following a complaint from a passenger, but he was a victim of a 'common informer', one of the more notorious ones, Richard John Carter. Standen argued that "It [was] very hard that a fellow like a common informer, who was not aggrieved, and who had not the public welfare at heart, but who was seeking to put money in his pocket, should be permitted to prowl about the streets and complain of men who were living by honest industry. …Every person in the metropolis knew that a cabman was bound to take two persons, and [I] regret to say that they were frequently, in consequence of the depressed state of the trade, obliged to carry more at the same price." When Burrell the magistrate mentioned that he was not too sure of the penalty for such an offence, he was informed by Carter that it carried a maximum fine of 40s – the informer's moiety being half of that plus his expenses. As Standen pleaded guilty to the charge Burrell fined him 10s, a nominal fine but the severity of which, as Standen saw it, far exceeded the offence. He pleaded for further mitigation but to no effect, and even asked, in an attempt to prevent Carter benefitting from his "prowling around" if the fine could go straight into the poor box. "If the City of London magistrates did not entertain information from informers, why do it so in this court?" argued Standen. It was all to no avail and Standen reluctantly paid the fine and costs to the clerk of the court.[1]

If any person uses or has in his possession without lawful authority any altered or irregular plate, notice or mark required for the purposes of the Order of 1934, or any counterfeit of any such plate, notice or mark he shall be guilty of a breach of the Order as well as an offence under the Forgery and Counterfeiting Act 1981.

In 1817 the owner and driver of a hackney chariot number 668, Charles Gates, was before a magistrate charged with extortion and adding a surcharge to the legal fare. Gates expressed astonishment at the charges, saying that he knew nothing at all about the fare. He even provided an alibi for the period of the alleged offence which was accepted by the court. He also came up with a theory as to how an innocent man was before the court. He told the magistrate that if he turned his plate upside down, the number would then become 899. He believed that the driver of 899 was working with his plates upside down, and that he, Gates, was getting the blame for the other driver's misdemeanours. The driver of 899 was subsequently summoned and he was found guilty on several charges of extortion. One of which he was fined £5, which could well be the highest fine levied against a hackney coachman to that date; he was also imprisoned for two months in Horsemonger Gaol for a separate offence.[2]

A simple remedy to prevent plates being turned upside down would be to include wording or a crown on the plate, neither of which seems to have been adopted for some time. When Major General Sir Ronald Ferguson took a hackney chariot from Cockspur Street, Trafalgar Square, to his home in Clarges Street, Piccadilly. The fare should have been 1s 6d (1s for distance plus 6d for being after midnight) but the driver insisted on being paid 10s for the journey. After suffering a large amount of verbal abuse from the driver the General decided to pay the exorbitant charge and report the driver after taking the number of his plate, 144. At the subsequent court hearing in Marlborough Street, a proprietor named Smith stated that he was the owner of twelve coaches, one of which was number 144. None of his plates were on a hackney chariot and he could show that hackney coach 144 was engaged at the time the General was overcharged. He further explained that recently the plate of the coach had been reported lost, they were easily removed, and the Hackney Coach Office had replaced the lost plate with a new one with the same number, so there were evidently two vehicles plying in London, one a hackney coach, one a hackney chariot, but both with the same number, 144.[3]

Proposals for the proprietor to carry their plate number inside the coach were adopted but only after a lengthy debate. Some protagonists saw the gesture as futile as the number was already on the outside in a number of places and would be just as impossible to see with the onset of darkness. Nethertheless, the proposal was implemented and soon after some of the more disreputable drivers and proprietors were inventing ways of confusing the public. There was the usual malpractice of turning the number upside down or the more ingenious method of having figures painted onto individual pieces of wood that could then be slid into place. The proprietors argued that there was nothing wrong with this method as the numbers could be moved to another vehicle if one was off the road, and if they had more than one coach then the figures could be re-arranged to agree with the plate number on the rear of the coach. They could also be re-arranged by the driver to sow confusion into the mind of the passenger.

From January 5th 1832 every hackney coach was to carry four plates, one on the rear, one on each side and one inside. The plate fixed to the rear of the carriage was the Stamp Office Plate, the adjunct of the Treasury had been given control of hackney carriages under the 1831 Act. It was down to the proprietor to supply the other three plates. The Act specified that one of them, containing the same number as the plate number must have figures "projecting from the plate" (so it could be 'read' in the dark by touch) of 1½ inches in length, with no other wording or figures upon it and must be fixed inside the carriage. The two side plates can be painted, black figures on a white background and were to display the name of the proprietor as well as the plate number. The Stamp Office Plate on the rear of the carriage, also stated how many passengers the carriage could legally carry, the forerunner of today's "licensed to carry …persons".

Despite the thoroughness of the 1831 Act to bring reform to the trade, proprietors were still endeavouring to put their own interpretation of the

Act to good use. In 1832, an extensive hackney coach and cab proprietor by the name of Willis had to answer a summons by Seagrave, an inspector appointed by the Hackney Coach Commissioners. Seagrave testified that he "…saw the Defendant's cabriolet with a circular piece of wood, so constructed as to have a sliding plate, on which the number and name were printed in legible characters. This plate could be taken in and out at the pleasure of the driver, who could commit frauds upon the public with impunity; whereas the Act of Parliament required that the plate was to be so affixed as to render it immoveable at will or pleasure." Willis argued that although the plate could be taken out, he felt he had not broken the law as every cab proprietor in the capital was using a similar system – which was probably true enough given the large number of cab proprietors who attended the court to hear the case.

Seagrave admitted that the sliding plates were in common use but the drivers "… can take out the plate and with red chalk make a different number, and afterwards substitute their own number on the plate if they have imposed upon their fare." According to Seagrave, the plate was not properly affixed as per section 28 of the recent Act and therefore the prosecution should stand. After a reading of the relevant section, the magistrate could see no reference to plates being immoveable and said he would dismiss the charge. Seagrave fired one more shot across the bows, "hackney coachmen and cabmen can demand and take 3s or 4s for a eight-penny fare, or ask whatever they please; they can play tricks with the plates and the customers." The magistrate informed the inspector that his duty was to find the drivers in the commission of fraud, not depend on anticipation of it. If he felt the law was insufficient in this respect he should apply to the legislature for change. As a warning to all the other proprietors present, Seagrave informed the magistrate that he would be watching out for them as he knew the "frauds practised every day were numerous."[4]

"It appears," wrote a reporter for the *Morning Post*, in March 1832, "that by the precious jumble of nonsense and absurdity called the "New Hackney Coach Act," which appears to have been framed for the purpose of perplexing the public, that all carts, waggons and vans, must have the name of the owner and his place of abode painted either in white letters

on a black ground, or in black letters on a white, and the letters must be an inch in length. Byers [an informer] has, however, discovered by another clause all hackney coaches, chariots, cabs, &c., must have the name of the owner painted *only* in black letters on a white ground..."
Proprietor William Cripps informed the magistrate that he was under the impression that he had complied with the law in painting the required information on either side of his cab, but as it was white letters on a black background, the magistrate fined him 20s plus costs.[5] Such cases go to show the intelligence of the informers who studied the laws to the level of a barrister, and were probably one-time students of law.

Wardle, a Westminster proprietor, was summoned by Byers in March 1833, for having an illegible Stamp Office Plate. Wardle denied the charge and produced the plate in court showing that all the figures upon it were perfectly legible. Byers argued that the plate had since been touched up, making the figures distinct. Wardle emphatically denied the charge as did his driver. On careful examination, Byers pointed out where the plate had recently been painted and the magistrate agreed with him. Wardle was fined the maximum £10 penalty and suffered the wrath of the magistrate in committing perjury. Later that day Wardle tried to have the fine reduced by admitting to altering the plate and apologising to the court. His apology was accepted but his attempt in getting the fine reduced was unsuccessful.[6] It was not until the Act of 1853 that legislation prevented informers, the bain of the cabman's life, from benefitting financially by bringing charges against cabmen.

John Allen was charged with dangerous driving by a policeman in September 1850. Allen denied the charge and said at the time of the alleged offence he was nowhere near the Surrey Gardens but was in Cheapside. The arresting officer admitted that Allen, badge 393, was not the driver, who had badge 7703. The officer said he was absolutely certain however that he had the right cab as he made doubly sure he recorded the plate number. Allen drove a privileged railway cab and had "Eastern Counties Railways" painted above the plate number. The policeman was equally certain that there was no such legend on the cab he had stopped. It was clear to the magistrate that there were two cabs working with the same number plate. Elliott dismissed the charge against

Allen but also stated that he "hoped the police would lose no time following up the inquiry, as it was most important that the practice of changing the numbers, which was so subversive to public justice, should be put an end to.[7]

The practice to which Elliott was alluding to was called "bishoping" and only the most detailed inspection of the plate, could it be detected. "The mode by which this ingenious process is applied is by plugging up the numbers on their plates with a black adhesive composition, and by obliterating the first or last, or transforming one of the centre figures, totally change the number. The consequence is that the person whose number happens to agree with that to which the 'bishoping' alters that of the delinquent is the person summoned, while the real guilty party escapes scot free."[8]

Stamp Office Duty had been abolished once the Metropolitan Police took over the control of London's hackney carriages, the fee remained the same, it just became known as the licence fee. Proposals for the 1853 Act, which led to the trade's first all-out strike, saw the licence fee changed to the equivalent of a shilling a day. There was much agitation at the time to have a Sunday as a rest day. Not working on the Sabbath was deemed fine for the gentry, but not for cabmen, who received a lot of work on a Sunday by ferrying passengers to and from church. This led to another grievance from the trade, the chastisement they received from the public, who, having used their services, criticised them for not being in church themselves. Pressure was mounting for drivers to have a six-day week but many of the proprietors were against the idea. Food and stabling for horses had to be paid for seven days a week and they could ill-afford to lose one-seventh of their annual income, just so the driver could spend all day in a tavern. Not every driver was so inclined to waste away their days at a local hostelry and one cabman, John Cockram, actually paid his master five shillings in order not to work on a Sunday. Bowing to moral and political pressure, the government relented and allowed those who wished to have Sundays as a rest day without having to pay duty for their day off – or did they?

New licences were based on the number of days the carriage would be required to work, six or seven days being the only choice. It was widely held that the new rate was equivalent to a shilling a day, no matter what the licence, the actual cost was slightly higher. A six-day plate cost £16 19s a year, equivalent to 339 days at a shilling a day, in effect, a six-day man was paying duty for every alternate Sunday getting only 26 days free. A seven-day licence cost £19 11s, or the equivalent to 391 days at a shilling a day – exactly twenty-six more days than in a year. So as long as there were more seven-day than six-day licences, the government made a profit whilst maintaining the sanctity of not working on a Sabbath. To differentiate between the two sets of duty paid, any carriage that only had a six-day licence would be numbered 10,000 or higher, all seven-day plates were numbered below 10,000. It was a simple and effective remedy to stop a carriage which only paid a licence for six days, working a full week. The numbering system also stopped anybody who for one reason or another had a day off during the week, from actually working the Sunday to make up the loss as the high number of the plate actually precluded such workings.

To aid identification even further, the colour of the plates was different. In a move similar to the old tax discs, once the six and seven day plates were phased out in 1869, each year's new plate was a different colour to the preceding year.

The importance of maintaining the plate was highlighted by the case of William Adams, an owner driver, in 1852. Several weeks prior to the renewal of his plate he was thrown from the cab and badly injured. Whilst he was off work his wife had not only to look after their large family but also find sufficient funds to pay for the following year's Stamp Office plate. Failure to pay would see the cab seized, the plates removed, and the horse, carriage and harness, sold to pay the accumulated debt. In order to prevent this, Adams's wife pawned all their furniture and managed to raise the necessary sum. She gave this to their ostler, who promptly absconded with the money. Fortunately, the neighbours rallied round and enough money was raised to retain the plate. A year later, the now healthy Adams and his wife were strolling in Greenwich when they chanced upon their ostler who was promptly arrested and admitted to the theft. Though what become of him is not recorded.[9]

To the outside world Moses Moses was very much the "Government Contractor, General Agent, Exporter & co." that the name plate on his premises in Bell Lane, Spitalfields, proclaimed. His wife sold clothes on a market stall in Petticoat Lane which perhaps showed that the world of government contracts and exports was not profitable. His wife may have been of the same opinion but she did not know of the £20,000 he had stashed in a bank. Next door to Moses's office was a cab yard, the proprietor of which was also Moses's landlord. It was these cabs that were the secret of Moses's wealth. By day, the cabs would be worked as a normal cab but, at night, the plates would be removed and replaced with false ones. With accomplices, the cabmen, who were licensed, would "assist in the successful plundering of London warehouses. In many instances, the vigilance of the police has been frustrated by their carrying sliding plates bearing different numbers, and substituting one plate for another..."[10] It confirmed the accusations of many that a large number of hackney coachmen were of a criminal class. Numerous robberies could only be effective with the use of a carriage, and what better carriage than a London hackney coach to drive anonymously through the streets of the capital. Acting on information, the City of London police raided a warehouse rented by Moses and found so much stolen property that it took up most of the space in the vaults of the Mansion House. Moses's defence was that he was just a buyer and seller of property and had no prior knowledge of the articles he held. With no paperwork to back up his defence he was found guilty and sentenced to transportation for 14 years. He returned after serving only six years away, having benefitted from a "ticket of leave" which enabled his return. He was soon up to his old ways and in 1866 was found guilty of receiving a large amount of stolen jewellery (and seventeen elephant's 'teeth') and was sentenced to twenty years imprisonment. There does not appear to have been any action taken against his "organised gang of cabmen" or their proprietor, possibly for want of evidence.

When PC Stancombe attempted to stop a cab in Hampstead Road in 1869, the driver of the cab whipped his horse and drove off but was soon stopped by Stancombe who gave chase and caught hold of the horse's head. After a brief struggle, the driver was arrested and the plate, 1807, was seized. Plate 1807 was legally held by a proprietor named Lawrence of Ledbury Mews, Notting Hill. The plate the policeman had seized from the cab was forged. The driver pleaded guilty to knowingly using fraudulent plates and thus defrauding the Stamp Office out of £1 1s plus a subsequent 7s a week during the time the plate was used. With the law more concerned about defrauding the revenue offices, instead of hackney carriage law, the driver was sentenced to six month's hard labour.[11]

Before a cab could receive its plate both it and the horse were inspected as to their conditions of fitness. Once passed, the stamp office plate was fixed and the cab could legally ply for hire. There was nothing to prevent the proprietor taking the plate from a good cab and fixing it onto another cab that would not have passed the inspection. "There is some chicanery" wrote *The Times* in 1865, "in letting out tinkered-up cabs, and there is some chicanery in substituting cabs which have not been inspected and passed for those that have." The following year the Commissioner of Police, Sir Richard Mayne informed a parliamentary committee that "…cab proprietors brought one decent cab to be certified, and applied the certificate to a hundred others." The problem is exemplified by the fact that in 1865, 2,934 cabs were reported as being unfit for public use.[12] That was just the carriages, if the horses were considered as well the number is very easily doubled.

The "tinkered-up cabs" and 'horses that could only stand because they were supported by the shafts' were synonymous with the night cab and in many instances both cab and horse were consigned to night work as their appearance was reportedly "too shameful" to be seen by day. The efforts of inspectors from the RSPCA helped reduce the number of horses that were unfit for such work. The unfortunate animals did not end their days in a field but were despatched to a local slaughterer in order for the proprietor, in many cases, to avoid prosecution. As for the cabs, from 1872 the police instigated a system of stencilling directly onto the body of the cab which included the month the cab had passed its inspection, as well as the initials of the police commissioner and prevented the plate being removed and put onto a "tinkered-up cab". The stencil marks remained until 1960 when they were gradually phased out and a new series of plates, where the plate number itself could identify the month the cab was passed. In effect, a cab passed in January would have a plate number beginning with "1" followed by two or three other digits; one passed in May would begin a with a "5". A five-digit plate beginning with a "1" would signify October, November or December, depending whether the second digit was a "0", "1" or "2" respectively. As the number of cabs increased in the early seventies, the series was extended in a similar way to the 24-hour clock; a cab passed in May would begin "17xxx" and one in December with "24xxx". As a further security check a taxi would have alternate year plates, so a taxi passed one year (in May), with a plate beginning with a "5" would have a plate the following year beginning with a "17" and revert to a "5" in the third year.[13]

The plating system was computerised in 1998 and galvanised steel gave way to plastic. The numbering system of the plates also changed in favour of a strict numerical sequence which also contained the actual date the plate would expire plus a hologram to prevent forgery.

3 Plying for Hire

Restrictions on plying on hire

A taxi driver may not ply for hire elsewhere than at some standing or place appointed for that purpose.

There have always been more cabs than ranks spaces but the problem was exacerbated after 1832 when limitation on the number of drivers ended, from a maximum of 1200, but the number of stands within the Metropolis was not increased. In 1834 it was stated that there were 1700 hackney cabs and coaches but only enough room on the stands for 291 of them at any one time, nearly six vehicles for each space. If drivers could be fined for picking up anywhere than elsewhere on a stand, then it was imperative they found a space on a rank. This created "creeping up" – slowly driving along a street, thereby causing an obstruction, in the hope that a space may occur on a nearby stand. Once the informers had realised there were rich pickings to be had just by waiting near a stand, the summons began to roll in. Alderman Kelly was told that when he had a driver before him for 'creeping up', there were nearly seventy other cases of a similar nature outstanding. Staples, the informer, told the magistrate that he himself was only responsible for four of those summons. Kelly accused the informant of creeping up himself in a furtive manner so as to get the number of the cab. Not wishing to set some form of precedent for the remaining cases, Kelly said he would look further into the matter but it appears to have been dropped, much to the disappointment of the informers.[1]

Buck was another informer, and one who had slightly more success than his compatriot. Originally, stands were not marked out on the roadway, and hackney carriages could form a stand in any street that was at least thirty-two feet wide. The carriages would park in the centre of the roadway, leaving enough space on either side for passing traffic. Buck managed to bring charges against "a considerable number" of proprietors for allowing their coaches to stand, plying for hire, within eight foot of the kerb. Buck, who received a moiety, or percentage of the fine imposed, perhaps did not receive the pay-day he was expecting. The law had only just become enforceable under the recently passed Act of 1838 and the magistrate fined each of the proprietors, who were responsible for the actions of their drivers, just 3s plus costs in each case.[2]

John Webb was accused of acting as a witness for the prosecution in a case at the Old Bailey in order to re-establish his character and have his cab licence, that had been revoked for misconduct, re-issued to him. He had been accused of many crimes but the only time he served a sentence of imprisonment was for hackney carriage related crimes; the first being two months for using a cab licence under a false name, "It was no false name at all – they said it was and I was convicted." He was also fined, "7s, 8s, or 10s for plying for hire within eight feet of the kerb; that is what I have been in prison for, not for dishonesty." Whatever the merits of John Webb's character, or lack of them, the example highlights the dangers a cabman faced when charged with a hackney carriage offence. As in this case a small fine could easily see a cab driver unable to pay and being imprisoned as forfeit.[3]

We met another informer, Richard John Carter, in the previous chapter, where he was something of an expert in the law regarding hackney carriage plates. His expertise did not extend to the law on plying for hire. On Christmas Eve, 1838, several hackney coach proprietors answered a summons by Carter for plying for hire illegally in Trafalgar Square. The square had only been so named in 1835 and Nelson and his column were yet to make an appearance. Carter had based his prosecution on the basis that any hackney coaches standing stationary in the street were, according to the recent 1838 Act, plying for hire. Conant, the magistrate, read out aloud to the court, the relevant section; "It shall be unlawful to stand or ply for hire in any street, common passage, or alley." He then turned to Carter and informed him that the word "square" was missing. As a "square" was not, by definition, a street, common passage or alley, the summons against the proprietors would be dismissed. Having paid out the costs of a summons against each of the proprietors, Carter was considerably out of pocket. He warned however that every other square would soon be blocked up by hackney coaches and there would be very little the law could do.[4]

The problem of not enough spaces available on the stands for the number of cabs looking for work reared up again when a driver answered to the charge of driving slowly "...trying to get a fare." The cabman explained to Yardley, the magistrate, that he had no wish to violate the law. The cab rank was full and the whilst he could have put on at the rear of the rank, whilst not being on the stand ("putting on foul"), which would render him liable to a penalty, he thought his best plan of action was to drive slowly through the streets until a space occurred on the stand. He denied that by doing so he caused any congestion behind him. The driver also went onto explain that there were currently 3000 cabs and coaches, but spaces on the stands only amounted to 2000, although another 85 spaces were to be created within the next few weeks.

Yardley had sympathy for the plight of the cabmen and could not see how a magistrate, could fine a cabman for the offence cited whilst there were not sufficient spaces for the cabs. A police inspector all but confirmed the figures given by the driver but he stated that at any one time, approximately 1000 would be hired, thus leaving sufficient space on the ranks for those looking for work. Just how much use a space on a rank in Kensington is to a driver looking for a space in Whitechapel, as the cabman was, was not entered into. Yardley dismissed the summons against the driver, and informed the inspector that more ranks were needed and at some date in the near future, he would like to be given all the relevant data.[5]

The situation became so intolerable that the drivers said they were forced to pick up in the streets in order to support their families. Drivers always had picked up in the streets, whenever they thought they could get away with it; but now the numbers doing so were so great that the law had to be enforced. When, in 1849, a number of drivers were brought before Broughton the magistrate, for 'gagging' (plying for hire whilst moving along) he sympathised with the plight of the cabmen and blamed the government for the situation; "Government licensed all who applied, while the number of cab ranks were limited, and, therefore, not half of the licensed cabmen could find business in a legal way." By fining each of the drivers a nominal 1s plus costs, it was the magisterial method of telling the police not to bring charges like these before me again.[6]

Notwithstanding the feelings of the magistrate, the police soon after charged over 30 drivers for plying for hire in the streets or leaving cabs unattended, but this time at a different court. One driver, named Lizard, gave a long oration from the stand about the system of granting licences by the Stamp Office and Metropolitan Carriage Office (both within one year to be relieved of their duties regarding the hackney carriage trade). The magistrate Bingham expressed some sympathy to the "considerable hardship inflicted on cabmen as the law now stood [but he could not] alter the Act of Parliament. Bingham was not as sympathetic to the plight of the cabman as Broughton and fined the drivers 2s 6d each plus costs.[7]

Christopher Small was said to be travelling at walking pace along Sloane Street when a pedestrian called out to him. The pedestrian had been refused by several cabmen, all of whom wanted to pick up at the Great Exhibition, the Crystal Palace, then in Hyde Park. Small's defence, put forward by his solicitor, Mr Long, was that when refusing to be hired, "the vehicle must either be at the usual place where vehicles to be hired are standing, or in some other place." The magistrate, Arnold, countered that if the cabman was not plying for hire, then why had he stopped. This was done, according to the solicitor, out of convenience and politeness. Small was coming to the end of his shift and the horse had a loose shoe, hence the walking pace of the cab. An ostler testified that on returning to the yard, the horse did have a loose shoe which he repaired. Arnold was still not satisfied. If the defence of a loose shoe had been given to the prosecutor, then he, Arnold, would have no problem saying that it was a reasonable excuse in which to refuse a fare. However, as he stopped in the street to enquire which direction the pedestrian was going, he was deemed to be plying for hire and was fined 20s for refusing a fare.[8]

Arnold was once more the magistrate in 1856 when Joseph Fellingham was summoned "entirely upon public grounds" – a 'catch-all' designed to punish for trivial offences without appearing vexatious. Fellingham was outside the Cremorne Pleasure Gardens when he was hailed by a gentleman. Fellingham did not stop, nor enquire in which direction the gentleman was travelling in. For his part, the pedestrian accused the cabman of picking and choosing his fares, it was raining heavily that night and it was well known that cabmen outside the Cremorne only wanted to carry parties of three or four people, as the drivers could charge more. The driver denied the charge. He had been out with the same horse since two o'clock in the afternoon, it was now half-past eleven. His master testified that he returned the cab to the yard within ten minutes of the alleged refusal. Arnold asked the prosecutor whether Fellingham was holding his whip upright, indicating that he was plying for hire, to which the pedestrian replied he had not. Fellingham was not on a stand, he had not stopped and he had not signalled to the prosecutor that he was actually plying for hire. Arnold said he had no alternative other than to dismiss the summons.[9] Fellingham was fortunate, doubly so with Arnold, who usually came down strongly against cabmen, another cabman in another court, may not have been so lucky.

The *Morning Chronicle*, in 1857, highlighted the number of cases against cab drivers at Marlborough Street (whose jurisdiction covered the popular Oxford and Regent streets). The magistrates were tied up for several hours in dealing with complaints made by the police regarding cabs illegally plying for hire and/or obstruction. The newspaper had some sympathy for the plight of the cabmen who were being fined for what could only be described as minor offences but which the clothes of the wife and children had to be pawned just so the fine could be paid. In order to emphasise the trivial offences that cabmen were fined under, thus delaying the more important business of the court, the newspaper highlighted the case of Henry Wisdom. Wisdom had had his number taken by a policeman who saw him "hold up his finger" toward some gentlemen, an action which he alleged, constituted illegal plying for hire. Wisdom denied the charge and the three gentlemen concerned even turned up in court to back the cabman. The policeman replied that they were not the gentlemen he had seen Wisdom approach, to which they replied that at the time the driver's number was taken, they were the only people in that part of Regent Street. The magistrate, Beadon, had no doubt about the honesty of the three witnesses, but they must be mistaken as to the time the (honest) policeman was referring to. The only person whose honesty was impinged was Wisdom, and for "holding up his finger" he was fined five shillings, with 2s costs.[10]

John Webster was charged with several offences after refusing a fare at

Fenchurch Street Station in 1858. The prosecutor alleged that as he approached a line of cabs Webster "held up his hand in the usual way, as if he wanted a fare". Webster called the waterman who swore that "...on that stand, the cabmen never held up their hands for fares." This merited a sharp rebuke from the Lord Mayor, sitting as chief magistrate in the City of London, "Why, man, I wonder you dare say such a thing. Cabmen do so on all stands." After accusing the prosecutor of perjury and using a false name to summon him under, Webster was perhaps fortunate only to be fined a total of 40s plus costs, which he paid "with a surly air."[11]

James Green, 13438, did not hold up any of his appendages when he was accused of refusing a fare. He was holding up his whip, which again, was deemed to be a sign of plying for hire. Green tried to protest that he hadn't stopped when the prosecutor climbed into the cab, but he was not believed. He was fined 10s with 3s costs, and Green could only watch with indignation as his hard-earned money was paid into the poor box.[12]

George Taylor did not move any parts of his body either whilst he was waiting outside Liverpool Street Station – his passenger did. At least a prospective passenger. Taylor saw a gentleman walking towards his cab who had made a motion with his hand. Taylor assumed the man was to get into his cab, and out of politeness called out, "Cab, sir?" The gentleman replied that he did not require a cab, and a nearby policeman who heard the exchange, arrested Taylor for plying for hire. In court, he had a good solicitor; "Of course cabmen took their vehicles out to get fares. The ranks were crowded, and what was a man to do? He wanted to earn a living... Cabmen had a hard life, out in all weathers, for the benefit of the public as well as themselves, and he thought it very hard for one to lose a day's work to answer such a summons as this. [Edmunds the solicitor] thought if the defendant were ordered to pay costs it would be ample." Alderman Pound agreed. The summons against Taylor was dismissed on payment of costs.[13]

When taxi driver Colin A Hunt was driving through Victoria in the early hours of July 8th 1947, he was flagged down by a pedestrian. Hunt, believing the pedestrian was drunk, did not stop, did not slow down to enquire which direction the pedestrian wanted to go, nor did he raise a finger or hand to suggest he was for hire. The number of the taxi was taken and at his subsequent appearance at Bow St Magistrate's Court, he was fined 10s for refusal. Hunt was allowed to appeal to a higher court but the judges there not only agreed with the magistrate but doubled the fine to 20s. Hunt had been a driver since just after the Great War. Following the end of the Second World War he opened up a knowledge school, training demobbed servicemen into becoming taxi drivers. In 1958 he would publish *"Here It Is"* an essential guide to London for anyone undertaking the Knowledge. Undaunted by his lack of success thus far, Hunt took his case to the High Court and the Lord Chief Justice finally applied common sense to the issue. The relevant law was in section 7 of the Act of 1853 and provided that "every cab found standing in any street or place shall, unless actually hired, be deemed to be plying for hire..." The Lord Chief Justice took this to mean that a cab had to be stationary to be plying for hire. If a driver sets down a fare and somebody approached the taxi wishing to hire it before the driver moved off, the driver was compelled to take the passenger anywhere within six miles, even if he was about to go home. A member of the public could no longer compel a taxi to stop when hailed, but if the driver does stop, then they are deemed to be plying for hire.[14] If, however, a taxi is stationary in traffic then he is not deemed to be plying for hire. This remains TfL's definition of plying for hire, at least with regards to taxis.

An unintended consequence of the above clause from the Act of 1853 was that no cabman could buy his own taxi unless he could have it garaged when it was not working. If a driver lived outside the Metropolitan Police District (MPD) he could park his taxi outside his house on the road as a London taxi could not ply for hire outside the MPD. A driver who lived within the confines of the MPD was open to prosecution for plying for hire than elsewhere than on a rank and leaving his cab unattended. Both of which could carry hefty fines.

Section 7 of the 1853 Act was finally revised in 1968 and allowed a taxi to be parked in a recognised parking space and legally be unavailable for hire. This allowed a large number of drivers to purchase a taxi for the first time in their working life. Numbers were so great that the waiting list for a new taxi from Mann & Overton, then the only manufacturer of

London taxis, grew from a few weeks to two years. The fleet garages became smaller and the federation of proprietors, the LMCPA, was weakened as drivers departed from the garages to venture out on their own and some yards closed their doors for good.

Since the dawn of the motorcab the driver had worked on a commission basis on the meter, ranging from 25% in 1907 up to 40% and over by 1968. It was always a source of dispute between the drivers and the owners and was responsible for several strikes within the trade. Now that the cabs did not have to be returned to the yard at the end of the shift, the commission- based "on the clock" was replaced with the "full-flat system". A driver would pay an agreed weekly sum and would have no need to return to the garage until the following week's rental was due. The proprietor was now only responsible for the maintenance of the taxi, whilst the driver could work as many hours as he, and now she, liked. The TGWU (Cab Section) also lost out. The garages were their mainstay within the trade, with many of the yards being closed shops. Many would put the decline of the Union within the cab trade down to its ineffectiveness during the early years of the minicab crisis from 1961 onwards but the number of union men within the trade has dwindled and whilst it is no longer the force it once was, numbers have increased in recent years due to organised recruitment drives.

A taxi driver is thus prohibited from taking up a position in any other place and remaining there for the purpose of plying for hire.

In cab driver parlance this is called "hanging up". It is a hackney carriage offence that, if anything, is on the increase. With a severe lack of taxi ranks, where a taxi driver could gather a few minutes rest (if he's lucky, or longer if he is not), many drivers take the opportunity of parking outside an office block or a place of entertainment. They run the risk of getting a parking ticket, particularly from a camera, or being moved on by the police but many feel it is a chance worth taking. A problem arises however when a prospective passenger hails a passing cab, assuming that a cab parked, say on double yellow lines, is not available. The passing cab has every right to accept the fare, but it is a fare which the cab that has been "hanging up" feels that it should, by either right or convention, be theirs.

Eli Smith was a frequent practitioner of "hanging up", though in 1895 the term itself had not entered the cabman's vocabulary, the legal definition being "unlawfully and in a clandestine manner taking a fare from another cabman". Smith would park his cab up outside the Langham Hotel, but remain out of sight of the nearby cab rank. If he was asked by a policeman if he was engaged he would answer that he was, but when a prospective fare emerged from the lobby of the hotel he would announce to them that he was available for hire and he would take the fare that should have gone to the rank. The porter of the hotel must have been in on the scheme, it would have been his job to notify the rank, by means of the then ultra-modern, electric bell. This would be the signal for the first cab on the rank to pull round to the main entrance. Today, the last week of August can be a very quiet week with most of the taxi travelling public on their summer holidays. In 1895 the last week of August was the last week of "the season" when London was full of visitors, both foreign and domestic. Many who lived in the country at various times of the year could be found in London doing the social rounds during "the season". It was a very lucrative period for the cabmen. August 24th however was uncommonly quiet, so quiet in fact, that the cabman on point of the rank, first cab, had been there between two and three hours. Whilst Smith was able to convince the police that he was lawfully engaged, his fellow cabmen were more suspicious. Six of them left their cabs and walked around to the side of the hotel and confronted him. Smith informed them that he was engaged but the cabmen were not convinced. They kept a watch on him and it was not long before he accepted a fare, no doubt to the shouts and insults of the watching cab drivers. It is not uncommon for cab drivers who have had work stolen from under them to block the culprit in and convince the passenger that they should leave the cab and get into the cab that has been abiding by the law on the rank. Smith was allowed to drive off with the fare but his number was taken and a summons was taken out. In court Smith explained that he had a number of friends who were employed at the hotel and when there were social gatherings he liked to think that he too was a member of staff and would agree to convey the guests at the behest of the hotel and for a nominal fee. He admitted that on the day in question he was waiting for a party of men when a gentleman came out and asked to be driven a short distance. It was a lame excuse. Plowden the magistrate, was not easily taken in; "What the defendant had done was illegal; it was more than that, for he [Plowden] considered his conduct shabby towards his fellow cabmen. Unless there was absolute fairness all round, those cabmen who acted legally would be handicapped by those who behave illegally." Many cabmen, then and now, would agree with these sentiments. Eli Smith was fined 10s 6d with 4s costs.[15]

Duty of taxi driver to accept a fare

A taxi driver, unless required by the hirer to drive more than 12 miles...or for a longer time than one hour, is under a duty to accept a fare:

An Oxford Street linen draper, John Reed, was not a happy man in late November 1853. He had been to a music hall in Store Street, Tottenham Court Road, and now, no doubt due to the fog, could not find a cab to take him to his home in Rotherhithe. Every cab stand he passed was devoid of cabs and those that passed him on the street were driving slowly, looking, according to him, for a more profitable fare than a single gentleman. No doubt the cabmen would argue that they were driving slowly due to the thickness of the "London Particular". As he approached London Bridge he espied a cab heading westward; he called out to the driver if he was engaged? The driver, Anthony Cooper, 6906, replied that he was not engaged but on hearing the destination was Rotherhithe, Cooper allegedly told Reed that he was willing to pick him up, but only if he was going in the same direction that he was going. At no point during this exchange did Cooper stop his cab. Under the Act of 1853 a passenger could insist on being taken to a police station, at no extra cost, to have any dispute with the driver settled. Cooper would have been within his rights to refuse Reed on this point, as he was not a passenger, but informed him that if he was willing to pay for it, then he would convey him to the nearest police station. Once inside the cab, Reed probably thought his chances of convincing the driver to take him to Rotherhithe were increased. On this his hopes faded. Cooper took him to a police station, and after telling an inspector the story so far, they were both requested to attend Southwark police court to have the matter settled. Reed never did get a cab and had to walk the remaining couple of miles.

In court before A'Beckett, Reed related the previous night's events, "I now want to know whether a cabman can legally refuse to take a fare under such circumstances." Before adding, "I would not have attended to make the complaint had I known the trouble." People did not mind bringing errant cab drivers to justice in the name of public duty, but many regretted the inconvenience it caused to them. In his defence, Cooper alleged that he had a pre-booking from the Surrey Theatre, Blackfriars Road. He had no proof of the fare but due to taking Reed to the police station, he was too late and "lost the fare". "I contend that I was not actually plying for hire, and that I was not compelled to take you." A'Beckett then read through the relevant clauses from the 1831 Act; "That any hackney carriage which shall be found standing in any street or place… shall, unless actually hired, be deemed to be plying for hire." On the prosecution's own account, Cooper was creeping along the road, so was not standing. The emphasis was on Cooper however to show that he was already booked, which he failed to do. A'Beckett dismissed the charge against Cooper and awarded him costs of 2s 6d. "Mr Reed thanked the magistrate for his decision, and left the court." No doubt ruing his attempt at performing his public duty.[16]

It was most probably the Act of 1831 that the Chief Clerk of the Court had in mind when Richard Cope was fined for not wearing his badge. As we saw earlier (in Chapter 1), he was driving his cab but had members of his family as his passengers. Although not fined, it was stated that "whenever a taxicab was in a public street it was deemed to be plying for hire." What the Chief Clerk failed to mention was the caveat regarding being already booked. With his family in the back of the taxi, it could be argued that he could not accept another fare – even so, the magistrate decreed that he should have been wearing his badge at the time and he was probably fortunate in having the case dismissed on payment of costs.[17]

When, in 2000, the Mayor of London, Ken Livingstone, doubled the compellable distance a driver was liable to take a fare he stated that the previous six-mile limit was an anachronism dating back one hundred fifty years and was only made legal to spare the harsh working conditions that the cab horse laboured under. In truth the horse was rarely considered, see the section on extra passengers in Chapter 9 for instance. In reality, it was for the benefit of the driver rather than his horse. A long journey was not necessarily a lucrative job to a hackney coachman. A busy driver doing short jobs in town was always better off financially than a driver who would take a fare out of town and risk coming back empty.

Hackney coach drivers could ply for hire anywhere in the City of London, Westminster, Southwark "and its environs". If a driver took a passenger out past the environs, then he was allowed to charge, what was originally called, back fare. Defining London "and its environs" was something of a challenge. For many years the defences of the Lines of Communication built by Oliver Cromwell which, at least north of the river mirrors the present-day Congestion Charge Zone. As London grew so did its road network and London soon came to be defined as the area "within the stones" – where the streets consisted of hammered stones, forming a rudimentary road surface. Once the stones gave way to a dirt track, you were no longer in London – and the driver could charge extra for the journey back to a stand "within the stones". A legal definition of the extent of London, at least for the purpose of fares for hackney carriages was laid down in 1831 with a radius of three miles centred on the General Post Office in St Martin le Grand, though drivers could not refuse a fare that went up to five miles from the GPO (the compellable distance). A driver taking a fare past the three-mile radius could charge a passenger extra for the journey back to a stand within the radius. In 1843 Metropolitan London was defined as the area within a five-mile radius of the GPO – thus eliminating the charging of back fares up to that distance.

Constant complaints of overcharging by drivers who were claiming back fare for journeys that did not warrant them led to the introduction of a compellable distance. A driver who was for hire from "any place" within five miles of the GPO was obliged to carry a person five miles to any place within or without the radius. The penalty for refusing to go such a distance if found guilty, was 40 shillings.

The compellable distance was increased to six miles with the Act of 1853, the radius was reduced later that year to four miles but it's centre shifted westward to Charing Cross. A driver was under obligation to take a passenger up to six miles, but could refuse to take him any distance over six miles – unless a price can be agreed. Refusals under the six-mile limit were treated as refusals but it was the adjunct to the above abstract, a maximum time of one hour, that caused problems for both.

The Act of 1853 stipulated that if a driver was hired by the hour, then the driver was under no compulsion to drive faster than four miles an hour, a brisk walking pace. In 1862, an un-named driver, but with badge 14549 was brought to court by his passenger after refusing to continue with a journey. The passenger stated that he had hired the driver by the hour and after a couple of stops in which several packages were picked up, the cabman refused to go any further. The magistrate at Southwark addressed the driver; "Why do you refuse to take the gentleman any further?"

"Because the gentleman can't compel me."

"That is not an answer. Tell me the reason you object to carry the gentleman any further?"

"The gentleman engaged me by the hour and I could terminate the agreement at the end of the hour if I liked, but he kept me two hours, and then I found that it would not suit to continue as it would not pay me to do so, as I have to pay 24s a day for my cab and horse."

The driver could only charge 2s an hour so even if kept for twelve hours by a customer he may have earned enough to pay his master but would still have no money left to pay for food for himself and his family, as well as his rent. After having looked at the legislation, Combe found the driver to be in the right, he could terminate a hiring after one hour. Combe, it will be remembered from Chapter 1, was the magistrate who seemed to thrive on sending cab drivers to prison for being in debt for just a few shillings, especially if they were in the employ of the Solomon brothers. After having informed the passenger that the driver was right and he would have to be paid, he, rather vexatiously, advised him that if a similar occurrence should happen in the future, he should pay the driver and immediately rehire him – because, as we have seen, if a cab is stationary in a street it must be plying for hire. If the driver refuses the rehiring, then he can be summoned for refusal.[18]

A few months later, in November 1862, another driver was brought to court by Richard Brinsley Sheridan MP, grandson of the playwright. He had engaged the driver by the hour and was in his house when the driver knocked at the door and demanded from the servant 2s for the hour just passed. Sheridan had wanted to engage the cab for another journey but the driver was adamant that he had the right to drive away and look for another fare. The magistrate, Paynter, enquired why he had waited fifteen minutes before knocking at the door. The driver replied that the hour was not completed when he had set the politician down. He waited for the hour to elapse before he sent in for his 2s. Another magistrate in another court may have found for the driver but Paynter told him that he was wrong in terminating the fare. He should have waited and continued and charged accordingly. If he was paying as high a rental as the previous driver, then being paid by the hour was obviously no good to him though in this instance that defence was not used.[19]

Journeys "by the hour" all but disappeared with the arrival of the taximeter but many drivers were still aware of their rights, even if the public were not. In 1919 Charles Forey was summoned, principally for abusive language but the dispute arose once he decided to terminate the hiring after having gone more than six miles. His passenger, a barrister, had hired him in Russell Square and taken him to Elgin Avenue. From there he was taken to the Adelphi Theatre in the Strand. Forey had calculated that he had gone over six miles, there were no odometers in the taxicabs then but such information could be calculated from the meter. His passenger had wanted Forey to continue onto the Conservative Club in Pall Mall but Forey flatly refused. He had seen another, more potentially lucrative fare, so he used his right to terminate the hiring. The passenger asked the linkman at the theatre to make a note of Forey's plate number and it was the altercation between Forey and the linkman that resulted in the summons for abusive language. In court a police inspector informed the magistrate that Forey had several convictions for using abusive language and for refusing to be hired. The magistrate acquiesced that Forey did have the right to refuse to carry a fare more than six miles "but it was a law that not one person in a hundred is aware of." Had he explained this to his passenger the present dispute may never have arose, nethertheless he was satisfied that Forey was extremely abusive and fined him 40s with costs.[20]

The post-Second World War expansion of London led to many people desiring to get a taxi home after a night out in central London. Taxi drivers were only willing to do it for a price and, especially from 1961 onwards, resented the fact that they were losing many of these types of jobs to the minicabs. In 1964 Rupert Speir MP, a major advocate of minicabs and credited with first calling them "minicabs" asked that in the light of a fare increase for London Taxis, the six-mile limit should be abandoned. Albeit, the main problem regarding the six-mile limit was centred on Heathrow, drivers could, and usually did, charge what they liked for every journey – as nearly every journey from the airport had to go more than six miles.

After a series of "confidential discussions" the government announced in August 1965 that they were ready to legislate on the matter using a graduated tariff on journeys over six miles. Such a tariff required not only a change in law but also the development of more sophisticated meters. "Haggling over taxi fares to be banned" ran the headline in the *Daily Mirror* which proclaimed, wrongly, that drivers will be compelled to travel any distance within the Metropolitan Police District.[21] The law was finally changed in 1968, a four-year gestation period that was something of a record when it came to hackney carriage legislation. A driver was still obliged to take a fare up to six miles (or 20 miles if the journey originated at Heathrow); however, he could legally refuse to carry a person more than six miles if he so wished, but having agreed to carry such a fare, he must abide by the meter if the journey is within the MPD. If a journey took him outside the boundaries of the Met, he was at liberty to "haggle" for an agreed price.

4 Offences Relating to the Conduct of Drivers and Management of Taxis

Causing offence by loitering in any public street

It is an offence for a taxi driver to cause obstruction by loitering or misbehaviour in any public street or place.

When a taxi driver, one of several that day, was summoned to appear at Marylebone police court for loitering, he asked Bingley, the magistrate, for a definition of the charge. "You must not ask me conundrums" came the reply, after which, the un-named driver was fined an unspecified amount.[1] A cabman from a previous generation gave his definition to a reporter; "… the police call it loiterin' – we call it lookin' for a livin'."[2]

The answer that satisfies Bingley's 'conundrum' and cabmen 'looking for a living' falls into two distinct states. In each case, the driver is looking for work. He can either do that by remaining stationary on a rank or by 'hanging up' outside a location that may produce a fare – as seen in the last Chapter – or he can be mobile. The stationary cab fulfils the dictionary definition of standing aimlessly or idly, but what of the moving cab? Apparently, the dictionary definition of loitering, is not exactly the same as the legal definition. A cab can be loitering if it is moving slowly and causing a build-up of traffic behind it. One man's careful driving, is another man's obstruction.

Alderman Rose described the crawling cabs as "an intolerable evil". Anybody could see that the City of London was "greatly impeded by the creeping up and down" of cabs. He, like many of his fellow aldermen and magistrates, realised that there were not enough spaces on the stands for all the cabs in London. The authorities were continually issuing licences, but were very slow in appointing new stands. Alderman Rose knew this and usually dismissed the summons, on payment of costs, against the cabman, deeming that a day spent in court, with its subsequent loss of income was punishment enough. By 1857, he had had enough and gave notice that he would be levying fines against cabmen who promoted the "intolerable evil".[3]

The *Morning Chronicle*, in 1861, after highlighting the plight of girls selling oranges in the City, who had never hindered the progress of anybody, should put the causation of traffic congestion within the City, firmly with the cabs. "If the Lord Mayor will step out to the front of Mansion House and look around upon the open space beneath him, he will find a large number of empty cabs, so erratic in their movements that he will be unable to count them, performing all sorts of gyrations in a style that utterly baffles the pedestrians. He will find this to be especially so about four o'clock in the afternoon, at which hour the description of the figure 8 by a procession of cabs around the two lamps which are intended to serve as resting-places for timid pedestrians while making the long sweep across, is a favourite amusement with cabby. He will also find that this process is varied from time to time by a division of the cabs into two sets – each set taking possession of a lamp, and performing a circle around it. He will also find that, in this case, some of the cabs go round in one direction, while others trail the reverse way, so that an unfortunate pedestrian is utterly bewildered, and positively cannot get to his resting-place at all."[4] One can accept the exaggeration of the piece, but the editorial must have struck a chord with its readers to be in anyway plausible.

Three months later there was no let-up in the *Morning Chronicle's* campaign; "There is a law to prevent cabmen from loitering in the streets with their vehicles when unemployed – how is it that this is so seldom acted upon? Day after day the regulation is actively broken – a bony and lazy horse, guided by a touting driver, and followed by a rickety cab, may be met with every fifty paces in any leading thoroughfare. The unsavoury disreputable-looking vehicle and the pertinacious, half-insolent driver are nearly the greatest nuisances in London."[5] It's refreshing to see London cabs are 'nearly the greatest nuisance', even the editor of the *Chronicle* must have realised that disease, starvation and poverty were greater problems for London over cabmen looking for a living. *The Era* newspaper also joined in by complaining that Piccadilly,

Regent Street and Bond Street, where fashionable Londoners shopped, could see that those thoroughfares were "literally infested by lines of crawling cabs."[6] Thus establishing a link between cabmen, disease and the upper classes.

The City authorities laid down new traffic regulations in 1863, primarily aimed at crawling omnibuses within the square mile, cabmen were told that after setting down a fare, they must either put on a rank, or leave the City by a "different route", a totally impractical, if impossible solution to enforce. More beneficial was a suggestion from the Commissioner of the Metropolitan Police, Sir Richard Mayne, that all cabs carry a flag on the roof of their cab to signify they were available for hire.[7] It was the first (official) "for hire" sign of its kind, and when, on being hired, the flag was lowered, it gave rise to the expression "flag-fall" signifying the initial fare.

The "flag-fall" was embodied in law with the Metropolitan Public Carriage Act, 1869, which called for flags to be either hinged or socketed. The question of crawling cabs was also addressed; a hackney carriage cannot ply for hire other than on a stand, and if a driver picked up a fare as he drove along the street, the passenger was under no compulsion to pay. *The Standard* described the Act as "the Home Secretary's crowning exploit in the way of imbecility" for banning cabs from picking up elsewhere than on a stand. Whilst it agreed that crawling cabs were a problem, there was not a single cab stand in the whole length of Fleet Street, "it is impossible to get a cab, except in one of those crawlers"[8] cried the editor of *The Standard*.

Thomas Edwards was not crawling, but had parked outside a pub in Piccadilly when he was hired by a Reverend Holden. After the legal profession, clergymen were responsible for summoning more cabmen for overcharging than any other calling. Barristers and solicitors were aware of the law, clergymen were impinged upon for their beliefs and Christian forgiveness against an overcharging cabman. When Edwards dropped his passenger off in Addison Road, he was paid 2s, but demanded an extra shilling. Reverend Holden paid the extra shilling but warned him that he would be summoned. Edwards' evidently laughed at the threat and assured the reverend that he would not be summoned. The clergyman was as good as his word. They duly appeared before the Hammersmith magistrate, Dayman, who informed Reverend Holden that the new Act prohibited hiring a cab that was not on a stand, but if so hired, a cabman could not recover his fare. Dayman also added that he thought such a regulation could not stand in a court of law, which would have been good news to cabmen. For his part, Edwards said that he charged a shilling a mile as he was allowed to, under the new act. Dayman pointed out that the new fares had not yet come into force, and only applied to cabs hired from a stand. The fare he had demanded was twice the legal fare, he was fined 5s for overcharging, 2s costs of summons and ordered to repay the 1s 6d overcharge. Reverend Holden asked that the costs be placed into the poor box, but Edwards said he had no money to pay either the fine or costs, and was no doubt waiting for the reverend to intervene on his behalf but Dayman would not allow it. Edwards was sent to jail for seven days.[9]

The magistrate's assumption that there was no legal validity in not paying a cabman proved to be correct. Within days of Edwards being fined, the phrase, "nor shall any Fare be recoverable in respect of any hiring... unless from an authorised stand" was dropped from the revised Act, published on February 1st 1870.

The Marlborough Street magistrate, Knox, noted that he was seeing about 200 cabmen a week, all summonsed by the police for loitering. This translated to around 10,000 cases a year which he believed probably amounted to around £4,000 a year being taken out of the pockets of cabmen, "who were, after all, just trying to earn a living." Knox observed that most of the summons appeared for loitering at specific locations, notably outside theatres. He now suggested that the police, instead of summoning offenders, should direct them to leave the area. If they failed to do so, then they should be summoned and he would fine each driver, the maximum of 20s - until now Knox had only been laying down fines of 5s. It was hoped that after a few drivers had been fined the maximum fine, the practice would stop. Both the police and cabmen appreciated the common-sense approach and for good measure, Knox dismissed all the loitering charges before him that day on payment of costs.[10]

Despite Knox's, all too real, reluctance to fine a driver 20s for loitering, he felt he had to back the police when a case came before him as the situation was still becoming intolerable. When a solicitor, a Mr Johnson, addressed him with respect to his client in the dock, he took on the mantle of being a spokesman for the trade; "The cabmen felt the hardship of their position, inasmuch as they had to pay as heavy a fine occasionally as 20s and costs, and because they could only bring their denial against the unsupported testimony of the police. The charges in the majority of instances were for loitering – an indefinite act – but one respecting which the police appeared to constitute themselves the sole judges. The cabmen were really desirous of obeying the law, but they hardly knew how to do so, now that the police appeared to be invested with such almost unlimited powers."[11] The solicitor had a sympathetic ear in Knox, who reiterated his regret at taking money from cabmen, but the question of loitering and crawling cabs had to be addressed. The number of summons against cabmen for such offences had drastically reduced but had not been eradicated entirely. He asked that Johnson go back to the drivers and proprietors and let them know that the magistrates had no wish to inflict fines at all upon cabmen but they must come up with something to alleviate the situation.

With more drivers becoming licensed and no increase in the number of spaces on stands, the situation only became worse. Legislation had failed but that did not stop the authorities from trying something new – banning empty cabs from central London.

If the police could not stop a cabman driving slowly looking for a fare, the easiest solution was to ban them from looking. They had the power, under the Metropolitan Streets Act 1867, to ban vehicles from what were later described as Scheduled Streets. The ban did not extend to private vehicles, or even commercial ones, just to cabs and omnibuses; but as the latter were driving along prescribed routes, it was not they who were banned, just cabs. For a long while only certain streets, usually near the theatres, were allocated as Scheduled.

A cab could only enter proscribed streets if they had a passenger, many complained that the regulations prevented them from picking up a pre-booked job. One way of getting past the policeman at one end of a scheduled thoroughfare was to find a pedestrian walking in the same direction and offer them a free ride past the policeman. The pedestrian gets a short cab ride for nothing, and does the cabman a favour by getting his entry into a restricted zone. It was a common enough occurrence that could have taken place several hundred times each night, some drivers were happy with just entering the restricted area for nothing. P Echlin warned other members of the public of a trick played upon him by a cabman. He had been walking along the Strand when a cabman asked if he was going towards Charing Cross. He replied he was and after the cab driver explained his position he entered the cab and was driven without any problem past the policeman. The cab only went as far as Catherine Street, which means Echlin only travelled a matter of yards when the cabman turned him out and demanded a shilling for his fare. No doubt intimidated and fearing he might get into greater trouble, he paid the shilling and walked off. Warning other readers to be on their guard against such a trick[12]

The drivers suffered the inconvenience of certain streets being restricted. After all, if you could get into a street, whether with a legitimate fare paying passenger or one who was offered a free ride round the corner, and if you could then get onto a rank, you at least knew a passing cab was not going to take your job. The police were convinced that such measures kept the traffic moving and so, in 1899, they decided to extend it to a large swathe of central London. At a well-attended meeting of drivers and proprietors at Exeter Hall, Fred Simmons, president of the London Cabdrivers Union told those present that there were 11,506 hackney carriages in London (7,925 hansoms, 3,583 four-wheelers), but only rank accommodation for 5,795 of them. It elicited a loud cheer from the drivers when Simmons noted that this figure included the cab rank of 100 spaces in Russell Square – which was perennially empty as there was no work to be had from there. The Commissioner of Police had the power to appoint ranks, but now he was preventing drivers from entering central London because there were not enough ranks. Between the proprietors and the drivers, £40,000 per annum was raised in revenue for the right to ply for hire on the streets of London, a right being denied to them. Simmons went on to say that he had a meeting with the Commissioner, Sir Edward Bradford, who expressed that he had no desire to injure the cabmen – cue for loud jeering from the assembly. It was not the Commissioner's wish that cabmen should be prevented from driving through London with empty cabs, just that they wanted to stop the 'crawling cab menace'. Which meant, according to Simmons, that they would "leave it to the discretion of a twenty-four-shillings-a-week policeman whether a man was loitering (laughter)."[13] In one respect, the police had succeeded in clearing the streets of cabs. The two thousand drivers who had attended the meeting had left their cabs in the yard, with the full agreement of their masters. It was one of those rare occasions when driver and proprietor were in complete agreement with each other.

The Commissioner tried to back track, the last thing he wanted was to be blamed for an all-out cab strike; politicians and important people relied on cabs and he did not want to be the one to bear the wrath of why they could not get a cab on a cold and wet night. It was reiterated that an empty cab going at a trot would not be prevented from passing through the scheduled streets, but the drivers said otherwise – all empty cabs were being forced to drive down side streets. Sir Charles Howard, speaking on behalf of the Home Office, "denied most emphatically that any such order as was supposed had been issued, and he could not understand, how the idea had got abroad." He also stated that any cabman who was prevented from driving down certain streets should take the constables number, and report him, "when he could be dealt with by the department."[14]

At one point, over 3,000 cabs were left in the yard, the drivers, with the agreement of the proprietors, each taking only one horse out – effectively a half-day strike. The notion that only crawling cabs would be re-directed, assuaged the feelings of many, but not many drivers would go to the lengths of reporting a policeman for fear of retribution.

Joseph Keen had had enough of the police regulations when he was stopped a few days after Sir Charles Howards' proclamation. He had been driving empty along the Strand at two in the afternoon, when he was directed by a policeman to drive up Bedford Street. Keen refused. "You have stopped the cab" he told the officer, "and you can move it on." Keen was charged with obstruction, as well as refusing to show his badge. At Bow Street police court, before Lushington, Keen's solicitor, on behalf of the Cabdrivers Union tried to object using legal argument that the prohibition against cabs had not been enacted legally. Lushington dismissed this defence and Keen was found guilty of causing an obstruction and fined 15s with 2s costs.[15] That was not the end of the matter.

A week later the solicitor was back in court and applied to Lushington to state a special case in order that the opinion of the Court of Queen's Bench might be heard. Lushington had no time for the defence, "I convicted the man on a matter of fact. He was causing an obstruction, by wilful misbehaviour. I shall not grant a special case."[16]

Lushington's acquiescence in granting a special case would have been helpful, but it was not essential. The Union went ahead anyway and had a hearing before two judges at the Court of Queen's Bench. Keen's solicitor now showed that no obstruction was proven, nor was he loitering as all he desired was to go home and his nearest way home was via Chancery Lane, and not through Bedford Street, as he was directed. Justices Grantham & Kennedy agreed that there may have been a miscarriage and granted a *rule nisi* calling upon Lushington why he "should not state a case raising the correctness of his decision."[17]

Keen's case went to the Court of Appeal and despite a spirited defence by his barrister, the appeal was dismissed by the two judges. Scheduled streets were here to stay.[18]

The police again applied their powers to ban empty cabs from scheduled streets in 1903 "like a bolt from the blue". Twenty additional officers were drafted into principle streets in the West End to turn cab drivers back in the direction they came from. Only when Sam Michaels, the newly-elected president of the Cabdrivers Trade Union threatened to call all the cabs out on strike did the police agree to temporarily suspending the order.[19] Before the truce came into effect, one luckless cabby told of his attempts, after setting down a fare, to get to Piccadilly via Vigo Street. He was turned around by one policeman and tried to go another route, but was again turned around. Exacerbated after being turned around a third time, he climbed down from his seat, and handed the reins to the policeman, telling him he could do with it as he wished. He had had enough. It worked. The policeman let him drive his cab through to

Piccadilly. The truce lasted three days, in which time the Union put forward several proposals such as the rank in Berkeley Square, which can hold 70 cabs is "practically useless" as no work comes to it. The Union wanted the Berkeley Square rank to act as a feeder to smaller, better positioned ranks in the area. More ranks should be established in suitable spots, where cabs would be required. These two proposals were both moderate and sensible, and the police could easily have accommodated them. The third proposal flew in the face of what the police were trying to achieve; "An absolute claim on the part of the drivers to drive through any street in the metropolitan area [as they were compelled to do so]." The police would never agree to it. Sam Michaels responded by stating that whilst the men would not be called out on strike, they would take action which would "seriously inconvenience the public."[20]

The arrival of the taxicab, being much shorter in length than a hansom cab, was believed by many to be the end of traffic congestion in London but the popularity of mechanised transport just increased the number of vehicles on the road. When Alexander Barrett, an owner driver and partner in a small yard that had just two taxis, spoke before a Home Office Committee looking into taxi fares, he thought the police might let "more drivers into the charmed circle of Piccadilly Circus." He explained, "Between 10pm and 1am empty cabs were excluded, and they could not stand on the rank in Shaftesbury Avenue as horse cabs occupied it. People who wished for motor-cabs had to whistle for some minutes without obtaining one, although there were any number on the outskirts of the Circus."[21]

Barrett highlights two problems with the scheduled streets policy. First, the very streets cabs and taxis were prohibited from, were the streets where the cabs and taxis were needed most. Complaints from owners of, in the first instance, private broughams and Victoria's, and later, private motor cars, blamed cabs and taxis from preventing them from making a quick getaway from the theatre, which is probably true. The police were only getting complaints against taxis, added to the fact that the Home Office could only act against cabs and taxis, the only form of public transport within their remit. The second problem was whistling for cabs.

The public were at one location, and empty cabs were at another. Porters, linkmen and cab touts etc would give several blasts on a whistle to summon a cab. After a while, a type of coding was introduced; one blast for a hansom and two blasts for a four-wheeler. With the arrival of the taxi, three blasts were introduced but because of its popularity, the taxi was given primacy with a single blast, two blasts called for a hansom and three for a growler. The rhetorical question of how many blasts for a cab that does not turn up, was soon answered. The sound of the high-pitched whistle incessantly trying to find a cab became probably the greatest real nuisance to those who lived in central London. The problem became even more acute during the Great War when injured officers were kept awake at all hours by the cacophony of the shrill whistle. Attempts to ban whistling for a cab proved useless and it was only when it was totally banned under the temporary provisions of the Defence of the Realm Act (DORA) that the practice was finally ended. Some places reverted to a visual signal, a large flag etc but technology soon allowed a visible light to show that a taxi was required, which soon became the norm.

The problem of scheduled streets was a cyclical one, even though they never went away. When traffic congestion became too much, the taxis were blamed, when there was a dearth of work, the drivers complained that they could not get to the public who wanted a cab. The problem arose again in 1926 when the authorities promised to place new ranks to alleviate the problem. The ranks were not forthcoming but the convictions were, as thirteen drivers in one day were each fined for loitering. The London Traffic Advisory Committee proposed that certain streets within a three-mile radius of Charing Cross, which probably accounted for 90% of the work, should be prohibited to taxis unless they were on a taxi rank. The law was about to be turned full circle. Where, as seen in the previous Chapter, a driver could be summoned for not responding to a hail whilst he was driving down the street, a cab driver could now be summoned for picking up a passenger, even if he was the only vehicle in the street.

Despite there being over 7,000 taxis on the streets of London, neither the views of the drivers, nor the proprietors had any representation within the advisory committee. The chairman was Lord Ashfield, who was also chairman of the London General Omnibus Company, who saw taxis as a direct threat to the profitability of his own company.

The advisory committee succeeded where many had tried before in uniting the trade into a single focus group. All the relevant sections reformed the Joint Trade Committee and a letter condemning the proposals was addressed to the Traffic Advisory Committee. Their argument fell on deaf ears. It took the advisory committee another seven months to publish their results, in which they were "satisfied that [crawling taxis] cause serious congestion and delay to other traffic and that all practicable and reasonable steps should be taken to prohibit or restrict this practice." What they described as "practicable and reasonable" included, from between the hours of 8am to 7pm, the banning of cruising taxis from; Buckingham Palace Rd, Kensington High St [part] New Bond St, New Oxford St, Old Bond St, Oxford St [west of Oxford Circus], Regent St and Wigmore St. The list did not end there; from 8am to midnight cruising taxis were banned from Charing Cross Road, Coventry St, Kingsway, Oxford St [east of Oxford Circus], Piccadilly [east of Stratton St], Shaftesbury Avenue [from south of Cambridge Circus], Strand, Tottenham Court Rd & Wilton Rd. Not only did these streets represent the busier streets where a taxi driver was likely to find a job, they were also important arteries to getting across London. It was a blanket ban on empty taxis. If a driver was pre-booked by a regular customer, he could not get to them; if he dropped off his last job and wanted to go home he faced a long diversion.

Common sense may have prevailed either amongst the police or the magistrates as there appears to be very little reporting of drivers being fined. Two drivers however were fined 5s each at Marylebone for having the temerity to reverse their cabs in Welbeck Street. This only happened to be against the law as Welbeck St was within three miles of Charing Cross. The magistrate described it as an "unusual charge" which was probably a coded reference to the police to stop blocking up the duty of the court with such trivial offences.

In 1931 an organisation called the Taxi League prevailed upon the taxi-going public to make their concerns heard. They printed a circular which was carried by most taxis: "Unless the Minister of Transport and those who advise him are made to realize by the force and weight of public opinion that such an unjustifiable restriction of public liberty will not be tolerated, you will no longer be able to hail a passing disengaged taxicab in any of the following streets:-" there then followed a longer list than that already given which also included Basil St, Fulham Rd, Hans Rd, High Holborn, St Martin's Lane, Southampton Row, Terminus Pl [Victoria], Victoria St and Vauxhall Bridge Rd.

If the Taxi League hoped the public would tear down the walls of the Ministry of Transport they were sorely disappointed. The concept of Scheduled Streets was reinforced in 1933 with the Hired Cab Regulations. By the end of that year 543 taxi drivers had been arrested for loitering and 324 were arrested just for stopping in a scheduled street.[22] It appears that the only people who were inconvenienced by scheduled streets were the taxi drivers, and even then, many of them seem to like the situation. If after setting down, a driver could make his way to a rank, he was more than happy to know that the next fare would come to the rank, instead of hailing a passing cab. Drivers like Herbert Hodge, Maurice Levinson, and Robert Buckley, all of whom were driving at the time and who later wrote their memoirs, did not have a problem with scheduled streets. Hodge however, did sum it up, "... what it amounts to in practice is that if another passenger vehicle is going faster than I am, I'm liable to be summoned. Whether I think that vehicle is going too fast for safety in that particular stretch of street at that particular time is apparently beside the point."[23]

For those drivers who were not happy with the situation, the Second World War may have provided a brief interlude as petrol rationing and the decimation of the cab trade allowed for the free movement of what vehicles that remained. The austere days of rationing and deprivation did not last long as by the end of the 1950's when Britain "had never had it so good" the public had sufficient means to buy a car – only to find their journey in London was disrupted once more by cruising taxis. To be fair to Ernest Marples, the Minister of Transport, the Pink Zone was not primarily aimed at cruising cabs but, as taxi drivers had been saying for years, at parked cars. Marples initiated his plan in the run up to Christmas 1959 when he banned cars from parking in central London.

Car parks were laid out, outside the Pink Zone, but shoppers etc would have to make their own way, preferably by taxi, from the car park to the shops. The Pink Zone was a success with traffic reportedly moving at twice its average speed and taxi drivers could work a shift without being stuck in any "real traffic".[24] It did not take long however for the Minister of Transport to find a way to upset the drivers.

Just over two weeks into the Pink Zone scheme, U-turns were banned within its cordon. The ban applied to every vehicle, in every street throughout the day. The taxi drivers were up in arms over the new regulation. Taxis were designed specifically for doing a quick U-turn, it was a condition of fitness which added greatly to the cost of the vehicle. Many taxi ranks were in the middle of the road and by law had to face in a specific direction. No longer could a driver pull off to pick a fare going "in the wrong direction", but the passenger had now to cross the road and pay extra for the taxi to negotiate several turns before he would be back where he started but with the possibility of a extra shilling on the meter.

The Pink Zone may have been a temporary measure to cope with the extra traffic at Christmas but the ban on vehicles doing U-turns remained. Five weeks after the U-turn ban had been initiated, over 200 taxis laid siege to the House of Commons. Many left their cabs parked up in side streets, which in itself was still illegal at the time, and lobbied MP's within the House. A week later the problem was addressed in a Commons debate but the Ministry of Transport were still wanting to see how the "experiment would work" and that segregating different categories of vehicles, such as taxis, would present many problems and blur the whole picture."[25] Six weeks later the "problems" had apparently been overcome when Marples announced to the Commons that the restriction on taxis doing U-turns would be lifted on the assurance that "they make U-turns with the minimum of inconvenience to other traffic."[26]

The *Abstract of Laws* still contained a list of Scheduled Streets at least to around 1990 but then were dropped in favour of local traffic enforcement.

Obstructing other vehicles

A taxi driver must not obstruct or hinder the driver of another taxi in taking up or setting down a passenger or take away from another taxi hirer his legitimate fare.

Or as we say, "nicking a job". When it is particularly quiet on the streets cab drivers are always looking for the raised hand that signifies a hiring. The longer you have been driving around trying to get a fare, the more acute your eyes become and when you espy the signal, everything else is blocked from your senses and you are determined to get to the fare before anyone else can. George Inwood, badge 8665 was no different to thousands of other cabmen before and since. At about half past midnight on 21st September 1871, two gentlemen emerged from Three Crown Square (now demolished but then on the north-west corner of Southwark Street and Borough High Street where the old administrative offices of the Borough Market now stand) and hailed a cab. Two cabs raced to the upstretched hand with Inwood winning. Having lost, the other driver continued on his way, hunting for another opportunity. One of the gentlemen got into Inwood's cab whilst the other remained on the pavement, it was as they said goodbye to each other and were shaking hands that a third cabman came up and remonstrated with Inwood for stealing his job. Inwood, not willing to give up the fare urged his horse to move but the other driver, James Bristow, badge 10245, grabbed hold of the horse's reins. As he did so, he slipped and fell under the wheel of Inwood's Hansom cab. Inwood was stopped straight away by a policeman who had witnessed the whole event. Bristow was insensible. He was placed in a four-wheeler and taken to nearby Guy's Hospital but was found to be dead on arrival. At Southwark police court later that day, the attendant of the rank testified that Bristow had been waiting on the stand for nearly three hours waiting for a fare, so was naturally angry when a passing cab stole what he felt was his. The rank itself was said by one witness to be opposite Three Crown Square, in which case Inwood should have been aware of it, though another witness stated it was sixty yards away, in which case it could be argued that Inwood believed it was his legitimate fare. Inwood was said to be deeply upset by the tragedy and insisted that he had not seen Bristow until after the wheel of his cab had gone over him. Both men were said to be sober.[27] A week later all charges against Inwood were dropped after it was found that the coroner's inquest had exonerated him from blame and gave a verdict of "accidental death".[28]

Various acts of misbehaviour by taxi driver.

The following offences are punishable by penalty or two months imprisonment:

(a) Wanton or furious driving.

The name "Jehu" is all but forgotten these days. The late Simon Hogan used it as his pen name for his long series of articles for *Taxi* magazine up to his death in 2000. In Victorian times 'Jehu' and 'Jarvey' were synonymous for cabmen. Jarvey was a descriptive noun that applied to most drivers and was favoured by the press. If a cabman got the better of someone, or even came off worse, the newspapers applied the epithet 'Jarvey', promoting the point that all cab drivers were roguish but likeable. Sometimes 'Jehu' was used in similar circumstances but more specifically it applied to those drivers who were guilty of furious driving.

It is in the Old Testament book of II Kings Chapter 9 that Jehu, (pronounced Yeh-hu), having been appointed King drives in a chariot towards the city of Jezreel. A watchman on the city walls warns that "...the driving is like that of Jehu the son of Nimshi; for he driveth furiously." Jehu is then reported as killing King Joram who came out from the city in his own chariot; then he chased after and killed King Ahaziah, the king of Judah, who tried to flee from Jezreel. Once inside the city walls, Jehu, observing Joram's mother, Jezebel, looking out from an upper window, ordered three eunuchs attending to her to throw her from the window down into the street. Jehu then drove his chariot over her body and "trod her underfoot" – before going to have a celebratory feast.

It did not take a lot of effort on the part of detractors to label the early hackney coachmen as 'Jehus'. In 1636, just two years after Captain Baily put four hackney coaches on an impromptu rank in the Strand (see

Chapter 5) a pamphlet penned by one Henry Peacham and entitled *'Coach and Sedan Pleasantly Disputing for Place and Precedence'* which was a diatribe against the fledgling hackney coach service accusing the personified hackney coach that he is responsible for many robberies in the city, is always drunk and that "…like Jehu, ye drive as if you were mad and become very dangerous in the night."[29] Even before Parliament recognised the role of hackney coaches to the City, it appears that hackney coaches had a reputation that preceded them. Samuel Pepys, in 1663 records; "Thence by coach, with a mad coachman, that drove like mad, and down bye ways, through Bucklesbury home, everybody through the street cursing him, being ready to run them over."[30]

Sometimes a cabman would drive fast as the passenger was in a hurry and there was the hope, or expectation, that the passenger would give a large tip. When cabman Thomas Harrison took a fare from Albany Street, Regents Park, to the Tower of London, the fare in 1832 was reckoned to be 4s. Harrison demanded, at first 10s, then reduced the demand to 8s. When asked by the magistrate what induced him to charge such a fare, Harrison replied that his fare was in a hurry so he drove fast, therefore he was entitled to double fare. Rawlinson the magistrate was not impressed by this logic; "And double then shall be the penalty, for I shall fine you 20s at once." Harrison paid up but to add insult to injury the passenger gave his share of the fine to the poor box.[31] Whether this was the same Thomas Harrison mentioned in Chapter 1 as overcharging whilst he was only 12 years old cannot be confirmed, but in the intervening 22 years, he could have gained a lot of experience both of overcharging and driving.

Whilst the race to beat another cab to a potential job could be seen as a spur of the moment event, some races between cabs were organised, though on a limited scale. In 1837 William Sergeant challenged Thomas Hill to a race from Blackfriars Road, by Stamford Street, to The [St. George's] Circus at the southern end of Blackfriars Road. The wager was for 5s and each of the cabs were to carry two passengers. The race began and the two cabs raced along Blackfriars Road "at great violence". As they were passing Rowland Hill's chapel, TfL's offices at Palestra House now stand on the site, an elderly woman walked out into the road and was struck by Sergeant's cab. This was seen as no reason to halt the race. A man named Mullen witnessed the accident and called out for the cabmen to stop, which the drivers ignored. Somehow, and the report does not state how, Mullen chased after and caught up with Sergeant's cab at the junction of Wellington Street (now Webber Street) which would require a superhuman effort on his part, or that the cabs were not being driven as furiously as was alleged. However he managed it, Mullen did succeed in grabbing hold of the horse's harness, forcing Sergeant to stop. Goaded by one of his passengers, Sergeant then began using his whip on Mullen forcing him to release his grip. Just as he was about to drive off again, a policeman appeared and arrested Sergeant and his two passengers. Hill was also arrested after he came upon the scene and was heard to exclaim "A ____ old woman has been run over." Hill was acquitted of the manslaughter charge as there was insufficient proof that it was actually him who was racing with Sergeant. Sergeant himself was found guilty of manslaughter and his two passengers guilty of being accessories to the fact.[32]

A couple of weeks after that race, Henry Boatright was driving his hackney coach "at a slow pace" down Albany Street, Regent's Park, when he observed two cabs "coming towards him at a most tremendous rate". He could see that the two cabmen were whipping their horses into a frenzy and trying to cut in front of each other. Boatright shouted out a warning but it was too late. The shaft of one the cabs, struck Boatright's horse, fatally injuring the animal. The driver of the cab that had collided with Boatright, William Ward, attempted to make his escape but was apprehended. The other driver managed to slip away. Boatright's master enquired of the magistrate, Hoskins, as to how he could be recompensed for the loss of the horse. Hoskins informed him that there was very little he could do but he advised the master to contact his solicitor and bring an action against Ward's master through the county court. As for Ward he was fined £5, a fine he had no chance of paying so in default he was committed to prison for two months.[33]

Until the recent construction of Portcullis House at Westminster, a policeman would be situated near the pedestrian crossing on Bridge Street and would stop the traffic to allow a Member of Parliament to cross the road in order to get to the Palace of Westminster. It was another example of the 'them and us' culture. Today, a tunnel links the two buildings and members of the Metropolitan Police can get on with more important things. But the system of having a policeman on traffic duty at that point had prevailed for sometime. In 1870 a cabman named Day was summoned on a charge of furious driving as he was said to be too close to William Gladstone, the then Prime Minister. The police said Day was travelling at 10 mph, Day said it was closer 8 mph. Not only did Day's passenger not think him guilty of furious driving but Gladstone himself believed there was no misconduct. Despite all this, Shiel, the magistrate, sided with the police but Day only had to pay the 2s costs of the summons. It was tantamount to saying that you are not guilty of anything, but we have to back the police. Another driver was not so lucky. As the Speaker of the House of Commons crossed the road he had to stop and allow a cab to pass. The Speaker alerted a constable to this heinous act and the driver, Giles, was fined 5s and costs.[34]

Three months after he had struck a child in St Martin's Lane, William Patterson was sentenced to six month's hard labour in July 1874. The fact sentencing occurred so long after the accident gives an indication that the injuries suffered by the child were life threatening and only once it appeared he was out of danger could the original charge of furious driving be pursued. The Assistant Judge at Middlesex Sessions gave a "severe admonition...to London cabmen in general" as to how they drove through the streets to the danger of the common public.[35] Patterson's sentence was raised by a Colonel Learmouth in a question to the Home Secretary in the House of Commons, as to its severity, but nothing appears to have come from that line of appeal.[36]

The admonition given by the Patterson case was not a rare example. Magistrates often used their position to warn about cabmen, knowing that their words would be recorded by the court reporter. Newton, magistrate at Marlborough Street was no exception. Before him was Robert Fijett, the driver of a hansom cab. Although he was charged with reckless, and not furious driving, it transpired that the three gentlemen had asked him to drive as fast as he could. This he did but he collided with Lord Ernest Bruce's victoria coach, slightly injuring his lordship.

Fijett denied that he was at fault for the accident, it was the responsibility of Lord Bruce's coachman to get out of his way once he shouted at a warning. Newton asked Fijett "...if he thought that all the world were to get out of the way to please hansom cab drivers who chose to drive at reckless speed because told by a fare to do so." In reply, Fijett stated that he tried to pull up but couldn't, to which Newton countered with that he was not fit then to drive a cab. Fijett received no help from his master who informed the magistrate that Fijett had been locked up the previous Saturday night at Marylebone Police Court for being drunk and that his last master had discharged him for being drunk and ill-using the horse. "Such a man ought not be allowed to drive a cab." Newton agreed. He fined Fijett 40s or one month's imprisonment if he could not pay and suspended his cab driver's licence, his bill, for six months. Newton added that he "...was determined, as far as lay in his power, to check the practice of cabmen driving about the streets of London in a reckless manner."[37]

It was not just the magistrates. When cab driver Joseph Hurford was charged with furious driving in 1874, after crashing into a victoria coach and pitching Lady Stanley of Alderley and her sister out onto the street, prosecuting counsel argued that if such conduct by the defendant was to be tolerated, no one would be safe on the streets. The fact that the charge against Hurford was dismissed did not abrogate him, or the trade, from driving furiously in the streets. It transpired that Hurford's horse had been purchased just three weeks previously, it was not a hackney horse but a thoroughbred racer. Totally unsuited for hackney work but such horses, after their racing days were over, were frequently purchased by cab proprietors as they were fit for nothing else. Hurford denied the charge of furious driving, saying that the horse had bolted and he could not pull it up as he himself was suffering from dropsy at the time. Woolrych the magistrate said he had no option other than to dismiss the charge against Hurford but Lady Stanley, who was said to be close to death because of her injuries, could take the case to a higher court, not only seeking compensation for her injuries but for the damage sustained to her victoria coach which was wrecked in the collision.[38]

The following offences are punishable by penalty or two months

135

imprisonment:

(c) Drunkenness during employment.

It is, to excuse the pun, refreshing to note that "drunkenness" is now the third bullet point in the list of Various Acts of Misbehaviour – after "Wanton & Furious Driving" and "Causing hurt or damage to any person... (not included here). An indication that the problem is not so acute as it once was. Drinking and driving a hackney carriage was seen not so much as something that could be frowned upon, or even deemed dangerous or anti-social, it was seen as part of the job, not just by the drivers but by many passengers as well. The long periods between jobs could be spent sharing a beer (literally) with one or more other cabmen. There were obvious benefits to being inside a warm tap room than sitting on top of a cab in all weathers waiting for a fare. So great was the consumption of alcohol by cab drivers that the value of a pub was said to be greatly enhanced by its proximity to a cab stand.[39] A common feature of many fares was to stop off at a pub along the way, usually at the instigation of the passenger but it was not unheard of for the driver to suggest a similar idea. Ladies would remain in the cab, sending the driver into the beerhouse with enough to get himself a drink. Men would often be accompanied by the driver to the bar where they would both partake; such perquisites were called "skinks" by the drivers.

In the anti-hackney coach pamphlet, *Coach and Sedan Pleasantly Disputing for Place and Precedence* (1636), there are numerous allegations by "Coach's" protagonists who accuse him of being drunk whilst at work, being in a tavern on a Sunday when he should be listening to divine service in a church and that a hackney coachman "... is good for nothing, except to marry some old Ale-wife..." The fact that an embodiment of a brewer's cart is the moderator in the 'pleasant dispute' only highlights the notion that a hackney coach was a greater evil than beer and that the drivers already had a reputation for drink even in their embryonic days. What follows is just a small selection of drunken episodes through the years.

Christmas was usually a period when the cab & coachmen would over indulge. In 1828 William Amos was hired by a gentleman in Leadenhall

Street and was told to go to the Strand. The passenger noticed almost immediately that Amos was drunk but before he could say anything, Amos crashed his cabriolet into an errand cart. Undeterred he carried on with the passenger asking, then pleading, to be allowed to get out but Amos responded by saying he would "Drive him to the Devil". As they passed the Royal Exchange the passenger asked to be allowed to purchase a newspaper. With difficulty the passenger managed to extricate himself from the cab but not before Amos was trying to force him back into it, or pay him his 8d. The passenger paid the 8d and reported the matter. In court Amos denied being drunk and stated that afterwards he took another gentleman from the City to Charing Cross and back "safely" and that his master would swear that when he brought the cab back he was sober. This was corroborated by the owner who said Amos was a very sober man but "If he had had a drop this Christmas time he thought the Gentleman ought to excuse it." The Lord Mayor, as chief magistrate of the City, said he "was disposed to make every allowance for the indulgence of the season, but we were not to have all our necks broke because it was Christmas time. Amos was fined 5s for being abusive (twice telling his passenger he would drive him to the devil) and 5s for being drunk.[40]

As previously stated, the hackney coachmen and cabmen became licensed following the introduction of the Hackney Carriages Act, 1838. The enforcement of the act began on 7th October, and it was not long before the first licensed cabmen were appearing before a magistrate. On October 11th 1838 Daniel Hill, whose badge number is not recorded but was driver of cab number 368, was charged with being drunk and incapable of looking after his vehicle. A policeman stated that he observed Hill close to the Surrey Theatre in Blackfriars Road, and was so intoxicated that he nearly fell from the box as the cab was moving down the road. The magistrate informed Hill that, under the new Act, he would commit him for one month's imprisonment. "Pray don't do it this time" pleaded Hill, "it is the first instance of my being brought here for intoxication. I have two families to support, and what will they do without my assistance? I am well known to Mr Daniel Whittle Harvey as a man not accustomed to drink and to have a respectable character." Hill's only association with Harvey was probably no more than the interview he had to become licensed. The magistrate remitted the punishment but told Hill his licence would be sent to the Registrar, who of course was Harvey, with details of the conviction entered upon it.[41]

Thomas Morse has the distinction of being the first cabman charged with being drunk, whose badge number is recorded – 1763. Although drunkenness was a factor, that was not the reason why he had been stopped by the police in the first place in October 1838. Instead of plying for hire as formerly, presumably on a stand, or the surreptitious raising of the whip, Morse displayed a board with "Not Hired" written upon it. When he was engaged, he turned the board over. This early version of the "For Hire" sign was frowned upon by the Alderman, who perhaps thought that once licensed they would be easily controlled. "Is there no conquering these men" he exclaimed, before informing Morse that he was facing a charge that could see him imprisoned for two months. Instead, and taking previous good character into consideration, he was let off without even a fine.[42]

John Hopkins' (badge 3373) claim to fame may be even less salubrious. He could possibly be a contender for the first licensed cabman in London to be imprisoned with hard labour for one month for being drunk and driving furiously.[43]

A policeman witnessed David Hutchinson fall from his box whilst his cab was in Hampstead Road at three o'clock in the morning. Hutchinson was so drunk he could not get back on the box so the policeman assisted him, but no sooner having accomplished this, than Hutchinson pitched forward onto his horse's back before falling down onto the street. This time the policeman put Hutchinson into the back of the cab and he drove to Albany Street police station. Once there however, Hutchinson demanded to be paid his 6d he was now due as his fare. With no money forthcoming, Hutchinson began lashing out at the policeman and landed "many severe blows" and kicks before he was subdued. In court, and full of contrition, Hutchinson blamed his predicament on one of his passengers who had treated him to a drink. "I never pass over drunkenness", warned Broughton the magistrate, "when a cabman is brought before me for misconduct such as yours." Hutchinson was fined 20s or one month for assaulting the policeman and 10s or a fortnight for being drunk in charge of a cab.[44]

In 1854, Mark Horlock "a drunken cabman" was fined 30s or 15 days imprisonment after attempting to drive his cab down the Duke of York steps into the Mall. He got half-way before being thrown and was picked up from underneath his own cab.[45]

There is a perennial urban myth that black cabs can also be used as hearses but other than the majority of cabs being black, the same colour as a hearse, it is no more than an urban myth. That said, the myth itself has foundation; mourning coaches were required to carry hackney coach plates from 1715. This duopoly lasted over a hundred years until the Act of 1831 which defined a hackney carriage as a vehicle "that could ply for hire in the streets, which funeral carriages patently could not do!"[46]

Whether George Peters thought his job in 1855 was unusual is not recorded but in the back of his cab he had two funereal 'mutes' and a coffin. The 'mutes' – not living up to their status – had persuaded Peters to join them for a "gin and rum". They spent too long in the public house and now there was a rush to get to the cemetery in time. As he was driving over Westminster Bridge "at a furious pace" he collided with an omnibus. He, the two 'mutes' and the coffin were all thrown out onto the bridge. Fortunately, none were hurt. The coffin, presumably with the two 'mutes' was put into another cab and proceed to the burial ground, Peters was taken to a police station. Henry, the magistrate at Bow Street, described it as a "disgraceful occurrence" but on hearing that Peters would have to pay his master £3 for the damage sustained to the cab, he "let him off" with a fine of 10s which was immediately paid.[47]

That same magistrate, Henry, was lambasted by the editorial in *The Standard* on April 14th 1858, after it transpired that he had had five cabmen before him on charges of being drunk the previous day. Each of the cabmen were given the mitigated fines of 10s because of the "trying state of the weather". The previous day had seen rain, described by *The Standard* as being "of Biblical proportions", not a cab could be had anywhere as all the drivers would be sitting in the warm and dry tap room of a public house close to a stand. "Five cabmen" wrote the editor, "actually became inebriated within the precincts of a single police-office, and this heart-rending spectacle was ascribed by Mr Henry to the "trying state of the weather." Whilst Henry was finally endearing himself to the trade (following the cabman Phillips episode - see Chapter 6), *The Standard* wondered if there were another wet Thursday, such as the last one, there might be "a frightful train of inebriated cabmen" brought with it.[48]

In November 1861, Tyrwhitt, the magistrate sitting at Marlborough Street, had two separate cases before him of drunk cabmen. In the first case, 70-year-old James Neave, "a weather-beaten cabman" was charged with being "quite overcome" with drink after turning his cab over in Pall Mall. "I own I was in liquor," admitted Neave, "but I'm blessed if you could have helped it yourself such a night, your worship." Tyrwhitt agreed, the rain "made it a dreadful day" and for that he discharged the summons against Neave. Isaac Moore was similarly charged. He was found very drunk "and like a drowned rat" at eleven o'clock the previous night. Moore confirmed as to how wet the night was, "Why, I'm still wet now." He was also discharged.[49] Tyrwhitt appears to have escaped the opprobrium heaped on fellow magistrate Henry.

Magistrates invariably sided with the policeman's version of events if a cab driver denied being drunk as Richard Nobbs, 4169, was about to find. His last passenger got out of the cab after being driven around in circles by Nobbs, who did not appear to know where he was going. Nobbs was arrested for being drunk, which he denied in court. Nobbs' master confirmed that he was a teetotaller but he suffered from paralysis of the brain. Even the master admitted that he did not think Hobbs was fit to drive a cab. De Rutzen agreed with him and revoked the licence straight away. As for the drunk charge, de Rutzen noted that it was the third time he had been convicted of such an offence, but did not appear to take the paralysis into consideration, he fined the now-out-of-work cabman 10s.[50]

Benjamin Pearce was a cabman who took an active role in cab trade politics. In 1867 he was a member of a delegation that met with the then Home Secretary in order to try and bring about an end of a strike by the cabmen. Lately he had been vociferous with the Lord's-day Rest Association, advocating Sunday as a rest day. He may well have been considered a thorn in the side to the police, particularly over his union activities. On April 1st 1879, PC Hackett observed Pearce refusing to carry two ladies who hailed him from [Great] Portland Street Station. Pearce had told the ladies that he could not take them, he was there to pick up two gentlemen who had pre-booked him. Before he knew it, PC Hackett was unbuckling the horse's reins and accusing Pearce of being drunk, which was a surprise to Pearce as he was a total abstainer. He was arrested and taken to the police station. The two gentlemen followed and spoke of his sobriety, a surgeon was sent for who proclaimed him not only sober but had not even been drinking. The Inspector at the police station even refused to take the charge. With no evidence against him, Pearce was released. Most people would have let the matter rest there but not Pearce. He took a summons out against the policeman at Clerkenwell county court. The jury found in his favour and he was awarded £5 damages "with costs on that scale". PC Hackett was allowed to pay the debt back at the rate of £1 a month.[51]

John Bettinson felt he was doing the 'honest thing' when on Christmas Day 1879 he found a package in his cab. He took it to the nearest police station, Clapham, but instead of being thanked for his honesty he was arrested for being drunk. In court the following morning, Paget, the magistrate, may have felt some sympathy for the cabman and stated that he was not too drunk to find his way to the police station. A police sergeant explained that Bettinson had not waited for his passenger to return out of his house but instead drove straight to the police station. The passenger then had to walk to the station to report the loss but was re-united with his package. Seeing that no harm had been done Paget dismissed the charge.[52]

William Sells was so drunk that in November 1889, he pulled up outside a police station, stumbled up the steps, then asked the policeman behind the counter "for a beer". Unimpressed, the policeman asked him what he wanted, but Sells was quite affable, "Come on old chap; I'll treat you." Realising that Sells had mistaken the red-bricked Hornsey police station for a pub, "You had better come into the tap-room" advised the policeman, as he opened a door and led Sells into the dock of the neighbouring police court. After hearing that he only partook of the drink because of the bitterly cold weather, Sells was released on payment of a 5s fine.[53]

When a 70-year old cabdriver, Thomas Cole, appeared before the magistrate at Westminster police court in 1890, even the police were keen to admit that he had been a cabman a good many years and was highly respectable. The magistrate, D'Eyncourt noticed however that the cabman was shaking as he stood in the dock, and enquired if his condition was due to drink? "No, sir," replied Cole, "I am a shaky customer naturally, sir, and belong to a highly nervous family (loud laughter). There is my daughter, sir, at the back, and if you call her up, I am sure she will shake as much as I do." D'Eyncourt never took up the offer; he dismissed the charge telling Cole to, "Well, go away this time, and don't shake any more."[54]

The word of the policeman is, as has been seen, usually taken as the real version of events when there was a conflict. A magistrate would only have the word of a policeman testifying that the prisoner was drunk and this would be accepted, though as we have seen there were a few exceptions. A cabman, or any other person for that matter, who was arrested for being drunk could ask to be examined by an independent doctor, which carried with it a fee of 7s 6d. Henry Ellerington availed himself of a doctor after being charged with being drunk and causing an obstruction outside the Haymarket Theatre. The doctor said that although Ellerington had been drinking, he was perfectly sober. Fortunately for Ellerington, the cost of the doctor's visit would now have to be paid for by the police. Ellerington still faced the charge of obstruction but he counter-summoned the arresting police officer for assault. Ellerington alleged that on the way to the police station he was punched and kicked several times. In the witness box he was seen to have several marks on him that were consistent with being beaten. The magistrate refused to take the charge. He fully accepted that a dishonest policeman could do what was alleged but felt that there would be too many witnesses for a policeman to launch an attack on a man in his custody. The summons was dismissed. Ellerington then climbed into the dock and after a brief summary of events was fined 10s for obstruction.[55]

Sir Edmund Henderson KCB, Commissioner of the Metropolitan Police, addressed a large meeting of cab drivers at the Cabmen's Mission Hall, King's Cross [the Lighthouse Building, entrance on Grays Inn Road] in November 1880. The mission had over 1000 members, all of whom had taken the pledge towards abstention from drink. Henderson, wished that another 10,000 cabmen would take a similar pledge. He gave his audience a few salient facts from the previous year's statistics; "Out of 4,400 omnibus men, there were only 11 convictions for drunkenness in the year [0.25%], and of 3,200 stage drivers, only 26 [0.8%]; but of the 11,000 cabmen there were 1,100 convictions [10%] – a decrease of 250 from the previous year."[56] ¬ `1   No doubt the cabmen would argue that the large numbers attributable to them was from police persecution. From an outside perspective however, it is hard to find fault with a 10% conviction rate for the time.

In 1897, George Smith entered the record books as the first motorist to be convicted of drink driving. Smith was driving a Bersey Electric Cab, known at the time as a "humming-bird" due to the quietness of its engine. As he was driving down New Bond Street, his vehicle suddenly swerved, mounted the pavement and crashed into a shop front at number 165. He admitted to have drunk "two or three glasses of beer" and further offered that it was the first time he had been charged with being drunk in charge of a cab. Which was evidently true as the magistrate looked at his list of convictions and whilst he had been fined for being drunk, it was never whilst in charge of a cab. The magistrate, De Rutzen, summed up a warning to all future motor car drivers; "You ought to be very careful, for if anything happens to you – well, the police have a very happy knack of stopping a runaway horse, but to stop a motor car is a very different thing." Smith was fined 20s, and a place in the history books.[57]

John Tottman got so drunk in February 1904, he could not remember how he got home, but he supposed he was assisted. As he usually did, he took his boots off outside the house, but could not open the front door. He knew the latch on the window was loose and he managed to slide it open. He climbed in and walked upstairs to his room. He sat down in his chair and fell asleep. He awoke to loud screams coming from a woman, whom he'd never seen before. Her son burst in to the room and found Tottman sitting in a chair, without his boots. The police were called and

Tottman was charged with burglary. Whether he was a tired burglar who fell asleep on the job, or really a drunk cabman who entered the wrong house, only he knows. The jury believed him and he was found not guilty of burglary.[58]

A large meeting of suffragettes at the Albert Hall in June 1908 caused a lot of disruption to the traffic, especially at Hyde Park Corner, over a mile to the east. In order to alleviate the congestion, westbound traffic in Piccadilly was directed by the police to turn north up Hamilton Place, and thence into Park Lane. Alfred Chaplin was driving a motorcab and was stuck in the line of traffic that was being directed up Hamilton Place. Chaplin's passengers had directed him to drive down to the end of Piccadilly, and not realising the road was closed, he pulled out of the line. PC John Boarmann saw Chaplin's motorcab coming towards him and directed him to turn right, instead, Chaplin drove straight into the policeman, pinning him against the wheels. Boarmann was perhaps fortunate in not being the first fatality of a taxicab. Although he was injured, a large number of people came to his assistance and lifted the cab from his injured body. Chaplin was charged being drunk, the first taxicab driver so charged, and also of causing bodily harm to PC Boarmann. Chaplin denied being drunk but did admit to having drunk two glasses of beer on an empty stomach. The accident was due to a misunderstanding of the officer's directions. Despite such a confession, the jury were not convinced that Chaplin drove wilfully into the policeman through drunkenness but as a result of a misunderstanding, and found him not guilty.[59]

George Thomas Goldsmith probably has the distinction of being the first taxi driver to be sentenced and imprisoned for being drunk in charge of a motor cab. The 41-year old driver was allegedly zig-zagging down Knightsbridge when he crashed into a stationary taxicab on a rank, telescoping that vehicle and badly injuring its driver, who was taken to nearby St George's Hospital. One of Goldsmith's two passengers was also cut badly on her arm and lip as she was pitched through the glass of the taxi. Goldsmith denied being drunk, but like Chaplin before him, admitted to having "two or three glasses". Unfortunately, he was before Horace Smith, the Westminster magistrate, who for a long time had been punishing drunken horse cab drivers. Horace Smith reiterated that it was an inflexible rule of his to send drunken motor car drivers to prison; Goldsmith was sentenced to one month with hard labour.[60]

Before the advent of the breathalyser the doctors themselves had no more to go on than their own judgement and likewise, the drivers themselves had methods that could show they were sober. There were a variety of methods used. Henry Cates, 11624, was one of a group of cabmen who were causing a disturbance at a cab rank in Notting Hill Gate. The men were "swearing about Lord Palmerston" and when asked to get back to their cabs only Cates desisted from doing so. As the policeman was taking the number of Cates's cab a stone was thrown at the officer which badly damaged his helmet. Cates was arrested for being drunk and disorderly. He denied being drunk. "In the army, if a man had been drinking he was taken to the guardhouse, and if he went through his facings, he was not considered drunk." Cates had been in the Army and asked the sergeant to put him "through the facings", something the police sergeant, who had not served in the Army, was unwilling to do. Cates was fined 20s.[61]

Alfred Fitter denied being drunk, "he had spelt the word 'Belvidere' [sic] at the station, and offered to write his name and address," - according to the court reporter, Fitter lived in Belvidere Buildings – the reporter may have been drunk. There was conflicting evidence and Selfe, the magistrate, had misgivings about the policeman's version of events but it was enough for the charges against Fitter to be dismissed.[62]

A cabman only named as Russell denied being drunk and incapable, and the following conversation was reported by the *Pall Mall Gazette*:

Russell: "At the police-station, I said to the inspector 'Now chalk a mark along the floor. If I'm drunk, I can't walk it. A drunken man your worship, can't walk a chalk line.'

The defendant, the reporter says, amid much laughter, imitated the swerving of a drunken man in his attempt to walk the mark. Sir Robert Carden asked whether the police made a chalk mark?"

Russell: "No, they wouldn't."

Sir Robert: Then you did not have a fair trial?"

Russell: "I did not your worship."

Sir Robert said he had been a magistrate many years, and never heard such a test as that put before. He thought the inspector should have applied the test.

Russell: "Certainly he should."

Sir Robert: But perhaps they had no chalk."

Russell: "I offered to lend them a pencil. Here it is. I put it down like that" (suiting the action to the word).

"Sir Robert Carden said that as the defendant had had a good character for thirty years he would not then take it from him by fining him, and also, considering all the circumstances, he should remit the greenyard fees. The defendant, however, must be careful in future."[63]

A pencil featured in Henry Wickstead's defence when he was accused of being "...undoubtedly drunk, very drunk" by a police inspector.

"How can you say such a thing?" exclaimed Wickstead, "Why," he continued, "I considered the constable acted so improperly when he interfered with me that I asked him to lend me a pencil in order that I might take his number. Could a drunken man do that? (A roar of laughter.) There is the number as I took it down. Is that like a drunken man's writing? (Laughter.) Sir Robert Carden looked at Wickstead's licence and saw that he had been fined for being drunk just two weeks previously. "Ah, that was the fog" replied Wickstead, "I was not drunk at all, but the fog got down in my throat and it made me stupid." Carden did wonder if Wickstead was a fit and proper person to drive a cab but gave him the benefit of the doubt, Carden was one of the few magistrates who had a genuine liking for cabmen. Wickstead was fined 10 shillings or seven days. Unfortunately, he could not pay the fine so he was locked up for a week.[64]

James Brooks denied that he was drunk, and magistrate Mansfield asked if the doctor had not certified him drunk? "Yes," Cried out Brooks from the dock, "the doctor said, "Put out your tongue." and as soon as I did so he said, "Oh, yes, he's drunk." I could not have been drunk, as I remember everything that occurred, and I even "interpreted" for a foreign gentleman."

Mansfield asked if this were true, to which the policeman who took the charge replied, "No, sir; all the prisoner, who made himself very busy, did was to say to the gentleman, "Parlez-vous, Francais?" an expression which he kept on repeating." Whether it was the lack of scientific analysis in determining if Brooks was drunk, or his efforts towards entente cordiale, Mansfield let him walk out of the court a free man.[65]

The doctor who examined Charles Fairclough after he was found to be drunk and driving furiously down Gordon House Road, Kentish Town, had a better scientific method than sticking out a tongue. He allegedly took one look at Fairclough, felt his pulse and declared him to be drunk. Fairclough interjected, "Didn't the doctor ask me to feel my own pulse?" To which the arresting officer conceded as being true. Fairclough explained that he was not drunk, the horse had bolted as it passed under a railway bridge. He had not asked for a doctor, and when he asked him what was the point of feeling his own pulse the doctor just said "drunk" and left the room. The magistrate, Plowden believed the cabman's story totally and criticised the police for employing a doctor who worked in such an unsatisfactory manner." The charge against Fairclough was dismissed.[66]

A Dr Lloyd, according to the *Daily News*, was on record as stating that if a person could not repeat "Say, now, Constantinople" without mistake, then that person is probably drunk. No cabman appears to have been convicted for failing to utter such a sentence, though other doctors utilised similar methods.

An un-named elderly cabman was charged with being drunk on the evening of Christmas Eve, 1895. The cabman denied the charge, saying he had had one glass of ale all evening and the cold and exposure was mistaken for him being drunk. At the police station he requested an independent doctor to examine him. Despite the festivities, one was found and he was examined by the doctor and the police surgeon. He walked a straight line and both doctors pronounced him sober at the time they examined him, but could not be sure if he was not drunk at the time of arrest. The independent doctor then added that the cabman was able to repeat, without a mistake, the sentence, "The artillery extinguished the conflagration early." Which, he added, even someone recovering from drink could not successfully pass. The cabman was discharged after paying the doctor's fees of 18s 6d – which was probably more than a fine had he pleaded guilty. The 'discharge' meant that the case had not been decided one way or the other. If further evidence arises, he could still face a retrial. Nobody seemed to consider the fortuitous effect the charge had for the arresting police officer, who now found himself in a warm police station as the bells tolled on a very cold Christmas Day.[67]

Another, albeit un-named, cabman, was at least found to be drunk after the doctor examined him with a scientific instrument. "He got a magnifying glass." Explained the arresting officer. The magistrate at Marlborough Street asked the police witness, "Could he not see him without?" The policeman explained that the doctor used the magnifying glass to examine the pupils of the cabman's eyes. It was enough for Plowden, given the cabman's previous convictions to impose a fine of 10 shillings. The editorial of the *Daily News*, thought the use of a magnifying glass was "about as bad as 'Constantinople.' A man whose drunkenness can only be discerned microscopically cannot have erred very deeply in his cups, and might even be justified in driving a cab."[68]

Tests did not improve with the arrival of the taxicab. Sidney Manley was told to walk along a line on tip-toes, after being arrested for being drunk in charge of a taxi in 1914. His solicitor thought that such a test difficult for a sober man, which the doctor disagreed with. The magistrate agreed with the doctor and thought it an easy task. Manley was sentenced to a month's imprisonment with hard labour.[69] When a policeman was asked what tests were applied to Edward Fiddler, who was accused of being drunk after hitting a lamp post, the officer replied, "He was told to shut his eyes, but he could not keep them shut. He was then blindfolded and told to follow the doctor, but he could not do it. He was then asked to say "constitutional" and "truly rural". He was then asked, "What are eleven fours?" He replied, "Eleven fours were forty-four when I was at school." Fiddler denied he was drunk and that he later drove his taxi from Hornsey to Acton. The magistrate remanded the case for the attendance of the two doctors.[70] Though no further action appears to have been taken. When another driver appeared at Marylebone police court, the doctor was asked how he determined the driver was drunk. "He could not stand straight, walk straight, talk straight or think straight" was his medical opinion. The driver was fined £2 with 10s costs.[71]

The following offences are punishable by penalty or two months imprisonment:

(d) Use of insulting or abusive language during employment.

Insulting or abusive language was probably more prolific among the cab drivers than drink was – a sober driver can abuse his passenger every bit as much as a drunk one. The abuse usually came after the passenger paid for the journey and what was received was not to the cabman's liking. Alderman Kennedy, in a case at the Guildhall in 1855, where the passenger gave the driver a 6d tip, but, because of the severity of the weather, the driver demanded more and used insulting and abusive language to try and obtain it. This prompted the alderman to remark, "It is an old saying, that if you want a little abuse from a cabman, you must give him 6d under his fare; but if you want some special abuse, you must give him 6d more than his fare.[72]

Thomas Crew told his passenger that the "next time he might walk instead", this despite being given a tip of 8d. For this "special abuse", according to the Alderman Kennedy doctrine, Crew was fined 20s.[73]

George Turner was paid the 8d legal fare by his passenger in 1853. The cab driver "looked at the money contemptuously, told him to put it back in his pocket as he might want it, and repeatedly called him no gentleman..." The Marlborough Street magistrate, Bingham, addressed the court and informed all that he "...was by no means a timid man, but he never yet, knowing the character of the class, was able to muster courage enough to offer a cabman 8d, however trifling the service he might have required from the man." Bingham thanked the passenger in bringing the case to court and as if to get his own back on all the tips he had to give, he fined Turner the maximum penalty of 40s plus costs or 21 days.[74]

A couple of months later, Henry Brett was to suffer a greater penalty for abuse and demanding more than his fare. With the introduction of the 1853 Act, the new minimum fare was reduced from 8d to 6d. Brett's passenger travelled less than a mile and so offered the legal fare of 6d. Brett said he refused to take anything less than a shilling, as well as the usual mantra of "Call yourself a gentleman?" In the hearing of several bystanders, Brett exclaimed "I will make you a present of the 6d." and drove off slowly without taking any fare at all. In court Brett stated that he did not know the new Act had come into operation. "He did not use any abusive language to the gent, as he know'd of. He certainly did laugh at him when he offered a sixpence (and he couldn't help laughing at that), and he also said he would make him a present of it." The magistrate, Henry, stated, with some justification, that there was not a cabman in London who was not aware of the day when the new act came into force, and even under the old law he could only charge 8d and not a shilling. For demanding more than his fare, Brett was fined £2 or a month's imprisonment. No fine was imposed by Henry for the insulting language, instead, he sent Brett to jail for three weeks.[75] This was on the same day that Henry sent cabman Phillips to jail (see Chapter 6). In one day, Henry had earned a reputation for penalising London's cabmen. The sentence of Cabman Phillips saw questions raised in the House of Commons, that of Henry Brett never raised an eyebrow.

In July 1856, George Mather Andrews, 2585, took a fare from Hamilton Terrace, St John's Wood, to Highbury Place, Islington. The passenger, Frederick Ward, thought the journey to be less than four miles, tendered Andrews 2s. Andrews contested this and said the distance was nearer six miles and that the fare was 3s. Andrews showed no insolence and gave Ward his ticket, stating that he would call at his home for the money once Ward had reconsidered. Andrews twice went around to Ward's house to collect the money but was twice refused and it was with some reluctance that he took out a summons against Ward, whom he had carried many times in his cab.

In court Andrews was described as being "very respectfully attired, and who gave his evidence in a fair and impartial manner". The dispute was one of distance but as the passenger was not willing to have the ground measured, Corrie, the magistrate found for the cabman and awarded the 1s disputed fare, 2s for the cost of the summons, and 3s for loss of a day's work in attending court. It was then that Ward, the passenger, asked for a summons against Andrews for abusive language, which Corrie granted straight away. Andrews then made his way from the witness box and into the dock. According to Ward, the abusive language from Andrews was, "Two shillings are not enough for a 3s fare." For this, Andrews was fined 2s. His net profit in taking out a summons and spending a day in court was just one shilling. Andrews paid the fine and left court mumbling that "it was not justice".[76]

Neither did the newspapers believe it was justice. *The Examiner* called the decision "preposterous" and the passenger, Ward, took his copy of that paper to Corrie to complain about the reporting of the case. Corrie read the report in *The Examiner* and agreed that to fine a man for saying such a thing was indeed preposterous. "The facts were, that the cabman called out that 2s was not enough for four miles, but according to the act of parliament it was enough." That was why Andrews was fined 2s.[77] Ward was still not happy that the cabman came out of the court case as some kind of martyr and he managed to get a retraction into *The Standard*, giving his version of events. He stated that he had done the journey many times before and had always paid 2s but Andrews had taken him a longer way around than was usual. When Andrews called at his home the first time it was straight away after he had been set down at Highbury so Andrews knew he would not be there. On the second occasion he was told to return in the evening, which he never did. Ward contested that the abuse he received was far greater than that published and the magistrate threatened to withdraw Andrews' licence because of his turbulent attitude in court.[78] None of this outburst was reported at the time, the court report having remarked that Andrews gave his evidence in a 'fair and impartial manner'. Andrews never got the right to reply, but at the end of the day, a cabman could be fined just for voicing his disagreement of an act of parliament.

A cab driver named Watts, 9744, was ordered to stop by PC George Cross outside the Mansion House in August of 1895. PC Cross alleged that Watts was driving dangerously and he himself had prevented two females from being struck by the cab. At first, Watts would not stop but the policeman gave chase and pulled him over. When he asked for the cabman's badge, Watts became very excited and exclaimed, "You're a liar. Who cares for you, you monkey-faced puppy?" Watts was summoned for insulting and abusive language and driving to the common danger. In court, the constable was cross examined by Watts's solicitor, "You thought it insulting to be called "monkey-face"?"

"I did"

"And yet you know we are all descended from monkeys."

"You might be, I'm not." Replied the constable to the laughter of the court. The magistrate, Alderman Truscott, added to the levity by observing that the policeman did not take it as a compliment. It transpired that Watts had travelled to the court from Southend, where he was on honeymoon. After re-iterating that according to Darwin we were all descended from monkeys, Watts was told he must pay the 5s costs on each charge. "Will you give me a week to pay in" asked the cabman, "I'm still on my honeymoon." Alderman Truscott allowed him the privilege of a week.[79]

A number of cab drivers, and cab proprietors for that matter, were fined for sending a horse that was unfit, out to work a shift. The worst horses came out at night, hidden by darkness. It was not unusual for horses to have open sores, broken knees, starved, or to be lame. To make matters worse, a cabman could often be seen whipping such a horse for not moving fast enough, only adding to its injuries. A cabman's defence was that he was told if he didn't take a particular horse out, another man would and he would lose a day's work. The masters often stated that the horse was sent out by mistake and should have been left resting in the stable. To counter this, and look after the welfare of the horses, RSPCA officers would patrol the streets and inspect horses whilst they stood on ranks, "Like roaring lions, seeking whom they may devour." If they found a horse was being treated cruelly, they would issue a summons against the driver. William Lowe suffered one such inspection but he no doubt felt his horse would pass muster, it was looked after and well fed. "You can get inside that horse," called out Lowe, alluding to the fact that his horse was more than just skin and bones, "If there is anything wrong with him, I will give him to you." For making such a generous offer, Lowe was summoned for abusive language. He may have felt the charges were to be dropped when the magistrate said it was nothing more than "... cab rank language, which came perfectly natural to cabmen, and which no one thought anything about." Except obviously, officers of the RSPCA. The magistrate could see no reason why officers of the society had to suffer at the witticism of cabmen whilst they were performing a necessary public service. Lowe was fined 5s with 2s costs.[80]

The same day as Lowe was fined for insulting two RSPCA officers, Isidore Charik (erroneously spelt Sharrick by the press) was before a magistrate in the City for using insulting language to a policeman. Charik and several other cabmen were standing by their cabs on a rank in Aldgate. According to a policeman they were causing an obstruction to pedestrians, and were asked to make room for people to pass by. Charik followed the policeman and told him, "You are too good to be a policeman. You ought to be something better. I don't get three suits of clothes a year, and don't live on the rates and tax-payers." For this advice and observation, and for causing an obstruction, Charik was summoned. The City Alderman was more sympathetic than the Lambeth Magistrate that heard Lowe's case. He felt that cabmen "must stand somewhere. They had to be out all night and deserved some sympathy. He should not have made such remarks, but he can go this time.[81] A case that elicited very little sympathy from the magistrate, when it was much needed was that of Henry King.

King had driven up to the National Hospital in Queen's Square in the early hours of November 13th 1902. His passenger was suffering from paralysis and was begging him to find medical attention for her. The hall porter at the hospital refused her admittance until a surgeon could be found who could certify whether the woman should be admitted or not. King and the woman were kept waiting outside the hospital in the freezing cold with the woman pleading to be allowed inside to at least be warm. By the time a surgeon did arrive, King had lost his temper and was shouting abuse at everyone and no one. The woman was admitted but died within a few hours. In court Henry King stated that in the fifteen years he had been a cab driver he had never been summoned before and had never used bad language in his life. The magistrate could have dismissed the summons but there was no doubt that King had verbally abused the hall porter of the hospital. In the end he was told to pay the 2s costs of the summons. With no fine imposed there was no endorsement on his cab licence.[82]

The following offences are punishable by penalty or two months imprisonment:

(e) Use of insulting gestures during employment.

Inspector Charles Jeeks of the Hackney Carriage Department, was inspecting cab horses on a stand in Tower Hill when he found that two of the horses had cab sores that rendered them unfit for work. Joseph Peck tried to discredit Jeeks by asking him if the animal was a horse or a mare. Peck said it was a horse, but Jeeks said it was a mare but as he made this observation he also saw Peck stick his tongue out in his direction. The two cabmen Jeeks pulled up that day were each fined 5s plus costs, for working a horse unfit for hackney carriage work. Peck was also fined a further 5s plus costs, for sticking his tongue out, a charge he denied.[83]

An un-named cabman was summoned to appear at the City Summons Court on a charge of loitering. The Policeman stated that he told the cabman to move on but was ignored and laughed at him. The cabman explained that he was laughing at something in the street when the officer came up to him and said, "I shall summon you for laughing." The alderman could not believe a policeman would say that but the cabman got off lightly on the loitering charge with a fine of just 1s plus costs.[84]

The following offences are punishable by penalty or two months imprisonment:

(f) Any misbehaviour during employment.

With so many rules, laws and regulations against a cabman, it is hard to imagine if there was any kind of action left that could be construed as misbehaviour but that did not stop the police and magistrates from finding some.

James Rogers was accused of misbehaviour in 1866 when he refused to accept any money for his fare. The journey was only "about 600 yards" and Rogers was paid 6d by his passenger, Sir Frederick Roe, one-time chief magistrate and brother of leading cab proprietor, Francis Roe. On being handed the 6d, Rogers proclaimed that he "...was surprised the gentleman should offer 6d and that he did not understand what it meant." Rogers put the 6d back into Roe's hand and said he would drive him for nothing. He added, he may have been aware who the passenger was, "Mind, I did not ask you for more than my legal fare." Roe stated that it was not for refusing to take his legal fare that Rogers was summoned but for misbehaviour. The magistrate was Knox, who felt that Rogers had been guilty of "an infinitesimal amount of misbehaviour" but not enough to convict under the 1853 Act. "The defendant had not given one word of abuse, though he had certainly made use of a stupid remark, and he thought allowance ought to be made for a person in the defendant's position in life." The summons was dismissed.[85] A rare occurrence of not only a magistrate disagreeing with a respected former magistrate, but also for Roe not to get a cabman punished.

Ebenezer Williams, badge 3138, was charged with misbehaviour and extortion. In early January 1880 "a respectable man" and his wife had been dining with friends at Peckham. Having missed the last omnibus they engaged Williams to drive them home to Leicester Square. Williams said he could not go that far but agreed to take them to the Elephant and Castle for 1s, where they could get another cab. On arrival there, Williams was handed his shilling but then "made use of the most disgusting language and accused the [respectable man] with having conducted himself improperly." The passenger resented this and iterated that the woman was his wife but Williams said "he knew better than that" and demanded more money. A policeman arrived and the accusation from Williams was repeated, as well as the foul language. In court, Williams was warned that he was lucky his licence was not suspended for his "disgraceful conduct" and he was fined 50s with 10s costs or six weeks' imprisonment.[86]

5 Taxi Ranks

Appointment of and Regulations for taxi ranks

TfL may appoint taxi ranks and make regulations as to the limits of the ranks, the number of taxis to be allowed to ply for hire there, the time during which they may ply for hire and also for enforcing order at the ranks, and removing any person unnecessarily loitering there.

A problem facing the embryonic hackney coachman in the 17th Century was where to find the work. Driving around looking for a passenger was tiresome for both man and beast. Alternatively, a coachman could wait at some point of his choosing and let the passenger find him. The second option was more problematic; the Aldermen in the City of London had forbidden coach stands whilst drivers waiting outside Shakespeare's Playhouse theatre in Blackfriars were threatened with being incarcerated in Newgate if, having once set down a fare, they continued to wait for the end of the performance to pick up the same or another passenger.

A standing for a carriage was not a new concept. The carmen of London, who delivered goods and cargo, had their own system of having space for a carriage to await the arrival of a boat laden with cargo. A carroom was, as the name implies, a space for a cart, where it could wait in the street until required to move cargo from a nearby supplier. They were at one time privately owned and could be hired or sold, or even bequeathed to a widow. Once the Woodmonger's Company took control of carmen, the carroom lost its commercial value and was held on licence, though in future years the carmen did win the right to treat them as an asset once more.[1]

Despite the rise in the number of hackney coaches in the first quarter of the seventeenth century, the Aldermen of the City of London and its environs, which pretty much included all the places a hackney coachman was likely to find work, steadfastly refused to sanction standings for hackney coaches. When a petition was raised to prevent a private house becoming a playhouse, it was the arrival of so many coaches that seemed to be the biggest fear: "...to which there was daily such a resort of people and such a multitude of coaches (many of them hackney coaches bringing people of all sorts), that at times the streets could not contain them, they clogged up Ludgate Hill also, so that they endangered one another, broke down stalls, threw down goods, and the inhabitants were unable to get to their houses, or bring in their provisions, the trademen to utter their wares, of passengers to get to the common water stairs without danger of life and limb; quarrels and effusion of blood had followed, and other dangers might be occasioned by the broils, plots, and practices of such an unruly multitude."[2]

Notwithstanding petitions against "unruly coaches" and a propaganda campaign led by John Taylor, a waterman-cum-poet-cum-publicist, who complained of the waterman's profit "running away on wheels", the hackney coachmen persisted in their calling. Even the introduction of sedan chairs, which were given a monopoly in London, Westminster and the suburbs, could not quash the need of the public to travel by coach despite how uncomfortable the journeys must have been given the conditions of the roads.

Unable to stand in the street, many parked their coach and horses in the yard of an inn and waited in the tap room to be called, thus starting a tradition that would last two hundred years. It took a certain Captain Baily to upset the status quo and revolutionise the hackney coach trade. We know very little about Baily who appears to be a retired mariner. There is speculation that he is the same captain John Bailey that sailed with Raleigh on his expeditions to find gold in Guiana but there is no corroboration that they are the same person. What we do know about Baily is in a letter from a Reverend George Garrard, who was master of Charterhouse in London, to the earl of Strafford, the Lord Lieutenant of Ireland. In the letter, one of many Garrard sent, enlightening Strafford on all that was happening in London. He described an experiment of Captain Baily, "an old sea-captain", where "He hath erected, accg to his ability, some four hackney coaches, put his men in livery, and appointed them to stand at 'The Maypole,' in the Strand, giving them instructions at what rates to carry men into several parts of the town, where all day they may be had. Other hackneymen seeing this way, they flocked to the same place, and perform their journeys at the same rate, so that sometimes there is twenty of them together, which disperse up and down, so that they and others are to be had everywhere, as watermen are to be had at the waterside. Everybody is much pleased with it, for whereas before coaches could not be had but at great rates, now a man may have one much cheaper."

The Maypole was equidistant between the City and Westminster and thus outside the jurisdiction of the City Aldermen. The enterprise was a success but no more is heard of Baily but he has the distinction of being the earliest named proprietor.

If the City Aldermen were powerless to prevent the hackney coachmen ranking up outside the City walls, then the Crown was not. Eager to protect the sedan chair monopoly he had bestowed upon Sir Sanders Duncombe, King Charles initiated a set of proposals that were designed to eradicate hackney coaches from London altogether by making them uneconomic. Amongst the conditions, no coach could be hired "in or about London" unless the journey was at least three miles; the coach must be pulled by at least four horses; no unmarried gentlemen or sons of noblemen shall be allowed in a coach unless accompanied by their parents. The coachmen had until Michaelmas (September 29th) for which to dispose of their coaches[3]; a period they took full advantage of. The following month after the proposals were drawn up by Lord Cottington, the watermen on the Thames petitioned Parliament complaining that "hackney coaches are so many in number that they pester the streets and make leather exceedingly dear, and moreover carry every common person, to the great prejudice of the petitioners."[4]

The King's subsequent proclamation, in January 1636, had the desired effect of bringing the coachmen, of which there would have been about one hundred, to their knees. They subsequently petitioned Parliament for a charter of incorporation which would give them a legal status. Their removal from the streets had not prevented "chandlers, innkeepers, brokers and other tradesmen [intruding] into the profession of coachmen." The petitioners alleged that the "intruders" "have set up coaches and hired men to drive them"[5] presumably from their own yards and in a furtive manner as not to be seen defying the King's proclamation.

As the numbers of intruders, providing a clandestine hackney carriage service increased, the *bona fide* hackneymen returned to the streets and were once more openly ranking up in defiance of the law. The drivers did not have it all their own way, as James Thompson found out in 1648. Thompson has the distinction of possibly being the earliest known hackney coach driver to be named. On December 1st he was bailed, in the sum of forty pounds, to appear before the next sessions to answer a charge of "estoping and annoying the King's highway over against the new Exchange in the Strand by standing with his coach in the streete there to waite for faires." Although he was the only coachman named, a further six others were also bailed to appear at the next sessions having illegally ranked up at the same location waiting for fares.[6] Their arrest follows a petition from the scavengers and street-sweepers of the Strand who, now that that thoroughfare was blocked with, at times, twenty coaches, they had more than their work cut out in dealing with the natural waste of forty extra horses. The fate of those seven hackney coachmen does not appear to have survived.

In 1654 Oliver Cromwell consented to the formation of the Fellowship of Master Hackney Coachmen. For the first time the hackney coaches were to be licensed. The licensing authority was to be the Court of Aldermen of the City of London and besides limiting licences, laying down the rates they could charge, they were also responsible for "places of Standing" – the very first official ranks.

The Aldermen had the authority to establish, or remove stands within the area of their jurisdiction, which would not only include the City, but Southwark "and its environs". Outside of their domain it was left to individual parishes and interested bodies such as the Woods and Forests Commissioners who owned much of the land that coach stands stood upon, even though the Commissioners had not given permission for many of these stands to be created in the first place. From 1771 a regulation allowed hackney coachmen to form a stand in any street that was over thirty-foot wide and possession being nine-tenths of the law, once such stands were established, the hackneymen were reluctant to have them taken away from them. In 1826 the Commissioners of St Pancras Parish sought to remove a rank from Howland Street, and move it into nearby Tottenham Court Road. "The Knights of the Whip being refractory, several were summoned to appear at the police court." The case against the hackney coachmen was thrown out by the magistrate who remarked that the Parish had the power under law to "direct and regulate" a coach stand, but not authorise its removal. St Pancras appealed against the decision and the Lord Chief Justice ruled in their favour. The Parish Commissioners did have the power to remove the stand in Howland Street but were warned that trying to remove a stand in Tottenham Court Road, being wider than thirty-foot, was a different matter.[7]

The Act of 1831, which saw the abolition of limitation of licences but no increase in the number of cab and coach stands to accommodate the new influx, also reinforced the thirty-foot rule. An informer had summoned a coachman for obstruction in Charlotte Street, now part of Bloomsbury Street. The thoroughfare was more than the required thirty-foot wide but the case had been brought by the Commissioners of Pavements for the parish of St George's Hanover Square who had not given permission for the rank to be established on their land. The Board of Stamps, the governing body of Hackney Coaches and cabs under the 1831 Act, had authorised the stand and the court case developed into one of jurisdiction. The coachman was fined 40s for obstruction but the penalty was allowed to stand over to see if the Commissioner of Stamps would appeal against the decision. He didn't, and the coachman was left high and dry having to pay his own fine and costs. Buoyed by their success, the Commissioners of Pavements summoned a cabriolet driver for causing an obstruction from the same stand. It would be another six years before the drivers were badged and licensed and, as was in accordance with the law, it was the owner of the cabriolet who was summoned. By a pre-arranged agreement, the owner did not appear, though his driver did, but in the owner's place was cab and coach proprietor, Francis Roe, who we earlier met in Chapter 1 when he "had the lowest regard for his drivers than anyone could imagine". Roe informed the magistrate that he wished to take on the case on behalf of the defendant and would abide by any decisions or fines imposed by the court. Whilst the magistrate and the prosecution were keen to test the case, there were legal problems that could arise. To combat this, Roe got into one of his cabs and was driven to the stand in Charlotte Street where he was promptly told he would be summoned.[8]

In Marlborough Street police court the following day, Roe argued that it was "a most extraordinary thing for a hackney coachman or cab driver [to be summoned] for that which is allowed under the Act." The Commissioner of Pavements responded by stating the "bungling manner" under which the Hackney Carriage Act was framed - neither the first, or last time, such an accusation was levelled against a hackney carriage act. The Act only laid down the law to the Stamp Office for receiving revenue and granting licences, it had no authority in the appointment of stands. Dyer, the magistrate, found in favour of Roe but said he would allow an appeal by the Commissioner of Pavement's should they want a higher court to decide on the matter.[9] Roe was slightly hesitant with regards to fighting the case further at an appeals court. He had, for the time being, ensured that hackneymen had the right to ply for hire on a stand in any street of at least thirty-foot width. Fighting an appeal was not inexpensive but a week later Roe was back in court with the news that should the Commissioner of Pavement's wish to pursue the matter, Roe had been given assurances by the Stamp Office to fight the appeal from which he would be indemnified from any of its results.[10] The Commissioner of Pavement's, no doubt fearing the cost of such an action themselves let the matter drop and hoped that by lobbying Parliament they could negotiate a change in any future legislation.

When the London and Birmingham Railway Company opened its terminus at Euston in 1837, the streets surrounding the station proved to be a lucrative spot for hackney coaches and cabs to pick up fares. The hackney coach stand in Seymour Street [now Eversholt St] was said to be of "extraordinary and unprecedented proportions". Further north along the same thoroughfare, in what was then Upper Seymour Street, "...the respectable residents were all leaving their homes as fast as possible, as the minds of their families were liable to become polluted by the disgraceful language and conduct of the coachmen, who, instead of keeping to their horse's heads, were continually assembling in groups, playing at pitch and toss, and other low amusements. They would keep at this until the second bell of the railway announced the arrival of the train, when they would drive about to get up to the train first, regardless either of their own necks or the lives of the public."[11]

Earlier complaints from the local inhabitants had gained a compromise from the railway company that hackney coaches would be permitted to rank up on one side of the yard to the rear of the station and private carriages on the other. This idea soon collapsed owing to the multitudes of coaches trying to get into the yard. The railway company then promised to employ three men at their own expense, as rank marshals. This appeased the local tenants for a while until they realised that the railway company had no intention of going to such expenditure. To make matters worse, the London & Birmingham Railway Company were planning to erect posts and chains at the front of the railway station (this would have been in Drummond Street, the New Road (now Euston Road), was a further three blocks to the south) which would prevent hackney coaches ranking along there and forcing even more coaches to park along Seymour Street.

Seymour Street was forty-nine-foot wide from building to building, the carriageway itself was 33 foot wide. The hackney coachmen were using the law that allowed them to ply for hire in any street wider than thirty-foot but the commissioners of the parish and the Southampton Estate Paving Estate were to use that law against the coachmen. Seymour Street was a busy shopping street, the busiest in the area, but it only had a pavement on either side of the carriageway of 8 foot. By increasing the pavement out onto the road, they would make it safer for pedestrians and also reduce the width of the road to below thirty foot, thus making it illegal for any hackney coach to stand and ply for hire.

Before they followed through with that threat, a different tact was tried. The hackney coach stand in Seymour Street had been there as long as any of the residents could remember, and it's official status was confirmed by the fact that the Commissioner of Hackney Coaches had appointed three watermen to attend the stand, supposedly to maintain good order. The stand in Upper Seymour Street however, had only appeared since the opening of what is now Euston Station. There were no posts or markings to designate an official stand. If watermen were appointed to it, it was official, if they were not, then it had not been sanctioned by the Hackney Coach Commissioners. The stand in Seymour Street was perfectly legal, despite the problems it was causing the local residents, the Upper Seymour Street stand was however illegal, and any hackney coachman standing there was liable to be prosecuted for obstruction.

Hackney coachman John Emery, was to be the test case for any such prosecution. His trial excited great interest, not only with the local residents but with the cab trade as a whole. After the magistrate, Combe, had heard all the legal arguments as to whether the Upper Seymour Street stand was a legal feed to the authorised stand in Seymour Street, and deciding it was not, he had no option than to find Emery guilty of causing an obstruction. Emery was fined 20s with the threat of imprisonment [presumably for a month] if the fine were not paid. Combe, no doubt realising that the residents just wanted to prove a point and had no animosity towards a particular cabman, reduced the fine to one of 10s. Emery however, expressed to the court that he could not pay the reduced fine. In such circumstances, his master, a proprietor named Jarvis, was asked to pay the fine for his 'servant', but he, rather magnanimously, declared that as his driver had done nothing wrong, he refused to pay the fine 'on principle', so Emery was led away to the cells.[12]

John Emery had no inkling that he was about to be a martyr, albeit an unknown one, but his conviction was about to change cab trade history. The residents of St. Pancras and Somers Town followed through with their threat to extend the pavements, thus making it illegal, for hackney carriages to stand in Seymour Street. With no ready supply of cabs to take their passengers away from the stations at the sound of a bell, the railway companies had to come up with a plan. It was called the "privilege system" and by limiting the work coming out of the station to just a few cab yards that could cope with that work, for a price, the railway companies had full control over the number of cabs, and their condition. It seemed like a good idea but it caused not only a strike but seventy years of grief and would come close to splitting the trade into two separate entities before the system was finally abolished by the Act of 1907.

Drivers to be with taxis

The drivers of the first two taxis on a standing or any portion thereof must be with their taxis and available for hiring immediately.

This regulation was originally brought in by Winston Churchill when Home Secretary in 1910. Prior to this, and going as far back as 1853, drivers were compelled to remain on the seat of their cab whilst it was on a stand, in all weathers, without so much as a cigarette to enjoy. Churchill proved to be a great favourite among the cabmen as he allowed them, for the first time in 60 years, to smoke whilst seated on their cab waiting for a fare, and also, more importantly, the right to leave their cab on a stand whilst they took some refreshment. At first, the regulation only applied to those ranks where a cab shelter was attached with the rank being divided into "ordinary" and "reserve". Those on the reserve portion had thirty minutes for their refreshment but there always had to be at least two cabs on the "ordinary" part of the rank, available for immediate hire. If either or both of these two cabs pulled off the rank for a hiring then the next available cab had to be moved up and the driver, no matter what part of his meal was before him, had to go sit in his cab to await the next fare. Prior to Churchill's intervention a cab left unattended on a stand, or for that matter in any street, could be seized by the police.

The police had found a cab left unattended on a rank in Oxford Street at 11 o'clock in the evening of Boxing Day, 1835, and drove it round to the local green yard. They returned to the same stand and found a hackney chariot, likewise left unattended. They were about to remove this to the green yard when its owner, James Lewis, approached them and began haranguing the officers. Lewis was joined by James Reece, who was the driver of the cab that had already been removed from the rank. The pair created so much disturbance that the police had to obtain assistance by calling for officers with their rattles, the police of the day not yet issued with whistles. The commotion also brought other members of the public to the scene and Lewis called out to them on the "tyranny of the police" and excited the assembled mob so much that in order to prevent the chariot from being removed, they unharnessed the horses. The chariot was still taken to the greenyard, but pulled by several officers and not the two horses. Whilst this was going on Lewis and Reeves were joined in inciting the mob by Charles Greenwood, an ex-policeman. All three were charged with riot. In court they each denied the charge, Lewis stated that "he did not address the mob until after witnessing the violent conduct of the police, and then he said but a few words." The magistrates were unconvinced and fined each of the men £3. Lewis, being a proprietor could pay his fine but the other two were committed to the House of Correction for one month in default.[13]

In 1845 Edward Cooper, Francis Neville and Henry Ware, left their cabs on the stand in Piccadilly, for what they claimed were "urgent necessities". As far as they were concerned, they had left their cabs in charge of the waterman on the rank but the police said the act, as it then stood, unequivocally stated that no cabs should be left unattended on a stand. The drivers stated that such a condition was not only cruel but impossible to deliver. The men had to leave their cabs at some point of the day to answer a call of nature. The case was adjourned to hear from the Hackney Coach Office. A deputy registrar confirmed that a licensed waterman was the only person who could be left in charge of an unattended cab. A cabman could be fined if he left his cab under the control of an unlicensed person. The three cabmen were home and dry. They had left their cabs on the stand in charge of the licensed waterman. If Catch-22's existed in the 1840's, the three were about to find out. The deputy registrar then informed the court that a licensed waterman was the only person allowed by law to look after a cab. If the drivers left the cab on a stand then they could be subjected to a fine as once they were on the stand they were deemed to be plying for hire. They could park elsewhere off the stand – but the licensed waterman was only empowered to look after those cabs and coaches on the stand. On the basis of this, it is difficult to see exactly what the watermen were there for. The magistrate failed to see the full implication of what the deputy registrar was saying. As far as the law was concerned, the Act was passed to stop people coming up to a hackney coach stand where all the cabs were unattended with the drivers smoking and drinking in the nearest public house. Cooper and Neville were fined 5s each plus costs, Ware was fined 3s plus costs.[14]

The absurdity was allowed to continue. The police knew they could get an easy arrest from any unattended cab left on a stand. It caused great hardship among the cabmen who contrived ways of getting around the law. In November 1846, a full 22 months after Cooper, Neville & Ware were fined, two other cabmen appeared before magistrate George Long. As far as Long was concerned, a cab left in the care of a waterman on a stand was not unattended, he felt that that was one of the primary reasons for the existence of watermen. If anybody countered this by saying that a lone waterman could not possibly control a stand full of cabs then the Commissioners had the power to employ more watermen. The charges against the two cabmen were dismissed and some semblance of common sense was restored to the cab stands.[15] But not much.

Fifty-two-year old James Cook did not have any money to spend in a warm tap room a month after magistrate Long had applied some common sense among the stands. He had been struggling lately to earn enough to pay for the cab, in fact he had fallen behind and owed his master a sum of money over and above his daily rental. He went to work on the morning of Monday 14th December, 1846. He made his way to the stand in Davies Street, Mayfair, and there he waited on his box, on a freezing cold day for four hours before he was called off the rank. As he was about to carry a trunk down a flight of stairs he keeled over and died instantly. Death was from "natural causes" but exhaustion was thought to have been a major factor. The plight of Cook so touched those people who were in the coroners' court that a collection was made for his widow which totalled £2 18s.[16]

There was a major review of hackney carriage ranks in 1850 which saw a number of them taken out from the main streets, such as Oxford Street, where they impeded traffic flow, and into nearby side-streets, where they were a nuisance to the local residents. It was an old adage that everyone wanted a hackney coach stand close by, but nobody wanted one outside their front door. In order to obviate the nuisance, the Commissioners also enacted several regulations in April 1853 for all stands within the Metropolitan Police District. These included that drivers were not allowed to stand on the footway or cause any obstruction or annoyance to persons passing; drivers or watermen are not to use any offensive or insulting language, or improper behaviour or gestures; they are not allowed to smoke or drink spirits or malt liquor; they are not allowed to wash or clean their cabs upon any standing; they must cause no dirt or litter by feeding or watering their horses; and they must move their vehicle if it is found to be obstructing a private vehicle. *The Era* newspaper, generally sympathetic to the trade, believed that many reforms were needed but described the new regulations as "...a more unwarrantable and unreasonable mandate was never issued by any Jacks-in-office." It continued, "If the cabman is prevented from leaving his vehicle to obtain refreshment, it must be presumed that he is to have no dinner, or that he is to carry his dinner with him and eat it on the box. A pleasant meal he would have on many days on which the rain would pelt down upon his cold meat, and fill up his half-emptied beer jug. But we have forgotten; the cabman, when on duty, is forbidden to drink. ...actually to prohibit a man's purchasing a tankard of beer because he wears a badge and pays for a licence to drive a cab is rather going too far in the career of cab reform.[17]

These hardships were epitomised in a letter to *Lloyds' Weekly Newspaper* by E.B. Chesney who professed to be unconnected with the cab trade. "A poor man named George Clayton, a cab driver for these last twenty years, and living, or rather starving and dying, at 69 Alfred Place, New-road, Chelsea, was on the Sloane-square rank on Tuesday. Under the new, tyrannical, and inconsistent regulation, he was strictly confined to his cab. This rank being in the open square, is more exposed to the weather than many are. He sat on his box, shivering and shaking (and with a hungry belly) from one till four o'clock in the afternoon, surrounded by bleak winds and a bitter nipping frost. Poor cabby suffered much, but did not complain. How dare he?...But he was a cabman and not allowed to speak of a grievance. Cabbies are poor, and, as is often the case, uneducated, and therefore must be kept down. This degraded man...has five young children (too young to earn a penny), and a sober, hard-working, prudent wife at home, anxiously waiting with craving appetites, the return of their provider. After three hours of subdued grief and suffering, he gets off with a little job. Scarcely does this benumbed victim of oppression set down his fare, than he is compelled to seek his poverty stricken home, being too ill to put again on the rank."[18] Chesney called on the editor, "…in the name of God", to do something to right the wrong under which cabmen were suffering. By including Clayton's address, Chesney was no doubt hoping the public would relieve the suffering of his family by donating money. Clayton was listed in the 1851 Census as a proprietor, though he possibly owned just the one cab. The Census records that he had seven children in 1851, the oldest was eleven years old, so not even thirteen by the time Chesney told of Clayton's ordeal. Tragedy seems to have struck the family in 1852 when the two youngest children, William (3) and Louisa (2) both died. Clayton himself appears to have survived the ordeal and lived another nine years dying at the age of 58.

On 6th February 1875 a crowd of dignitaries from the trade, parliament and the press assembled at the cab stand in Acacia Road, St John's Wood. At the head of the stand stood a green wooden building, the first cabman's shelter in London. Captain Armstrong, editor of *The Globe* newspaper, is credited with the erection of the shelter after sending his servant out for a cab on a cold snowy night. After a lengthy period of time the servant returned empty handed. There were plenty of empty cabs on the stands but all the drivers preferred to remain in the warm tap rooms, supping beer and smoking. It had given Armstrong the idea that if the cabmen had somewhere warm and dry to wait upon jobs, somewhere they could get a hot drink and hot food, they may shun the public houses. His faith in the London cabman abstaining from drink was not totally unfounded. For the last few years or so, the cab trade had initiated a renaissance from within the ranks. The Cabmen's Benevolent Association had been formed, where, for a small weekly subscription, cabmen could look forward to a retirement instead of dying at the reins or in the workhouse; there was also the Cabmen's Mission at King's Cross, spreading the evangelical word and promoting abstention from drink; there was the Lord's-day Rest Association who for some time had been advocating a six-day week, a luxury enjoyed by most of the cabmen in mid-1870's London.

Although new to London, the shelters were not a new idea. The first cab shelter had opened in Manchester in 1862 which was more a waiting room for drivers to await a fare, and for the public to wait for a cab. In

1872 a cabman's shelter with wheels, opened in Birmingham exclusively for the cabmen, a gift of the town mission. A stove was planned for the drivers to have hot food, and a curtain was needed to give the driver's more privacy. Literature to enhance the "instructive and moral tendency" of the cabmen was to be on hand.

Attempts had been made by George Stormont Murphy, Secretary of the Cabmen's Benevolent Association, to have a shelter, first at the stand in Hyde Park Corner, then later at the top of Sloane Street. Both ideas failed due to opposition from local residents. Stormont Murphy had written to the Commissioner of Police at Scotland Yard to find out if he could authorise such buildings and override the complaints from the local population. Henderson replied that whilst he had the power to appoint and remove stands, he had no authority in having the shelters erected. Then, as a teaser, he added, that he also did not have the power to order their removal.

Despite local opposition, the press thought the idea of cab shelters was a good one. After all, other than sitting in the cab itself, which many of the cab riding public did not like to see, a cabman's only other place of refuge was usually a pub.

On that foggy Saturday, all opposition had been overcome and the first shelter was erected in the middle of Acacia Road, St John's Wood. The shelter, which contained "conveniences for cooking and a supply of hot coffee" was formerly opened by the Hon. Arthur Kinnaird MP, a philanthropic member of parliament who was frequently championing the cause of the London cabmen. Also present were Stormont Murphy, who was on the committee of the newly formed Cabmen's Shelter Fund which was also represented by cab drivers Macnamara and Dennistoun, treasurer and secretary respectively to the Fund. Kinnaird also thanked Captain Armstrong who had been a principle mover in obtaining permission for the shelter to be erected, especially for his campaign through the pages of *The Globe*. He remarked on the role of the building, was it a place of shelter, protecting the cabman from the elements, the foggy morning no doubt enhancing his words; or was it a place of rest, where a cabman could find tranquillity inside from what was happening outside. *Punch* magazine would shortly after identify the shelters as a place of retreat from a particular customer, but more about her in the next Chapter.

Continuing with the theme of rest, Kinnaird pointed out a cab proprietor in the crowd, John Cockram. Cockram had long advocated that cabmen would be in a much better position if they took one day a week off, preferably Sunday's. Up until he had started his one-man crusade, most cabmen worked seven days a week. This, he believed, exhausted them, and they spent longer and longer in the ale-houses than trying to work. In taking a day off, a man would feel recharged, as would his horse. In 1860 he used his £20 prize money, from his 19,000 word essay on the evils of working on a Sunday, to start up his own cab business. Cockram would not allow any of his men to take out a cab on a Sunday, and with the courage of his convictions, by the time the Acacia Road shelter was opened, Cockram and his partner owned a fleet of eighty cabs.[19]

More shelters soon followed. Whilst Acacia Road shelter enjoyed its first working day, construction on two other shelters, one at Langham Place, the other near St Clement Danes Church in the Strand, were well under way.

Owing to the success of the Acacia Road shelter, the Board of Works for St George's, Hanover Square debated erecting a stand in fashionable Belgravia. The only objection, as one member saw it, would be from the local licensed victuallers of the area who would stand to lose a lot of custom by not having cabmen within their walls. Another member felt that the publicans might welcome the introduction of a shelter, there would be cabs on hand to take away drunk customers. Another objection was that the "cabmen cooked onions and herrings in these rests, and that was not very nice for Belgravia." Colonel Ogilvy remonstrated on that member by telling him that he had obviously not been to the Acacia Road shelter, "or he would not give utterance to such a remark." A motion to delay the erection of a shelter was defeated and the committee agreed to have a shelter placed in Eaton Square for a month on trial.[20]

The temporary status of the cab shelters was reinforced by the shelter in Belgravia. From Eaton Square it was moved to the corner of Grosvenor Place, and from there into nearby Hobart Place, a trip of no more than a couple of hundred yards. But it raised objections from wherever it was sited. A resident named Ratcliffe, of 19 Hobart Place, now objected that the shelter was placed as close as was possible to his house, impeding his view from his window. The shelter had been placed in the centre of the carriageway above the gutter than ran down the centre of the road. This allowed "filthy water" to accumulate and stand. He desired its removal either to its earlier site of the corner of Grosvenor Place or in the neighbourhood of those people who had consented to the shelter in the first place. It was agreed that the matter should be looked further into and a report to be drawn up.[21] The hut was eventually moved around the corner from Hobart Place into Grosvenor Gardens, where the temporary structure remains to this day, over 140 years later.

Alexandra Palace held what could be termed the Victorian equivalent of the Taxi Driver of the Year Show in October 1875. Prizes were given in a number of categories, best horse, best cab, for drivers who had not been convicted of any offence, for those who had abstained from drinking alcohol the longest, etc. One category was for the best design of cab shelter, the only provisos being they had to meet the current regulations of being no wider than a horse and cab, and to be of a temporary structure that could be moved. A further condition was that they should cost no more than £75. All in all, nine different designs were submitted, including "a very capital design" from a builder in Norwich, but which was disqualified when it was found that it failed the maximum cost of £75. [22]

Drivers to be willing to be hired

A taxi must not be left on a standing or portion thereof unless the driver is willing to be hired.

Despite these regulations, drivers still persisted in leaving their cabs on a stand, ostensibly in charge of a waterman, whilst they sat in a warm tavern. Which is what John Bull, badge 7367, had done on a cold December night in 1853. He had been in the Globe tavern in Moorgate, it's still there today, and when he left and sat upon his seat, he was approached by two gentlemen who wished to go to Myddleton Square, just over a mile away. Bull refused, claiming that his horse had already been a great distance and that he could not go. Thomas Glover, the complainant, informed him that as he was on the rank he was therefore plying for hire but Bull countered this by alleging that Glover and the other gentleman, Glover's brother, were both drunk. Glover admitted to having had a drink but he was not drunk "he knew what he was about". He informed the court that he and his brother had spent an evening with ex-Sheriff Croll in Finsbury Circus, a person who would have been well known to the magistrate hearing the case, Alderman Wilson. The brothers had left Croll's residence at 10:30 in the evening and proceeded to the cab rank in Moorgate, which was full of cabs but no drivers or even a watchman could be found. After threatening to summon Bull for the refusal and taking his number, Glover's brother interjected and concerned that Bull might have a family to look after, asked him to apologise for saying they were drunk. Bull refused to apologise and as they argued, all the drivers who had been in the Globe now came out and accused the brothers of not only being drunk but of assaulting Bull. It was suggested, by a policeman on patrol, that they should all go to a nearby police station where the Glover's could be charged. This was probably more agreeable to the brothers than having to face the wrath of a large group of cabmen who had had a drink. The charge against the Glovers was not taken by the inspector at the station, who did not think the brothers were drunk, nor did the policeman who accompanied them. The Glovers did follow through with their threat to summon Bull, and it was the cabman's unlucky day when he found out the magistrate at Guildhall was Alderman Wilson.

Alderman Wilson had a reputation for having a low regard for cabmen. He was convinced that if they knowingly drove over a pedestrian the cabman, especially if he had a fare, would not stop but continue, just so he would get paid. Several drivers had had their licences suspended and even revoked by him and he even called for all drivers striking in 1853 to have their licences revoked. He was not a stranger to taking out the odd summons against a cabman himself for various reasons such as overcharging, refusing to wait and refusing to give a ticket (see Chapter 6). Conversely, he admitted that he would never think of giving a cabman anything less than a shilling, no matter how short the ride. In reviewing the evidence against Bull before him, he deemed it "a very grave offence" and fined him 20s or seven days' imprisonment. He also would suspend his licence for fourteen days. If Bull was going down, he was going down as a martyr. He refused to pay the fine, "It is very cruel to convict me of this offence. It is not justice." The martyrdom was short-lived as Bull's master paid the fine for him. Later that day, Bull was back before Alderman Wilson in an attempt to summon the Glovers for the alleged assault. Wilson replied that it "would be extremely inconsistent" to allow such a summons after he had been guilty himself of misconduct. Bull then tried to get the fourteen-day suspension of his licence lifted. He had a wife and two children who depended upon him for support and had been a cabman for thirteen years and had never been summoned before the present case. Taking into consideration his previous good conduct and the fact that his family would suffer, Alderman Wilson agreed to lift the suspension of the licence. Bull "expressed himself perfectly happy, and retired."[23] But that was not the end of the matter.

Two weeks later the Glovers were back before Alderman Wilson asking for further charges to be made out. They hired a detective who found out that far from being married and with a large family to support, Bull was a single man. As for Bull's witnesses, a gold penmaker, who came across as a respectable tradesman was "in the habit of frequenting the Green Gate public house in City Road and was seen recently to be drinking with John Bull for over three hours; such conduct threw doubt on his respectability they added. A second witness, who described himself as a respectable butcher, was in fact just a slaughterman who worked only two days a week and had no address where he could be contacted as he often slept in six-penny lodging houses. The third witness, a cabman who lived in Red Lion Street, Barbican, could not be traced as there was no record of his living there and a search at Scotland Yard revealed that he did not even live in the district. "Mr Glover said he understood that there were always a number of persons called "mounters" attached to every cab stand, who were ready to get up in the witness box and swear whichever way the cabman wanted them; and if such was the case, he thought it extremely desirable, both for the protection of the public and the ends of justice, that in every instance where a "mounter" appeared to give evidence, that the case should be adjourned for inquiry as to character."[24] Alderman Wilson agreed and confirmed that he had indeed heard of the existence of "mounters". In the present case, he thought the only sustainable charge was against the butcher and a summons would be granted for him – but they would have to find him first. No further action appears to have been taken against Bull for alleging he had a wife and two children.

An entire rank of cabmen was summoned for not being willing to be hired in 1854. A Mr and Mrs Wigan had been to the Olympic Theatre and asked the staff there to procure a cab from the nearby stand. A couple of drivers flatly refused to take them whilst others just walked away from their cab and slouched into a nearby public house. 'The ringleader exclaimed, " "Oh, ah! Brompton for eighteen pence. Don't you wish you may get it?" Indeed, the entire rank, with one reluctant exception, refused to take the fare, and as the occurrence was by no means unusual, Mr Wigan directed that summonses should be taken out against the whole of them." In court, a policeman explained that the rank also served the Drury Lane theatre where it was more likely a family of four would want a cab. Due to the recent act there were no extras in carrying just two people. The drivers wanted families as they could charge for all persons numbering more than two. It may also be that the drivers recognised Wigan as someone who only paid the legal fare. It was not recorded just how many drivers he did summon; the alleged ringleader was fined 20s or twenty days, whilst all the others were fined 10s or ten days.[25]

Drivers not to cause annoyance, etc.

Drivers must not obstruct the carriageway or footway to cause annoyance or disturbance to residents or persons in the vicinity.

Whilst the "*Interesting Adventures*" described by Henry Beauchamp in 1813 may rely more on his fertile imagination than on his "auricular powers" (listening to the conversation of his passengers), he does relate how his master, on obtaining a reconditioned coach, "without much difficulty procured for it a respectable stand."[26] By a respectable stand,

Beauchamp is probably referring to the drivers who frequented the stand were polite and smart, and likewise kept not only their cabs clean and smart but the area surrounding the stand as well. No doubt ladies and gentlemen could walk past the stand without being accosted or jeered. Presumably as a mark of their respectability, the men would not be getting drunk in a nearby public house or gambling. By residing on a respectable rank, Beauchamp wants to convey that his passengers, who he no doubt also think may well be his readers, are likewise, respectable. There were a few stands that were not only disreputable, but notoriously so.

One of the most notorious stands in London was "the coach rank in the Haymarket [which] had been a most serious nuisance to the respectable inhabitants of that place. The cabmen in particular [as opposed to hackney coachmen], generally young men of bad character, assembled together on the pavement during the day, and, by their filthy language, and numbers, deterred passengers, especially females, from passing along. At night the nuisance was still more intolerable, for, as the fellows were mostly connected with the low prostitutes who abound in that quarter, it was utterly impossible to walk through the Haymarket without witnessing scenes of the grossest profligacy, and hearing the vilest language. Sometimes there were upwards of fifty vehicles on the rank, and as nearly each driver was provided with a substitute (a "buck" - see Chapter 1), there were from eighty to one hundred of the lowest ruffians in the metropolis, congregated in the street." A bookseller named White had complained to the police on many occasions about the nuisance caused by the drivers, which of course was resented by the drivers themselves. One, a hackney coachman named Crossley, went into White's bookshop "in a state of intoxication" during the day and fired off a torrent of abuse at the bookseller. White filed charges against him and Crossley was fined 40 shillings plus costs.[27]

If the bookseller was hoping that a forty shilling fine would dampen down the behaviour of the cabmen, he was sadly disillusioned. Five years later the police were reporting that the Haymarket stand was completely in the hands of the "bucks", and the law could do very little against them. When, in 1843, Thomas Vorgen was bilked by two young men he picked up from the Haymarket stand, the magistrate, Rawlinson, called it the "thieves" rank, such was its reputation among the magistracy, and had been so called by them for many years.[28]

Marylebone Vestry had a long running battle with the hackney coaches and cabs that ranked up in Oxford Street. Over four hundred rate payers had signed a petition to rid the thoroughfare of all the hackney coaches and other vehicles plying for hire – presumably omnibuses and stage coaches "The coach stands in Oxford Street had not only the effect of prejudicing the interests of the inhabitants… but their moral and social feelings, were disgusted by gangs of ruffians lounging about their windows, using the most obscene and disgraceful language."[29]

There was illegal activity of a different kind when Westminster Board of Works decided to enhance Knightsbridge Green during the Spring of 1879. Following a bequest, it was decided to beautify the area by planting some trees. Parish workers came and dug sufficient holes for the trees to be planted the following day. The only problem for the local cabmen was that many of these holes were dug right through the cab stand. That night, 150 to 200 cabmen took hold of the shovels used by the workmen and in "a systematic, but not in a disorderly manner" filled in all the holes. Two men, Henry William Rowland, secretary to the Amalgamated Society of Metropolitan Cab Drivers and Robert Dennistoun, a cab driver who was mentioned earlier regarding the opening of the Acacia Road shelter, voluntarily gave their names to the police when they arrived. In court there was a debate over who had jurisdiction over the stand, Westminster Parish or the Commissioner of Police. Similar questions of jurisdiction had been raised several times before and it has previously been found that the Commissioner of Police had the sole discretion to appoint or remove ranks. It seems Westminster Board of Works would have to find somewhere else to plant their trees.[30]

6 Fares

Demanding more than proper fare

It is an offence for a driver to demand or take more than the proper fare

Mention has been made in the previous Chapter of the letter sent by the Reverend George Garrard in 1634, to the Earl of Strafford describing the experiment by Captain Baily in setting up a coach stand by the Maypole in the Strand. Garrard wrote that Baily's liveried coachmen were a success and were undercutting many of their contemporaries; "Everybody is much pleased with it, for whereas before coaches could not be had but at great rates, now a man may have one much cheaper."[1] It is an indication that hackney coachmen were willing to charge whatever they thought the public would pay but it would be twenty years before a structured fare was laid down.

Later that same year, a petition from the Watermen of the Thames complained that their traditional work, between London and Westminster, was being undermined by the hackney coaches "that pester the streets...[and]...they ply in term time at Temple Gate, and carry sometimes three men for 4d each, or four men for 12d to Westminster, or back again..."[2] It would seem then, at least from the Watermen's point of view, that the hackney coachmen were providing a service by undercutting their fare structure, a tariff enforced on them by Parliament. Over three hundred years later, taxi drivers would be saying much the same about mini-cabs.

The Act of 1654 saw the first set rate; "sixpence a mile there, and sixpence back"[3] was charged for all fares that began and ended within the Lines of Communication, Cromwell's fortifications – roughly reflecting the present-day boundary of the Congestion Charge Zone to the north of the Thames. The '6d back' is also of importance for other reasons, it later became known as "back fare", and many people, passengers and drivers, will be surprised to know that it still exists today as the "unofficial" rate 4 for journeys over six miles though there is speculation that it will soon be abolished.

Typical fares in 1654 would be "From the Guildhall to Temple Barre or any part of Chancery Lane, Gray's Inn or other place of like distance, not above 12d. From Westminster to Whitechapel or the like place or thereabouts 2s 6d. From the Old Exchange to Whitechapel or the like distance or place 12d".[4] So the basic fare structure of a shilling a mile was laid down in 1654, it would not be until 1951 that the rate would rise to more than a shilling a mile, every mile.

Once a fare structure was in place then hackney carriage drivers could be punished for overcharging. By no means the first person to overcharge, but one of the earliest surviving records from that period, is of John Saltmarsh charging more than he was entitled to for a journey from the Royal Exchange to Hoxton. Saltmarsh, who was one of the overseers of The Fellowship of Master Hackney Coachmen, the London hackney trades first, and last, attempt to govern itself, argued that the prosecution was politically motivated. Whether there was an underlying cause behind the claim is not known, Saltmarsh was found guilty of the overcharge, and was removed from his position as an overseer.

In 1662, a hackney coachman was allowed to charge 10s if booked for the whole day, a day being defined as twelve hours; or, if hired by the hour he could charge 1s 6d for the first hour, then 1s for every hour thereafter. No doubt that if the driver was booked for the day he would try and opt for the latter tariff as he would be 2s 6d better off after twelve hours. The Act of 1662 also stipulated a few fares by distance, all seemingly to or from the Inns of Court. It is not clear whether the architects of the Act were trying to ensure solicitors paid the correct fare or that the solicitors themselves felt they would benefit from a standardised tariff. If the drivers were found guilty of overcharging, the Act stipulated that they could be fined a maximum 10s for every such offence.

Throughout his diaries, Samuel Pepys proves to be a regular user of hackney coaches; in one week in April 1668, where, uniquely, his diaries give a day by day expenditure, he pays out 28s 6d for their hire, which not only included regular journeys but hiring a coach by the day to go to Hyde Park where his social status warranted him being seen by other people in their coaches. As his wealth accrued, Pepys contemplated purchasing his own coach and once the idea had set in, his mind was made up, "I am almost ashamed to be seen in a hackney"[5] he confessed to his diary one day, and "...it is a greater charge to me now in hackneys, and I am a little dishonoured by going in them..."[6] Dishonoured or not, Pepys continued using hackneys, even when he had his own coach, including visits to Hyde Park (his wife was in their coach with friends, Pepys in a hackney with other friends behind her but still ashamed to be seen).

The hazards of asking more than the prescribed fare had its dangers. In April 1680 hackney coachman Philip Caps dropped his passenger off at Palace Yard, Westminster. His passenger, a gentleman by the name of Samuel Doughty, was visiting the house of a "person of quality" but the Old Bailey trial does not enlighten us as to who this person actually is. Doughty offered Caps what he thought was a reasonable fare, but Caps argued otherwise. The argument became heated and the two began exchanging blows. Doughty had the upper hand in the exchange and Caps was knocked down to the floor. From out of the 'person of quality's' house came a Mr Hambleton and seeing the fracas, implored his friend Doughty to chastise the coachman and have him on his knees and beg for mercy. Doughty did not push his luck too far and retired into the home of the "person of quality". Caps however was not as beaten as Doughty or Hambleton had assumed, before the door could be closed he put his foot in the way and pushed it open. Doughty, no doubt enraged and embarrassed by the actions of the coachman, then drew his sword and before he knew it, Caps was staggering backwards into the street. Bystanders rushed to Caps' aid and unbuttoning his coat found that he had been stabbed in the chest, with what a surgeon would later say was a deep wound but one that Doughty insisted was only a flesh wound and that the rapier had glanced of his rib cage. Besides the chest wound, Caps was also cut in the thigh, nose and forehead. Doughty, now realising that he had gone too far, assisted in getting Caps to a surgeon, whom he paid for. Over the next few weeks Caps seemed to make a recovery, with Doughty paying for his medical bills and supplying his family with money to support themselves whilst Caps was off work. Soon Caps was back at work but he had never fully recovered. On a particularly wet day he began coughing up a lot of blood. Some said he had contracted a fever, Caps himself said it was from the sword attack. Caps died shortly after and as he had died from injuries received within a year and a day, Samuel Doughty was to be tried for murder. Following their trial at the Old Bailey, Doughty was found guilty and sentenced to death, Hambleton was likewise charged but the jury found him innocent, there being insufficient proof that he drew his sword. Doughty was not the first, nor the last, to be capitally indicted for murdering a hackney coachman, but like several before him, and many others after, a gentleman killing a hackney coachman must have been under some form of provocation and his death sentence was remitted but how long he remained in prison was not given.[7]

A similar fate befell Henry Mead when he set down a fare in Coventry Street in June 1714. Mead wanted 2s for his fare, which involved a couple of stops but was no longer than half an hour from beginning to end. His passenger offered him 18d and when Mead realised that he was not going to receive the extra 6d became very insolent towards the passenger. The verbal assault soon gave way to a physical assault and the passenger, armed with a walking stick, struck Mead over the head with it. The fighting died down and common sense prevailed. The passenger took the number of the coach and Mead was given the address of the passenger. Despite the blow to the head, Mead felt he had got the upper hand and told several of the witnesses that the rip he had occasioned in the passenger's coat would cost more to repair than the 6d they were arguing over. By the time Mead got home that night he was feeling a lot worse. He told his wife about the fight and that he had received a mortal blow. The panacea for all ailments at the time was to be bled, usually with an incision under an armpit. Mead languished for a few days before he succumbed and died of his injuries. At his trial for murder, the passenger, recorded only as C.G. produced the cane which he had with him on the night of the attack. It was light and had previously been split, and it was pretty evident that such a cane could not produce the blow suffered to Henry Mead's head. With the possibility that the fatal blow to Mead had come from when he hit the ground in the fight, the jury had no option but to find C.G. not guilty.[8]

As seen earlier, the rates for the fares were set by Act of Parliament and in several cases the rates a hackney coachman could charge between any two points was fixed by law. The problem naturally arose that passengers did not want to go from the Inns of Court to Westminster and it was from these peripheral journeys that disputes would arise over the actual distance travelled and the resultant fare for that distance. Many cases were settled by the Hackney Coach Office who sent an officer out to measure the disputed route. These measurements were kept, though the Commissioners acknowledged that this was pretty futile as the same journey "seldom [happens] twice". Nevertheless, they continued compiling the distances measured and ended up, in 1725, with the first fares book, "226 pages in folio of large paper". The Hackney Coach Commissioners were responding to a request from magistrates to be supplied with all the by-laws relating to Hackney Carriages and a copy of the rates. The reply would not have best pleased the magistrates, the law books were of little problem, they had already been sent out and there had been no new laws since then, but to prove a point they included a copy. Because of the large size of the hackney coach rates book, the Commissioners felt it would be unjust to have the government pay for them (by which they meant out of their own budget) but, if the magistrates were willing to purchase copies at their own expense, they could, if so desired.

The Hackney Coach Act of 1786 established a new tariff for hackney coaches over distance or time. This provoked a few entrepreneurial publishers to assist the public by producing books of fares. Wallis's *New Hackney Coach Rates*, priced at 1s 6d or 2s 3d depending on the choice of cover, was a pocket-sized compendium with "alphabetical lists of all the principal fares in and about the Metropolis, with their measurement and price."[9]

One of the earliest surviving book of fares was published about the same time by John Fielding. Although sometimes attributed to Sir John Fielding, the 'Blind Beak of Bow Street' fame (who, incidentally, died in 1780), this Fielding was a bookseller of Paternoster Row. *"Fielding's Hackney Coach Rates"*, published in 1786, contained a purported

'...twenty thousand fares' which were obtained by "actual measurement". Fielding's was not the first book of fares but, as he acknowledged, that the recent Act of Parliament has "rendered all former publications of this nature entirely useless." Fielding was clearly not just aiming his publication at the long-suffering public, but the drivers as well: "Experience shows how frequent disputes arise between hackney coachmen and their employers [the passengers], which is always attended with great inconvenience and loss of time to both parties." Fielding chose 76 stands as the beginning or ending point to a number of destinations. His claim to have measured nearly 20,000 routes was an act of contrivance on his part. The actual number of fares is just above 9,700 and he arrives at the exaggerated figure by advising the reader that fares from the junction of Fetter Lane and Fleet Street, are the same as from the Fleet Street Obelisk 'being but one furlong further west' and as such, depending whether the journey is eastwards or westwards, 6d should be added or subtracted. Similar instructions are repeated through the book, and trying to find the proper fare in a jostling hackney coach without any light must have been near impossible.

Fielding's was followed very shortly after by Carington Bowles' "*Hackney Coach Directory*". Bowles acknowledged the necessity of a book such as his because for so long the fares had remained unchanged, 'impositions were not so frequently attempted'. Like Fielding he gives advice for the novice traveller, "A Coach should be taken possession of, before the coachman is told where to drive, if he then refuses to proceed he is liable to be punished..." Both Bowles and Fielding advise that in the case of refusal or of overcharge the number of the coach should be taken and a complaint made to the Hackney Coach Office. When faced with an overcharge the passenger is advised to hold out the money in his hand and offer the coachman to take his fare. If he takes more than the legal fare he can be charged with theft. This course of action was adopted by many passengers and quite a few drivers were charged accordingly.

With competition in the publishing and selling of fares books being rife, laying claim to have measured the greatest number of fares was the great selling point. Where we have seen that Fielding had a contrived 20,000 fares, Carington Bowles claimed no less than 50,000. Unlike Fielding he did not give the actual distance, just the price of the fare, but included a table in the frontispiece showing how far a driver would go for 1s (1¼ miles) or 1s 6d for up to two miles etc. Bowles took his measurements from 102 coach stands and public places (such as the theatres, the Vauxhall and Ranelagh pleasure gardens etc.). Bowles' Directory may be easier to find a particular fare over Fielding's but his claims to the number of routes measured was a greater exaggeration. Even allowing for a maximum 86 destinations per page, a quick calculation over 170 pages shows that there could not be more than 14,620 fares actually measured.

Clearly there was a need for some form of standardisation for the hackney carriage travelling public with which they could use cabs and coaches without being imposed upon by the trepidations of a greedy and argumentative driver. Ideas such as boundary markers, milestones and even lamp posts were utilised as some form of measuring device for each journey. Such ideas worked for the simplest of journeys but fares, as pointed out by many, were never as simple as portrayed in a fares book. Despite this, the fares book prevailed.

The Quaife family had a long running connection with the Hackney Coach Office spanning three decades. Thomas Quaife was appointed surveyor to the office in 1800 and five years later, he was succeeded by his son, James. In 1815 James became chief clerk whilst his son, Thomas, became Streetkeeper (a form of director of traffic), a position James's father had held for the previous ten years.[10] By 1828 there were reported to be six men and one woman, all having the name Quaife, working at the Hackney Coach Office.[11] Whatever the rights or wrongs of perceived Quaife nepotism, and even Parliament pondered that it did not appear to be right, at least James was industrious. In 1821 he published, under the authority of the Hackney Coach Commissioners, *The Hackney Coach Directory*, which he claimed had 18,000 distinct fares. A sign of its fidelity could be judged, he claimed, "that the coachman have not been able, in the course of the three years my work has been published, to discover a single error, although they have looked sharp after it."[12] The Quaife dynasty at the Hackney Coach Office ended when the office was dissolved in 1832 and the day to day running of hackney carriages was put into the hands of the Stamp Office, who in turn would gradually cede control to Scotland Yard from 1850. The family were not all together turned away following their years of service as at least one member was working at the Stamp Office following the transition.

Drivers that were prone to overcharge their passengers usually received their come-uppance when their passenger knew more than them. When William Addison set down his passenger in Regent Street in 1829, the passenger informed him that if his charge was moderate, he would give him extra for his civility. Addison was not leaving nothing to chance, he demanded 5s for his fare. His passenger was Frederick Roe, a magistrate at Marlborough Street. It was to that court that Addison was summoned for overcharging by 2s. Roe's fellow magistrate, Dyer, heard the case and Addison, who was now full of contrition, was fined 10s plus costs.[13]

Robert Chiswell was caught in similar circumstances a few months later. He had overcharged, Hoskins, a Marylebone magistrate, by 3s 8d. Chiswell was described as a young man and was among the new breed of drivers working a cabriolet. The fare in this instance was complicated, Hoskins having used Chiswell for over seven hours. Neither the complexity of the fare, Chiswell's inexperience, or, as he stated, his lack of a book of fares, did him any favours and he was fined 20s plus costs.[14]

Dyer, fellow magistrate of Roe at Marlborough Street, was himself witness to the extortion of cab drivers. In 1831 he had been in a hurry to get to his home in Devonshire Place, when he jumped into a cabriolet on a stand in Oxford Street. It was some minutes before the cab driver, John Cross, came ambling up and "without a word of an apology" took him to his residence. Once there, Dyer tendered the legal fare of 8d, the journey being of less than a mile, but John Cross was not satisfied; "You're a pretty sort of gentleman, ain't you." Along with a torrent of abuse, Dyer was intimidated enough to hand over a shilling – although it was not stated whether this was a shilling inclusive of the 8d fare, or a shilling on top of the 8d he had already paid. Evidently, once Cross found out who his victim was, he tried to return the overcharge but to no avail, Dyer wanted the cabman in court. He had his wish and Cross was fined 10s plus costs.[15] The fine was small, but Dyer was to exact his revenge on the trade as a whole, starting with any cabman who had the misfortune to come before him

One of the first cabmen to feel his wrath was a driver named Mulford, who was summoned for overcharging a woman and using abusive language towards her. She had taken a cab from Oxford Street to Haymarket, and proffered 8d legal fare. She then received a torrent of abuse so bad, she had to leave the court to allow her father who, "recapitulated the expressions, too disgusting to be applied to anyone, much less to a respectable female." In his defence, Mulford argued that it was raining hard at the time and he was the only driver willing to pull off the rank to take her. As for the abuse, "*If*, he offended anybody, he was sorry for it." Dyer reminded him that he was there for the convenience of the public and it was his duty to take a fare at all times, and in all weathers. As for the apology, Dyer remarked that it was always the case, especially when overcharging lone females that when the victim had the courage to see the case come to court, the driver was always full of contrition. "The Worthy Magistrate was determined when cases of that nature came before him to make a severe example of such infamous conduct; and the defendant must therefore pay a fine of 40s, and costs, or be committed to the fullest period allowed by law."[16]

It appears that Dyer made his crusade against the cabmen his New Year resolution for 1832. A driver who overcharged by a shilling was fined twenty shillings plus costs, a fine he could not afford to pay. He pleaded with the magistrate to mitigate the fine. "Mr Dyer observed that he should do no such thing, and if the money was not paid, he should commit him to one month. Hackney coachmen were always repentant when brought up before a magistrate, but he had made up his mind never to mitigate the penalty. The coachman was then locked up in default of payment."[17]

Two weeks later he dismissed a test case brought by proprietor, Francis Roe, to see if the powers of the Commissioners exceeded those of local governments, in which case, his driver was allowed to rank up in the middle of Regent Street, as there was more than eight foot of roadway either side. Dyer dismissed the case, saying that the local governments still held jurisdiction over the cab stands in their area. Roe, was fined 20s plus costs, having agreed to pay all fines levied against the actual driver.[18]

On the same day, "a new hand to the whip" or, in today's parlance, a "butterboy" who erroneously charged 'backfare' (see later in this Chapter) was fined 20s, as opposed to the maximum 40s he could impose. "Myself and the rest of the Magistrates," Dyer informed the court, "are determined not to flinch from our duty, and such as are guilty of these extortions, shall be punished with the utmost severity, and in such we are doing a public duty."[19]

Leaving aside Dyer for the time being, he crops up elsewhere in several chapters, another man who could be described as having a crusade against overcharging cabmen was a William Peters. Nothing is known of the gentleman except that on August 5th 1838 he summoned thirteen drivers in one day for overcharging him. The case against each of the men was examined and every one of them was found guilty by the magistrate with fines ranging from 7s 6d and costs, to 20s and costs. The fact that none of the thirteen were fined the maximum amount indicates that the unnamed magistrate was probably not H.M.C. Dyer.[20]

The first badged driver to be convicted of overcharging was William Burn, badge 291. He was paid 2s for a 1s 6d fare, but forced himself past the front door of his passenger's home and would not leave until he was given another shilling. Burn pleaded guilty and was fined 40s plus costs which was paid by his master, albeit after some hesitation. Burn's licence was also endorsed and his master was informed that he could take out a summons against Burn for the return of the fine and costs and if this was not forthcoming, Burn would be committed to two month's hard labour at the House of Correction.[21]

In 1839, William Watson probably saw more court rooms than he cared to remember. In August he was summoned for not wearing his badge. The prosecution came from an informer and despite a "stubborn defence" he was fined 10s plus costs.[22] In October he was brought up on a charge of taking more than his fare from a lady on a journey from London Bridge to Hammersmith. He had primarily agreed to do the journey for 10s but when he dropped his passenger off he said his fare was now 15s. The lady paid the money and took out a summons against him. In court Watson denied he was the driver, in fact he could prove that at the time he was supposedly setting down in Hammersmith, he was in the east of

London, taking a fare to Blackwall. The lady was adamant that not only had she taken the right number of the coach, she was just as certain that Watson was the driver. Watson produced one witness to back his story up and said he could produce the other passengers if the case were adjourned. Likewise, the passenger also wanted an adjournment so she could produce her fellow passengers and two servants who helped unload the luggage. Burrell the magistrate said he would adjourn the case for a week in order for both sides to bring forward their witnesses.[23] The magistrate would be meeting the cabman sooner than he expected.

The following day, Watson was before Burrell on another overcharging case. "[Watson] is one of the coachmen in the habit of attending at the steam-packet wharfs, and the complaints of impositions upon persons returning from watering places have been of late loud and frequent." On this occasion he pleaded guilty to charging 9s from London Bridge to Eaton Square. There was no evidence of abuse but the magistrate, no doubt remembering Watson from the previous day, fined him the maximum 40s plus costs. At the request of a man from the Registrar of Hackney Carriages, Watson's licence was also endorsed.[24] Six days later, the original players were back in court, with the exception of Watson. After awaiting two hours for his arrival, the lady asked Burrell to proceed in his absence. After hearing one side of the case, Burrell announced that there was little doubt as to Watson's guilt and to compound matter's he reminded the court that Watson produced a witness who blatantly committed perjury. Watson was fined the maximum 40s again, this time in his absence. Half an hour after the judgement, Watson turned up in court where he was ordered to be committed for two months unless he came up with the 40s plus costs.[25]

A writer to *The Times* in 1843 estimated that he was charged double in every three out of five journeys he made by hackney coach or cab, and that was from a man; a woman travelling alone or with children was at a much greater risk to her purse, as well as her safety, from "rough" cabmen.

"The best piece of fun" exclaimed Jonas Chuzzlewit, cousin of the eponymous Martin in Dickens' novel of 1844, is "a joke of a practical kind, and its humour lay in taking a hackney-coach to the extreme limits of possibility for a shilling." Which is exactly what a young gentleman did in January 1872, when he emerged from Putney Station and asked to be driven exactly a mile towards Cliff Lodge, his home in Southfields. The cabman, William Hayden, duly obliged. Hayden stopped the cab at what he deemed to be a mile, but the young gentleman pointed to a mark on the wall and said, with confidence, that that mark was exactly one mile from the stand. Hayden pulled up outside the mark, and instead of asking for one shilling, he now asked for two shillings as the journey was over one mile. His passenger paid him the one shilling he believed was the legal fare and allowed Hayden to summon him for the remainder. In court, the passenger's father explained that the mark on the wall was as a result of a previous dispute from the same cab stand. On that occasion the father would not pay the extra shilling either and after the ground was measured, he was found to be in the wrong so had to pay the outstanding shilling plus the 5 shillings for the cost of measuring the ground. The line on the wall marked an exact mile from the head of the cab rank. The route was once again measured, both Hayden and the passenger depositing five shillings to cover the cost. The officer of the court who measured the route now proclaimed that the mark on the wall was one mile and nine yards from the rank. Unbeknown to the passenger, but which the drivers themselves well aware, the rank had been shifted along the road, by fourteen yards. Once again, the passenger had to pay out the 1s fare and forfeit the 5s measuring costs.[26]

The opening of the Great Exhibition in Hyde Park in 1851 brought with it an influx of visitors, most of whom were unwise to distances within London and were ripe for extortion from unscrupulous cabmen. *The Standard* believed that not one case of overcharging in over five hundred ever make it to the courts, a figure the paper, and most of the public, feared would only increase as tens of thousands of people visited the Crystal Palace. In order to combat this, at least for those who had visited the exhibition and now wanted to go elsewhere, Sir Richard Mayne, the Commissioner of Police, posted a list of fares at the cab stand in Prince's Gate to "places of public notoriety in the metropolis." Officers who policed the stand were issued with the list and visitors were urged to consult with the officer in order that there could be no overcharging. As to those visitors who could not speak English, a brief digest of hackney carriage laws, in German and French, was also posted on the stand. A similar list of fares, to and from a stand in Whitehall had already been published and it was hoped many of the principle stands would be covered. *The Standard* also proposed that drivers should furnish a ticket with their badge number and the fare charged upon it.[27] As will be seen later in this chapter, it was not a new idea. The law still required cabmen to give a ticket to the passenger at the commencement of the journey, though very few offered and probably even less were asked. Even the idea of having the fare, or multiples thereof, printed upon the ticket had never succeeded in curbing the activities of the cabmen.

Having authorised the fares for a number of routes, Sir Richard Mayne was becoming quite an expert in his knowledge of distances, which was bad luck for Edward Eaton badge number 2863. Eaton had picked up Mayne from his home in Hyde Park Square and taken him to the Botanical Gardens in Regent's Park. When he was set down, Mayne gave Eaton 1s 4d, which he later stated was a shilling for the fare and 4d extra "it being Sunday". Eaton demanded 1s 8d and appeared to use bad language once he realised that the extra 4d was not forthcoming. According to *The Standard*, Mayne even asked for the return of the "joey", though it is doubtful if the Police Commissioner ever resorted to slang. Eaton was summoned and the court was packed with a large number of cabmen who attended the court to hear Eaton found guilty "after a very patient and dispassionate investigation" and was sentenced to 20s or 14 days for the overcharge and 10s or 7 days for the rude behaviour, with the sentence to be served in the House of Correction if the fine were not paid.[28]

If the number of fares a fares book contained was said to be an indicator of its usefulness, then the pinnacle was reached in 1852 with the publication of Colonel Shrapnel's *Stradametric Survey of London*. Henry Needham Scrope Shrapnel was the eldest son of Lieutenant General Henry Shrapnel, the inventor of the shrapnel bomb, which was reported to have caused devastation during the Battle of Waterloo. Henry junior likewise followed his father into the army, rising to the rank of captain.[29] Volume One of his enterprise was based on the expected, and wholly justified, imposition of visitors to London for the Great Exhibition in

Hyde Park. In a series of tables, a visitor to the Great Exhibition would turn to the page which included the point where their journey began and read across the page to the column entitled "The Crystal Palace" and they would be informed of not only the distance but the legal fare the cab driver could charge. To whet the appetite of his potential customers, he proclaimed in the first volume that the second volume would be a complete survey of London and would include 6,200,000 cab fares. He was being modest. When volume two eventually hit the streets in 1852, it proclaimed to include a staggering 14,800,000 cab fares. What is perhaps hard to credit, is that for a pocket-sized book the claim was by no means an exaggeration.

In part one of the latter work, Shrapnel lists, over 50 pages, around 4,800 streets. Some of the longer streets are split into sections but taking the square root of 14,800,000, which gives around 3,847 streets it is easy to see how he arrives at such a large figure – assuming that every street listed has had its distance computed to every other street. "At first sight one is apt to shrink from the formidable mass of figures which he finds embedded in every page", wrote *The Times*, "but a single glance at the explanatory key satisfies him that the arrangement is simplicity itself, and that the distance between any two points in the metropolis, and the proper cab fare, may be ascertained without the smallest difficulty."[30] There were calls for every cabman to be compelled to carry a copy, no doubt at their own expense and Shrapnel's profits. Shrapnel himself even proclaimed that his work would lead to the reduction of 6d a mile in every cab journey – it was public knowledge that drivers always overcharged by at least that amount. In the second section of Volume Two he includes a list of 451 tables, to be used against the streets named in part one. The distances and fares, all 101,000 of them are laid out with the fares based on the 8d a mile basic charge. If, as parliament was hinting, that the fares were to be reduced to 6d a mile, all these calculated fares would be rendered null and void. As a precaution however, he added an addendum at the rear of the book where the 6d fares could be computed against the unchanging, distance. To be fair to Shrapnel he did state that he saw the book as being a benefit to both passenger and cabman. The former would be aware of the legal fare and thus should not be imposed upon nor be guilty of underpaying the driver; for the latter, the drivers were constantly at risk of being summoned for overcharging, a risk that could be prevented if the driver had their own copy of *Shrapnel's*.

If disputes arose, through either extortion or abusive language then Shrapnel informed his reader of the correct method of reporting a driver – to a policeman if the cab was hailed from a stand or in the street, or at the Secretary's Office if obtained at a privileged railway station. He also made quite useful observations regarding luggage and suggested the passenger offers a 2d surcharge on top of the fare for each piece of luggage within the cab that could not be carried in their hands. In his preface he stated; "An alteration in the system of proprietors contracting with drivers is most needed – at present, let a cabman be ever so honestly disposed, a premium for imposition is forced upon him by his being obliged to bring to the proprietor's office, every night, a certain amount, in default of which the balance is deducted from the deposit, (generally two pounds), placed in his custody for this purpose, consequently a bad day's work is followed up by public imposition. – Cabmen should be public servants, and not contractors for taking advantage of the unavoidable ignorance of the public."[31] Perhaps Shrapnel was more on the side of the honest cabman than the drivers themselves actually believed. A notice however in *The Observer* in May 1852 proclaimed that several magistrates were now using *Shrapnel's* fares book as an adjudicator in disputes. The warning was simple – cabmen beware!

One such disputed fare occurred when cabman William Wade took a barrister named Simpson from Paddington station to Victoria Road, Kensington. On arriving at the home of the barrister, Wade declared that his fare was 1s 8d, as the journey was over two miles. A similar journey today would be considerably shorter as a taxi would use the West Carriage Drive (separating Kensington Gardens from Hyde Park) which had not been built in 1852. Simpson offered the driver 1s 6d which he considered enough to cover the fare and including a tip of 2d. When Wade reiterated that his fare was 1s 8d, Simpson took the 6d piece back and gave him 4d instead. For imprudently demanding more than his actual fare Wade was about to be 'legalled off' – given the legal fare, thus losing out on a tip.

Having the strength of his convictions, Wade took out a summons against the barrister for the outstanding 4d. If Wade had kept abreast of the newspaper columns of the appearances of cabmen before certain magistrates, then he must have feared coming before Mr Paynter. Only recently Paynter declared in court that cabmen were very choosy about what fares they agreed to undertake and that he himself was continually being refused by them for short journeys, but he could not summon them to appear before him in court. Under oath, Wade informed Paynter of the journey and that he believed he was underpaid. Simpson the passenger/barrister was not in court, no doubt a better remuneration awaited him in a court elsewhere, he was said to be represented by a 'youth'. After the details of the case were gone into, the clerk of the court handed the magistrate a copy of *Shrapnel's* in which it was stated that the distance was indeed less than two miles and the correct fare was, as stated by Simpson, 1s 4d. This was disastrous for Wade who felt the journey was over two miles, he had lost out on the 4d, the cost of the summons (usually 2s sometimes 3s), and several hours sitting around in court when he could have been with his cab. Fortunately for Wade, help came from Paynter the magistrate. He doubted the correctness of the book and declared that he himself believed the journey to be more than two miles. The clerk countered by mentioning the numerous testimonies that had praised the works and that "Captain Shrapnel had measured all the distances". Paynter dismissed the accuracy of that particular claim and stated that such a work would have taken years to complete and that he himself had no doubt that Shrapnel had relied on nothing more than guess work. Without even offering to have the ground measured, Paynter declared that the distance was clearly over two miles and ordered 'the youth' representing Simpson to pay the outstanding 4d plus 7s costs.[32]

The following month, *Shrapnel's* was also used – to little avail - in a court room, this time under Mr Beadon at Hammersmith. Samuel Shingles, badge number 11,794 had been engaged from the Holland Arms rank and took a lady, Charlotte Heath, to her home in Hammersmith. From there they went to Tilbury's warehouse store in High Street, Marylebone, before returning back to her home in Hammersmith. For this lengthy journey Shingles demanded, a not unreasonable, 5s, but Miss Heath, armed with her copy of *Shrapnel's* had worked out that the legal fare was 4s 8d and that is what she gave him, to the penny. After having engaged Shingles for a good couple of hours at the least, a 4d tip would have prevented any further action, though no doubt Shingles would have complained about being legalled off.

Shingles summoned the lady over the outstanding 4d. In court he gave his side of events and Miss Heath, still armed with her copy of *Shrapnel's*, stated she was in the right to pay the 4s 8d as stated by Shrapnel. Beadon the magistrate was not prepared to come down on either side and advised having the ground measured if both driver and passenger were willing to deposit 5s each with the court. Miss Heath readily agreed, as did Shingles but wise heads must have entreated the lady to back down as it was clear that *Shrapnel's* was wrong. Having acceded to the advice, Charlotte Heath withdrew her defence and had to pay Samuel Shingles the outstanding 4d and 7s costs.[33]

Despite these setbacks, *Shrapnel's Stradametric Survey* was still being used in courts to arbitrate on disputes. Like many other fares books before him, with the possible exception of *Quaife's*, *Shrapnel's* lacked the authority for the measurements it contained within, an authority that could not be questioned at a police or magisterial court. *Shrapnel's* was still being advertised within the pages of *The Times* in 1853 and attributed the Commissioner of Police as being full of praise for it, "in cases in which he has referred to it, has found the information accurate..."[34] Perhaps Shrapnel may have been less than willing to carry the Commissioner of Police's endorsement if he had known that the latter was producing his own book of fares, that not only would be authorised, but the law would also require that every cab driver would have to carry a copy. Despite all his professed hard work in compiling his list of 14,800,000 routes, *Shrapnel's Stradametric Survey of London* had its use for just over a year and would never have a second edition published.

Paragraph five of the 1853 Act stipulated that every cab and hackney coach was to display the rate of fares (6d a mile, or 8d a mile for a coach with two horses) and the rate for waiting time of 6d for every 15 minutes. Every driver was to carry a book of fares which must be produced when asked for by the passenger. Paragraph six stated that in disputes over distance, the book of fares, when signed by the Commissioner will be deemed to be "absolute proof".

The 1853 Hackney Carriages Act proved to be a pivotal document in the history of the trade, it united both drivers and their masters and provoked the first ever strike by London cabmen. The two most decisive elements to the Act were the introduction of the 6d a mile fare, reduced from 8d, and the abolition of 'back fare'. The latter had been introduced in the 17th century to make it worthwhile for drivers to take a fare out into the then suburbs of Kensington, Islington, Lisson Green etc. and where the drivers were prevented by law from picking up after having crossed the "limitation of London." The limitation was originally set at a three-mile radius from the General Post Office in St Martin's Le Grand but in later years a four, then a six-mile radius from Charing Cross defined that as the centre of London. As London grew, drivers had more reason to go past the radius but they wanted extra money for doing so. "Back fare" entitled a driver to be paid to come back within the radius, thus making a run to the suburbs economically viable. A driver was legally entitled to charge extra, depending on how far past the radius he travelled, so that he would effectively be paid to travel back into the radius and thus pick up from the first available stand. Soon this rule only applied to journeys past the radius after 8pm and before 5am, much to the chagrin of the cab riding members of the public who often mistook a demand for back fare as an extortion which often resulted in a summons and a trip to a police court.

The problems concerning back fare arose in a case just prior to the introduction of the 1853 Act. James Tuxberry had been called off the stand in Pont Street, to pick up at the nearby Cadogan Institute in Sloane Street and take a Mr and Mrs Roach to their home in Princes Terrace (now Ennismore Gardens). The journey, Tuxberry could add the distance from the stand to the pick up as part of the fare, was still under a mile so the legal fare was 8d. Roach gave a shilling, which included a 4d tip. Tuxberry argued that it was not enough and said his fare was 1s 4d, - 8d for the fare plus 8d back fare. Roach snatched the shilling back from Tuxberry and gave him 9d. Tuxberry summoned him for the difference. In court Tuxberry explained to the magistrate that as the journey was after 8pm and "beyond the limits" he was fully entitled to charge for back carriage. Roach agreed that he lived beyond the radius but only by 150 yards. If the driver had warned him that back fare would have been charged, then he would do as his neighbours do and get out of the cab at the three- mile marker stone. The magistrate, Paynter, informed Roach that the cabman was under no obligation to state that he was going to charge back fare and, looking at a map he thought the distance travelled was over a mile anyway. Roach had to pay the outstanding 7d plus costs of 9s 6d.[35] Such were the inconsistencies with back fare that sometimes it was actually cheaper to get a cab to take you home, if like Roach you were just past the radius, and then send it back on a fool's errand to just inside the radius. If the whole was within a mile, then only 8d could be charged. As Roach found out once the contract was terminated at the destination, outside the radius, the driver could charge a further 8d, the minimum fare, just to travel a matter of yards.

When Roach had snatched back the original shilling, he paid Tuxberry with two coins, a 6d "tanner" and a 3d "thrupenny bit" to cover what he felt was the minimum fare. The 8d fare was considered to be "broken money" i.e. there was not a 8d coin so at least two coins had to be tendered or, more usually, a shilling coin from which the change was never forthcoming unless given with a torrent of abuse. The early months of 1853 had seen an unprecedented onslaught from the trade press against the extortionate and exacting cabmen. All cabmen, the generalisation was so great they did not even accuse *most* of the cabmen, all cabmen, were daily robbing their passengers of at least 4d on every journey, usually more.

The 1853 Act did away with broken money by reducing the tariff to 6d a mile which the government believed would lead to more people using cabs and as the duty on the hackney carriage plates had been reduced by 25% and the price of oats had reduced by the same amount, they, the government, stated that there was no reduction in real terms as all their costs had fallen. It can be safely surmised that the drivers and their masters did not agree with the government and their view of the potential of a reduced fare.

The Act of 1853 came into force on July 10th and little could cabman Thomas Phillips be aware of the implications the Act would have upon him. On July 18th Phillips was called off his stand in Brompton to go to the home of a Mr Bond, of Victoria Grove [now Netherton Grove], Fulham Road. Bond did not want a cab there and then but would require one the following morning. This was acceptable to Phillips – if it had not have been, he could have charged Bond 6d for calling him from the stand. Accordingly, the following morning, Phillips arrived at the appointed time and carried Bond to several stops before finally finishing up at Wellington Street, Strand. Phillips stated that his fare was 5s but Bond disagreed and said it should only be 4s. Fortunately for Bond, the 1853 Act gave the passenger the power to compel the driver to take him to the nearest police court, or, if at night, a police station, where the dispute could be settled according to Sir Richard Mayne's official book of cab fares. The idea behind the clause was to prevent needless summons being taken out by the passenger when the matter could be easily decided and without the costs of a summons. The problem with the clause was that it was one sided – the driver could not compel the passenger to go to a police court, only the other way round, and, more importantly, the driver could be fined, or imprisoned, for being in the wrong, whereas the passenger was asked just to pay the disputed amount.

It was Phillips' bad luck that the fare was to be adjudicated by Mr Henry at Bow Street, who had already dealt with several cases under the new Hackney Carriages Act. In several of the disputes, Henry deemed the cabman to be in the right, with no punishment directed at the passenger who had brought the case to court. When a cabman was found to be in the wrong, then his punishment was generally far worse than would be meted out by his fellow magistrates. After taking the oath, Bond stated that there was no dispute about the various stoppages which amounted to one hour, or two shillings. He had no complaints about the route, though he felt Phillips going via Birdcage Walk was slightly circuitous but felt the whole of the journey was under three miles, which was 1s 6d. Bond generously allowed an extra 6d for an extra passenger, which Phillips did not charge for as it would have been illegal – the 6d for an extra passenger could only be charged when the number of passengers exceed two. Phillips then took his turn on the stand, and stated that as the distance exceeded four miles, and including the three-quarters of a mile he travelled from the stand the previous night, he believed his legal charge was 5s.

Henry could not refer to that final arbiter, Commissioner Mayne's book of fares, as only one book had been published and which was of little use in the present dispute. Instead, he reverted to the tried and tested method of having the ground measured. Both Bond and Phillips agreed to this course and Bond subsequently slapped his 5s down on the desk. Phillips however was in a quandary. Bond was his first fare of the day, he had no money on him at all. Phillips was so sure of his case he argued that if the passenger paid him what he believed to be the right fare, 5s, he would then deposit that with court for the ground measuring. Given the consequences if he was wrong, Phillips had to be pretty sure he was in the right. Henry, however, was not interested. "As you cannot pay the 5s deposit I shall take Mr Bond's statement as evidence of the fact, and convict you of the overcharge, for which you must pay the penalty of 40s, or go to prison for a month." Even Bond was staggered by this turn of events. Phillips pleaded with Henry not to impose the penalty but the magistrate refused to go back on his judgement. Unable to pay the 5s to have the ground measured, Phillips had no chance of paying the 40s fine and he was immediately taken to jail. His horse and cab, which was parked outside Bow Street court was taken to a nearby green yard - the predecessors of modern-day car pounds – where an initial fee, usually of 8s was payable once it entered the yard but would also accrue daily costs.[36]

Two days later the case of cabman Phillips was brought up in the House of Commons by Radical MP, John Bright, architect of the Anti-Corn Laws. He questioned whether such punitive action against Phillips was more reminiscent of living in Turkey or Russia but not for anyone living in Britain. The Home Secretary, and future Prime Minister, Lord Palmerston, replied that he had been made aware of the case as of that very morning and has launched an inquiry into it. He, like many members of the house, found the facts hard to swallow and asked everyone to suspend judgement until the truth could be ascertained as though court reporting was usually very reliable there may have been errors in this instance.[37]

Thomas Phillips was now becoming an unwilling martyr to the cause, that cause being the ending of the vilification that had recently plagued the trade from all sections of the press. The *Daily News* which had been calling for a total change in the trade, without coming up with a workable alternative, now stated that "It now seems to have fallen to us to vindicate the cause of the drivers..."[38]

The following day, Lord Palmerston informed the House that he had communicated with Henry, the magistrate at Bow Street, and his initial cautiousness about believing the court report as published had been vindicated. The real truth of the matter, Palmerston stated, was that the magistrate offered both parties to have the ground measured but which the cabman declined to do so. His only interest in declining to have the ground measured was because the distance was not as great as he had stated and that therefore the cabman was guilty of exaction and that is why the magistrate had no other option than to follow the course of the law and impose a fine on the cabman which was defaulted to the one month's imprisonment. No doubt the members of the House were relieved that the laws of the land were not being used in a tyrannical way reminiscent of Turkey or Russia. It was all lies, Palmerston had, albeit unknowingly, mislead the House but its members were placated and saved their biggest cheer for the news that the cabman's fine had subsequently been paid and he had now been released from jail.[39]

There was further support for Phillips, and by default his fellow drivers, in the press over the ensuing weekend. *Reynolds' Newspaper* described the actions of Henry as, "A more monstrous, scandalous, infamous, and atrocious exercise of arbitrary power from the magisterial bench, we never remember."[40] The reportage over the weekend prompted Thomas Phillips to compile a letter to the editor of the *Daily News*. Phillips confirmed that he had now been released from prison, his fine being paid after a collection among his friends. He stated that he had since had the ground measured and the distance was found to be over seven miles, far more than Phillips had been charging for. He reiterated that the passenger, Bond, had sworn on oath that the distance was not above three miles "... and on whose word I was knocked down". Phillips ended his letter by confirming that he did not refuse to have the ground measured, and that he would be able to put down the 5s deposit if Bond paid the fare, which Henry refused to accept.[41]

A second letter that was published in more than one newspaper that day was from the anonymous court reporter who filed the original story. Maintaining his anonymity "The Reporter" said he had no option after Lord Palmerston informed the House that the whole matter was an error in the reporting. Palmerston's statement had cast doubt on his own integrity as a reporter and one who could not now be trusted to report on the true events. The reporter asked to what purpose he would have in portraying Mr Henry in such a poor light, a man whom he had the utmost respect for and had received every courtesy from him. On the same hand why would he pronounce himself on the side of cabmen, after reporting all the previous week and "exposing their extortionate demands upon the public." It was clear that the reporter was no friend of the cab trade and felt that the magistrate's zest on enforcing the regulations under the new Act was a "grave mistake". The story would not have even been filed by him had the magistrate listened to the pleadings, not of Phillips but from his passenger Mr Bond, who asked for a reversal or postponement of the decision. Astonished at this sudden turn in events the court reporter assiduously took down Henry's words when sentencing Phillips, as far as he was concerned there was no room for error, Henry clearly stated that Phillips "cannot" pay the 5s deposit, not that he "refused" to pay. When the first reports of the case hit the news-stands several people came to Bow Street to pay the cabman's fine. Not once following the publication did Henry express any disapproval over the reporter's work. It was not until Friday morning, after the matter had been raised in the House of Commons that Henry and the reporter discussed the subject. Even now, Henry appeared to be back tracking. "It is a pity" he told the reporter, "you did not make it appear, that I decided the case upon my own knowledge that the distance was under three miles." The reporter was shocked to hear this, as nothing of the kind had been mentioned in court and in fact the question of the 5s deposit, whether Phillips would not or could not pay it, had now, according to Henry, had not even been raised in court.[42]

The day after the publication of the letter, the cab trade, for the first time in its history, went on strike. The main reason behind the strike, which was more of a lock out by the cab proprietors but with the backing of the drivers, was the reduction in the rate from 8d to 6d a mile and the loss of back fare. There was generally little sympathy for the drivers, or for the reasons behind the strike but the case of cabman Phillips was never far from the surface and whilst cabmen were facing injustices such as that, then perhaps it was understandable that they had such grievances. On the second day of the strike a deputation of the trade attended the House of Commons and met with Henry Fitzroy, the member who had drawn up the 1853 Act, and Sir Richard Mayne, the police commissioner. Fitzroy informed the delegation that the house would have been more amenable to their demands if they had not gone on strike, Hider, "an ordinary cabman" as he liked to describe himself and spokesman for the delegation informed them that had it not been for the treatment handed out on cabman Phillips they would never have gone on strike in the first place. Mayne agreed that the magistrate's decision had been "very bad", Fitzroy completely went on the defensive, "You ought not to come here and blame me for any decision of a magistrate." Which struck Hider as odd, as Fitzroy was Under-secretary to the Home Office and any appeals would come to him in the first instance. Despite the inference from the court reporter that Lord Palmerston had, albeit unknowingly, misled the house, he still insisted that the problem was nothing more than an incorrect report of the actual facts. Using a pair of compasses, Palmerston himself had measured out the route on a map and found the distance to be under three miles and therefore the complainant was right and Phillips was guilty of overcharging.[43] In fact the Home Secretary went as far as stating that no matter how circuitous the route Phillips had taken, there was no reasonable way that that journey could have been anywhere near to the five miles as claimed by the cabman.

Phillips had made an overcharge and that was the end of the story, except, just to settle the matter, the police decided to measure the exact route and, with unquestionable authority, they stated that the actual distance was a shade under seven miles – as Phillips himself had stated when he had the ground measured. Finally, the truth was out, Phillips was exonerated

On August 19th 1853, a month after Phillips was imprisoned, Lord Palmerston addressed the commons. Palmerston sang the praises not of Phillips but of the passenger, Mr Bond, "who acted in the most-handsomest manner", neglecting to mention that Phillips' problems arose after Bond swore on oath the journey was not more than three miles. With regards to Phillips he informed the Commons that the police had measured the route which was just under seven miles and as a result Phillips "having been erroneously fined, [had] therefore been erroneously imprisoned for a few hours." Quite how many hours Phillips was incarcerated is not recorded. Once he had been carted off to prison and his cab to the green yard, he had no way of letting his wife know what had befallen to him. Somehow, he had managed to get a message back to her and she raised the requisite 40 shillings to secure his release. Even before the news of the sentence had been published word of mouth in the neighbourhood of Bow Street Court "a shrine of inhumanity"[44] had seen several well-wishers donating money to go towards his release. Once he was released he would have needed further money to withdraw his cab from the green yard. Palmerston's response to this was to return the forty-shilling fine that had been paid, plus a further forty shillings as compensation, and there the matter ended.

Was the wrongful incarceration of Phillips the cause of the first strike of cab drivers in London? The idea that it was, gained momentum in the weeks following the dispute, which lasted four days. The cab trade was quick to point out that they never would have struck were it not for cabman Phillips. Even the editorials saw the Phillips case as the 'ostensible' reason behind the strike. The introduction of the 6d a mile fare had been first introduced in Edinburgh before sweeping southward to London via Manchester and Birmingham. In each of these cities the cabmen went on strike and it was likely, Phillips or not, that the London cabmen would follow suit. The drivers argued that it was hard enough trying to pay their daily cab rental when a rate of 8d a mile was charged. If the drivers could not pay their masters, then the masters themselves would eventually lose out. With the reduced rate and the loss of back fare it was the masters who struck by refusing to allow their cabs to leave the stables. In all the subsequent negotiations it was the owners of fleets of cabs that set out their demands, not the journeymen cab drivers. For the strike to have any effect then it would require the joint enterprise of both proprietors and drivers, something that was never easily achieved, but with what was seen as a pernicious attack upon their earnings, the government succeeded in uniting the two uneasy bed-fellows. What the case of cabman Phillips added to the dispute was a third demand, that of the right of appeal following the decision of a magistrate. When the cab proprietors voted to return to work and put their cabs out on the street they had already been told that a new rate for back fare would be introduced, as well as a 6d hiring charge that would be added to every journey, thus making 1s the price for any journey for the first mile but allowing cabmen to appeal a magistrate's decision was seen as going too far and was outright rejected.

When the furore over Phillips was at its height, cabman Thomas Asker found himself in a similar position to his fellow whip. Asker had taken his passenger from the Consumption Hospital in Brompton to New Bond Street. On arrival the passenger paid the driver a shilling but Asker argued, politely, that the distance was over two miles and therefore he would require a further 6d. Using his powers under the Act the passenger told Asker to drive to the nearby Marlborough Street Court where the matter would be adjudicated upon. There, the sitting magistrate, Bingham, looked at a map and informed the passenger that it looked like the cabman was right, the journey was considerably over two miles by a few furlongs. Unperturbed, the passenger insisted on having the ground measured "for his own satisfaction" and laid down the five-shilling deposit. Like Phillips, Asker did not have the required sum to hand but informed the magistrate that he would be able to raise it within a few hours. No doubt fearing the ignominy that had been hoisted upon his fellow magistrate at Bow Street, Bingham allowed for the ground to be measured as soon as possible.[45]

The first volume of Commissioner Mayne's book of fares had been published the day after the 1853 Act had itself been published, July 11th, but the fares themselves were all based upon the stand at Palace Yard, the first beneficiaries therefore being the politicians who had passed the law in the first place. Now the legislators had absolute proof that the fare from Parliament to their club in Pall Mall really was within a mile and because it was they who reduced the rate, they could go there for the price they ordained and not what the cabman thought he should charge. By the beginning of August, fares to and from various points based on stands at Whitehall, Haymarket, Piccadilly and Knightsbridge had been measured and published. The authority of the distances and fares was unquestionable and Mayne's book of fares was rippling across London.

By early 1854 all distances had been measured under the authority of the Commissioners and all that remained was to have the tables published and distributed to all the magistrate's courts as well as the drivers. In February of that year, William Henry Case, 10372, an owner driver who had been prominent in the previous year's strike was summoned to appear at Worship Street police court for overcharging Stephen Corbett 1s more than the published fare. The journey in question was from the Cremorne Pleasure Gardens at World's End, Chelsea to the Eastern Counties terminus at Shoreditch (now Shoreditch overground station). The fare for such a journey, according to Commissioner Mayne was 2s but Case argued that the journey was nearer six miles and the correct fare was 3s. The magistrate L.C.T. D'Eyncourt looking at a map could only concur with the cabman that the distance was over six miles. It was during an adjournment of the proceedings that the magistrate was furnished with an erratum of corrected fares that should be appended to the end of each book. D'Eyncourt declared that the errata showed that the true fare was 3s 6d and far from overcharging the passenger, Case had demanded less than he was legally entitled to. That appeared to settle the matter but an objection was then raised by the passenger's solicitor who argued that whilst the book of fares was authorised under the signature of the Commissioner as legal evidence, the errata did not carry such a signature and therefore cannot be construed as legal evidence so must be withdrawn. D'Eyncourt thought this last observation was fatal to the cabman's claim. The book of fares which the Act of Parliament stated was the arbiter of such disputes was clearly in error and listed a journey that was clearly over six miles as being under four. It was whilst perched on the horns of this dilemma that D'Eyncourt had a revelation. He asked Stephen Corbett, the passenger, if he had had any acquaintance with the cabman prior to the journey. Still under oath, Corbet replied that he had known William Case for a couple of months. When asked if the cabman was aware that the present proceedings would be enacted upon, Corbett replied that as he was in the public house when the matter was raised, he was only too aware. Now that the cloak of surreptitiousness had been removed Case informed D'Eyncourt that the matter had been taken up by a body of cab proprietors who considered themselves fully justified in putting the question before the court for a judicial decision. He added that a cabman could be imprisoned "unless they strictly conformed to the commissioner's book of fares, which contained several errors." D'Eyncourt decided in favour of the driver and so for the first time the legal book of fares was shown to be in error.[46] The errata soon after carried the signature of the commissioners and so could be deemed to be legal evidence. In a letter to D'Eyncourt, Sir Richard Mayne pointed out that if alternative starting points to the journey had been used other than Cremorne Gardens, such as the Man in the Moon or Beaufort Street, both nearer to Shoreditch, the distance could be seen to be greater than six miles.[47] The error within the book of fares was a clerical one and not a problem with the measuring. But measuring problems were about to come to the fore, and all because of a Sparrow.

In February 1854 Thomas Sparrow took a Mr Sherman from the Coach and Horses in Dover Street, Piccadilly, to the Bag of Nails, Arabella Row (now Lower Grosvenor Place). At journey's end, Sherman tendered 6d, signifying he thought the distance was under a mile. Sparrow however argued, civilly, that the route taken was over mile – cabs were not allowed through the Royal Parks at this time so the route would have been via Hyde Park Corner. As per the Act of 1853, Sherman directed the cabman to take him to the nearest police court and Sparrow obliged. At Westminster police court they found no joy as neither the official book of fares – the final arbiter in the eyes of the law – nor any lists of fares, nor an Ordnance Survey map could decide the problem. It was then decided to resort to the old-fashioned method of 'using the wheel', the measuring device which Mayne's book of fares should have consigned to history. Having located it within the dusty confines of the court, Sparrow, Sherman and a court official retraced the route. With both men having deposited their five shillings the measuring device showed that not only was the cabman wrong in this instance he was wrong by a margin of 110 yards – a very high margin of error. Sparrow did not accept defeat gracefully. Not only did he stand to lose his deposit, he could also be fined by the magistrate for overcharging which, if he could not pay, would result in him being sent to jail. Lack of funds however was not Sparrow's immediate concern. Somehow, he managed to locate another measuring wheel and after paying five shillings for its hire, the route was re-measured. This time the wheel measured the distance as one mile 270 yards – a difference of 380 yards from the previous device. Of course, the passenger, Sherman, did not want to act upon the wheel that Sparrow had magically appeared with and wanted the original device, the official court measuring wheel, to decide the case. The court messenger informed Broderip the magistrate that there may indeed be an error with their court's measuring wheel as it appeared to stick every now and then. Weddle, the court official, was then despatched to Marlborough Street police court to borrow their measuring wheel. The route was then measured for a third time – and remember, all this was for a dispute over a sixpence. This third device measured the distance as one mile 270 yards, exactly the same as the device procured by Sparrow. Sherman was still not happy and asked for a fourth device to be used but Broderip told him as the latter two perambulators had measured the same to the yard there was little room for dispute, the cabman was right to charge a shilling. Having faced the possibility of jail had he been proven wrong, Sparrow could do no more than accept the extra 6d he fought so hard for, whether he was awarded costs for the time taken in settling the dispute were not recorded by the court reporter. He did complain at losing out on the five shillings it had cost him to hire the second measuring wheel.[48]

It was soon realised that if the Westminster police court wheel was wrong, then measurements that were used with wheel could also be in error. Weddle, the court official told Broderip that the wheel had not been used to settle a dispute for some time. The last time that it had been used was by the Metropolitan Police when they began their massive task of compiling all the distances for the fares book. The very first routes measured were from Palace yard in front of the houses of parliament. As no complaints about those particular measurements had been made it is more likely that the police did not look after the instrument as well as they should and that the measurements actually made were sound.

As already mentioned, the book of fares, according to the Act of Parliament, was to be the final arbiter on disputes over distance. So, when one unfortunate cabman was summoned for overcharging he may have thought that he had the law on his side. The actual route was not covered by the book of fares and both parties paid a five shillings deposit to have the ground measured, which being done appeared to show that the cabman had indeed overcharged. The cabman argued that the book of fares did cover a journey that followed most of the route that he took, and all he did was to compound the distance he further travelled onto that route and charged accordingly. When the ground had been measured it was found that the distance given in the book was evidently wrong but, as the cabman pointed out, by law he had not only to purchase the book but had to be guided by its pricing. Arnold, the Westminster magistrate, had some sympathy for the cabman. He himself had noticed that the distance from Cadogan Place to the British Museum was 2 miles 670 yards whilst the fare was listed only as 1s (equivalent to a distance of under two miles). Clearly either the measurement or the pricing was wrong. Although the cabman in this instance had lost his 5s deposit, Arnold was in no mood to convict the man and informed him that if he paid back the 1s overcharge, and paid the 2s costs of the summons he would be free to go.[49]

The report of this case prompted another lengthy response from Sir Richard Mayne who defended his measurements. As for the journey to the British Museum highlighted by the magistrate, this was no more than a clerical error. The correct fare had been entered in the proof sheet as 1s 6d - the errant 6d "must have dropped out from the rest of the type". Mayne further reiterated than any discrepancies in the true measurements had been covered by the errata. All remaining distances must be deemed to be accurate. There was no mention of the faulty wheel at Westminster police court, or that the wheel at Marlborough St police court, which had been used as an arbiter when the Westminster wheel was found to be in error, had itself a spoke missing and the measurement was seen to 'jump'.[50]

If the magistrates were kept busy by cab passengers exercising their right to have any disputes between themselves and the driver adjudicated upon by the sitting magistrate, then they were about to have before them whole shoals of cabmen following a police clampdown. On June 1st 1854 the commissioner of police, Sir Richard Mayne, issued a notice that the second edition of his book of fares had been published and drivers were instructed to purchase one under the directions of the 1853 Act. Many drivers saw this as a further tax upon their income, it was down to them to purchase the book, priced 1s, but this was a shilling many of them could ill afford. They could also be forgiven for wondering just how many books they would eventually be forced to carry with them. Seeing that the books were not being taken up by cabmen as quickly as he liked, Mayne instructed each of the police divisions to enforce the regulations by having a uniformed officer demand to see the driver's badge and his two book of fares he was now obliged by law to carry.

John Williams, the 'Cabmen's Attorney-General' as he liked to be styled – but with a singular lack of success, was charged with having neither a badge or a book of fares. He contended that under the 24-hour rule, an unlicensed person could drive a cab – which was true, but was only as an emergency measure when a licensed driver failed to show. He proclaimed to own several badges, only one was legitimate, but that matter was not pursued by the magistrate.

As for the book of fares, Williams contended that he was under no obligation to show the book to a policeman when so demanded. He was only bound by law to show the book to a hirer, and the policeman had not hired his cab. Hammill, after consulting the Act of 1853 was inclined to agree with the cabman and the summons was dismissed. A victory for the 'Cabmen's Attorney-General'.[51]

The Metropolitan Police, and Sir Richard Mayne, were not to be so easily beaten, especially by a cab driver. They intensified their efforts against the trade. Uniformed officers were now instructed to approach a cab on a stand and demand to see the drivers badge and his book of fares. If neither could be produced the policeman would then hire the driver to drive no more than half a mile in one direction, and then half a mile back, being a 6d minimum fare. Mayne probably realised that most drivers, rather than risking their position on the stand for a 6d fare, would then produce their badge or books. Any driver refusing the 6d fare would then be summoned for that offence as well.

In August 1854 Inspector March of H Division informed the sitting magistrate at Thames Court, Tooley Street, that he had the names of 30 drivers he wished to apply for a summons against. He further informed the magistrate, Ingham, that in the recent crackdown over 700 violations of the hackney carriage Acts had been discovered. These were a mixture of offences including not producing a badge, having only one of the required two books of fares and the inevitable refusals for the 6d minimum ride. March predicted that about half of the cabmen in London would soon appear before the courts unless they obeyed the law. Undaunted in the task before him, Ingram asked March to call out the names of the drivers he wished a summons against and he would grant it. Here he was interrupted by the clerk of the court who informed the magistrate that it would be impossible to deal with an extra thirty summons on top of the normal day-to-day business of the court. Ingram felt that the laws of the land could not be ignored and planned that the summons for the drivers should take place over several days. It was then that March informed the magistrate that there was a further batch of driver's names he would be coming to court with the following day. To which Ingram could only raise a smile of reluctant acceptance. It was going to be a long hot summer for the cab trade.

Beadon, the magistrate at Hammersmith, was not as complacent as his fellow judge at Thames police court. He was confronted with just seven similar offences at his bench and castigated Inspector Cooke for bringing them in front of him without any prior notice. A fellow magistrate had previously granted the summons and now it was left to Beadon to hear the cases. Beadon informed Cooke that if it had been down to him he would have granted just the one summons, which would then have had the case decided upon in that court and all similar cases could then be summarily dispensed with. He was aware that similar cases were appearing in other courts and, as per usual, there were differences in how each court approached the subject. He himself would have liked more time to consider the question so in the circumstances he would hear just the one case today and the remaining six, being similar, would all fall to the same judgement.

The unlucky guinea-pig was Edward Longley. He was charged with "...unlawfully neglect[ing] to have with you, when plying for hire with such carriage, a book, in the form directed by the commissioners of police, of the fares for the hire of such carriage." Beadon made the court aware that as far as he was concerned, the Act only provided for the cabman to be compelled to show the hirer the book of fares, so much had been agreed upon by his fellow magistrates. But Longley, having refused to show his book to the policeman, was then hired by the policeman for his 6d ride, Beadon gave his interpretation of this new modus operandi. "If the constable intended to hire the man and he failed to produce his book of fares when called upon to do so, then he would be clearly liable to a penalty of 40s. Now if I were to swear the constable in this case, it would amount to moral perjury, for I do not believe that his instructions were to hire the cab provided he had the proper book of fares." Inspector Cooke confirmed that if the book of fares had been shown at the first request, then the policeman would not have hired the cab. "Then how," argued Beadon, "can he be an intended hirer within the meaning of the Act? Then how can I swear the constable? The first question I should ask him would be if he intended to hire the cab. If his answer would be, "Yes, I did." That would amount to perjury, at least moral perjury, and I am not going to put him on the box to do that." Beadon advised Inspector Cooke that his best plan of action would be to hire a cab and then ask the driver for his book of fares. If the driver cannot produce a book then Beadon would ensure that the full weight of the law, a fine of 40 shillings, or imprisonment, would willingly be levied against the cabman concerned. Beadon was making it quite clear that he was no friend of the cabman, just a stickler for the law. The case against Longley and his fellow cabmen was dismissed and Inspector Cooke had to retire to consider a new plan of action.[52]

Much the same was happening in the police courts across London. Back at Thames Court the magistrate Ingham began dealing with the first of the batch of thirty cab drivers that his clerk had warned him would be a burden to the system. First up before him was Joseph Romaine, 2286. Romaine had been charged with not having either of his two fares books, but in court he informed the magistrate that as the policeman was not the intended hirer he had every right to refuse to show him. Such a defence was well founded given recent events but Ingham asked if he was actually in possession of both the books. Romaine admitted that he was not, he had the first but not the second and he also added "One book has printed one journey at two miles and 1s., and the other book states the same journey to be two miles 760 yards, and the fare to be 1s 6d. Which book are we to go by your worship? Notwithstanding this, Ingham reminded him that under the directions of Sir Richard Mayne he was bound to carry both copies. On questioning Inspector March, the officer could not prove that Romaine had actually received the notices from Scotland Yard informing them as to their legal duties in purchasing and carrying with them both editions of the book of fares. Ingham then dismissed the charge against Romaine and the Inspector withdrew the charges from the ten other cabmen who were awaiting their fate outside the court room. No doubt the clerk breathed a sigh of relief.[53]

As the eleven cabmen left the court, one had been heard to cry out in triumph at how the cab trade had struck a blow against the vexatious commissioners of police. Just how vexatious the police could be is highlighted by the case of Edward Frostick, badge 2720. he had been waiting on the stand at Boston Street, Marylebone, when PC Beckett approached him and asked him to produce the second edition of the book of fares. By now the attitude of the police had been the talk of all the cab stands as well as how the drivers should react to such a demand. Frostick refused to show the policeman his book as he believed he was not going to be hired by him. Beckett then climbed into the cab and informed Frostick that he wished to be taken to Gloucester Place, a short trip. Frostick complied and when Beckett asked him for a second time for his book of fares, Frostick told him to look under the cushion of the seat he was sitting on and he would find it. The policeman looked and indeed there was the book. Having followed the instructions of the magistrate that he had done nothing wrong in not showing the book in the first instance, Frostick was surprised to find himself summoned but no sooner had he gave his version of events to the magistrate than he was discharged and allowed to go back to work. The two shillings cost of the summons, the 6d for the fare from Boston Street to Gloucester Place, the paperwork and the police officer's time in pursuit of offending cabmen and attendance at court was all for nought.[54]

If the fare structure could not satisfy a hackney coachman's income, then he had to rely on the generosity of the public in supplementing his earnings. This was achieved by cajoling or, depending on the type of passenger, threats or intimidation. None were more open prey to the hackney coachman than the lone female. A correspondent to *The Times* wrote that, "At least, three times in five, you have to pay 50 per cent. over your fare when you employ them [hackney coaches], or to dispute (i.e. a fight); and it really becomes a serious inconvenience, that a lady cannot take a coach from the Bank to Charing-cross, without the moral certainty, if she be alone, of being plundered or insulted."[55]

After punishing one cabman for the attempted extortion of two women, Ingham the the Surrey-based magistrate, "then gave notice to cabmen that he should inflict the full penalty in every case of imposition, Ladies, when not attended by gentlemen, must be protected."[56]

Despite the threat of Ingham's and other like-minded magistrates, the imposition continued. Soon however there was a champion to fight the cause for the lone female, a rather eccentric woman by the name of Caroline Giacometti Prodgers.

Some would indeed describe Caroline Prodgers as eccentric, but according to one contemporary who professed to know her well "she was as mad as a hatter"[57]. Her father was a rector at the Hertfordshire village of Ayot St Peter near Ware, and one fortuitous day he happened to save the life of a young woman from drowning. They soon fell in love and were married. It was indeed fortuitous for the reverend Edwin Prodgers as the young lady he saved was heiress to a huge fortune. [58]

Caroline herself was born in Brixton in 1829 and was the eldest of four children born to the said Edwin and his wife. Whatever the source of the family income, there is no doubt that they had money. The 1841 census shows that the family were living at Clarence Lodge, Brixton, a large house in its own grounds, the BMX track in Brockwell Park is said to be on the same site. Caroline's father is described as a rector and magistrate and they have a staff of four maids, two male servants and a governess.

By 1851 the family were living in the hamlet of Ayott St Peter, Hertfordshire. In 1853 Caroline was admitted as a private patient into the asylum at Wood End. It is unclear how long she remained in there but it nethertheless shows that her eccentricity may have stemmed from an early age.

In 1861 she went on a tour of Europe, no doubt funded by her allowance of £2000 per year but quite an adventurous undertaking for a young lady, especially a young rich lady. In Europe she met and fell in love with Captain Giovanni Giacometti, an officer in the Austro-Hungarian navy. He was completely smitten by her and she convinced him to return with her to England. This he duly did and the couple were married shortly after at St Mary's Church, Bryanston Square, London on February 15th 1862, just two months after the death of her father. And that was just the beginning of Giovanni Giacometti's downfall.

With income secure from her dowry Caroline convinced her husband to resign his commission from the Hungarian navy so as to devote his life to looking after her, this he did but it was claimed that she did not "appreciate his attentions".[59] With her being of the Anglican faith and he being Roman Catholic, it was thought that the marriage was not legal, at least in the eyes of the Catholic Church. They planned an extended honeymoon in Europe where they would get married again, but this time in a Catholic chapel. However, a papal bull had forbidden such marriages between the differing religions and so the original service would suffice. It was just as well. Two months after the marriage, she banned her husband from the matrimonial bed; two years after that, she kicked him out of the house. Giacometti was now destitute, he was in a strange land, had no job and nowhere to live. Salvation actually came from Caroline's brother, Edwin, who felt that the treatment of his brother-in-law was heartless and settled an allowance of £200 a year on him.

Giovanni Giacometti sought a divorce from his wife, in the eyes of the Catholic church the marriage had not been consummated, but the court found no evidence of this. It would be hard not to disagree with the judges, as by this time the couple had two sons, Ferdinand and Ernest. Lord Penzance actually criticised the couple for coming to court and seeking a judicial decision on whether their marriage was legal. According to the law of the land it was indeed legal and all they had done was feather the pockets of the lawyers involved. Whilst her exploits in the divorce courts brought her to prominence, it was her entanglements with cab drivers that would set her on the path of a crusade.

Her first recorded "victim" William Southwell, badge 1785 who, in January 1871, she accused of overcharging her by 6d in a fare from Victoria Station to Ludgate Hill station. Southwell had picked her up from the station at 12:35 pm, no doubt to the relief of all the other cabmen on the rank. Mrs Prodgers was well known to them. Southwell drove her to Gray's Inn Square where he waited 15 minutes and from there he took her to Ludgate Hill. He demanded 4s as his fare but Mrs Prodgers was only willing to tender 3s 6d and not a penny more. He asked for her name and address but she refused to give it. She went into a shop and Southwell waited for her. The argument continued once she left the shop and a passing policeman came to Southwell's assistance. Even he could not solicit her to furnish him with her name and address and he advised her that one way or another she would either give it to him where they stood or at the police station – she chose the latter option. Even the Inspector at the station was hard pressed to obtain her details but then he came up with an idea to get rid of her. Instead of Southwell summoning her, she was to summon him for demanding more than his legal fare and for misconduct (badgering her over trying to get her name and address).

The next day at Guildhall, Prodgers, as the cabmen always referred to her, dogmatically insisted that she was in the right, a faith that would she would follow throughout her litigious lifetime. She informed Alderman Sir Robert Carden that everyone believed she was right, even Southwell; but according to Southwell's solicitor, Knight, far from overcharging her he had undercharged her and therefore had every right to obtain her name and address. A cab driver from Victoria Station was produced as a witness as to the time Southwell actually left the station. When asked how he could be so sure he replied that all the drivers knew Prodgers and several of them looked at the clock just in case there was a dispute. When Knight asked Mrs Prodgers how many cabmen had she summoned to date, she replied that it was several but was not quite sure how many exactly. Sir Robert informed Mrs Prodgers that she was indeed in the wrong and should pay 2s 6d to Southwell and 10s 6d to his solicitor. Mrs

Prodgers protested; "I paid him his legal fare and he demanded more."

"You have committed an offence yourself" replied Sir Robert, "by not supplying your name and address when asked." When told there was no appeal against his decision Mrs Prodgers paid the 13s and left the court, by cab. Later on that same day, the driver of that cab returned to court to take a summons out against her for not paying him the legal fare from the Guildhall to Ludgate Hill Station.

She had a similar lack of success the following day at Bow Street court with her defence resting on the pretence that if a cab driver should not receive more than the legal fare why was she being asked to pay extra by the courts. The magistrate there informed her that he had no jurisdiction over the actions of Sir Robert Carden. A few days later cab driver Richard Jones, badge 7470, picked up Mrs Prodgers from the King Street rank and took her to Ludgate Hill station, there he waited for her before taking her on to Chancery Lane. She went to pay the fare of 1s but Jones said his fare was 1s 6d because of the waiting at Ludgate Hill. Despite protestations from her son to pay the cabdriver, no doubt inspired by her lack of success so far, and with a self-belief that she will be found right, she refused to pay the full fare. Jones refused to accept less, and summoned her to appear at the Guildhall the next day, once more in front of Alderman Sir Robert Carden.

Jones took to the witness stand and testified that Mrs Prodgers had kept him waiting nineteen minutes at Ludgate Hill. When asked how could he be so precise as to the time, he replied, to laughter from everyone in the court, that a porter and a policeman came up to him and warned him about his passenger, saying how bad her reputation was. There then followed a dialogue between the Alderman and Mrs Prodgers that was widely reported in the press:

Alderman Sir Robert Carden "I believe I must decide against you Mrs Prodgers"

Mrs Prodgers "It is not of the slightest consequence to me what you decide Sir Robert Carden"

"My decision is that his fare is 1s 6d"

"Will you explain how that is"

"Certainly. There is 6d for waiting nineteen minutes-"

"Nine minutes…why cannot my word be taken as well as his"

"Because he is on oath and you are not"

"Then why cannot I be put on my oath?"

"Because the law does not allow it"

"But when I was here before, I was put into the witness box and sworn"

"That was because you were the complainant"

After having his decision explained to her yet again, Mrs Prodgers tried a different tact with the Alderman; "This is the cheapest mode for me to pursue, because I have the honour of seeing Sir Robert Carden"

"If you consider it an honour, I hope you will not have to indulge in it frequently" replied Sir Robert, again to fits of laughter from the court. Mrs Prodgers was not finished. When the clerk of the court stepped up to receive the 19s she was ordered to pay, she refused to hand over any money to him as he was not the same person she paid the money to the previous week. It was then agreed that she would go into another room and pay Jones' fare and costs, but before she left, Sir Robert advised "…Mrs Prodgers in future […] pay the cabmen their fares", to which Mrs Prodgers responded, "My name is not Mrs Prodgers".

Sir Robert; "Well I have no wish to call you by your wrong name, Mrs Gi-a-co-metti Prodgers but you better pay the cabmen"

"That is not my name"

"Well, what is it?"

Mrs Prodgers; "Giacometti" [pronouncing it as Jacometti]

"Well Mrs Giacometti Prodgers, I beg your pardon. I hope I have it now right." To more laughter from the court, Mrs Giacometti Prodgers paid the money and left.[60]

She was still having a dispute on the domestic front which had far greater consequences for her than her battles with the cab trade. Her husband went to court to obtain an order for him to access his right to the matrimonial bed, literally a judicial decree for him to have sex with his wife whether she consented or not. Despite the order of the court being in his favour, Mrs Prodgers still refused the advances of her husband and was found in contempt of court for not obeying the court order. She was incarcerated in Horsemonger Lane Gaol, but not for very long. Giovanni Giacometti agreed to relinquish all claims to his wife in return for an allowance of £300 per annum during her life time, and £100 per year thereafter (she herself was beneficial in her parents will her father died leaving £80,000, her mother died the following year with an estate of £18,000) and was receiving £1700 a year, a figure that would take a cabman a lifetime to earn).

After a further dispute with her husband over a share in a fund of an intestate will of £6000, Mrs Prodgers was once again in court opposite a cabdriver. In October 1871 Edwin Castro, badge 9180, took Mrs Prodgers from Victoria Station to Euston Station, the legal fare, according to the book of fares "that she always carries with her" was 3s 6d., Castro demanded 4s. The clerk of the court looked up the fare in the book and surprised everyone by stating that the police had not yet found a place in London called Victoria (the station was at least ten years old). The magistrate attempted to locate places listed within the fare charts that were close to Victoria and surmised that the cab driver could indeed be right, but Mrs Prodgers could have the ground measured if she so wished. This she agreed to, but not at her expense. The magistrate informed her that both she and the cabman should deposit 5s to have the ground measured and whoever was in the wrong would forfeit their 5s with the victor having their money returned. A week later all the parties returned to Marylebone Magistrates Court, all except Mrs Prodgers who had already heard the findings. Police constable Osborne had measured the distance and found it to be three miles, four furlongs and twenty-three yards, Castro was right to charge 4s and Mrs Prodgers was ordered to pay the 6d outstanding fare plus 12s costs (as well as losing the 5s costs in measuring the ground).[61]

By now Mrs Prodgers, or Mrs Giacometti, as some papers were rightly calling her, was becoming a national treasure in the eyes of everyone except cab drivers. The *Pall Mall Gazette* was frequently praising her, not only for taking on the rude and overcharging cabmen (though it failed to mention her lack of success) but to bringing the attention to how badly the book of cab fares was, not only its printing quality but in its calculations. To some she was on a mission for the "unprotected female" armed with just an umbrella[62] (and a book of fares), she was undaunted by the overbearing magistrates that, she believed continually sided with the cabmen. Even provincial newspapers were reporting on her episodes; there were songs being sung, such as "Mrs Prodgers and the Cabman" at music halls across the country. The historian J.E. Cussans remarked, after travelling down by train to Kings Cross with her, that if he was in any doubt as to who she was, it would not have been for long. The porters knew her (they were only allowed to pick up her children if they had clean clothes) and the cry of "Prodgers", "Prodgers" could be heard resonating down the cab rank as the drivers warned their colleagues and each manoeuvred themselves to avoid her and grab hold of another fare.[63]

Her next summons was against an owner driver, John Challis, who refused to carry her from St James's Street to Balham, a distance, as she reported, of less than six miles. In court it indeed transpired that Challis agreed to carry Mrs Giacometti Prodgers to Balham but she insisted on having the windows open and whilst she was all wrapped up, the wind was blowing the rain into his cab, saturating the cushions and panelling. As she continually refused to close the window and he felt that he would not be compensated for any damage he ordered her out of the cab and forfeited the 2s 6d fare. A passing policeman took the details of all concerned and informed Challis that his cab was not fit for use due to the dampness inside and he had to return to the yard. Mrs Giacometti Prodgers had to get another cab home. The magistrate dismissed her summons against Challis saying that the law did allow a justifiable excuse, and Prodgers had provided him with one. Another defeat for Caroline Giacometti Prodgers.

Her defeats kept on mounting. A shorthand writer she employed to take notes of her many appearances in the divorce courts successfully summoned her for non-payment and another, unknown, cabdriver, who in May 1872, picked her up from opposite the police court in Southwark, no doubt after yet another confrontation with a cab driver, summoned her for non-payment. She was willing only to depart with 1s 6d and he said his fare to Balham was 2s 6d. Mrs Prodgers had asked the cabman for his book of fares that he was legally obliged to carry and did not have, and, reminding the magistrate of his powers, believed that such an offence carried a fine of 40 shillings. The magistrate informed Mrs Prodgers that she had not summoned him over not carrying a fares book but on overcharging. Once again Mrs Prodgers could have the distance measured but she "wisely", as reported in the press, declined and paid the driver his 2s 6d fare plus 7s costs.

Days later she was in court again, this time it was her nine-year-old son who had been summoned, for throwing a bucket of water over a neighbour's coachman, he appeared to have slightly better success than his mother as the case was thrown out by the magistrate.[64] There was a compromising solution to further action by her husband who said that in the eyes of the law he was entitled to the £6000 that had been bequeathed to her by her sister, which was now sitting in a fund. Vice Chancellor Malin, who was judging the case, actually stated that Mrs Prodgers was of doubtful sound mind as an earlier action by her, to see if she was legitimately married could have ended with her son being declared a bastard. In the end Malin settled the case by awarding £1000 to Giovanni Giacometti straight away with the balance to be settled between the pair of them and for the two children to receive the balance when they came of age.

In November 1872 it was Stephen Boucher's (6481), misfortune to carry Mrs Prodgers. He appears to have been one of the few cabdrivers in London who did not recognise her, and the journey from London Bridge station to (what is now) Liverpool Street station, was one that even the irrepressible Mrs Prodgers could not doubt the stated fare of 1s – but fate decreed otherwise. First of all, an obstruction on London Bridge necessitated Boucher going via Southwark Bridge which added an extra 6d on the fare. Boucher also asked for an extra 3d, which was his entitlement, as, along with Mrs Prodgers there was a nurse and a small baby. Drivers had previously been summoned to court for charging for an infant under ten, when the law stated, quite categorically, that two children under ten were to be charged as one adult. The cabdrivers argued, and won the argument, that if only one child under ten was to be carried then it should be charged for, as they were liable to any accident that befell the child when inside the cab. As the inevitable dispute began once they set down at the Great Eastern station, Mrs Prodgers asked Boucher for a ticket which he could not give but he did furnish her with all the details that such a ticket would provide. Sensing success in the forthcoming summons that she knew was about to happen she agreed to give her name and address to the driver. In court, Mrs Prodgers informed the magistrate that the driver had no right to charge for a baby, and had refused to give her a ticket and would not let her board the train until she had provided him with her address. She believed that it was not necessary for her to give such information as she was well known. The magistrate agreed that she was indeed well known but the cabdriver was right to charge 1s 9d instead of 1s and his excuse for not providing a ticket, he had given the last one away to an earlier fare was a valid excuse. He advised Mrs Prodgers that he could not proceed with the summons in its present form and she should go away and restructure it. Mrs Prodgers left the court minus another victory and Boucher left the court empty handed, still without his 9d and probably owing more in costs.

Just before Christmas 1872 she was back before the magistrates in Westminster, this time complaining of the fact that no cabmen were willing to pick her up. Over the previous two or three weeks she had had trouble trying to get a cab from Victoria station. On the last occasion a porter got her a cab from the rank but when the driver saw who his fare was he turned the cab around and drove off. She complained to the inspector of the cabs at Victoria and despite the rank being full of cabs he could not get a cab to leave the stand to come and pick her up. In desperation the inspector went out into the street and hailed a non-privileged cab, but Mrs Prodgers' reputation was so great that on seeing his fare, he too abruptly turned his cab around and left the station. Now at the Westminster police court Mrs Prodgers demanded that something should be done about all the trouble she had been put to in trying hire a cab. However, she was to be disappointed by the power of the law, the cabs were private property and the stations were also private property and despite being governed by hackney carriage legislation he had no authority over them whilst they were within the station, and it was to the station manager that she should seek redress.

In February 1873 Mrs Prodgers appealed against Vice-Chancellor Malin's decision to allow her husband access to money that was bequeathed to her by her deceased sister. The appeal judge threw the case out saying it was an idle appeal and had caused an unjustifiable waste of time.[65] In November of that year Giovanni Giacometti had had enough and finally sued his wife for a divorce. It appears that her frequent actions against the cabdrivers may have precipitated Giacometti's decision, and could well have been the Boucher case described above. It had been reported in the newspapers that Mrs Giacometti Prodgers appeared in the witness box at Worship Street with a baby in her arms. It transpired the child was born in September 1872 and as there was no way he could be the father. He was granted a *decree nisi* on the grounds of her adultery.[66]

The problems for Mrs Prodgers continued on the domestic front. Her cook, "a violent and strong Irishwoman" as described by Mrs Prodgers, would not leave the house even though she had been dismissed from her service. She would sit in front of the fire all day and sing. Ingham, the magistrate at Wandsworth police court, said there was nothing he could do about the matter but perhaps she could employ a strong man to remove the cook. Without seeing the need to go to the expense of employing some strong-arm muscle, Mrs Prodgers and her ten-year old son Ferdinand attempted to do it between them – but found themselves up before the magistrate on a charge of assault. Despite a witness to the attack, it could not be found whether the cook was still in the employ of Mrs Prodgers, in which case no crime had taken place, or attacked her after dismissing her, in which case an assault had occurred. The magistrate refused to come down on one side or the other and dismissed the case for want of jurisdiction.

In September 1874, the now divorced Mrs Prodgers applied to Alderman

Besley for a number of summons against one cabdriver. When asked how many she wished to have she replied four; "one for demanding more than his legal fare" – he wanted 3s 6d from the Consumption Hospital in Fulham Road to the Bank, and she said the legal fare was only 2s 6d; "one for abusive language" – when she refused to pay, he allegedly said "You swindle all the cabmen; you are only fit to ride in a dung cart"; "one for not giving a ticket, and one for not producing the authorised book of fares". All the summons were duly issued.[67] Of the four, Robert Chalk was only fined a shilling on each of the charges for not having a book of fares or handing her a ticket – he had actually written his details on the back of a tobacconist's card, then later that night delivered to her address a proper ticket, telling her that he would summon her for the outstanding 1s 2d, which probably precipitated Mrs Prodgers in going to court first thing the following morning to take out the quadruple summons against him. Alderman Finnis dismissed the overcharge claim as there was conflicting evidence on both sides, to waiting time, not for the actual distance. The charge of abusive language was also dismissed.[68]

Less than a fortnight later she was back in the courts again, seeking another application for a summons. She had taken a cab from Kings Cross station to London Bridge station the previous day and paid the cab driver the legal fare of 1s 6d, saying he became abusive and demanded more. The following day she was at York Rd station (Kings Cross) where the same cab driver was waiting on a rank. He warned all his fellow cab drivers about her, as if they needed to be told, and she was forced to walk out of the station and into the street to get a cab. She said "She was determined not to be cheated or annoyed by the London Cabman, who seemed to have combined for the purpose of putting [her] to every inconvenience."[69]

Charles Eagle was summoned for refusing to pick up Mrs Prodgers from York Road station. As Mrs Prodgers had not turned up, he, quite reasonably, asked for costs to be awarded, including a loss of a day's wages in attending the summons. Not only had he no recollection of the offence but he did not even drive a cab – he was a bus driver. It transpired that somebody had taken down the cab number as 89 but entered it into the space for a badge number, it appeared to be a mistake made by the court. He was further disappointed to find that as Mrs Prodgers had not attended the court no costs could be awarded. Just then, the irrepressible Mrs Prodgers made her grand entrance, (no doubt she found it hard to get a cab) and at once confirmed that Eagle was not the man who insulted her. The case was adjourned though it was not recorded whether Charles Eagle was ever remunerated.[70]

The following week was a busy one for Mrs Prodgers and her crusade. On Thursday October 8th 1874 she was summoned by Isaac Gruby, 11,678, it was believed that she had now appeared in front of a magistrate about fifty times.[71] It transpired that Mrs Prodgers had originally summoned him for demanding 6d more than the legal fare, but, no doubt having been warned of her imminent failure, indignantly left the court. Gruby was then allowed to summons Mrs Prodgers over the 6d, and for his time lost in attending the original summons, he had waited from 10am until 6pm and he assured the magistrate that the distance from Kings Cross station, to London Bridge was indeed over three miles and that he had proof. Mrs Prodgers was ordered to pay a guinea to Gruby.[72] Two days later, cabdriver 8568 asked for a summons against her for non-payment. He had driven her around for four hours and ten minutes and all she was willing to pay was 8s 6d, when he demanded 11s. If he had stuck around he could have handed the summons to Mrs Prodgers personally, as she had taken a summons against a driver of the badge 2597 who drove for a John Harvey of Boston Place, Marylebone. Having arrived at the York Road station the driver, having been warned that Mrs Prodgers would legal him off, demanded the fare of 2s 6d up front. A not too unreasonable request given the nature of the passenger but one that was illegal under hackney carriage legislation. In fact, part of the driver's defence was that although he was guilty, as Mrs Prodgers was continually summoning cabdrivers the magistrate may like to impose only a small fine which would meet the justice of the case.[73] Nothing doing, the driver was fined 20s and costs or, in default of payment, 14 days' hard labour. A singular success for Mrs Prodgers, which would not have been her first, but it did highlight the scale of punishment meted out to cabdrivers when they were wrong and the absence of any punishment when the passenger was at fault.[74]

Mrs Prodgers was on the crest of a wave. She had not attended the first (counter) summons made on her by Isaac Gruby the previous week. She had been ordered to pay him a guinea for the extra 6d he demanded for the fare and for sitting around for eight hours waiting for her to turn up. Gruby, it was remembered said he had proof that the distance from Kings Cross station to London Bridge was over three miles. The distance was measured and found to be under three miles but then it transpired that the assistant gaoler who carried out the measurement with a pedometer was not trained in its use and the distance was to be measured again. At this point Gruby backed down and declined to have the ground measured. Many took it to be an admission of guilt. No further action appears to be taken against Gruby even though he was technically guilty of overcharging, and Mrs Prodgers was allowed to keep her guinea that had originally been taken from her. She had her ever-present ally in the *Pall Mall Gazette* which reported; "Patience, perseverance, probity, pedometers and Prodgers were triumphant. When it is remembered how frequently the public are imposed upon by cabmen, and how few people take the trouble to bring them into court, the result of such impunity being increased audacity on their part, anyone who attempts to keep them in order is a benefactor to society, or at least cab-hiring society. From Caroline Giacometti Prodgers, at least, whether they deserve it or not, none but the brave will get the fare."[75]

On October 9th 1874, and this may give an indication of the frenetic mind of Mrs Prodgers, the day after the initial court appearance against Isaac Gruby and the day before her successful appearance at Clerkenwell (when the driver asked for the fare in advance), she employed Charles Redgrave, 4557, but at the end of the journey she refused to pay him the 2s he demanded. For once the magistrates were getting tougher. She had to pay the 2s to Redgrave and 5s costs or face seven days in the House of Correction. Naturally the fine was duly paid, it was a pittance to her, but there were many cabdrivers who could not pay such a fine and were incarcerated.

An application for a summons for refusal was denied her by Arnold the magistrate in November, 1874, on the basis that, like her previous experience, the cabman was on private property within the station and could basically do as he pleased. Mrs Prodgers evidently left the court "much dissatisfied".[76]

The following month she was back inside a courtroom seeking a summons against a cabdriver who refused to pick her up from Victoria station. It would appear that the drivers there had a long memory for faces and the law, as Mrs Prodgers was informed, and not for the first time, that the court had no jurisdiction against cabs that were on private property.

The first cabmen's shelter was opened in Acacia Road, St John's Wood (not very far from Queen's Road (now Grove) where Mrs Prodgers lived), in January 1875. They were designed with the view of keeping the cabmen out of the public houses as well as being somewhere to shelter from inclement weather. It was soon realised that they could give the cabby a further role.

A cartoon in *Punch* showed Mrs Prodgers entering the cabmen's shelter and the inhabitants of which are either stupefied by fear, hiding under the table or clambering out of the window in a bid to escape.[77]

Benjamin William Coombe picked up Mrs Prodgers in the Strand and took her to several destinations, waiting for her each time. In no doubt of who she was, after the expiration of one hour twenty minutes he asked for his fare, as his horse had been out all day. Mrs Prodgers refused to pay the 2s 6d he demanded, not because it was an excessive charge, just on the fact that a cabman should not be allowed to terminate a journey when he saw fit. Coombe summoned Prodgers to appear before the Westminster police court magistrate, Arnold. In court, Arnold asked Coombe if he had been hired by time or distance. Coombe replied that it was by distance and provided the court with his own *Abstract of Laws* but Arnold intervened stating that whilst he was aware that a cabman could not be compelled to go more than six miles by distance, or an hour by time, he felt the *Abstract* was enough to confuse anybody. Anybody except Mrs Prodgers. Coombe answered that if "an hour by time and six miles by distance were to be relied on separately, then a fare could take a man by distance and keeping him waiting all day so, long as the six miles were not completed. It was a perfectly valid argument and Arnold did not know the answer, so he asked the only person in the court room who he thought was more aware of hackney carriage law than himself – Mrs Caroline Giacometti Prodgers. Unfortunately, she did not know the answer either, which prompted Arnold to state that as it was such an important matter he would adjourn until a future date. Mrs Prodgers was not too happy about this. She had a cabman waiting outside the court and she feared that he might adopt the same tactics as Coombe and terminate the hiring at his own satisfaction. Arnold warned her that if the question was settled as once, as she desired, he would have to rule against her. Mrs Prodgers then agreed to an adjournment but left the court not wholly satisfied with Arnold; an earlier ruling against her by him she stated, had, according to Civil Service people, been wrong.[78]

When the case resumed, it was a complete fudge by Arnold who by some Solomonite judgement allowed Mrs Prodgers to lose, but denied Coombe all but a complete victory. Coombe stated that at the termination of one hour, Mrs Prodgers was inside the Austrian Embassy, and he had to wait for her to emerge before he could terminate the hiring. Coombe was at the end of his working day and had taken 11s up till that point, and felt his horse was at the end of its limit. Mrs Prodgers protested that Coombe had made no such mention of his horse having been tired, and if he had done so, she was in the waiting room when this protest was raised. A constable of the London, Chatham and Dover Railway testified that he had heard Coombe tell Mrs Prodgers that his horse was tired, and not fit to be worked. His testimony alone should have been enough for Arnold, who simply stated that if this argument had been put forward earlier, he would have found in Coombe's favour. Coombe's replied that if he had been aware of Mrs Prodgers defence, the railway constable would have been produced at the earlier hearing. Coombes's victory was a pyrrhic one, Mrs Prodgers had to pay him the disputed 2s 6d, which in fact she did not dispute, but he was only allowed the 2s costs of the summons.[79] Technically it was a result for Coombe, but he had lost two day's income sitting in court for the matter to be decided. The money he could have earned over those two days was important to him and his family, it meant absolutely nothing to Caroline Giacometti Prodgers.

There is a slight adjunct to this case that has a bearing on the personal life of Mrs Prodgers and her estranged husband, Giovanni Giacometti. Coombe had been waiting for Mrs Prodgers to emerge from the Austrian Embassy before he could terminate the hiring. When she married Giacometti in 1862, Caroline Prodgers became a subject of the Hungarian Empire. In the mid-1870's both she, who was seeking re-admission, and Giovanni, were both applying for application to become British Subjects. Caroline Giacometti Prodgers, as she signed herself on the oath of allegiance was re-granted citizenship in 1875, Giovanni, who not only had the custody of the two children from the marriage but actually swore on oath that he was a widower, received his citizenship in 1876. Did he lie under oath that he was a widower? Probably not. The divorce was a high profile one that had been for many the talk of the town. Most likely it was a mistake by Richard Cross who took the oath, widowers were far more common than divorcees. When the final judgement came before a magistrate, in this case it was Arnold, who could not be under any illusion that Caroline Giacometti Prodgers was alive, allowed the process to continue without raising any questions.

Having been granted a divorce on the grounds of his wife's adultery, Giovanni Giacometti now had custody of the two boys, who were at a private school in the country, and Mrs Prodgers had no access to them at all. She produced witnesses who stated that the children had never been harmed under her care and she had sympathy from the court who did not want to be seen to keep an adulterous mother from her children (even though by this time the couple had been separated from each other for over five years) where an adulterous husband would be granted access. After adjourning so that further affidavits could be filed the court ruled against Caroline Prodgers, it seems the most damning evidence was from her own two brothers who swore that it "would not be to the advantage of the children" for them to see their mother.[80]

The next to feel her wrath was Robert Harvey, the publisher of the *Daily Telegraph*. She went down to the offices of the newspaper and asked to purchase a back issue, no doubt concerning her custody case. The paper was produced and being told it would cost 1d, the cover price of the paper, she was indignant and felt it a gross imposition that a paper that was three weeks old should be the same price as a newly printed paper.

The paper contained old news and should only be worth ½d or three farthings. By now Harvey, on hearing the commotion, came into the office and refused to let her have the paper for less than a penny. With that she threw onto the counter a half-sovereign (ten shillings, or for that matter 120 old pennies). Harvey refused to change the money for her and with that she took up the paper, and the half-sovereign and went to go to her coachman (it is not stated whether this was a private coachman or a hackney coachman, but either way he was not willing to provide a penny). Harvey grabbed hold of her shoulder and doing so, stood on the train of her dress "which was very long" creating a tear in it. Harvey now found himself up before a magistrate on a charge of assault. He apologised for standing on the dress, which was quite accidental but he was only reacting to her belligerent attitude. The magistrate agreed and dismissed the summons.[81]

In September 1875 she was summoned by cab driver Charles Weedon, 4992, for refusing to pay him 1s 6d, the fare from Paddington Station to her home in Queen's Road, St John's Wood, she of course disagreed with him and was only prepared to pay 1s. Having had the ground measured and the distance found to be two miles and 90 yards, a 1s 6d fare, Weedon must have felt himself on safe ground, but the indomitable Mrs Prodgers, armed with the official book of fares, showed that the distance was under two miles. The Act of 1853 stated that in cases of dispute, the fares book was the final arbiter. In this instance, the distance as measured in the fares book was clearly wrong, but the Commissioner of Police's signature endorsed the entries, thus giving assurance to their validity. The magistrate, Mr D'Eyncourt, who had sided with the cabmen on numerous issues in the past had to dismiss the summons. He had to go by the fares book, "even if that was wrong". Weedon not only had to pay Mrs Prodgers' costs of 4s 6d, he also had to pay to have the ground measured, and lost a day's earnings whilst waiting around in court.[82] She was even losing her main ally, The *Pall Mall Gazette* who remarked a few weeks later that another cabdriver had summoned Mrs Prodgers but just before the case was heard, she paid the amount demanded, leaving the cabdriver lumbered with the costs of having the ground measured and, after seeking legal advice, found that none of it could be claimed.

There were to be repercussions for Mrs Prodgers following the Weedon case. Two weeks after Weedon had lost, Mrs Prodgers was due back in court again. A cabman named only as Walker, had summoned her for underpaying him but just before the case came before the magistrate, Mrs Prodgers paid the outstanding amount. The barrister who appeared for the cabman said it was very hard on his client, "that he should be debarred from claiming the costs of measuring the distance and of engaging legal assistance to which he had been put." He continued, "The question was identical with that presented to the court a fortnight since, when Mrs Prodgers obtained 4s 6d from a poor cabman for summoning her for sixpence, the balance of a fare from Paddington Station to her house at St John's Wood, although that lady now admitted she was wrong. The complainant had been, he contended, perfectly justified in taking steps to finally settle this question, and prove to the public that Mrs Prodgers was not infallible. He was in a position clearly to prove that Mrs Prodgers was in the wrong in this case, and in the other, when the poor cabman was severely mulcted."[83] The magistrate, Mansfield, may well have been in full agreement with the barrister. It highlighted how one-sided the law was. There was the rich Mrs Prodgers underpaying cabmen, but then paying only what they had asked for in the first place if she thought they would take it to court, which, as we will see in Chapter 8, would make her a professional bilker. The money was not important to Mrs Prodgers, it was the fame that went with her position. She was being championed as an indomitable female fighting the greed and abuse of the hackney carriage trade. If Britannia on the back of the very pennies she was so keen to wrestle from a cabman's grasp had her shield and trident, then Mrs Caroline Prodgers went into battle armed with her fares book and her umbrella. She may well have seen herself as wearing a crown upon her head - if there were one, it was about to slip.

Her trusted ally, *The Pall Mall Gazette,* reported the last case as unbiased as it could, letting the readers decide on its merits. Even *The Daily News,* which earlier in the year described Mrs Prodgers as "a kind of Joan of Arc...and is by herself enough to vindicate the courage and maintain the rights of her sex,"[84] could see the absurdity and one-sidedness the cabmen faced. Mansfield the magistrate had given one piece of advice after stating that the cabman before him could not be helped; he advised that Weedon might be able to apply to the magistrate who heard that case, D'Eyncourt, to look again into it. And that is exactly what happened. Weedon's appeal had been taken up by The Amalgamated Society of Metropolitan Cabdrivers, a trade union. They may well have been behind the attempted prosecution of Weedon's earlier summons, and the subsequent one of Walker. The society retained the same barrister who described Mrs Prodgers as not being 'infallible'. It transpired that the journey involving Walker, was identical to the one undertaken by Weedon, Paddington Station to Queen's Road. As Mrs Prodgers had paid Walker his just demand, she was admitting she was in error. If she was in error with Walker, she had to be in error with Weedon. The barrister now asked for a summons against Mrs Prodgers for the 6d balance of the fare and the 4s 6d costs that he was erroneously forced into paying her. D'Eyncourt said he was not prepared to issue a summons but, he would have the ground measured by an officer of the court, the original measurement was undertaken by the Amalgamated Society, and, if it was shown that the distance was over two miles, Weedon would be re-imbursed. He then added, totally contradicting his earlier stance, "I find it is not imperative to rule by the Distance Guide Book." The distance was measured that day and the officer of the court stated that the measured distance was two miles and 95 yards. Weedon was proven correct. He was repaid his 6d, the 4s 6d he had to pay for her costs and he was also awarded costs for all the time he had lost in obtaining justice.[85] The money came from the court, not from Mrs Prodgers. Every cab driver taking her from Paddington Station to her home knew the fare was 1s 6d, her days of 'mulcting' a cabman of a tanner were over, at least on that particular journey.

The following Guy Fawkes night allowed the cab trade to pay due homage to Mrs Prodgers in their own inimitable manner. An effigy of Mrs Prodgers was created and placed on top of a cab and paraded throughout the streets of London. It appears that it was permissible to display effigies of Guy Fawkes and even the Pope, but it was the police who objected to the display of the cabman's terror, Mrs Prodgers. George Hughes, the driver in charge of the cab, was arrested for begging, but the magistrate would throw the case out saying that the police were being "frivolous and vexatious" and that the cabman was providing amusement for the public.[86]

The crown had slipped. You could now burn effigies of Mrs Prodgers for public amusement. Her façade had been cracked and her actions against the cabmen could be seen to be "frivolous and vexatious" just like the police in trying to stop a bit of fun. She was no longer Britannia, no longer Joan of Arc, she was plain old Mother Prodgers who liked to complain against cabmen.

Her reign of terror, at least it was so-called from the popular press's point of view, had lasted a little over four years. She took to travelling abroad but even after a hiatus of several years she was not forgotten. The *Morning Post* in January 1881 gave out a warning to cabdrivers that "Mrs Giacometti Prodgers has returned" from Malta, saying that such news would make the cabmen wary "and frighten them away altogether from the ranks", but she appears to have had no arguments with cabdrivers on her return.[87] The following year she went on a more extensive trip taking in India and Ceylon. An indication of her global fame can be seen from a report in the *Straits Times of Singapore*, describing her as the lady from London who took on the "extortionate 'cabbies'", though like the *Morning Post* before them, they did give a hint that her mission was to obtain information on the native "gharry-wallah".[88]

By the mid-1880's Mrs Prodgers was perhaps part of the folk lore on the ranks, a tale or two told by an old cabdriver to a bright spark with a shiny badge. Then, in November 1886, like a dormant volcano, she awoke. Mrs Prodgers took a cab from Finchley Rd to Victoria station. The cabdriver asked for 3s but she only offered 2s, and he followed her into the ladies waiting room. In attempting to get somebody else to eject him and stop bothering her she asked the female attendant for assistance but was told "I suppose he wants his money", a remark which Mrs Prodgers thought "very improper" under the circumstances. The magistrate, Mr Partridge, informed her that in his opinion the journey in question was more than a two-shilling fare. "Oh no!" replied Mrs Prodgers, "It's under two shillings; I ought to know". After the laughter in the court died down, Partridge reminded her, as if she needed reminding, that she would have to pay the costs if she was wrong. "I am positive I am right" asserted Mrs Prodgers, "Not only that, I was abused. He told me I was not fit for anyone's company. This was when he wanted my name and address."

"Did he not know you?"

"I should think not."

Partridge allowed her to take a summons out for overcharging but not for abusive language, but she would have the opportunity to do so later if she could show that he was uncivil.[89] There appears to be no follow up to this case which probably indicates Prodgers let the matter drop once she realised she would lose.

One of her last reported actions against a cab driver was of alleged insulting language. She explained to the magistrate that she was riding down Edgware Rd in a carriage when a cabdriver shouted out at the top of his voice "Old Mother Prodgers". She explained that this was the sort of treatment she was constantly being subjected to. She took the number of the cab, 97, and stated that the defendant, John Burgess, looked like the driver who shouted the abuse. When questioned by Burgess as to the time of the day of the incident Burgess replied, and produced witnesses to show, that as he was a nightman he could not be driving a cab at one o'clock in the afternoon. The magistrate dismissed the case leaving Mrs Prodgers complaining that the railway people must have given her the wrong name and address.

Eternal respite from Mrs Caroline Giacometti Prodgers was finally achieved by the cab trade in 1890 when she died at the age of 61. According to the *Pall Mall Gazette*, one cabman was reported as saying, "Whichever place she's gone too, she'll be quarrelling about the fare."[90]

Provision of a receipt on request

The driver of a taxi must if requested by a passenger during or immediately after a journey, provide the passenger with a receipt for the fare paid by the passenger for that journey.

The idea of making the driver give a receipt goes back to the end of the late 18th century, when it was suggested that if a driver be compelled to give the hirer a ticket with a number that corresponded with the plate number of the coach then items that may be inadvertently left behind could, in theory, be traced.[91] Despite addressing the suggestion to the Commissioners for Regulating Hackney Coaches, the idea appears to have been ignored. It would be another three decades before the idea would be adopted.

The Hackney Coach Act 1814 gave a legal standing to the issuing of tickets, which a driver was compelled to give to every person who hired him. "To be at all useful, everyone ought to insist on these tickets before they pay."[92] The proposed design upon the tickets went much further than was when first suggested in 1786; each ticket was to include the number of the coach, the name address of the proprietor as well as the name of the driver. In the event, neither name of proprietor or driver would appear. The tickets would also have on them, in words or figures, "one shilling" or "one shilling and sixpence", which between them could cover all multiples of fares. The last item, which appeared above all other information was His Majesty's coat of arms. Anybody falsely printing up their own tickets could be faced with a charge of treason in using the crest for their own illegal needs, which carried a maximum penalty of a £300 fine or up to 12 months in prison. There was also a second clause attached to the issuing of tickets, and one which proved to be a greater burden to the driver than the tickets themselves, the driver was legally bound to give, not offer, a ticket or tickets to the hirer. The government could also foresee that the hirer may not wish to have their pockets stuffed full of tickets and may not want one. The government placed the onus on the passenger to ensure that unless they accepted the proffered ticket there would be no redress against a driver for abuse, or overcharging or even the return of property. The driver had no choice but to give a ticket, the passenger no choice but to accept one.[93]

Whilst redress against the driver for abuse or exaction, or the return of property left in the vehicle, may have been the primary cause behind the idea, there is a suspicion that the proprietors may have had a vested interest in the legislation. By giving out a certain number of tickets to the driver, they could easily establish his earnings at the end of the day –

which would allow them to adjust the rental charges, preferably upwards.

Almost straight away, the act was seen to be completely useless. A Mr Hatchett, who gave his address as the White Horse Cellars, Piccadilly (a coaching inn), hired hackney coach numbered 878 from Conduit Street for the short distance to Cavendish Square. On arrival there, the coachman asked for his shilling fare and Hatcham asked him for a ticket. The driver replied that he did not have any, it being the first day of their enforcement, and there was some confusion as to whether they came into effect. Hatchett refused to hand over any money unless he was given a ticket, to which the driver then began a torrent of abuse. After some minutes of the tirade, the coachman drove off without any money. Not satisfied with having a free ride, Hatcham summoned the driver for the abuse he received. After hearing Hatchett's complaint, the four sitting magistrates at Bow Street read from the 3rd clause of the recent Act; "That no person...who shall have hired any hackney coach shall be entitled to any redress...relating to any laws relating to any hackney coaches, ...or for any other offence whatsoever...unless such persons...shall produce...one or more of the tickets."[94] The hackney coachmen may lose out on a fare but they had literally been given Crown immunity from prosecution as long as they did not give a ticket. In one fell swoop, every punishment for offences committed by a hackney coachman was made obsolete – every one of them barring refusing to undertake the job in the first place. If there was no hiring, the driver did not have to give a ticket and the would-be hirer could still not prosecute. After seeing his prosecution fail, Hatcham may have left the court more crestfallen than one would expect. The *Morning Chronicle* had called the Hackney Coach Act "one of the most bungling pieces of work that ever came out of Parliament. It is a matter of surprise how it was able to pass through all its stages."[95] It was no wonder Hatchett was crestfallen, it was he who had proposed the law in the first place, and his attempt at getting hackney coachmen to obey the law had been totally ridiculed.

Even though Hatchett's fiasco had been publicised, though his involvement in the legislation was not widely known at this point, drivers were still refusing to give tickets and passengers were refusing to pay the fare. John Toncham and Thomas Nelson were two such drivers. In each case their passenger refused to pay and in each case the passenger was physically grabbed and forced to settle.[96] Both drivers were remanded in custody and what became of them is not too apparent. If they were prosecuted for assault, which is not a hackney carriage offence, then they were still liable for prosecution.

"In the matter of Hatchett," wrote a correspondent to *The Examiner*, "against one of the Knights of the Whip, it appears the descendants of Jehu knew the extent of the new Hackney Coach Act better than the man that framed it, and had, I find, before it took effect, determined to resist it altogether. The Act, in effect, according to this case, has released these gentry from all the former laws on the subject, without subjecting them to any new one that can be enforced by any other means than refusing to pay the fare; so that a hackney coachman may now abuse any Lady or Gentleman as much as he pleases for a shilling or eighteen pence; for it appears that if a complainant has no ticket, which a coachman may withhold without penalty (other than the loss of his fare) is entitled to no redress. Was there anything so monstrous?"[97]

The hackney coachmen's carte blanche to run roughshod over the hackney carriage laws was short-lived, as this contemporary verse points out:

The *Jehus* in Town, for some weeks got on gaily,

Insulting their fares, and defrauding them daily,

And mocking the law of the land;

But now they no longer can get on so fast;

For FIELDING'S construction has check'd them at last,

And brought the whole tribe to a Stand.[98]

Fielding was William Fielding, son of John, the novelist (the "Blind

Beak of Bow Street") and nephew to Henry Fielding, the founder of the Bow Street Runners.[99] By 1814, William had been a magistrate for forty years and was not prepared to allow the hackney coachmen to denigrate his office with their apparent immunity from prosecution.

It is not known which of the father and son, both named William Carus Wilson, climbed into a hackney coach shortly after the introduction of the Act. The younger one, who would later be defamed as Mr Brocklehurst in Charlotte Bronte's *Jane Eyre*, is unlikely, he was in his early twenties and no reference was made to his age. The father is the more probable candidate, and was himself a senior magistrate in Westmoreland and later a member of parliament. Carus Wilson climbed into coach, plate 509, but the driver, Clark, refused to move until his passenger promised not to demand a ticket. Carus Wilson replied "I want tickets of course, an Act of Parliament says, and I have the Act in my pocket, the driver *shall* deliver tickets." As Clark was not prepared to issue any tickets, he refused to move the coach and waited for his passenger to give up and climb into another coach. Fifty-four minutes later Carus Wilson was still sitting in Clark's hackney coach, musing himself by reading a pamphlet. Realising that there could be no end to the stand-off, and the fact that he had not earned anything for over an hour, Clark began to get abusive. It was probably what Carus Wilson had been waiting for, and he took out a summons against Clark to appear before Fielding at the police court in Queen Square (now Queen Anne's Gate).

In court, Clark stated that he had no tickets and that the only language he used was only that which could be used against a gentleman. Fielding thought that this was very unlikely and that the Act stated that they must carry tickets, adding that he thought it was "abominable" that the hackney coachmen could set themselves up against the designs of the legislation. Clark reminded Fielding that under the third clause of the Act that "it imposed no penalty for the refusal of a ticket." Fielding feigned surprise at finding "the Lawyer and Coachman so admirably combined" but informed Clark, that under the new Act he was punished for the refusal by losing the fare, but he stood accused of abusive behaviour, which came under previous Acts of Parliament. Fielding's "construction" could only work if the driver was summoned for an offence other than the actual refusal. The Hackney Coach Act said nothing about abuse or insolence or physical violence, and whilst these offences may occur as a consequence of a refusal to give a ticket, the drivers to date had all been summoned for the actual refusal of giving a ticket, for which the magistrates had no power over. Clark was fined 20s for the abusive language but seeking martyrdom he said he would rather go to prison than pay the fine. When he was told that he would serve seven days in the House of Correction (hard labour, shaved head and a mask to prevent speech) he changed his mind and paid the fine. Carus Wilson placed his moiety of the fine into the poor box – a gesture that emphasised the public duty of bringing the case to court.[100] It is not a too great a leap of the imagination to believe that the case may have been contrived between Carus Wilson and Fielding to bring an end to the false immunity the hackney coachmen thought they now dwelled under. In reality, Carus Wilson reported the abuse originally to the Hackney Coach Office in Essex Street, Strand. They told him that as he had not a ticket, the driver could not be punished and they were powerless to act otherwise. Carus Wilson then heard of Fielding's interpretation and applied for a summons at Queen Square, where he received satisfaction.

Fielding had greatly embarrassed the Hackney Coach Office. They had turned away over 100 coach-masters and dozens of irate passengers. Telling them that unless a ticket was issued, they were powerless to act. Now Fielding made them look like a bunch of amateurs who had no idea of the laws they were empowered to enforce. They could do nothing more than confirm that the action taken by Fielding was the correct one. Any driver guilty of abuse or misbehaviour could be punished under the previous acts which were still in force.

Fielding may have created a rod for his own back. Passengers with complaints preferred to take the case to Queen Square, rather than risking failure at another police court.

A month after the tickets were first issued, the *Morning Post* remarks that the first case to appear in court where a ticket had actually been issued showed "what an extraordinary state" existed. Lieutenant Bernard Crump, of the 31st Regiment, applied for a summons having suffered abuse from his driver, Edward Broad, when he insisted on a ticket. Broad refused to issue one unless he was paid the 2s fare up front. Crump paid the money and was given a ticket for 1s 6d, which was also out of date – the first reference to tickets being dated and valid for a month at a time.[101]

On October 7th 1814, Fielding's fellow magistrate at Queen Square, Colquhuon, had several drivers before him, all accused of abuse following the request of a ticket. Joseph Bench was fined 20s plus costs as were two other unnamed drivers. Edward Broad was then brought up for issuing the wrong value ticket to Lt. Crump. Broad was found guilty and fined 20s plus costs which he refused to pay. He was not seeking martyrdom like Clark before him, he knew he was going to prison anyway. Earlier that week he had picked up a lady, who upon enquiry, was told the fare would be 2s. On arrival at the destination, Broad said he could not take less than 3s. The lady agreed to pay the exaction but requested that Broad accompany her to the house where she could obtain the extra shilling but she would require the appropriate tickets. Broad would not accede to the request and refused to let her leave the vicinity of his coach. He pushed her against some railings and also pinched and used abusive language against her and it was not until a passing gentleman chanced upon the scene that she was rescued. A warrant had been issued for Broad's arrest and now he was told that unless he could raise suitable bail he would be sent to Bridewell. Not being able to give any sureties, Broad was locked up.[102] Bernard Crump would be before Colquhuon again just a fortnight later after he was overcharged by a driver for carrying three large pieces of luggage. As the luggage did not weigh more than three persons, the coach was licensed to carry four people, and Crump was the only passenger, the driver was fined 20s plus costs.[103]

Even though Fielding and Colquhuon were fining drivers at Queen Square, their fellow magistrates at Bow Street said they were powerless to act. It was not the last time a driver could be innocent in one court, but guilty at another for the same offence. As a declaration of the ineptitude of the Act, the first clause of the 1815 Hackney Coach Act was to repeal the relevant clauses referring to tickets. The ticket system was dead and buried, a resounding success for a number of the drivers to continue their exorbitant demands.

The fiasco of the ticket system was all but forgotten when it was resurrected with Fitzroy's London Hackney Carriage Act of 1853. As already alluded to, this was the Act that created the first general strike of cabs in London, so was as good as any then, to bring in something that was controversial. This time, and showing that the legislature at least, had a long memory, the Act covered itself that offenders were liable to a fine of 40s for any offence covered by the Act, even if no penalty was appointed to it in the relevant clause. It was the wording of the relevant clause, the eighth in this instance, that would later cause problems for many cab drivers; "Every Driver of a Hackney Carriage...shall, on each Occasion when such Carriage shall be hired, deliver to the Hirer thereof a Card..." There was only one interpretation to be put to this clause - that the driver was compelled to give a ticket to his hirer as soon as he was hired.

The wording on the tickets was left to the Commissioner of Police and under the new Act, all proprietors were to ensure that their drivers had a sufficient amount of tickets for each shift. One of the first drivers to appear in court was George Downes, 11776. He had been summoned for overcharging by 6d and it was also stated in court that he refused to give a ticket. Downes admitted to the overcharge but denied that he had not given a ticket. He pulled from his pocket a piece of card with the plate number of his cab written on it in ink, which he proudly professed as being exactly the same as the one he offered the prosecutor. When the magistrate informed Downes that the ticket should be printed, and was therefore not authorised, he also thought that Downes' master should be brought up on a charge of issuing false tickets. Downes was fined 20s plus costs for the overcharge.[104]

At first the condition of having to give a ticket at the commencement of a fare was not accepted by the courts. Four drivers had been summoned by the police to appear at Marlborough Street for not having given a ticket to the passenger immediately on being hired. Bingham, the magistrate, threw all four cases out, as he interpreted the Act as meaning a ticket could be given at any point during the journey and the police had offered no proof that a ticket would not be offered at some point.

George Collyer found himself in the dock for not giving a ticket at the start of the hiring, but he did give one when prompted at the end. Collyer was not charged with any other offence than not giving a ticket at the start of the hiring. A contravention of the law that his passenger, a gentleman named Carlton, thought so great it was worth spending at least half a day in a police court. Hardwick the magistrate at Marlborough Street, stated that he was aware there were differences of opinion as to the legal interpretation of when the ticket should be given out. He, however, was in no doubt that it should be at the commencement of the hiring and he fined Collyer 10s with costs.[105] Similarly, William Walter was before a magistrate on the sole charge of not giving a ticket at the beginning of the hiring, he was fined 5s plus costs.[106] The only consolation for the drivers in these cases was that even the magistrates, as asserted by the fines, were loath to severely punish someone for a minor indiscretion of the law, especially when there was no evidence of abusive language.

A merchant took a cab in August 1853, from Kings Cross Station to Finsbury and was charged what he perceived to be an exaction. He requested a ticket and was given one, and the owner of the number given on the ticket, George Bolton, was summoned to bring the driver to court to answer to the charge. As the cab was doubled up, Bolton brought both drivers into court, but the passenger could not swear to either of them. Bolton informed the court that, "He was in the habit of furnishing his drivers every morning with a stated number of tickets to present to their passengers, but in nine cases out of ten they were regarded by the latter as mere useless encumbrances, and he generally found at night that the floor of his cabs were strewed with tickets which had been carelessly cast aside as soon as they were received. Every facility was thus afforded for the distribution of fictitious tickets amongst the unprincipled members of the fraternity, by means of which they were enabled to carry out their fraudulent practices with perfect impunity to themselves, but at the expense of a great deal of trouble and opprobrium to the owners and drivers of the cabs, whose tickets they had surreptitiously contrived to get into their possession."[107]

Perhaps the greatest grievance held by the cabmen on the issue of tickets was that they were virtual hostages to the whim of a vexatious public. True, if they abided by the law and gave a ticket at the beginning of the journey they may have spared a rod for their own back. The drivers would argue that in many cases the tickets would be refused by the passengers, many of whom had no need for them, so the driver usually waited for a request for a ticket before handing one out. A Mr Pritchard did not ask his driver, Richard Parsons, for a ticket, and it is quite unlikely that he made a mental note of the cab number. Pritchard had left a package inside Parsons' cab. The driver found the package and did what he was required by law to do – i.e., take it to a police station or the Lost Property Office at Scotland Yard. It should be noted that at this time, there was no provision in law for taking the item directly back to the passenger (see Chapter 10). The passenger was soon reunited with his package, but took great umbrage at having to pay 5s for his own neglect in having the parcel returned to him. Once having received his property, it was only a matter of looking at the details of the driver who deposited the item, for Pritchard to exact his revenge by summoning Parsons for not giving a ticket. It is no wonder that cab drivers had such a low opinion of the law. Even the magistrate stated that he "could not admire the spirit or the conduct of the complainant"[108] Somewhat reluctantly, the magistrate, Jardine, fined Parsons 5s with 2s costs. "But I have not yet received the 5s awarded to me by the commissioners." Parson's exclaimed. Jardine informed him that that will be paid to him in due course. For having done his duty and handed the parcel into the police, he was now 2s the poorer.[109]

George Bolton's assertion that drivers were exchanging tickets was exemplified when Joseph Clark, 8944, described as an old cabman, was charged with being drunk during his employment. A policeman testified that the cab pulled up alongside him and the passenger informed the officer that he asked the driver for a ticket but he refused to give him one. Which was ironic, as when Clark was taken to the police station and searched, he was found to have 18 different numbered tickets on him, none of which corresponded with the actual number of his cab. Ignoring the calls for leniency from Clark, Combe the magistrate had no doubt that drivers got together and exchanged tickets. This in turn would allow them to extort more than their fare from the public, with no redress to themselves, and an innocent driver hauled up before the court. Clark was fined just 5s for being drunk but his badge and licence were sent to the Commissioner (along with all the false tickets) for revocation.[110] Combe may have also been responsible for sending the first cabman to prison solely on the charge of not giving a ticket. John Davy had appeared before him and was informed by the prosecutor that due to the inclement weather, he gave the cabman 6d above his fare but the driver was continually uncivil and as he had not furnished a ticket, he took out the present summons. Davy was nominally fined 5s plus 2s costs but he could not pay so was locked up for seven days in default.[111]

There is little doubt of Combe's assertion that drivers were conspiring to confuse the public over tickets and even that they were a form of currency. When Thomas Iles, 611, was charged with being drunk, he gave the arresting policeman a ticket that did not correspond to his plate number. When asked how he came by having a wrongly numbered ticket, Iles replied that on the previous night he had taken a drunk cabman home and he paid for his fare with six bogus tickets. The magistrate had been prepared to nominally fine Iles because of the freezing weather he had worked through on the night of his arrest. On hearing from the potential fraud that could be played upon his fares, the magistrate fined him 30s or thirty days in default. The fine was paid.[112]

John Green was summoned for giving a ticket with the wrong number upon it. His cab was plate number 1397 and the ticket he gave was 3167. Fortunately, the passenger had heeded advice to check that the number on the ticket corresponded with the number on the plate. When the discrepancy was uncovered, Green offered his passenger the correct numbered ticket but the passenger retained both and took a summons out for giving the wrong ticket and incivility. In court, there was further confusion when it looked like Green's master was trying to pass himself off as the driver – in order to confuse the passenger. The master, Naish, apologised for giving that impression, how sincere the apology was, is not known. He stated that he was responsible for the mix up as he owned both plates 1397 and 3167 and it was nothing more than a mistake. The magistrate was not wholly convinced and fined Green 20s and costs.[113] William Moss was fined 20s plus costs for giving out a ticket with the number 3342 upon it, whilst his own plate number was 3432, showing a degree of collusion between drivers, especially ones with similar plate numbers.

The tickets were restyled in 1854 to include the name of the proprietor on the reverse. As the tickets were printed at cost to the proprietors there was a reluctance on their part to order up new sets of tickets whilst they still had old ones in stock. Some of the drivers of course were doing their bit by recycling tickets for their own use. Arnold suspected as much when a cabman came before him charged with extortion. The driver denied the claim and said at the time of the alleged offence he was miles away. Arnold asked the driver's master "...if he was aware of any collusion existing between drivers to interchange tickets, and so mislead the public?" The proprietor replied that he "did not know of any such practice existing."[114] Which may have been naive, but perhaps the men in his own garage were honest and it was the disreputable few who searched the back of empty cabs on a rank looking for discarded tickets on the floor.

Just how vexatious the public could be with the ticket system is exemplified with the case of James Martin who took his passenger to court for not paying him his proper and legal fare. The claim was for 5s but due to the wintry conditions Martin thought that 10s would not have compensated him enough for the conditions he had to drive in. Certain of his own case, Martin laid 5s on the table for the route to be measured, which the passenger declined to emulate. Martin was awarded 11s plus costs. His passenger then immediately applied for a summons against Martin for not supplying a ticket at the beginning of the journey. Unluckily for him, Elliott, the magistrate, was happy that as one had been given at some point in the journey, no offence had occurred.[115]

Michael Death had, in July 1871, taken up Lord Vivian from Brooke's Club, St James's, to Grays Inn and then back to the Albany, in Piccadilly. Having been warned by several other cabmen about his Lordship, the cab driver made a note of the times though Lord Vivian disputed the timings given by the cabman. At the end of the journey Lord Vivian had offered Michael Death 2s 6d, which was half the amount the cabman thought he was entitled to, namely 5s. Having listened to both sides, Arnold felt that the cabman was charging too much on the waiting time and accordingly awarded him 3s 10d. Arnold reinforced his earlier ruling, that had been reported in the papers that he would not award any costs, other than the cost of the summons, to a driver who had not offered a ticket at the commencement of the journey. As Michael Death had summoned Lord Vivian for too much, he would not allow him any costs at all, not even the cost of the summons. All he was to receive was 3s 10d. As a defiant gesture that the action was a matter of principle and not of greed, the cabman asked that the 3s 10d be put into the poor box.[116] One can only hope that Death's gesture made Arnold and Lord Vivian appreciate that not all cabmen were out to get every penny they could lay their hands on – some of them had principles as well.

For one cabman at least, the issuing of a ticket at the commencement of the fare proved his case. Cabman Higgs was waiting for a fare in a train station when a man came up to him and told him he would be hired come the arrival of a train in which he was meeting some people. Higgs, seeing that he was now hired, gave the gentleman a ticket and awaited the arrival of the train – which happened to be half-hour late. At the termination of the journey Higgs charged for the extra half-hour, 4d, but the hirer said it was not down to him that the train was late and he specifically told the cabman he would be hired as soon as the train arrived. Higgs summoned the hirer for non-payment of the half-hour waiting time and for the "six or seven minutes in disputing the fare." As far as magistrate Beadon was concerned, the time disputing the amount was dismissed but, the hiring began as soon as the ticket was accepted. Higgs walked away from court with his 4d and costs.[117]

The ticket system was soon reduced to a lame duck, passengers never requested them – technically they did not have to, and drivers rarely offered them. There only use was to satisfy the whims of a vexatious public who, as already noted, were apt to suddenly apply that particular law whenever they wished to punish a cabman. William Banks must have really angered his passenger, a solicitor, in January 1876 as the lawyer took out no less than five summonses out against him *viz*; assaulting him with a whip, being drunk, extortion, furious driving and, of course, refusing to give a ticket. Alderman Finnis dismissed the charges of being drunk and furious driving as they were not proven. As for the charge of not giving a ticket, "Although a cabman was bound to give his fare, one on entering his cab, it was so seldom required that he would not entertain it." That charge was dismissed as well. Fortunately, for the solicitor, he would have retrieved some of his costs as Banks was fined 5s for the overcharge plus 20s for the assault.[118]

Joseph Hoare, sitting at Hampstead police court was of much the same opinion as the Alderman. Before him in the dock was the poetically name William Wordsworth, badge 5628, who was charged by the police of not issuing a ticket. Wordsworth had to take an injured man from Hampstead police station to University College Hospital. The policeman accompanying the injured man needed a ticket so as to reclaim the costs of the cab fare, but Wordsworth, who usually had some on him, professed to not have any on that particular day. On hearing that Wordsworth had remained "very civil" after being charged, the magistrate dismissed the claim on payment of costs of 2s, he himself had been riding in cabs for ten years and had never asked for, nor received one. The police were unhappy with this outcome, especially with regards to their expenses. They wanted another shilling for "cost of service" and the costs of travelling down to Wimbledon to serve the summons (though Wordsworth lived in Lisson Grove). The magistrate would not budge and all Wordsworth had to pay was the 2s cost of the summons.[119]

The system appears to have never been repealed but the Act of 1907, which modernised the embryonic taxis of London by ensuring that all motor cabs carried a taxi-meter, still allowed for the issuing of tickets. The proprietor was still liable for ensuring that the driver had tickets on him but the driver would only be compelled to issue a ticket, if asked – a complete turnaround from earlier legislation. They no longer had to be individually printed with the cab number and proprietor's name upon them. Such details, along with the proprietor's address, could be written down on the pro-forma ticket by the driver, if and when required.

7 Taximeters

Taximeter to be fitted and sealed.

It has been stated that the term 'Taximeter' is named after Baron Von Thurn und Taxis - allegedly the inventor of the machine. The Baron may have had much to do with brewing, but absolutely nothing with taximeters. The term actually derives from the Latin *taxon* – to charge for, and the Greek *metron* – to measure. The introduction of taximeters was long heralded as a means of preventing drivers imposing upon passengers, particularly the lone female. Though would the cab drivers themselves allow such a machine to be used?

According to John Evelyn in 1657, his friend, Colonel Blount, "showed me the application of the way-wiser to a coach, exactly measuring the miles, and showing them by an index as we went on. It had three circles, one pointing to the number of rods [5½ yards], another to miles, by 10 to 1000, with all the subdivisions of quarters; very pretty and useful."[1] Despite its apparent usefulness, the way-wiser was never manufactured, its demise may have had more to do with the condition of the roads at the time than an unnecessary check by hackney coachmen.

It was with the latter in mind that a J.W. Lee saw the need for a device to rein in the hackney coachmen. In his pamphlet aimed at members of parliament, published in 1828, he denounced hackney coaches as "convenient nuisances" and that only those people who have to travel by them "can have any idea of the impositions that are continually practised by the drivers of them, when the *Fare* is charged by *Distance*, and which many, who are aware of the overcharge, submit to, rather than lose valuable time in an application to a police office; but when the great majority of persons who use these machines [hackney coaches] are known to be ladies, sailors, country people, and others, quite ignorant of the legal charges, it is quite within bounds to state, that one fourth of the *fares by distance* is imposition – that a 1s 6d fare is charged 2s – a 3s fare 4s – and in that proportion throughout." Lee went onto give a figure, in his mind a conservative one, that the amount the public are being robbed of each year was £40,950. Lee goes on to explain that his "Indicator" would be affixed to the rear axle of a coach, and be sturdy enough to survive "the shake of a carriage going over the stones, or any accidental blow" – such as from a hackney coachman with a large stick. He estimated that his "Indicators" could be built at a unit price of less than £5, and which would be paid for initially by the public by way of a surcharge on the legal fare. He envisaged the day however when a hackney coach or cabriolet would not be allowed on the streets unless an "Indicator" was fitted. He expected opposition to the initial costs from the proprietors, but "the money extorted by overcharge from the public; does not find its way to the proprietors of the Coaches, but is spent at the gin-shop by the drivers, who, from this cause, more than any other, are the drunken, dirty, dissolute set of beings, they too frequently are found to be." He had applied to the Hackney Coach Office but his invention was dismissed as being "unpractical" and so he was forced to appeal to members of Parliament to try and force the Hackney Coach Office to adopt his idea. As nothing appears to have been heard of the "Indicator" it appears the members also thought its implementation was "unpractical".[2]

There then followed a spate of such devices. "A single and ingenious contrivance" was how a newspaper described the Patent Mile Index machine in 1841. "Such an instrument would have the happy effect of preventing, or deciding, disputes with cabmen."[3] The public, however, would have to wait for the "happy effect". The editor of one national newspaper called for it to be installed in every cab in the kingdom, "It would relieve the public of an immense tax in the shape of overcharged fares. Candidly speaking, we believe the greatest curiosity in nature would be an honest cabman – one who only asked his legal fare, and no more. We should like to be introduced to such a man. He ought to be stuffed at the nation's expense, and deposited in the British Museum where he would rank as a sphynx, or a mummy in the visitors admiring wonder."[4]

A better class of driver was envisioned by the directors of the Economic

Cab Company in 1851. Only men who could provide security for their honesty, sobriety and civility were to be employed. Each man would wear a livery and any man found smoking would face instant dismissal. Each of the drivers would be paid wages and the cabs were to charge 4d a mile, half of the current fare. "To prevent any fraud or imposition being practised by [the drivers] on passengers...an indicator on a very simple principle will be attached to each vehicle, the dial plate of which will be in the interior of the carriage fronting the passenger, so that he can ascertain to a furlong the distance he has travelled; nor can the driver defraud the company, as the indicator will be secured on the cab leaving the yard in the morning, and on its return at night the dial will denote the number of miles passed over during the day."[5] Not being able to tell the difference between dead mileage and miles travelled with a fare-paying passenger probably led to much bad feeling between the drivers and the company. Either way, the Economic Cab Company proved to be uneconomic and the company, like their indicator, disappears from history after the company was dissolved in 1854.

Marcus Davies was a cab proprietor, and apparently a part-time inventor. He made, and patented a "cab indicator" which measured the miles travelled in a "Indicator cab". During the summer of 1852 he was suspicious that one of his drivers, 23-year old Charles Painter was not declaring his earnings, presumably increasing the number of dead miles allegedly looking for work, over miles with the proverbial "bums on seats". Davies sent out two men to engage Painter and they proved that he should be in receipt of at least 9s 6d at the end of the day. Painter only declared 7s and the balance, half-a-crown (2s 6d) he kept, and for this he was charged with embezzlement. The trial went before a jury who found Painter guilty but with a recommendation to mercy. The judge, unmoved by the jury, sentenced Painter to three months' hard labour.[6] Not engaging the meter when you had a fare paying passenger on board would later be called "stalking"; Charles Painter was therefore the first driver to be convicted of such an offence.

Despite the success of a conviction, the Indicator cabs failed to capitalise and appear to be consigned to oblivion, at least in London. A similar device was placed on cabs and omnibuses in Paris, much to the pleasure of the fare paying passengers, and despite calls for their standard introduction into London cabs, nothing was done. Impositions and disputes were to be maintained.

The Society of Arts, always looking at ways of improving the cab trade of London, had, in 1856, called for a device that could be placed in cabs that could measure time and distance. Despite the advances of Victorian ingenuity such a machine was, for the time being, beyond the scope of man. A correspondent to *The Times*, who signed himself "Cabophobia", and may have had an axe to grind with the trade, suggested the simplest solution of a device attached to the wheels to measure distance and a clock inside the carriage to measure time.[7]

Such a device as envisioned by the Society of Arts was actually invented, not by an Englishman as hoped, but by a Frenchman in Paris. His "Kilometric Reckoner" was capable of measuring time and distance as well as the number of jobs the driver undertook each day. *The Observer* may have felt the Reckoner's greatest role was not in ending disputes between the driver and the passenger but between the driver and the proprietor; their headline proclaimed, "New Cab Detector – The Cabmasters Friend." For the proprietor there was a guarantee that a driver could not defraud his master by declaring less miles travelled or a long time sitting on a rank without a fare. The reckoner recorded the number of kilometres travelled whilst engaged, the number of kilometres it might have travelled even though the cab was stationary, and the number of times the cab was engaged. A bell sounded to indicate the meter was engaged and there was a flag or "outer sign" which tells a prospective passenger whether the cab is engaged or not. The Kilometric Reckoner could even distinguish between the first, more expensive mile, than subsequent miles. When stationary the timer would register sufficient fare that would be the same if the cab was travelling at eight kilometres per hour. The benefit for the passenger was obvious. All they had to do was ensure the meter was engaged at the start of the fare, and stopped at the end. A fares sheet inside the cab would then be referred to and the corresponding figures from the dial of the meter would equate to a fare that could not be disputed by the driver.[8]

The *Birmingham Daily Post* reported in 1864 of the invention of a meter, again called an indicator, by a local man. As with the kilometric reckoner the device could measure time and distance and the number of jobs, the driver would have to lower a flag with the legend "For Hire" on it, which would start the meter and at the same time punch a hole in a roll of paper enclosed in the machine. The number of punched holes at the end of the day would indicate the number of jobs undertaken by the driver. The device was actually called "The Patent Cab-indicator and Tell-tale" which seems to indicate that the greatest beneficiaries of such a device would once more be the cab masters, who would be the purchasers of the machine, rather than for the convenience of the public.[9]

In the mid-1890's, "one of the most ingenious pieces of mechanism of the day" was being used by Berlin cab drivers. A third of the German drivers in Berlin had taken on the "taxameter", though not without a little opposition from the remaining two-thirds. But, it was reported that those drivers that had the taxameter installed had seen their income rise from between 30-50%. The public preferred using the taxameter cabs as there was no quibble over the fare, which was actually registered by a dial on the meter, and did not require a conversion chart. A syndicate in London was being formed to finance the importation and use of the taxameter in London cabs. "It not only registers the distance travelled in mileage" argued Charles Hyatt-Woolf, principle investor behind the syndicate, "but gives the equivalent in shillings and pence in accordance with the recognised cab tariff and includes in the amount the usual charge for waiting. The passenger is therefore left in no doubt as to the legal amount he is called upon to pay."[10]

It would be over two years before the first cabs, hansom cabs, would be plying for hire with a taxameter fitted. The meter itself had three dials, one for journeys that began within the radius, one for journeys that began without, and a separate window showing waiting time. The meter was engaged when the flag, now rather confusingly saying "Free", was lowered. The passenger had to make sure the correct tariff was engaged, journeys that begun outside the radius could be charged at a shilling a mile, as opposed to the 6d a mile for those jobs originating within the radius. "The instrument also registers the amount of the daily earnings, extras paid, journeys made and distance in miles travelled since leaving the yard. Altogether these cabs should prove a boon to owners, drivers and the public."[11] Note again the emphasis on the advantages to the owners. It was the masters of fleets, large or small, who the taxameter company had to convince of the advantages of having a meter fitted. As has been seen earlier, if the driver alleges he had a bad day and "came home short" i.e. he could not pay all of his daily rental, then the proprietor suffered from loss of income. Depending on the relationship between the two, the money was either found by the driver by some other means, held over as debt on top of the following days rental, or the proprietor just had to swallow the loss. Human nature being what it is, drivers would invariably plead poverty and try and depart with as little money as possible. The masters were well aware of the ploy and it was up to individual proprietors how they managed their drivers. However, if a driver had an exceptionally good day, the proprietor would not see any of that extra income come his way. The taxameter was capable of changing the system of renting cabs, a system that had survived for nearly three centuries.

Those who drove for the Taxameter Syndicate wore a livery of a brown driving coat and a silk coaching hat. Sat high on the top of a hansom cab they were noticeable, not only by the public but other cabmen. On Easter Monday, 1899, Sidney Crane, resplendent in his uniform supplied by the Taxameter Cab Syndicate, was sitting on his cab outside the Grand Theatre, in Islington. He was noticed by cabman James Wright, who began "chaffing" him and calling him a blackleg. The final straw was when Wright picked up some dirt from the road and threw it directly at Cranes' white coaching hat. For what was called a malicious assault, Wright was fined 40s plus 23s costs.[12]

Two months later hansom cabdriver Robert James Skinner, a member of the London Cab Driver's Trade Union, came across William Jeffreys, driving a horse-drawn taxameter cab along the Strand. Skinner "made some insulting reference to the white hat usually worn by taxameter drivers"; he then tried to force the taxameter cab onto the pavement, which he succeeded in doing but at the same time broke a lamp on the taxameter cab. In court, Skinner laid the blame for the incident firmly on Jeffreys, who he accused of coming out of Villiers Street at too fast a pace. The magistrate said bluntly that he did not believe him, "Taxameter cabs were introduced for the convenience of the public and it was not for any one cabman to oppose them." Skinner was fined 30s plus costs.[13]

Simms, the chairman of the Taxameter Syndicate had announced in 1899 that the cab drivers of London had prevented the syndicate from carrying on its projected business and in 1900 the company went into voluntary liquidation in the hope of starting afresh with a totally reconstructed company.[14]

Without the backing of the union, which at the turn of the twentieth century was stronger than it ever had been, the implementation of taxameters was doomed to failure. Times change. With the syndicate wound up in 1900 because of lack of orders, just five years later, officials from the Union and representatives of the proprietors were travelling to Paris and Berlin to see how the use of taxameters there prevailed. There were many reasons for the change. On the technological front, the first petrol cabs were about to be allowed to ply for hire in London. If a meter could be available for use with the gears of a motor cab, it could be much more reliable than one which relied on the revolutions of the wheels. The more important factor was financial. From 1899 to 1902 Britain had been involved in South Africa, fighting the Boers. A conflict, thousands of miles from London, created a recession that spread throughout the country. Money was harder to come by and the first luxury that went out the window was cab riding. Drivers to the west of London noticed that whereas once they would have had a couple of fares a day from Paddington to the City, they were now lucky to get one a week. Tips had dried up and were said to be either non-existent or at the best, meagre. In 1904 the cabmen went on strike to seek a re-negotiation of the Asquith Award, which set the price throughout the year at which a proprietor could charge on a daily basis for his cab.

Previously, whenever the proprietors had called for a reduction in the tariff, which they alleged would get more people taking cabs, the drivers usually opposed such an idea, as they felt they would lose out if the work did not increase. Now, both drivers and proprietors agreed that the initial fare should be lowered in a bid to take people away from the trams, omnibuses and underground trains that had taken much of the work away from the cabs.

In 1904, after much trepidation, the Metropolitan Police licensed the first motor cab, a French built, Prunel. It was driven by 34-year old James Howe from Hammersmith.[15] In recognition of his achievement, in 1933, when in failing health, he was given badge number 1, signifying his role as London's first motor cab driver. Following his death on Christmas day of that year, his obituary erroneously claimed that he was the first taxicab driver (the Prunel did not have a taximeter, so by definition, could not be a taxicab.) Howe had been one of the first proprietors to engage with the modern era and at one time owned a fleet of thirteen hansom cabs and thirty-three horses.[16]

The London Cab Driver's Trade Union were also happy to embrace the new technology and were running classes for horse cabmen and teaching them the basics of motor car driving from their premises in Gerrard Street. It was however the role of the taxameter in the future of the trade, and the financial impact it would have on its members that was their biggest concern.

The trade delegation that had visited Paris and Berlin to see the effect in those capital cities reported favourably. The taxameter was a success and "created a new class of customer". Quite exactly what was meant by this was not explained, presumably with the fare being incontestable, lone females, as easy prey for French and German cabmen as their London equivalent, were now once more returning to use cabs, exactly the sort of custom that was needed in London. In 1905 *The Daily Mirror* felt that such a seismic change in paying for a cab, needed further explanation:

"Suppose, for example, one takes a cab from Liverpool-street to Hyde Park Corner. As soon as he enters the cab the dial marks the minimum fare 1s. At the Bank it changes to 1s 2d., at Ludgate-circus to 1s 4d., at Wellington-street to 1s 6d., and so on.

Suppose the whole fare, for argument's sake, works out at 2s. One pays that, and 6d. extra to the cabman, and goes one's way rejoicing, without the squabble that is pretty sure to arise under the present circumstances."[17]

It was the prospective 'end of squabbling' that was proving to be the main attraction of the taxameter. Sam Michaels, ex-president of the London Cab Driver's Trade Union stated in 1906, that "Cabdrivers and masters are at present dead set against it... [but] They [the dissenters] will be forced to capitulate or see the utter extinction of the cab trade." He added, rather presciently, "I have no hesitation in saying that the next twelve months will see the taxameter in use in every cab in London." Acknowledging that fares would have to be reduced, he admitted that, "Sixpenny fares for short distances would save the situation."[18]

Not all cab proprietors were against the introduction of the taxameter, many may have thought they would work but at a unit cost of £7 10s, it was a gamble only a few were happy to take a venture with. One such company was one of the largest cab fleets, The London Improved Cab Company which had over 550 cabs and were the largest supplier of the privilege system to the railway stations. They had trialled the Berlin taxameter on hansoms back in 1898 and were always at the forefront of any conflict between the drivers and the proprietors; the manager of the company, James Scott, was also chairman of the Cab Proprietor's Mutual Protection Society (which would later amalgamate to become the LMCPA). The company now sent a circular to all its drivers proclaiming that the taxameter was the only way of rescuing the trade from its present recession. It is an indication of the changing times. Just a few years back Scott and Michaels were literally at each other's throats during the strikes of the 1890's, now they were in full agreement with each other.

The taxameter was a German design and had proved totally reliable. Inspector Bassom of the Public Carriage Office, talking before a Select Committee at the House of Commons, argued that such devices could be tampered with and so he was reluctant to pass any on a cab. The following day a technical advisor to the Metropolitan Police denied this was so. The early taxameters could be tampered with but these had been superseded by subsequent designs which were tamper-proof. It would be later conceded that no meter was completely tamper proof, but adaptions could be made to the meters if and when a problem arose.

1906 was to be a pivotal year in the history of the cab trade, three companies, The Anglo-French Herald Motor Company, The General Motor Cab Company and the Laudalette Motor Cab Company, were all launched, with others formed the following year. Several of them, particularly the General, would use the French equivalent of the taxameter, the similarly named "taximeter".

The Home Secretary, Herbert Gladstone, issued his draft proposals for the restructuring of cab fares in January 1907; it paved the way for 6d fares and taximeters and proved Sam Michaels correct in his prediction from the previous year. There were now, rather confusingly, three tariffs: A horse drawn hackney carriage without a taximeter may "if [the driver] so desires, notify in an approved manner that he is willing to accept a fare of 6d for any journey not exceeding half a mile." The driver still had the option of charging under the old rate of one shilling for up to two miles, then 6d a mile thereafter. A horse drawn hackney carriage that would eventually be fitted with a taximeter would be compelled to travel the first mile for 6d and then each subsequent half mile or part of was chargeable at 3d. It would be slightly more expensive to travel by a motorcab that was fitted with a taximeter, which could now charge 8d a mile, or, after the first mile, 2d every quarter-mile. Each of the three tariffs carried the same charge for extras, such as the carrying of luggage, bikes or extra persons and whilst the horse drawn carriages could charge double the usual rate for going past the radius, a motor cab was limited to the same tariff of 8d a mile, whether inside or outside the radius.

Gladstone also announced that motor cabs with taximeters fitted may be inspected for approval from March 1st, the date the draft order was to come into operation, but from July 1st 1907, only motor cabs fitted with an approved taximeter will be licensed to ply for hire on the streets of London.[19] Having different rates for different cabs was never an ideal method of operation, the public were sometimes easily confused by a single rate. The 6d fares were not universally welcomed by the drivers of hansoms and four-wheelers that did not have a taximeter fitted. They at least now had the option of taking up short fares, if they so desired. No doubt the drivers themselves were best placed to decide if a fare was willing to part with 6d under the new rules, or a shilling under the old ones. The hansoms that would eventually have a taximeter had no option but to charge 6d a mile once the meter was installed. They would lose out on short journeys, a journey of just less than a mile would only cost

6d in a taximeter horse cab, but would cost one shilling in a horse cab without a taximeter. It was hoped however that the loss of income would be supplemented by more people travelling in cabs throughout the day. Whilst the motor cab driver could charge 8d a mile, he had to pay for his own petrol, which was only deducted after his share of the meter reading had been paid to him. The motor cab driver lost out financially on any journeys that went outside the radius, but again, it was predicted that many more people would avail themselves of the opportunity on the longer fares at a pace that was much faster than a horse. Not everyone was happy with the new regulations.

As always, there were major disagreements within the various trade bodies, a situation that prevails to the present day. James Scott representing the Cab Proprietor's Mutual Protection Society said the regulations gave unfair advantage to motorcab drivers "and would utterly ruin horse-drawn cabs outside the four-mile radius and seriously damage the cab owners inside the radius." Alfred Mills, speaking for the Federation of London Cab Proprietors (more formally The LMCPA), whose members represented up to 5000 cab drivers in central London, but not any outside the radius, wanted the radius abolished, so a simpler tariff, in line with the motor cabs could be established. Fred Smith of the Union objected to the taximeter as it "was being introduced by a trust in the interest of a French company." Herbert Samuels MP, who listened to the arguments on behalf of the Home Secretary acknowledged that the three different tariffs were not ideal but it was the best of all worlds for all concerned. If every cab carried a meter, or if every cab became a motor cab the argument would settle itself. In the meantime however, the tariffs would remain, but he did hint that the government were looking into abolishing the four-mile radius, which would appease some quarters of the trade.[20]

Charles O'Donnell, the Liberal MP for Walworth, the area south of the Thames that held the most cabmen, highlighted the lack of taximeters that are available to cabmen still working with a horse. They were victims "of a monopoly by patent of a company in Paris which up to now has been able to supply them to few cab-owners except to the motor companies, which now have 120 motor cabs on the streets, and to a new company [The General] which will place 250 more motor-cabs on the streets on March 1." The one-hundred and twenty motor cabs with a meter fitted were most likely working to the old tariff of 1s for the first two miles, without having the meter engaged. O'Donnell further explained that having recently returned from Paris, he could see that the taximeter cabs were in high favour, and where the public had a choice, they always chose the motor taximeter cab. He warned that in seven days' time [March 1st] the horse cabs of London will not only lose out to several hundred motor cabs which have the attraction of great speed, but they are unable to provide themselves with the singular attraction of a taximeter. The horse cabmen predicted that the motor cabs would secure all their work in the profitable west end, a loss that they could never recover from. One remedy was to delay the introduction of the taximeter. O'Donnell suggested that if the taximeter not be introduced until August 1st, the end of the "London Season" – the most profitable time of year for the cab trade - and not made compulsory until November 1st, then the horse cabmen may avoid a "permanent injury [that would] deprive them of their livelihood."[21]

The government persisted with their timetable. The differentiation between horse cabs and motor cabs should help create work for the former with passengers who balked at paying a shilling, or now 8d, to travel half a mile. Taximeter cabs would not affect the four-wheelers, the Growlers, that worked from the railway stations as they had no capacity to carry luggage and were only licenced to carry two people – despite a number of motor cabs being capable of seating four passengers comfortably. There was nothing that was going to stop taximeter cabs plying for hire on March 1st. Nothing except the union.

March 1st 1907 should have been 'day one' in the history of the taxicab. The General Motor Cab Company had 250 motor cabs, with fully trained drivers, ready to leave the yard in Kennington, along with several other motor cab companies whose cabs were fitted with a taximeter, all of which were ready to invade London. New blood into the arteries of the city. On that day most of the cabs remained in the yard, those that left and went to work, did so without engaging their taximeters. The problem was two-fold. The London Cab Driver's Trade Union had negotiated with the motor cab companies that their drivers should receive a daily wage of five shillings, for six days, plus 10% of the meter reading. This ensured that even on a bad day, a driver would take enough home to provide for his family. The General Cab Company however, wanted to pay their men on a flat 25% commission basis. If the men have a good day, they take home extra; it was an incentive to do more work. Secondly, Gladstone, the Home Secretary, had his attention called to "certain provisions" of the 1853 Hackney Carriage Act regarding fares. It was therefore thought that part of his 1907 order may have to be reconsidered, which meant that the order allowing taximeter cabs to ply for hire could not be granted.

On March 15th the Home Office finally issued the order for taximeter cabs to ply on the streets. But still none could be seen. It is probable that this final hiccup was to do with the conflict between the union and the General Cab Company. The former were still trying to get the men what they deemed to be a reasonable working wage, the General responded by saying the drivers have signed up for 25% share of the meter. If the men were happy, they should be allowed to work. The last thing anyone wanted were pickets outside motor cab yards on what was supposed to be an epochal moment of history.

On Saturday 23rd March 1907 that moment of history arrived when taximeter cabs left the yard of The General, and took "London by storm". Depending on the source, there were between 70 and 76 taximeter cabs plying for hire on that day. The union were not entirely happy, they mounted pickets at selected cab ranks but it had very little effect on the new arrivals. The fares book, which the driver was still required by law to carry, was defunct. Not only had the tariff changed but Londoners now found themselves for the first time paying extra whilst sitting in a traffic jam. When the fare was calculated by distance, as had sufficed for the previous 250 years, no extra charge could be added for a block, or stop, what we now call a traffic jam. To many, having the meter tick away an extra 2d without the taxi moving was rather disconcerting, and possibly all was not lost for the hansom cab without a taximeter. It was also stated that it was in the driver's best interest to take a passenger the shortest distance as it was the driver who had to pay for the petrol. The General

Cab Company were ecstatic over the success of the first day of operations and they promised they would be releasing three new taximeter cabs a day until they reached their goal of 900.[22] The taxicab was here to stay - though not according to a judge at Southwark. A cabman before him had fallen into debt, "I have not averaged £1 a week since the taximeter cabs came along – they take all our work away." The un-named judge made an order that the cabman should pay off his debt at the rate of 2s a month, "It will take you three years to pay the amount. By that time these machines may have passed away."[23]

The problems facing the drivers of horse drawn cabs were all too real. In July 1907, E. H. Bayley, highlighted their plight in a letter to *The Times*. Bayley described himself as "the chairman of the largest cab company in London", which happened to be the London Improved Cab Company (he was also a director of the United Horseshoe and Nail Company). The London Improved Cab Co. had been at the forefront of introducing taximeters to London's horse-drawn cabs. As previously stated, they had backed the taxameter, but the taxameter had yet to be approved by Scotland Yard, and they could not get their hands on a French taximeter. Bayley blamed one person for the disaster happening to the hansom cabmen, Herbert Gladstone, the Home Secretary. "People ask why the ordinary hansoms are not fitted with taximeters, and the reply is that permission cannot be granted from the Home Secretary. The public are the losers as well as the cabmen and the proprietors, as my company [...] are prepared to put 400 cabs with taximeters on the streets and charge 6d per mile, whereas the French company charge 8d per mile." He further explained that all correspondence with the Home Secretary has not received any reply and in consequence, "the foreign company is enjoying the advantage of a lucrative monopoly and the English companies are being ruined."[24]

Bayley's letter elicited a response from Davison Dalziel, chairman of the London General Cab Company (The General Cab Company and the United Cab Company had recently amalgamated under the umbrella of the London General, but each company was to retain their own separate identity). His was the 'French Company' alluded to by Bayley, and he strongly asserted "that no French company is running taximeter motor cabs in London." He did admit that the cabs were built in France, and that the taximeter had a French patent, and even that some of the directors were French. Nevertheless, the General and the United Cab companies were English companies with limited liability, albeit with French co-operation. And anyone who doubted the fact were quite welcome to visit the Brixton Road garage of the General Motor Cab Company.[25]

Gladstone signed the order allowing horse cabs to ply for hire with a taximeter on August 25th 1907, but by the end of October there still was no sign of any of them. "The result being that," complained a xenophobic cab proprietor, "as everyone prefers a taximeter to an ordinary cab, the French company are enjoying an extraordinary lucrative monopoly while the unfortunate English companies are being squeezed out of existence."[26]

To many, it felt like the extinction of the horse cab was occurring by design, and not as an accidental by-product of technology. Horse cabmen were abandoning their hansoms and taking driving lessons in order to pass the harsh driving test supervised by Scotland Yard. A cabman was allowed three attempts at the driving test, if he had not passed by then he was forced to go back on the horses, or look for another profession all together.

The sixpenny hansoms, or "tannercabs" as they became quickly known by, eventually appeared on the streets in the beginning of February, 1908, when the London Improved Cab Company put 17 of their cabs out, with the men being paid a third of the daily meter reading.

The tannercabs were an instant success but it was too little, too late. The editor of the *Daily Express* recorded in his diary that the "horse cab was assured permanency", it was another forlorn hope. At their peak in 1898 there were 11,519 horse cabs plying for hire in London. There numbers fluctuated until 1907 when they began an irreversible fall. By the time of the outbreak of the Great War, there were less than 1400 horse cabs in the capital. Shortly after the Second World War they disappeared completely.[27]

The honeymoon period with the taximeter lasted less than a year. Soon passengers were complaining that there was a variation in the price they paid for the same journey. Questions were asked in the House of Commons. Scotland Yard responded by saying that only motor cabs with a seal supplied by the Physical Laboratory at Kew, where the meters were originally tested, would be passed at the annual inspection. Which begged the question of why the meters were not sealed in the first place. It is hard to ascertain just how accurate the meters were after they had been in use over a period of time. The public had been used to paying a specific sum of money for a given distance, it mattered not if the road was clear or packed. What they could not comprehend was that whenever the taximeter cab slowed down to below 6mph, or stopped completely in traffic, the timer mechanism of the meter would kick in and carry on adding the 2d increments. The public trusted the taximeter, the drivers had yet to win their confidence.

When a cabman summoned a doctor for bilking him, the doctor informed the court that the driver had "shaken him from the seat through...constantly applying the brakes." The doctor had heard that constantly hitting the brakes affected the meter. He must have had some sympathy from the magistrate who dismissed the summons from the cabman, who not only lost the fare, the 2s cost of the summons but a day's loss of earnings by going to court.[28] That particular story had been headlined "A New Terror", nobody could accuse the *Daily Mirror* of sensationalism, even back then. The more sedate *Times* was calling it "Robbery by Taximeter", the driver and the taximeter, the perfect symbiosis of a dastardly duo. "I have little doubt that some taxicab drivers are always "on the make" whenever the opportunity presents itself," wrote one correspondent.[29] In response, another frequent user of taxicabs suggested that it was the different types of meter that gave different readings, "I have repeatedly found that the small oblong type of meter records a lower fare over the same distance than the round type [both taxameters] and it has been a matter of some surprise to me for some time that the Scotland Yard officials have not taken notice before now of the higher fares recorded by the type of meter in use on a particular series of cabs, which I will not further identify, but which I always endeavour to avoid for that reason [possibly the taximeter in General Motor Cabs' Renaults].[30]

According to some taxi-cab drivers, "street Arabs", urchins, or what today would be called "teenagers" would creep up on a taxi when the driver was not looking and pull the flag down, thus starting the meter. Even if the flag was raised to the "stop" position immediately after, it would still register 8d, six-pence of which would have to be paid to the proprietor. No doubt some drivers used this as an excuse in order to keep more money than they were entitled to, but for a driver to be believed more than once was wishful thinking. It may have been a self-fulfilling prophesy.

Henry Charles Howell was on his way to pick up two ladies from the Drury Lane Theatre when he was hailed by the Marquis de Vallecerrato on a cold January night in 1911. Howell ignored the young man's hand but was forced to stop further up the road. The marquis ran up to Howell and demanded to be taken, but the cabman told him he was already engaged. With that, the marquis proclaimed that he, "...had had enough of you taxi-drivers," stood upon the running board and engaged the meter. Howell asked for the 8d that now registered on the meter and it was clear that de Vallecerrato was not willing to pay. When Howell got out of his cab, he was struck in the face. A policeman soon arrived and Howell said he would rather be allowed to punch the young man back than have his name and address. He was however prevailed upon to take the latter option. In court de Vallecerrato said the taxi driver acted like a madman and that he was only trying to defend himself. The magistrate told him that he was in the wrong from the very beginning and fined him 20s with 23s costs.[31]

Unauthorised seals etc

No unauthorised person shall seal or mark a taximeter or remove or tamper with a taximeter or its mechanism, or break, alter, deface or otherwise tamper with the seal or mark of a taximeter.

There proved to be several ways in which a dishonest driver could tamper with his meter and in doing so would be guilty of defrauding the cab company and possibly the passenger. One method, the 'wire trick' was to drill tiny holes into the glass fronting the totaliser dials, which were a small set of dials at the rear of the meter, the readings from which were taken at the end of each shift and the driver would then be told how much he had to pay in. A thin piece of wire could be inserted through the hole and the numbers on the dial could be forced backwards, thus ensuring the company received less money than they were entitled to. If the flag of a Bell type meter was pulled right down, then brought back up to "nearly level" it would register on the front (the passenger's side) but not on the rear. With the aid of a mechanic, employed by the cab company, the ratchet wheel of the Dreadnought meter could be reversed, so the totals were not entered on the back, On another type of meter, if a button was turned three times it would lower the flag and the meter would be legally operative, turn the button five times and this would disconnect the totalizer readings at the rear of the machine; a piece of India rubber between the flag and the bell would ensure that the 8d could be trapped. In all these types of tampering, the passenger would be none the wiser, in fact with several of the meters, even an honest driver would have been unaware that he could manipulate the dials. There were two 'nuclear' options, both of which needed the compliance of the passenger. Firstly, there was "stalking"; this was a matter of convincing the passenger that the meter was not working and that some arrangement could be made as regards the fare. This method was particularly successful to the driver even though, at the end of his shift, he would have to clock up several 8d minimum fares just to allay suspicion from the management. The second option involved "roaders", long journeys, usually outside the Metropolitan Police District. The star wheel would be disconnected from the drive gear which would completely incapacitate the meter. Once shown how to disconnect and reconnect the star wheel, a driver could do it themselves in a couple of minutes by crawling under the cab.

Prior, and some would say, continuing after the First World War, the motor car had a novelty attraction to many people. To most, owning such a vehicle was far beyond what they could afford; a taxi could fulfil the need of actually owning a motor vehicle when so many were at one's beck and call. In 1907, wedding parties were using the motor cab over the traditional horse cab. Other than weddings, the hire of a taxicab for an excursion out into the country, or to the coast was a favourite pastime of many people. Many of these jobs were done 'on the meter', the Fiat Motor Cab Company even produced a map book for its drivers, concentrating not on London, but on the home counties. There were other cabmen, like Henry Ellerington, who preferred to do these types of journeys 'off the meter' with a disconnected star wheel.

When the General Motor Cab Company sent out its first batch of motorcabs onto the streets in March 1907, Henry Ellerington may have feared the worst. He was in his 60th year and for many of them years he had been a hansom cabman. Henry was previously mentioned in Chapter 4 where he successfully defended himself against a charge of being drunk on duty, but was unsuccessful in bringing assault charges against the arresting police officer. In an effort to see if an old dog could learn new tricks, Henry applied to drive for the General in July 1909, a garage where his two sons, Harry and George were both employed as drivers. As the General's fleet expanded, they needed more drivers and were quite willing to train them. The London Cab Driver's Trade Union had been teaching drivers from its offices in Gerrard Street in conjunction with the General Cab Company, whose drivers were all union men. In October 1909, Henry Ellerington began learning to drive and three weeks later he passed the Metropolitan Police driving test and was re-issued with a 'bill' – his Motor Cab Licence.

If a meter had to be replaced, if one of the dials were not registering properly etc, there were mechanics on hand at the General who could replace the meter without having to have the cab re-inspected by Scotland Yard carriage officers. If the meter suffered a serious malfunction the driver would take the cab to the workshop of the Metropolitan Fare Register Company in Belvedere Road on the South Bank. If the machine was found to be defective through no fault of the driver, then the company would be charged the average daily takings of the driver, an incentive to get the cab back on the road as quick as possible. Some of the engineers at the General were actually employed by the Metropolitan Fare Register Company but permanently based at the cab yard. They soon discovered that they could make a few shillings on the side with certain drivers who were themselves willing to work with a meter that would give false readings.

George was apparently the first of the Ellerington's to work with a meter that had been "fixed" and when Harry was re-employed by the company, after having been in hospital, he was introduced to a mechanic at the General who fixed a meter to his cab that could be manipulated by careful positioning of the flag so as not to record the totals on the rear of the meter. With both sons now working with an illegal meter, it was not long before the father, Henry, was also boosting his income. He had known an out of work mechanic for several years, and there is some suggestion that the mechanic went around the various cab stands, offering to disconnect the star wheel from the gear box in return for remuneration. The same mechanic would say he also disconnected the star wheel on Harry Ellerington's cab as well.

In April 1910, Henry was taken off his regular cab because of his low earnings, whether this was due to constantly disconnecting the star wheel, or his age, was not known. He became an odd day man, sitting around in the yard hoping to take a cab out whose regular driver failed to turn up for work. Henry managed to survive being an odd day man but he supplemented his income by taking out Harry's cab on excursions out of London a number of Sundays throughout the summer. These journeys would include a wait and return to Windsor, for which he was paid £1 with a 2s tip; there was a job to Watford and several jobs to Hookwood in Surrey. On each of these trips the star wheel was disconnected, even though the meter was one that had been tampered with.

It was following the return from Hookwood on August 21st that it all began to unravel for the Ellerington's. As Henry, on one of his excursions, passed through Reigate, they were nearly in a collision with a horse and carriage, which was forced off the road by the taxicab. Several weeks later, by which time Henry had done other Sunday excursions, a manager at the General received a claim from the female driver of the carriage, who took the registration number of the taxi, and had traced it to their garage. Harry Ellerington was called into the office and asked why he had not reported the accident in Reigate. Harry denied all knowledge of it but did say that his father had worked the taxi that day. Henry was also questioned, as well as giving a statement, dictated and signed by Harry as his father was illiterate. Henry denied all knowledge of the accident or that he had even left town that day.

Henry Ellerington was arrested by the police as he was waiting to pick up a cab at the yard of the General on November 14th. When he was charged with fraud and larceny at Brixton police station, he told the arresting detective that he knows he was "given away", informed on, and in his first appearance in court the following day, he asked the magistrate for a remand for a week so he could inform on other people. The next day Henry Ellerington met with the arresting detective and informed him that not only was John Kay, the out of work mechanic, guilty, but he also named his son as being guilty as well.

On hearing that his name had been put forward by his father, Harry went to see the claims manager, Wilson, at the offices of the General at Kennington. Ellerington was asked why the meter of the cab that his father was driving had only registered 37 miles and 10s, Harry replied that his father always disconnected his star wheel. There was no doubt as to the illegality of such an action as there were notices placed around the cab yard stating that any driver found guilty of tampering with a meter, would be charged with fraud, Harry was taken to the general manager and asked to repeat his statement. The general manager did not like the idea of a son giving his father away, "My father has accused me of doing something which I did not do, and I am now going to accuse him of doing something that he has done."[32]

Henry Ellerington was perhaps fortunate that his son was not forced to testify against him. He faced over twenty counts of fraud and larceny and his defence team submitted that as he was not a servant of the company, the charges of defrauding that company should be dismissed. The jury had no problem finding him guilty but with a recommendation to mercy given his age, he was now 64. Henry Ellerington was sentenced to four months imprisonment on each charge, which mercifully were to be served concurrently.[33]

At the meeting when Harry had 'shopped' his father, he had been under the impression that the company knew that he had been defrauding them with tampered meters. He was given a verbal assurance that if he told them all he knew about the tampered meters, who was doing the tampering and which drivers were working with those meters he would not be prosecuted for any illegal activity on his part. Harry then named several drivers and the mechanic, Henry Allcorn. Shortly after the conviction of his father, Harry began to panic and asked Allcorn, who must have been under investigation since being named by Harry, to remove the meter that was rigged, with one that gave true readings.

The General Cab Company only became fully aware of the extent of the fraud when they had the meters on all the cabs tested and found a large number of them to be defective, not just at the Kennington yard but also at their Chiswick and Fulham yards.

It was probably Allcorn's arrest that prompted Harry to attempt to leave the country. He was arrested on board the SS Oceanic, whilst it was still in dock at Plymouth, about to set sail for New York, by Detective Inspector Ward from Scotland Yard, the same detective who had arrested his father. Harry informed Ward that, "Now you have got me again, I intend to plead guilty to the falsification and larceny, but I do not intend to be punished for what Allcorn has done. I have paid him sums of money for a faked meter, but I have never received anything from him." Following further questioning he named both the mechanics at the General as working the fraud between them (Allcorn and his predecessor, Thompson) and he also named "a considerable number of drivers who were implicated." When he appeared at Lambeth police court he justified giving names by stating, "I don't see why I should fall for 1500 drivers."[34]

Harry Ellerington and Henry Allcorn stood side by side in the dock at the subsequent trial at the Old Bailey. Harry pleaded guilty, Allcorn maintained his innocence, even with a number of drivers, named by Harry, testifying that the mechanic had tampered with their meters for a price. Harry Ellerington was sentenced to eight months' and Allcorn to nine, both with hard labour.

The General Cab Company was not alone in having taxi drivers trying to defraud them. Henry Hunter, 313, kept his cab out for three days, which was against the rules of the owners, the British Motor Cab Company. When he was arrested by a policeman who recognised the number of the cab from an earlier alert, he was charged with theft. He denied the charge on the basis that he had once before had a taxi for a couple of days (that time claiming illness) and also that he had never gone past the four-mile radius, as if to say the cab had never left its place of work. It was also found that the star wheel had been bent, and so nothing was being registered on the meter, and also that he had removed the lamps from the dials so the passenger could not read the meter. Hunter was sentenced to six month's imprisonment.[35]

Setting taximeter in motion

A taxi driver must set the taximeter mechanism in motion as soon as the taxi is hired and no sooner and stop it as soon as the hiring is terminated and no sooner.

If today's cab driver fails to initiate his meter at the beginning of a journey, it is probably nothing more sinister than forgetfulness. If he notices the fact shortly after and engages the meter, he may lose a fraction of the fare and hope that the passenger might rectify the difference with a larger tip. Alternatively, if his neglect was not noticed until the end of the journey he has to estimate the fare, by using either their own, or the passenger's, judgement. To avoid being accused of overcharging, the driver must always err on the side of caution and give a price that would be under the meter reading if the meter had been engaged the whole journey. Back in 1909, not engaging the meter was deemed a wilful criminal act. Drivers kept a quarter of the total money they received, or rather the total that was registered on the meter. We shall see later the problems of the "extras" caused to the trade. Once a taxi-cab was hired, the driver would lower the metal flag, attached to the side of the meter, which would engage the mechanism and 8d would be shown upon the dial, the 'flag-fall'. If a dishonest driver could agree a price for a journey "It goes 2s 6d on the taximeter, I'll do it for 2s without pulling the flag down" or such similar, the passenger benefits from saving 6d, whilst the driver keeps all the 2s for himself, defrauding his master out of 1s 11d, if the meter had been engaged. Alfred Solomons was one such driver. He had been asked to carry two people from Wardour Street to the Holborn Music Hall, wait for them whilst they performed their act, then take them on to the Crouch End Hippodrome (for another act), wait for them, bring them back via the Holborn Music Hall (and another act) and then home to Wardour Street. George and Emma Ross were the music hall artistes conveyed by Solomons. At the return to Wardour Street he said his fare was nine shillings, which Mr & Mrs Ross thought "very reasonable". Surprisingly, (and rather conveniently), neither had noticed that the dials on the clock had not moved all evening. Happy with the price they paid, they engaged Solomons the following night and subsequently for the rest of the week.

At the end of his shift, Solomons would return his taxi to the General Cab Company's yard at Kennington, and sign a declaration that the meter readings for the night were his true earnings. This declaration would form the basis of the prosecution against him under the Falsification of Accounts Act, 1875. The night-foreman at the yard would take readings from the dials at the rear of the meter, unseen by a passenger sitting in the taxi. The first dial counted the number of 2d increments made whilst the meter was engaged, the meter would add 2d every quarter of a mile or for every ten minutes whilst on the timer; the second counted the number of flag falls – the number of times the taxi was engaged; the third dial recorded the number of extras added to the meter; the fourth dial counted the number of half-miles travelled; the fifth counted the number of half-miles recorded, whilst the meter was engaged; the sixth dial was for non-recorded time, when the meter was not engaged.

It did not take long for the management at the General to become suspicious of Alfred Solomons. The money he paid into the General's cashier had dropped remarkably from his previous earnings. A quick look at the figures from the dials showed them that he was not engaging the meter for long periods of time. On the last day of March, 1909, Solomons was followed by management staff from the General in a private motor car, the car was owned by the General to provide, of all things, private hire work, when a car, and not a taxi was required. Any driver from the General would recognise the car, and possibly the taxi-driver at the wheel, Edward Leopold Coles, despite this, it was still felt the subterfuge would hold. The remarkable thing was it did. At the Holborn Music Hall, Solomons left his cab and a manager went to the taxi and recorded the figures on the dials. He also noticed that the flag was padlocked into position, a precaution against a prankster who thought it a laugh to engage the meter whilst the driver was at lunch, thereby costing him of 75% of whatever value was on the meter when he found out. The process was repeated again at the Crouch End Hippodrome and when Solomons walked away from his cab it was found that the numbers on the dials were exactly the same as what they were at Holborn. They had enough to have Solomons arrested but they needed to discover how the fraud was perpetuated, in order that it could be nullified. The answer came on the following night when Solomons was followed again. When a taxi was hired the flag was perpendicular to the meter in the "For Hire" (or rather confusingly "Free" position); the flag would be turned 90 degrees which would engage the meter. A taxi with passengers and with the flag in the upright position was an easy spot for a policeman. Solomons found that by tilting the flag to about 45 degrees, he could give the impression to any policeman that the meter was engaged when in fact nothing was registering at all on the meter.

Solomons was followed again by the management on the next two nights, they were if anything, thorough in their investigations. On the fourth night the police were also in the car. At one point, Coles, the driver of the private hire car was asked to overtake Solomons so the police could see the position of the flag. Solomons not only recognised the car and the driver, but actually waved at him. If his suspicions were raised, then they were confirmed whilst he waited outside the Holborn Music Hall. A uniformed policeman recorded the numbers on the dials as Solomons sat in the taxi, "routine information" was all that was explained to the now very nervous Solomons.

That was the last occasion he carried Mr & Mrs Ross and it is doubtful if the General let him have a cab again, but it would be three weeks before the police would arrest him in the yard of the General Cab Company. In June 1909 he was before a judge at the Old Bailey, charged with falsification of accounts and larceny. His legal team argued that the taximeter could not be seen in the same way as a ledger and so could not be falsified in the manner defined by the 1875 act, which the judge over-ruled citing modern technology. Solomons was the first driver to be found out in such a manner and nobody knew what sort of penalty he faced if found guilty. Solomons was found guilty on both counts and was sentenced to five months imprisonment with hard labour. Although he was given leave to appeal[36]

The following month Solomons was at the appeal court. His defence team tried to argue that as no contract had been signed between him and the General Cab Company, he was just a servant of the company, who were thus responsible for their employee's actions. It was an oft repeated argument and this case, and others involving the cab trade were to establish the precedent that once a taxi driver took a taxi out of the yard, he was his own free agent. Solomons lost the appeal and was returned to prison to see out the remainder of his sentence.[37]

In the pre-meter days, the amount in extras accrued by a driver had little import for the proprietor. As long as he received his daily rental from the driver he was not concerned whether the money was made from the fare, extras, tips or extortion. Once motorcabs and taximeters were married up, the status quo changed. Drivers no longer had to give a daily rental. Instead, they were guaranteed a wage, usually around £2 a week, and offered a commission of around 25% on what they took on the meter. Initially the drivers would have to pay for the petrol they used, as well as for their uniforms. There were immediate problems with such a system. Some drivers were more than happy with £2 a week and would do just a few fares a day to keep the garage happy. These were soon weeded out as the meters recorded everything the proprietors needed to know, how many miles the taxicab had travelled, how many miles the taxi had driven whilst engaged and how many times the meter was started. These early meters really were the pinnacle of technology as it then was.

The earlier meters had no method of recording extras, they did not need to as, by default, the earliest taxis could carry no more than two passengers (even though they could seat four), nor could any charge be made for luggage. A horse drawn Growler could charge for extra persons when there was more than two, and the motorcab drivers felt they should not be treated any differently. The arrival of the motorcab decimated the hansom cab trade of London, the two were in direct competition with each other. The drivers of the four-wheel Growlers had some respite; they could seat up to four people and carry a quantity of luggage at the same time, but it was only a matter of time before the taximeter drivers invaded their domain such as at the railway stations. When petrol driven cabs first appeared on the streets of London they were banned from entering stations by the railway companies who feared an explosion could result if the petrol was ignited by a burning ember.

It did not take long for the motorcab taximeter drivers to start charging extras, no doubt citing what the horse cabman could charge. A foot rest could be utilised as a seat for a third passenger and space for luggage, chargeable luggage, could be found. It soon became quite common for taxi drivers to be charging for extras, even though there was no method of entering or recording them on the meters. "The unwritten law of the cab trade was that the extras belonged to the drivers."[38]

The proprietors were not prepared to tolerate this much longer. Extra passengers and luggage equated to extra wear and tear upon a taxi – which they were at liberty to repair and make right.

One of the first companies to realise the potential in accruing the extras that a driver could receive was the General Motor Cab Company of Brixton Road. They had invested a lot of money in the motorcab trade of London and were most likely responsible through lobbying for the 1907 Act that compelled all motorcabs to have taximeters. Unlike earlier versions of the taximeter, the one employed by the General could record extras by the driver "punching" a button. From time immemorial, the drivers considered the "extras" to be theirs. Now they had to be registered on the meter and the driver would get a quarter of the total accrued. It was obvious to the drivers that if the extras were not "punched in", then they could keep every penny of the extras. In most cases the public would be unaware that the driver was doing anything untoward as there were several types of meter that did not record the extras at all. The management at the General noticed; and in September 1908 the drivers found, when they picked up their taxis, that the governors had placed a notice inside every taxi, informing the passenger that they should pay only what was added on the meter, and no more. To the drivers, this meant not only a loss in extras, but it was also advising passengers that they did not have to tip the driver. Whoever was responsible for the sign, was responsible for the subsequent industrial action. Of the 800 taxis run by the General, only 130 left the yard that day, and most of these returned once they were made aware of the situation. The General quickly backtracked and removed the offending notices. They insisted on their right to the extras, but they had no wish to deprive a driver of his tips.[39]

The arrival of the taximeter had eradicated the all-too familiar arguments over the fare, which prevented many people from using a cab in the first place. Back in 1906, drivers were literally pleading with the public to use cabs, guaranteeing to abide by the fares book and would be grateful for any tip they received, no matter how small. With the taximeter showing the fare, the public began using cabs again, so much so that even horse drawn cabs would start having them fitted. By not adding the extras to the meter, it reopened the old wounds of the belligerent cab driver at the end of the journey. The drivers maintained it was their perk, their money, so there was no need to enter it on the meter.

Robert James Heaslewood thought much the same. He refused to put 6d on to the extras of the meter after he carried three persons. "It was now a rule," Heaslewood stated, "which he thought was partly allowed by employers, that drivers should be entitled to keep all the extras. Heaslewood's solicitor pointed out that under the Act of 1907, it was stated that, "every motor-cab with an approved taximeter to indicate to the hirer either the fare chargeable or the distance travelled." The solicitor contended that the meter registered the distance travelled and that was sufficient to fulfil the legal requirements. The magistrate, Curtis Bennett, was not impressed with the legal argument. He thought the case was a "get up case" in order to "obtain a decision to legalize what was really a fraud." He dismissed the summons.[40]

What *The Times* described as "a convenient little pamphlet" was produced by *Commercial Motor* magazine and entitled "Twenty Points for London Taxicab Users"[41] Point number one was "DON'T PAY WITHOUT LOOKING AT THE TAXIMETER." Capitals were probably used for emphasis, and not for shouting as with modern day messaging. Point number two advised "EXTRAS MUST BE RECORDED BY THE METER in the space provided." Not many of the taxicab driving public would have been subscribers to *Commercial Motor* but its advice was widely circulated in the press. "It is by no means clear", wrote the editor of *The Times*, "that any arrangement of the kind [drivers keeping the extras without putting them on the meter] is recognised by the cab proprietors, but if it does exist, the sooner it is abrogated the better. The great advantage of the taximeter is, or should be, that it informs the passenger precisely what amount he can be legally called upon to pay..."[42] It was clear to the editor of *The Times*, that the bad days of when a cabman demanded a fare of his own choice, was not too far away.

The London Motor Cab Proprietor's Association (LMCPA), an amalgam of the leading taxi fleets, consulted with the Commissioner of Police on having a notice placed in every taxi advising passengers to pay only what was on the meter, exclusive of any tip. Fred Hill of the London Cab Drivers' Trade Union countered that drivers did not enter the extras "until they have received them as they might have to pay the amount out of their own pocket (not such an uncommon occurrence as the [public] may think)."[43]

Following the dismissal of a driver from the Waterloo Cab Company (the same company which Heaslewood drove for), the men there refused to take a taxi out unless they were allowed to keep the extras and their colleague was reinstated. The strike, at least in the beginning, remained just with the Waterloo cab men. It threatened to spread to other yards after the LMCPA stated drivers keeping the extras was defrauding the proprietors out of £150,000 a year, a figure which the men felt was preposterously high. But was it? Given that there were just over 5000 taxicabs in London at the time and the drivers worked a six-day week, the figure breaks down to just under two shillings per day per cab. Not an unreasonable estimate. The drivers would argue that they could only usually attain sums like that during the busy periods of the season, early May to the end of July. The strike at the Waterloo Cab Co, which involved about 100 drivers ended just after a week when the men agreed to take the taxis out in return for the company agreeing "to look at" the men retaining the extras. The man whose sacking had sparked the strike, he was only an "odd-man – taking out a taxi on the odd days when the regular driver was off sick etc - was reinstated.

The problems with settling the strike earlier were confounded by the fact that the men at Waterloo were subscribed to two different unions, the Motor Cab Drivers' Protection Association and the London Cab Drivers' Trade Union. The management stated from the early hours of the strike that they would only talk with a representative body of the drivers, not outsiders from two different unions. Both sides agreed that unification would put them in a much stronger position but many of the men, especially from the MCDPA were reluctant to form an alliance with the LCDTU whom they thought were too eager in calling men out on strike. The two bodies did eventually amalgamate and the dissatisfied proprietors formed a new body, the Motor Cab Owner Drivers Association, later just the Owner Drivers Association (ODA), and which would go onto form the Westminster Insurance Group (which in turn would develop its own taxi, the Winchester) and form its own radio taxi service ODRTS, which survived as a driver's co-operative, Dial-a-Cab, until it was decided by the members to sell up in 2018.

A second consequence of the publicity around the extras issue was regarding tips. The press was now arguing that if the extras were the perk of the driver, then why should a passenger tip as well. The taxi drivers were now being portrayed as greedy and willing to extract every penny they could from a gullible or timid passenger. The drivers countered by claiming that tips were not as forthcoming as the public believed. In fact, so many taxi drivers complained bitterly about just how small the tips they did receive were, it prompted those who usually gave larger tips to realise they had been over generous and would reduce their bounty accordingly.

The arguments over the extras rumbled on into the following year. A Home Office Departmental Committee looking into the issue of fares in general remarked that, "The whole system is unfortunate, as it leads an otherwise honourable class of men to appropriate under a claim of perquisites, that to which they know they are not entitled, and which they pay over only when detected."[44] The LMCPA, whose members now represented nearly 7000 taxis, announced that they would be sending out inspectors to railway stations and principle ranks, and take the numbers of any taxi where it was believed the driver did not punch in the extras at the commencement of the hiring. Taxi drivers who were caught were initially handed a warning, which could rise to a suspension before dismissal from the garage – with the unlikely prospect of gaining employment from another federation garage.

It did not take long for the inspectors to make their first 'kill'. Less than a week after the Waterloo men had returned to work, a driver named Bryant, who worked for the National Cab Company (about 500 taxis) was told that he had been seen at Paddington Station accepting a job that carried extras of 4d. He was now ordered to pay the company 3d, less his 25% commission, for those extras. Bryant denied that not only did he not do a job that involved extras, he had not been to Paddington Station at all the previous day. The company were not satisfied and told him he would not be able to take another cab out unless he paid the outstanding threepence. His fellow drivers in the yard, on hearing what had transpired, refused to take any cabs out from the yard. The unofficial stoppage soon spread from the Hammersmith Road depot to Harrow Road where the drivers at the Windsor Castle yard walked out in sympathy. Of course, the strike had nothing to do with a "thrupenny bit", it was the use of inspectors, spying on the men, that angered them more. An inspector might note that the extras were not 'punched in' but had no way of knowing if the driver had not charged for the extras at the end of the journey – although most would have done. By the following morning the strike had spread to all the federated garages under the LMCPA umbrella. With 5000 plus taxis remaining in their yards, the Motor Cab Owner Drivers Association were forced to issue a statement in sympathy with the journeymen drivers of the yards, whilst appreciating the hardship faced by proprietors in trying to run a fleet. "Cabs belonging to our members [about 2000] - and in taking which, the public may be sure of not using 'blacklegs' – are distinguished by a diamond-shape brass badge with the letters O.D.A. on it."[45]

Straightaway the strike was felt by the public, "it poured down in torrents" on the first full day of the strike, a Thursday. "Soon, thronging doorways, huddled under shop awnings, men gave up all hopes of a taxicab and decided to take a horse cab, but found that not at all an easy matter. Many hansoms and growlers had returned from an enforced seclusion, but all these were soon snapped up. The hansom cabby's air of dejection was gone, and he was evidently praying that the strike would last. Later, when the theatregoers came out, things were much worse. Not for years had so many people in evening dress been seen walking home..."[46] No doubt the men on strike were ruing the missed opportunity of a busy night, and whilst the inconvenience to the public was evident, a meeting of the drivers at the Empress Theatre in Earl's Court voted unanimously to remain on strike.

The proprietors belonging to the LMCPA were equally adamant that they were not going to open the yards until the dispute culminated in a satisfactory conclusion – for them.

A meeting chaired by Arthur Du Cros MP proved abortive. Du Cros was Managing Director of the Dunlop Pneumatic Tyre Company, founded by his father Harvey Du Cros (now chairman of the company) and J B Dunlop. He was also the brother of William and George, the eponymous W & G of W & G Taxis who owned a fleet of over 1150 cabs in west London. Du Cros announced that the absolute minimum to which the federation garages could agree to, was that the men keep all the extras, the observers are removed and the reinstatement of two men who had been sacked. "The sole condition on which they made that offer was that each driver would pay us 6d per day when he took out his cab, and they asked for that in order to retain the principle that we were entitled to the extras."[47] It was, by all accounts a generous offer, and easily affordable when there was plenty of work. What worried the men were the lean days when fares were few and extras even rarer.

Over 70 summons were issued at Lambeth Police Court following an application from the General Motor Cab Company. After coming out on strike, many men still held on to the previous day's takings, many using it as a safety net to buy food and pay the rent. At the outset of the strike the Union advised the men to "do the honourable thing" and pay in the money. Some did, many didn't. The action of the General was said to be the first of many that would be taken out by the proprietors, which the

Union felt was not helping matters. Cab driver John Fitzgerald was not one of the 70 drivers summoned by the General, he was already being held on remand for "converting to his own use £1 13s" which was his takings from his last day. After receiving a lecture on the ruination of the trade caused by strike action, Fitzgerald was sentenced to four weeks, which, due to time already served, effectively meant he was allowed his freedom.[48]

The British Motor Cab Company of Grosvenor Road, Pimlico, broke ranks from the LMCPA when it opened its doors to allow any driver to take a taxi out, on condition of agreeing to pay 6d, in lieu of the extras; exactly the same agreement the LMCPA were looking to establish but neither they, nor the Union, were happy that proprietor and driver had come to an agreement unitarily. Pickets from the Union were immediately sent down to the yard and there were threats to burn the premises down. A few cabs did leave the yard but the police had to be called to ensure the safety of the drivers who were breaking the strike. Two men were hurt and brothers Richard and Thomas Roberts were both arrested; "the former with insulting behaviour and the latter with obstructing the police."[49]

The following day the men from the other garages voted to return to work. In a statement issued by both sides it was stated "that the temporary settlement which has been arrived at is an eminently unsatisfactory one…" The two men who had been dismissed, were to get their jobs back; all the "observers" to be removed; no man to be reported as far as extras are concerned; no further action against the men who had summons taken out against them. In return the men were to pay 6d a day, though a penny was returned to them for rank charges to compensate for the 1d charge to enter a railway station to pick up a fare.[50]

Even though the extras were theirs to keep, the drivers were still not adding them to the meter. Christopher Warner summonsed his passenger, a Major Matheson, for not paying all of the fare. In court the Major stated that the driver demanded 4d for luggage, which he was quite willing to pay, but which were not on the meter. He had been advised that a driver could only charge what was showing on the meter. Horace Smith, the Westminster magistrate, soon educated him on the law; "Can you point to anything in the Act or Order which makes it obligatory for the driver to record his claim for extras?" When the Major replied he could not, he had "just assumed it to be a well-known fact." Horace Smith sympathised with the Major, "It is a very natural thing for the public to assume that the taximeter should record all they are called upon to pay. I thought so myself. If there is an omission in the Home Office Order, it ought to be amended." The Major was told he would have to pay Warner the outstanding 4d and the 2s costs of the summons. He refused any further costs, such as the legal fees Warner had paid for a solicitor to represent him. It was an expensive 4d to chase after.[51]

The LMCPA and the Union tried for the following fortnight to come to a more satisfactory and permanent settlement but were unable to. A Court of Arbitration at the Board of Trade, chaired by Lord St Aldwyn, was asked to settle the matter. They began meeting both sides shortly before Christmas 1911 but it was not until March 1912 that the court published its deliberations. The drivers were to keep the extras which were deemed to belong to them. The proprietors were not to demand any money in lieu of the extras but they no longer had to pay rank or station charges. In return, the men agreed to working a six-day week - many worked just five days of late - with a day being no longer than 15 hours. Whilst both sides agreed beforehand to abide by the decision of the Court of Arbitration, which of course the drivers were happy too, seeing as it met all their demands, the proprietors were none too happy about it. Davison Dalziel MP, a director of the General Motor Cab Company complained that Lord St Aldwyn had far exceeded his brief. The LMCPA held several meetings but reluctantly agreed to abide by the adjudication which would come into force from March 18th 1912.

On that day the men from the federated garages went to work in the full knowledge that the extras belonged to them. The men at the British Motor Company walked out on strike. Since the British Motor Company had broken ranks from the LMCPA, it was no longer a member of the federation. The men had agreed to pay 6d a day, a penny of which was returned for rank and station charges, and in return they kept the extras. Now, with the LMCPA divers keeping the extras for free, the British Motor Cab Company men saw no reason why they should pay 6d for a privilege that was now extended to all other journeymen. The company merely stated that as they were not members of the LMCPA, they were under no obligation to abide by the Court of Arbitration's findings.

Drivers at Bell & Co in Horseferry Road, also walked out, but their dispute was over the price of petrol and although they returned to work the following day, the issue of the price of petrol the drivers had to pay would lead to an all-out and acrimonious strike come 1913. The men from the British Motor Cab Company returned to work after six days, having supposedly won several concessions from the company, which was denied. An irony for the directors was that two days before the walk-out, the drivers had held an annual dinner and invited all the directors of the company and presented the vice-chairman with a gold watch. In response to the generosity of the men, the directors agreed to abandon a 5d "hiring charge" which all the garages charged. That same night Fred Smith, president of the Cabdrivers Union informed the drivers that the company would continue to charge them 6d a day in lieu of the extras, and that they would be the only drivers paying such a tax. Smith recommended that the men not work until the company accepted the terms of the St Aldwyn Award.[52]

The situation, which must have been confusing for those members of the public who were not regular taxi users was allowed to continue up until 1935 when the Cab Order of the previous year stated that extras were only chargeable when added to the meter.

8 Bilking by Hirers

Non-payment of fare

If a hirer refuses or omits to pay the fare, the driver may within 28 days complain to a justice, who may grant a summons against the hirer.

To the cab driver, non-payment of a fare is bilking and, other than as a term used in the card game cribbage, appears to be exclusive to the cab trade. The word itself has been around for nearly as long as hackney carriages and was brought into the English language by the playwright Ben Johnson in his 1637 play, *The Tale of Tub*:

Tub: Hee will ha' the last word, though he talke bilke for 't

Hugh: Bilke? What's that?

Tub: Why nothing, a word signifying Nothing; and borrow'd here to express nothing.

Once drivers began charging complete strangers to take them from one place to another, so those self-same strangers have been trying to evade the fare. And continue to do so.

In 1732 hackney coach driver Thomas Oulton was suspicious of his passengers after they had made several stops. He believed that "they wanted an Opportunity of jumping out of the Coach, and bilking me of my Fair [sic]". Oulton was right to be concerned. After taking the two men down to a public house in Wapping he had to follow them on foot through several tiny streets and alleys. When he was in the centre of a rookery, surrounded by thieves and prostitutes, he was robbed of the 3s, or 3s 6d, he had in his pocket. His assailant, a notorious character named William Flemming, had only that day been released from Newgate prison. Oulton managed to get out of the thieves' den with only the loss of his money. Flemming was captured shortly after and following his trial at the Old Bailey he was sentenced to death and executed.[1] Today, bilkers are fortunate that they may only face up to a month in prison.

Herbert Asquith, when acting as Home Secretary in 1893, once advised a deputation of cab drivers that was before him that in order to avoid being bilked – they should not pick up the bilkers in the first place. With such foresight, it is little wonder that he would eventually become Prime Minister. Bilkers, as we shall see, come in all shapes and sizes...

Robert Henry King was born in 1797 and educated at Oxford. He was an officer in the 5th Regiment of Foot and served in France after the fall of Napoleon. He became a member of Parliament for County Cork in 1826, the family seat, and succeeded to the title Earl of Kingston (now the City of Cork), following the death of his father in 1837. At various times he could be found at either Mickleston Castle in Cork or at 35 Alpha Road, Regent's Park. He was accused, in an alleyway of Oxford St, of what the *Morning Chronicle* described as "gross acts of a filthy and disgusting nature [with another man] to which it is impossible for us with any regard to decency further to allude". He was given bail of £10,000 but failed to turn up for his court appearance thus forfeiting his bail money, half of which was his, the remainder was from two sureties. Soon after, he had to sell 43,000 acres of land spread over several counties in Ireland to help clear his debt.

On the morning of July 31st 1855 William Ellom was driving down Portman Street when he was hailed by Kingston. The job would appear to be a very good one for Ellom; he drove Kingston around all day, making various stops and at a quarter to five was told to wait for him whilst he went inside the House of Lords. Ellom waited and waited. By nine o'clock he gave up. It was clear that Kingston had left Parliament and had missed Ellom, who had to take his horse back to the stables. The following morning Ellom went round to Kingston's London address, 35 Park Street in Mayfair, above a grocer's shop, to get paid but was told that as he, (Ellom), was not where he was supposed to be, the Earl was forced to get another cab and that therefore Ellom had forfeited his right to any of the fare. Undeterred, Ellom went to court and summoned Kingston for non-payment of a cab fare which he estimated, with waiting time to be 24 shillings.

The following week at Westminster Police Court, Ellom outlined, on oath, his journey with the Earl and how he had been kept waiting for four hours. A policeman who was on duty that day and had been talking to Ellom corroborated his story. When Kingston took to the stand he denied the whole thing – he came out of the Commons entrance and went around to Victoria Tower where Ellom should have been waiting and the only vehicle there was a private coach. He then accused Ellom and the policeman of committing perjury. The magistrate, Beadon agreed that perjury had indeed been committed, but he for one believed that the cabman and the policeman were telling the truth. A second policeman was also called and further corroborated the evidence given by Ellom and his colleague. Kingston was told he must pay the 24 shillings' fare plus the costs of 7s.

Reynolds, a weekly newspaper, was scathing of the "aristocratic arrogance" of the peer; "If justice were but equally administered in England, the cabman would receive a swinging sum in shape of damages for the defamatory charge [perjury] of the noble earl. But inasmuch as there is one law for the rich and another for the poor, the cabman was obliged to pocket the insult along with his day's wages."[2]

A fortnight later it was another police court and another cabman, though this time the noble earl failed to show up. Thomas Lawrence who drove cab plated 2,007 stated that he had a booking to be at 35 Park Street at 9:20 am. Quite why Lawrence was up for the job is something of a mystery as the previous day he had carried Kingston around London for over eleven hours, only to be bilked. He had returned to 35 Park Street and only managed to get his money after pleading and begging with the grocer (who owned the building) in the shop below Kingston's lodgings. He now described to Mr Arnold that he arrived outside the Park Street residence five minutes early but had not charged for that. Fifteen minutes after the time he was booked for, Kingston and a young man emerged and got into the cab. Lawrence drove to several addresses before ending up at the House of Lords at 12:40. He had worked out that his correct fare should be 6s 6d but Kingston disagreed, and said the actual total was closer to 5s 6d. Lawrence took what was offered, at least that day he got some money, and summoned his lordship for the outstanding balance of a shilling.

The magistrate asked Lawrence how he had come to the price of 6s 6d. Lawrence replied that he had charged by time alone. The magistrate asked Lawrence if Kingston had stipulated that he wanted to be paid by time or distance. Lawrence replied that Kingston had made no wish either way. Arnold remonstrated with the cabman that it was not up to him to decide whether to charge by time or distance, the Act of Parliament clearly stated that the option to pay by time or distance was for the hirer to decide, not the cabman. Fortunately, Lawrence also knew the law. The charge by distance, the whole being only four miles was 2s, but the Act of Parliament allowed him to accumulate all the waiting time accrued and charge extra for that. He explained to the magistrate that no matter which way it was calculated, the fare was 6s 6d, 2s for the distance, then a one hour forty-five minute wait at Wilton Place, a brief stay at Tichbourne Street (whilst Kingston had a shave), twenty minutes at the Union Club and a further half hour at Norfolk street. So the total waiting time was 2 hours 35 minutes which at the rate of 6d for every 15 minutes meant he should have charged 7s, so was actually guilty of undercharging his lordship, not overcharging him. After a few more questions the magistrate ordered that the Earl of Kingston was to pay the outstanding fare plus 5s costs.

Kingston appeared to have kept a low profile in the following couple of years. He had sold his commission and retired from the army and may have been spending time in Ireland trying to sell off his land. In April 1857 he was sentenced to ten days imprisonment for failing to obey a court order that he failed to comply with, namely payment for a piano he had hired for the sum of £10 4s.

Notwithstanding the reputation he was building among cabmen, Kingston changed tact – he bilked a train company. He was a frequent visitor to Brighton and would often travel down by train from London Bridge, with a friend, and they would travel at a cheap rate. However, on one Sunday morning in the summer of 1858 Kingston and a friend had arrived at London Bridge Station to find that they had missed the train and none were due for several hours. It is perhaps a sign of the times that Kingston asked for, and received, a special train to be laid on for him. A train was prepared for him and he wrote a cheque out for £15 10s - which bounced.

A cabdriver named Dape applied to a magistrate at Marlborough Street at the beginning of June 1858 and produced a bill run up by Kingston of "formidable length". Dape said that the hiring's took place over a month and that the total bill had been about £35 but £17 had since been paid and he was seeking the balance of £17 6s. The magistrate, Bingham, asked, no doubt incredulously, how he could trust anyone to such an extent? Dape replied "It is a month's cab work and how could I refuse to trust the gentleman when I was told at the House of Lords, where I used to take him from Park Lane, that he was the Earl of Kingston." Bingham replied that he could only grant a summons for the last unpaid fare, assuming it was within the time limit – it wasn't. Dape replied that it was over a fortnight since he had driven his Lordship. Bingham then informed Dape that there was little he could do as too long a period had passed. "It is precious hard on me." stated Dape, "His Lordship had my cab all day, and sometimes all night. About a fortnight ago his Lordship says to me says he, "Cabby, it's all right, you shall have your money; but I shan't want your cab any more just yet, as a friend has leant me his carriage – when I want you again I will write to you." Well, I had my suspicions, and I watched his Lordship's house in Park-lane the next morning, and, instead of a friend's carriage coming to the door, I see another cab drive up, and his Lordship get in. His Lordship has gone out every day in a cab and has run up another bill of £2. I've called and called at the house but it ain't no use." The only advice Bingham could give to Dape was, "Then don't call again" but he did advise that the luckless cabmen would have to go to the county court to seek recovery of the sum – a process he may not have been able to afford.[3]

It seems somewhat incredible that cabmen would continue to pick Kingston up, even though they knew what the likelihood may be. Perhaps even more astonishing was that the Brighton Railway Company, who was still pursuing Kingston through the County Court for the non-payment of the specially laid on train, allowed him to hire another train and present a cheque for £15 10s for this one also – though this time the cheque was honoured.

On June 14th 1858, John Benson, badge number 10,910, picked up Kingston at 7:40 in the morning from 35 Park Street. He was with him the whole day, setting down at Park Street thirteen hours later. Benson estimated that he would be happy with 30 shillings, though the fare should actually be more (he calculated that by distance alone he had gone 35 miles that day). Kingston of course disputed the amount and would only pay a sovereign (20s). Benson summoned him for the outstanding amount. At Marlborough Street, Kingston had sent an agent, but as there was another summons outstanding against Kingston from another cab driver, Beadon (the same magistrate who rebuffed Kingston for alleging perjury), adjourned the case. Not only were there now two outstanding cases for bilking cab drivers at Marlborough Street, there was also two or three from elsewhere as well. As nothing further is heard of these cases, it is presumed the drivers eventually got their money.

As far as the Earl of Kingston and the London cab trade were concerned, nothing more was heard for nearly two years and then normal relations between the two were resumed in April 1860, and it would prove to be Kingston's swansong. James Hoddenott had sought a summons over a fare for £1. He informed Arnold the magistrate, that a few days previously, he "took his Lordship up near Manchester Square, and after driving him about a good deal over the stones set him down at the House of Lords."[4] He was told to wait and that he, Kingston, would only be a few minutes. Hoddenott, like so many cab drivers before him, waited and waited, and after four hours he gave up. He asked the policeman the address of Kingston and was told "26 Duke St". As Kingston again had not bothered to turn up, Arnold wondered if the summons had been correctly served as the "Court Guide" had Kingston's address as 35 Park Street. His summoning officer, Edward Knowland, replied that he had gone to Duke Street but talking with the landlady, he ascertained that Kingston did not live there but was a frequent visitor. Arnold ordered that a fresh summons must be ordered against Kingston. Armed with this, Knowland returned to 26 Duke Street and this time the landlady admitted that the Earl did reside there but was not at home at that time. This time, a different magistrate, Paynter, was satisfied, and ordered that the Earl of Kingston would have to pay the fare of £1 plus 12s costs and that failure to do so would result in a distress warrant being issued.

The effect the bilking by Kingston had on some cab drivers can be seen with the case of a driver named J.F. Hall. He had picked up Kingston on April 17th 1860 and driven him about all day. Hall drove the Earl to several places and, as before, he was told to wait outside the House of Lords, which was the last he saw of him that day. Hall received a stern rebuke from his master for "coming home short" – not enough to pay the daily rental for the horse and cab, and was given a final warning. The following day, Hall managed to track down Kingston who offered him the paltry sum of 2s 6d for the previous day's work, which was nowhere near enough. Kingston told the cabman that if he again took him to the House of Lords he would be paid in full. They did not make it that far. Hall was told to wait whilst Kingston went into a house in Beak Street, Soho. After two hours he realised he had been duped again and took the cab back to the yard. He paid his master every penny he had on him but was still short of his rental money. Hall was dismissed by his master and was now without work or money.

A day later, Hall related his experiences to Paynter, the magistrate at Westminster and explained that he could not afford to pay 2s to pay for a summons against the Earl. Paynter took pity on him and allowed two gratuitous summons, one for 18s 6d, the other for 5s for waiting at Beak Street. Kingston was found guilty in his absence but Hall would have to wait for both of the summons to be served on the Earl before he could receive his money. He never did, at least not from Kingston.

A week later Hall returned to the court to hopefully get his money – but the summons could not be served as Kingston had gone to Ireland. "It is very hard upon me." stated Hall, "I am crippled with a bad leg, and it was as much as I could do to get here both last week and today."[5] Paynter took pity on Hall and gave him 5s from the poor box.

Hall's case was widely reported in the newspapers and many felt it reflected bad on the House of Lords that a poor cabman had been left destitute by a peer of the realm. Help finally arrived for Hall in the shape of an unknown gentleman who attended Westminster police court and paid the outstanding debt, Hall finally got his money, and presumably his job back. Three other cab drivers who were at the time waiting for money from Kingston were not so remunerated.

In September 1860 Paynter had another cabman in front of him that was owed money by Kingston, this time however, the noble earl was in court himself, and not by choice. On Thursday September 6th Kingston arrived at the Euston hotel in a cab and went into the dining area. He was well known at the hotel and most of the waiters doubted whether he was of sound mind. It is believed he had no control at this time over his bowel movements and several of the diners complained of the smell emanating from him. He ordered his dinner but ate with his fingers and a couple of times sent down to the cabman, who was still waiting, his favourite mode of payment – a piece of paper that usually had the words "pay the bearer £5 [or whatever]. Kingston", more often than not the handwriting was illegible. Soon the smell, the incoherent talking and maniacal laughing was too much for the staff and other guests and Kingston was ejected after paying for his meal with a real cheque, but which subsequently bounced. Kingston left the hotel and jumped into his long-waiting cab for the short ride to (the now) Euston station. He asked for a ticket to Holyhead but did not have the £5 to pay for it. He grabbed the ticket and began walking to the train. He was followed by an elderly clerk who was determined to retrieve the ticket, or get some money – he got neither. What he received was incoherent abuse and a punch to the chest. When asked later why he did not lay charges for assault against him, the clerk replied that he knew it was the Earl of Kingston and knew he was not of sound mind. A railway police officer, the delightfully named Sgt Swindle was called who managed to eject Kingston from the station, after receiving a punch to the face. He also did not take him into charge as it was clear that the earl was not sane (Swindle had worked for several years at Colney Hatch asylum and so recognised the signs) nor responsible for his actions. Sgt Swindle put him into the cab, the same cab that had brought him and he left the station.

Next evening, he was back at Euston again in a repeat performance of the previous day. Again with no money to pay for his ticket he actually made it inside a railway carriage and remained there for four hours, the train was going nowhere. He eventually was escorted out of the station and took a cab to Morley's Hotel in Trafalgar Square (on the site of the present South Africa House). He remained in the hotel until the early hours. The cabman, George Crambrook, fearing that the earl had gone to bed for the night sent a message via the staff that he was still waiting and would like to be paid off since he had to get his horse back to the yard. Kingston had asked for a room for the night but the hotel refused him on account of the disgusting smell he carried with him. To Crambrook's notes he replied with his now usual piece of paper with illegible writing. After a while Crambrook had had enough and went up himself to the dining area but was only met with a torrent of incoherent abuse. The police were called and Kingston was ejected from the hotel. Still not having been paid, Crambrook wanted to bring charges against Kingston for non-payment of his fare, so Crambrook agreed to take Kingston and the policeman the short trip to Scotland Yard. Kingston was happy himself to go as he wanted to bring charges against Mrs Morley, the proprietor of the hotel, as he objected to the way he was removed from the premises. Once at Scotland Yard the acting inspector, for whatever reason, refused to accept the charge of non-payment of the cab fare, but Crambrook was happy to be given Kingston's name and address with which he could get a summons served. Kingston had still not been arrested and, since he was a peer, such an arrest was unlikely and that the police would escort him home. After changing his mind a couple of times as to which friends' house he wanted to go to, Kingston suddenly turned on the policeman punched him in the face and kicked him twice on the shins. Now having due cause, Kingston was returned to the police station and charged with assaulting a police officer.

On Saturday September 8th the Earl of Kingston was in the dock of Westminster police court before Paynter the sitting magistrate. Also in attendance was PC Killick, whom Kingston assaulted and George Crambrook who was claiming 9s for his fare and waiting time. Once again, he accused all those who told against him that they were committing perjury, the policeman had collared him and that was no way to treat a peer of the realm. Killick replied that they were walking arm in arm as the earl was very drunk. He had no reason to hold him by the collar as he was not a prisoner. As for the charge of being drunk, Kingston replied that he had never been drunk in his life. When asked to explain why he had not paid the cabman Kingston went into a long incoherent ramble that bore no relevance to the charges. Paynter told him to confine himself to the charges before him and not waste the valuable time of the court. Kingston replied that by accusing him of wasting the time of the court that he not only insulted him but the whole of the House of Lords, this being one of his frequent refrains when he felt an injustice had been levelled against him. Paynter cut the proceedings short with respect to Crambrook and ordered that the Earl of Kingston pay the 9s demanded plus costs. At least Crambrook was in a much stronger position than many other cabmen who had won their case against the earl. Many had still not been paid and just gave up chasing what appeared to be a hopeless case, Crambrook would either be paid or Kingston would be sent to jail. Proceeding with the assault, the magistrate pointed out that the only defence offered was that the principle witnesses were all committing perjury and that he, Kingston, felt justified in insulting the judge of the court. Paynter described Kingston's action as a disgrace and had he been under arrest when he assaulted the constable then he would have no hesitation in sending him straight to gaol. Kingston's only reply was, "You disgrace the bench you sit upon." Which is probably not a wise course of action before sentence has been passed. Kingston was fined 40 shillings or one month's imprisonment if he failed to pay. Paynter ordered the gaoler to take him down to the cells. At that point an un-named cabman who had waited nine hours for the earl at Euston and elsewhere the previous Friday asked how was he going to be able to get his money. Fortunately for him a gentleman, possibly the same one as before, paid the unknown cabman his outstanding balance, settled with George Crambrook and paid the fine for the assault. Kingston was free once more, but not for long.

He immediately left London for Ireland but instead of arriving at Holyhead he was found wandering along the railway line at Chester, saying he was on his way to a luncheon with some eminent people. He was later ejected from Chester cathedral for refusing to take his hat off and the next morning was found walking 'naked' down the street. The authorities in Chester had no option but to incarcerate him in an asylum until he could be assessed. Despite a brief period shortly after, the Earl of Kingston never regained his sanity and remained in various asylums until his death in 1867. At the time of his last court appearance it was stated that he was literally a pauper himself. He had sold off much of his land in Ireland, land that had brought in a considerable annual rent, and even accused his brother, who succeeded to the title in 1867, of trying to kill him.

Henry Roland was totally unaware as to the sanity of the Countess of Carlisle when he picked her up from the Spanish Ambassador's chapel in April 1849. He took her to Warren Street where he waited "two or three hours", then to Eaton Place, where he waited three quarters of an hour, and finally to her residence in St Martin's Street, Leicester Square. However, when they arrived there, Roland was "told to go away" as there was no money for him. After trying to get his money a couple of more times he took out a summons. The Countess did not turn up at court, instead the magistrate read a letter: "The Countess of Carlisle presents her compliments to Mr Hardwick, [the magistrate], having received a summons with his signature attached, for money claimed by a person calling himself Henry Roland, begs to say she completely protests against the charge under the following grounds. In the first instance, as she is a married woman, she is not liable to be sued for any debts she may contract so…it was to the Earl of Carlisle [Roland] should have applied." She went onto say that she told the cabman she could not pay him until his Lordship returned to London as she had no money following the theft of her purse from within her lodgings. She was also rather indignant that the summons was not served personally on her but via one of her servants. Hardwick stated that he had never heard of the 'Countess of Carlisle' and wondered if she was of sound mind. He granted Roland a second summons and informed the officer of the court that her ladyship should be warned of the consequences if she failed to turn up a second time.[6]

When Roland turned up for the hearing of the second summons at Marlborough Street police court, he may have wondered why there were more people there than usual. When he found out that they too were owed money by the Countess, his heart must have sunk. The police had been looking into her background. She was Irish and had worked for the real Lord Carlisle, whilst he was Secretary of Ireland, but she obtained £40 by deception from him. She had recently been evicted from her lodgings in St Martin's Street, replying to the solicitor who drafted the notice that, "...she condescends to acquaint that weak minded individual that she is armed so strongly in virtue, probity, honour and honesty, though he and the whole body of 'Chartists' were 'coming', she would not for a moment flinch from the bright and unvarying path of propriety which she has heretofore followed. As to fear, such a word is a stranger to her vocabulary. Lady Carlisle is desirous that this ridiculous correspondence shall end." She could certainly pen a letter could the 'Countess of Carlisle', or Catherine Wetherelt, to give her, her real name. Several years back she had caused a disturbance which ended with her being declared insane and housed in an asylum for two years. Bingham, like Hardwick, had no doubt that the prisoner was insane and as such criminal proceedings would be terminated. Several businessmen and women came forward and informed the court they had been duped out of the wares, in some cases of several hundred pounds. In many instances the goods could be returned, she probably pawned most of them. Rowland however was completely out of pocket. He explained to Bingham that he had had to pay for two summons' at his own expense, he had been dismissed by his master for not being able to pay him, so was now out of work and had no prospect of being paid at all. Bingham agreed it was very hard upon the cabman but all he could do to assist him was give him 2s 6d from the poor box.[7]

Bingham could have been forgiven that the world was full of insane people passing themselves off as nobility and riding around London in cabs. The very next day he had another cabman before him, charging the Earl of Norfolk with bilking him. The earl said it was all a mistake and if the cabman took him directly from the court to the Bank of England, he would cash a £50,000 cheque he had in his pocket and pay his cab fare. He was taken to the infirmary instead to be assessed.[8]

Eight months later, presumably after a spell in an asylum, the 'Countess of Carlisle' was back in London. On December 14th 1849 the 'Countess' arrived at the magistrate's entrance to Worship Street police court, where she made a complaint directly to magistrate Arnold, about her son who had stolen certain documents from her. She then proceeded in the same cab to various police stations and other locations in an effort to find, and get her son arrested. She ended back at Worship Street after the cabman found out she had no money. Her son turned up for the summons and explained that he was mortified when he learned of his mother's exploits earlier in the year, when she defrauded many people. The son went onto explain that his father and grandfather had served in the army, both with distinction, and both having died in the service of their country. The documents his mother had accused him of stealing were pawn-broker's duplicates for items that belonged to his father. Arnold informed the son that the duplicates must be returned to his mother, he then allowed the cabman to make his charge. The 'Countess' proclaimed that as the cab fare was a matter of debt, Arnold had no jurisdiction to hear the case, it should be in a county court; "moreover, as a married woman, she was not legally liable." As her son had stated, she was in fact a widow. Arnold informed her that he did indeed have jurisdiction to hear the charge and unless she paid the cabman the 15s 6d she owed the cabman, she would be imprisoned for 14 days. Unfortunately for the cabman he was not to receive any money and the 'Countess of Carlisle' was taken to the police cells, and as far as the cab trade were concerned, never heard of again.[9]

Not all multiple, or serial bilkers, were insane. A man named Thompson hired a hackney coach at 10:30pm one night in March, 1823, in Oxford Street and told the coachman to drive to nearby Golden Square. When they arrived, Thompson told the coachman that he was to wait for "an hour and a half, but, if he is detained longer, you must wait longer." "Poor Coachee" wrote the *Morning Chronicle*, "having no suspicion that a man of the respectable appearance of the defendant would descend to anything like a trick, neglected to watch which house he went into and he waited there until three quarters past three in the morning." The coachman went home out of pocket. There is a saying that "London is so large, you forget how small it really is", and the coachman met Thompson accidently the following day and it was only then that a summons could be taken out. Thompson explained that when he returned after an hour and a half, the coachman was gone. "Upon my oath," exclaimed the driver, "I never moved half a yard in five hours and a quarter." After hearing the coachman's tale, Sir Robert Birnie informed Thompson that he would have to pay the fare and costs which amounted to 19s 6d. Acting with all the dignity he could muster, Thompson immediately paid over the money and bowed to the court, and was about to leave when another hackney coachman came forward and stated, "I has a little bit of a claim upon this here Gentleman, please your Worship. He hired me at exactly half-past ten o'clock at night, on the 26th of March last, to take him to Golden Square. It blowed cruel cold and snowed most *tremendious*. When I got to one corner of the square, says he to me, says he, 'Wait here,' says he 'till I return, which will be in one hour and a half,' says he. I waited, please your Worship, till half past two o'clock in the morning, and then I drove home, for it was so cruel cold that my poor *hosses* and me was very near *freezed* to death. I met the Gentleman since, and he paid me 7s in part, but he has never *gid* me the *overplush*." Thompson said he paid the 7s in satisfaction of the whole demand. "No, you Worship," cried out the coachman, "it an't true, I couldn't be such a flat as that, neither."

"Upon my word, Mr Thompson," proclaimed Sir Robert, "I would advise you to retire and settle with this man, or a third claimant may appear."

"There is a third, sir," countered the coachman, "a fellow servant of mine, who has the same demand, and he will be here in a day or two." The court reporter noted that Thompson, rather hastily, settled with the second coachman and left the court.[10]

When J Augustus Travis, "an elderly, shabby-genteel personage" appeared in court on a charge of bilking several cabmen, a driver was about to give his version of events when he was interrupted by the accused. "Don't trouble yourself, my good fellow. I own the debt. I only want to know how much I owe you all together, that I may clear it off at once. There's only eight of you who appear against me."

"There are twenty of us. You owe me twenty-four shillings for fares and expenses." After a rambling statement, it was found Travis could not pay the 24s and was sent to prison for twenty-one days, "at the expiration of which time, the defendant to be detained to meet the other cases."[11]

Charles Watson was perhaps as guilty as bilking as Travis was, but he went to extraordinary lengths to avoid paying his cab fare. In October 1851, Watson, a cloth worker of 59 London Wall engaged cabman Charles Martin to take him from the City to Stoke Newington, wait for him and bring him back. The fare was agreed to, and also the amount of time Martin would have to wait. Martin was joined on the box by a fellow cabman named Blowes who cadged a free lift. He was unemployed at the time, and was going up to Stoke Newington to visit his brother. The house in Stoke Newington that the cab was travelling to was an illegal gaming house, but Watson would later swear that he did not partake in the gambling, only witnessing it. Several times, cabman Martin had to remind Watson that the agreed waiting time had long passed. Watson fobbed the cabman off by supplying him with brandy and several pints of ale.

Eventually the party left the house in Stoke Newington and made their back home. During the journey Watson had to remonstrate several times with Martin to drive faster. It was soon apparent to him why Martin was driving slowly – running on foot behind the cab was Thomas Blowes, the cabman who had earlier cadged a free ride. When the cab reached Finsbury Pavement, Watson got out and began walking away. Martin asked about his fare but Watson replied that his friend had paid him at the house in Stoke Newington. By now Blowes had caught up with the cab and fearing that he might be bilked, Martin told Blowes to grab hold of Watson. A scuffle broke out and Watson cried out for assistance just as Blowes was standing in front of him and Martin had him by the collar. Fortunately for Watson help was at hand with the timely arrival of a policeman and the two cabmen were charged with highway robbery in attempting to steal Watson's gold watch and chain.

In Guildhall magistrates court before Alderman Sir Robert Carden the following morning, Watson reiterated his side of the story. The two "ruffianly-looking cabmen", as they were described in the press, gave their version, that Watson was walking away and was only stopped for fear that he was about to be bilked. Watson replied that Martin's statement was a tissue of lies and that he was attacked by Blowes just as he was about to pay Martin. Watson informed the magistrate that were it not for the fact that his watch was secured with a sturdy chain, it also would have been taken. He also missed a sovereign which he did not know how he had lost and could confirm to the magistrate that he was perfectly sober at the time.

The case was an easy matter for Carden to decide upon. In the dock were two 'ruffianly looking cabmen', one of whom was out of work and desperate for money, in the witness box was a smartly dressed businessman. "It appears to me," said Carden, "that this is a conspiracy of you both to rob Mr Watson of his watch and chain, and, had not the police rendered assistance in time, I have no doubt but that you would have succeeded. It is evident that Blowes had that object in view, and that Martin was co-operating with him on loitering on the road, to enable him to keep pace with the cab. Under these circumstances I shall deprive you both of your licenses as cab drivers; but I should not be doing my duty to the public if I allowed you to escape so easily. I shall, therefore, sentence you to fourteen days' imprisonment in the House of Correction, with hard labour."[12]

Alderman Sir Robert Carden was beginning to develop a reputation for not suffering fools gladly, though as we have seen in Chapter 6, he gave Mrs Prodgers the time of day but this case preceded Prodgers and was prior to his reputation being made. His maternal grandfather was John Walter the founder of *The Times*, and in 1855 Carden himself founded the City Bank, which would later become the Midland Bank before being taken over by HSBC. He became an Alderman in 1849 and the following year was made Aldermanic Sheriff. He was not well liked by the City Livery companies as he appeared to have been on a crusade to stamp out corruption. He was a particular a target of, "the longshore men" a group who dominated Common Hall but Carden would regularly defy their power and refuse their bribes. He was no disciple of tradition either. For over six hundred years the Lord Mayor's procession had been a spectacular event on the river Thames, Carden bucked with the trend and had his procession through the streets of the City, a parade that has continued on dry land ever since. Someone, somewhere, must have had a liking for him as he was knighted in July 1851 but the general public, at least those who had a vote, never took to him. He stood several times to be elected to Parliament, eventually succeeding in Gloucester (1857-59) and Barnstaple (1880-85). Many cabmen would find themselves up before him during his service as a magistrate and he could perhaps be described as firm but fair. In 1879 he was knocked over by a cab, the driver was fortunate only to be fined 20s. He was famous, or perhaps infamous, for sending vagrants to prison for three weeks, but he was also known to donate his own money to organisations in the east end and to open his house in West Molesey to orphan children from a home he was the patron of. His obituary described him as "frosty but fair" when he died at his town house, at 64 Wimpole Street in 1888 and he was buried, rather fittingly, at Kensal Green, one of a number of cemeteries designed and built by his brother George Carden.[13]

Having sent two cabmen to the notorious House of Correction on the previous Friday, Carden, perhaps preceding his epitaph of "frosty but fair" called all the parties back to court on the following Monday. He was, if anything, unconventional.

Carden informed the court that due to the publicity surrounding the trial, he had received several notices of information as not only justice for the cabmen was called into question but also the integrity of the victim, Mr Charles Watson. Watson's solicitor then enquired whether there was about to be a rehearing of the case. Carden replied that there would be and in more detail, but he assured Watson that the proceedings were more for his benefit to vindicate his character as a respectable tradesman.

Watson entered the witness box and elaborated on the evidence he gave on the previous Saturday. He had engaged Martin at nine pm, to meet at the Prince Albert public house, owned by his friend Mr Bilton. Under oath he denied gambling whilst he was there, or even seeing it take place, then promptly contradicted himself by saying he had a shilling bet on a game of cards. He stayed for an hour and a half, and the journey back took ninety minutes as well, given the leisurely pace Martin was travelling at in order for Blowes to keep up. He admitted to having had a drink but was perfectly sober as the station sergeant could testify.

Under cross examination he admitted to having £5 with him when he entered the cab, with that he paid off a debt he owed to Bilton and then paid for the drinks he had that night. He stated that he was unaware that his travelling companion who went with him to Stoke Newington, refused to come back in the coach with him as he was so drunk. He admitted not knowing how many drinks he had had, it may have been two or four glasses of brandy and two glasses of 'half and half'.

His travelling companion, Samuel Foster, a builder, was next sworn. He informed the court that Watson had asked him to go with him to Bilton's that night, and that he, Watson, would pay all his expenses. Foster said he was more interested in getting the 10s that Watson owed him and if that money was forthcoming he would go to Stoke Newington. Watson then tried to borrow money from a landlord of a public house but was refused. He then believed that Watson returned to his own house before coming back to Wormwood Street and finding Foster. Having paid Watson the 10s he owed him, they took a Hansom cab from the Bishopsgate stand and after negotiating with the driver, Charles Martin, they proceeded to Stoke Newington. Foster said he noticed that there were two men on the box and informed Watson (Charles Martin drove a cab – which did not have a box. Most likely Blowes was standing on the springs). Watson had previously sworn that the first he saw of Blowes was at Bilton's and had not been aware of another man next to the driver. Foster admitted to playing at cards but agreed that Watson did not play, but he was betting on the hands and that he purchased a lot of drink for the two of them and for the two cabmen, who were plied with more drink each time they reminded Watson that his agreed hour was up. When he did leave, Foster remained at the card table but Mrs Bilton informed him that he had left without paying for the drinks. "I told Watson it was always his way; when he went anywhere, he was sure to spill it." Carden asked him what he meant by that last remark. Foster replied, "That he always disputes cab affairs and other payments, and that such are constantly the subjects of altercations with him." Foster went on to say that he informed Watson himself that he was not returning in the cab with him as he was too drunk, he had been tipsy before they left Bishopsgate, having had several brandy's before they left. He also stated that he felt induced to attend the hearing today as a result of the newspaper reports he had read on Saturday. He also informed Carden that on a previous occasion Watson refused to pay a cabman the agreed fare, and told the driver to summons him. Fortunately, he and a third passenger had enough to pay the cabman, Watson just walked away.

Watson may have now been feeling a little hot under the collar, his so-called friend had contradicted nearly everything he had sworn under oath, and things were about to become decidedly hotter. A voice from the back of the court called out that he had been bilked by Watson a year ago. Carden replied that he would hear all the evidence, and pointing to the two "ruffianly looking cabmen, Martin and Blowes, stated "Here are two men that have been locked up since Friday on a most serious charge, therefore any evidence that can be produced I am bound to hear. From the communications I have received, I think it is my bounded duty to take every care of these men's interests – greater care than that of a nobleman for they are less protected."

Watson argued that he had a great many enemies in the neighbourhood who were prejudicial towards him. Carden allayed any fears he might have on that score as without evidence, prejudice would hold no sway with him. Two more witnesses were called; both stated that on Friday afternoon Watson, who was drunk at the time had asked to borrow money from them, both declined. With so many witnesses saying he was drunk Watson again stated that the station sergeant could testify to his sobriety. The police inspector who took the charge was called up and he informed the court that Watson was indeed intoxicated, the two cabmen were drunk also, but not as bad as Watson. As evidence of his drunken state, the inspector produced the charge sheet that contained a statement written by Watson, it was totally illegible. The police constable that arrested Martin and Blowes also stated that Watson was drunk at the time.

James Henwood, the cabman that had spoken out from the back of the court was called to the witness stand. he informed the court that he knew

Watson "perfectly well – to my sorrow." He stated that Watson had booked him for a journey to Waltham Cross, wait an hour and bring him back, all for 12 shillings. Henwood took him to Waltham Cross, then back to Stratford and then out to Cheshunt, picking up two friends on the way. Watson then wanted to go onto Rye House, to which Henwood objected as the horse had by now travelled many miles and he wanted to return home. Reluctantly he took Watson and his friends to Rye House before making the journey back to London. "I think I must have taken him almost 60 miles" Henwood told the court. On the journey from Rye House back to the City, "Mr Watson rode on the roof the whole time, but there was no one inside. When I asked for my fare he gave me in charge for being drunk, but the office refused to take me, and told Mr Watson it was a mistake, as he was the drunken man. Mr Watson gave me plenty to drink, but I threw it all under the cab. I called on him the following morning for my money, and he gave me in charge again."

Watson protested at this, stating that the cabman's evidence was absurd, he could never have travelled that distance in the time. To the laughter of the court Carden replied, "It is quite 50 miles, and when a cabman calls it 60, I think it is a very near calculation for a cabman." This was in reference to the many disputes that appear before the courts where the distance has come under scrutiny. Magistrates often advised complainants that if the cabman said it was over a mile, then it generally was, but this never stopped disputes arising.

Another cabman, Thomas Hitchman, then testified; "On the 16th of July last Mr Watson hired me to take him to Piccadilly and bring him back for 4s, but he "bilked" me by giving me a false address. He came again to me some time after, but I refused to take him. There are 20 cabmen outside who have all been done in various ways by him.

"Call them all in" replied Carden, "All these witnesses have come forward voluntarily to give evidence from what they have seen in the public papers." Watson by now was wondering whether he was about to be charged with an offence, it was evident that he had committed perjury. Perhaps with over twenty cab drivers baying for his blood, he might have been safer if he was held in custody.

Carden continued, "With respect to the men at the bar, I see nothing at all against the character of either of these. I only regret that they have been placed there innocently. I am quite sure they will acquit me of all blame in convicting them, for Mr Watson's bearing was such, and his evidence was given in such an apparently straightforward manner, that I was bound to convict. I am now induced to alter my former opinion and I think I cannot place any confidence in Mr Watson's word as the groundwork of a conviction...I shall however take immediate steps to procure the liberation of these two innocent men, and in the meantime, I will consider what further proceedings ought to be taken with regard to Mr Watson." Much of what Carden had said was accompanied by cheers from the public who were in attendance. Although Charles Martin and Thomas Blowes were taken back to the Giltspur Street Compter before the formalities regarding their release could be finalised, they were informed that their licences would be returned as they were found upon them – without a stain.[14]

If there was one thing worse than a multiple bilker, it was the professional bilker, the type that believed they were above the law, and certainly above the cabmen. Owner driver George Kite had picked up a painter by the name of George Smith at lunchtime on September 11th 1839. It was not until eight in the evening that he was discharged when Smith gave him, what he said was, a very generous sum, 3s 6d. Kite said his fare was at least 10 shillings more. A summons was issued, and ignored, as was the second one. Such disregard for the law is frowned upon by the courts and an officer was despatched to Smith's home to issue him with a warrant for his arrest. He was not at home but ignored the advice to appear in court the next morning. Eventually he was apprehended in the street and dragged into court. An officer of the Guildhall court informed Alderman White that "this was not the first or second time Mr Smith refused to pay his cab fares. He seemed to take a pleasure in annoying cabmen." Alderman White remarked that he had met such a person before, whom he cured of his folly by adjudging that he had to pay a much higher sum of money than he anticipated, which he would not pay, and so was marched off to the treadmill. He has not heard of him bilking any cabmen since. It had the desired effect on Smith. He explained that he only received one summons and had been out of town. If only the cabman had waited, he would have been paid. "When cab drivers committed offences," Alderman White informed Smith, "they were generally punished, and it was but fair they should be protected when they were imposed upon." It was not for the benefit of the cabmen Alderman White was alluding to, "If the cabmen were not protected they would naturally exact from some customers what they lost by the default of others." Unless Smith could pay the 6s 6d fare, and 17s for the cabman's loss of time, then he would go to prison for one month with hard labour. Smith paid and Alderman White cured another man of his folly.[15]

William John Nettleship Angerstein, habitué of Brook's Club, St James's, was the archetypal professional bilker and was known to have bilked 24 cabmen within a fortnight. John Coker, one of his victims, was on his way to Westminster police court when he saw Angerstein in a wine shop. Fully expecting to face him in the court room, he asked the bilker if he was going to pay all the cabmen he owed money to. Angerstein replied that it would be a waste of Coker's time to go to court, as he himself would not be there, and that his solicitor had informed him that "the cabmen do not have a leg to stand on." Coker relayed this conversation to the magistrate at Westminster, D'Eyncourt. The hall porter at Brook's confirmed that a large number of summons had been delivered to the Gentleman's club, and whilst he had a brother who was also a member, he refused to interfere with his brother's actions. Coker informed the court that he had been hired by Angerstein at eight o'clock one morning and drove him around to several places. In the afternoon he took him to Victoria Station where Angerstein took a train to Croydon for the horse racing, telling Coker to wait for him. More surprising than Coker waiting all that time was the fact Angerstein found him after his return at 8pm. After picking up a lady and visiting several other places, with the woman remaining in the cab at all times, Coker was finally discharged at one o'clock in the morning, and not paid. "Seventeen hours and not a farthing." D'Eyncourt wrote out an order for £2 9s.

Joseph Meakes related how Angerstein had ordered him to drive to a number of addresses in central London before stopping outside a house in Pimlico. Meakes informed his passenger that his horse was tired and he would like to get paid so he could finish up for the night. Angerstein kept him waiting till half past three in the morning before being told that he would not get any money until after 5am when he wished to be taken back to St James'. He never got paid. D'Eyncourt made an order for Angerstein to pay £1 11s. Next up was a cabman named Robinson, badge 8059. Angerstein had hired him for a total of 8½ hours, for which he was not paid. D'Eyncourt made an order of £1 14s 3d. John Hill told the court that Angerstein had hired him one evening and kept him until the following morning when he was told that as he (Angerstein) had lost all his money betting on horses, the cabman could not get paid until some of his more successful wagers were paid to him. Hill never got his money, and D'Eyncourt made an order for £1 plus costs.[16] As Angerstein was not arrested at some point in the future for ignoring the summons, it is quite probable that all the cabmen eventually were paid, and perhaps Angerstein took better advice from a change in solicitors.

Mrs Stancher was on her way with five other ladies to the Covent Garden Theatre in the first week of January, 1831. When they arrived at the theatre the ladies walked away, the hackney coachman, William Johnson, assumed that he was to remain outside the theatre and return them to where he picked them up. Such assumptions were all too real, and usually, instructions were not given if they did not have to be given. After all, why would a respectable lady want to converse with a hackney coachman. Johnson waited outside the theatre and when it "burst" (the audience leaves after the last performance) he saw the six women climbing into another coach. He first of all explained that they were getting into the wrong coach but when they said they had not requested him to wait for them, "and they would not pay him a farthing." He had no option than to summon them. Though the case was argued in court, the magistrate came down on the side of Johnson, he had not been paid off so was perfectly right to assume he was to be retained. He was awarded his 16s fare with 7s 6d costs. It was only after the money was paid over did the real reason for the bilk materialise; six ladies had travelled in the coach. Their husbands, however, walked on behind the coach, quite unbeknown to Johnson. The ladies had walked away from the coach believing that one of the husbands would not be so 'ungallant' as to let the ladies pay the fare. This of course could have been sorted out on the night, but believing that most hackney coachman were villains and trying it on, they would not admit to their mistake and Johnson was forced to go through the courts.[17]

Charles Henry Cutt was slightly dismayed when his passenger, Frederick Williams, who was charged with being drunk as well as bilking him, failed to turn up for the summons in December 1884. Bridge, the magistrate, ordered a warrant for his arrest but moments later Cutt pointed out his passenger in the public gallery of the court. The identity was also confirmed by the arresting policeman and a youth who had been assaulted. The onlooker protested his innocence, but now another witness came forward and said they were absolutely sure that he was the accused. The man continued to protest his innocence. He had only turned up in court out of curiosity as he was attempting to join the police force. He was placed in the dock and Cutt gave his evidence that the accused had hailed him at 3pm the previous afternoon and was engaged by him for the following five hours for which he had not been paid. The accused had an alibi, he was on the Metropolitan Police's drill ground between three and four o'clock, the same time he was allegedly riding around in Cutt's cab. Five fellow police candidates now came forward and confirmed what was stated and the police inspector who took the charge confirmed that the man in the dock was not the accused. The magistrate apologised to the police candidate and he was free to leave.[18] The real bilker appeared in court a few days later and was fined 40s with 13s costs, or one month's hard labour.[19]

Sometimes the cab driver can find himself at the centre of a matrimonial dispute – which usually ends with him not getting paid. In October 1900 a policeman was called to a scene in Praed Street, Paddington, where a crowd had assembled around a cab. It transpired that the couple inside the cab, an American lawyer and his wife, both of whom had imbibed several spirits, were arguing over who should pay the cab fare. The husband had no money on him to pay the cabman, and the wife, who had money on her, refused to pay as it was the duty of the husband to pay the fare. As neither could give a valid address, they were taken into custody. After a sobering night in a police cell, the husband apologised to the court and stated that he had no intention to "violate any of the ordinances" of the land. Plowden the magistrate was thinking more of the cabman than any constitutional crisis; "But have you settled between you who is to pay the fare – the husband who cannot, or the wife who won't." To the laughter of the court the husband ventured that he had found a sovereign in his pocket and would of course pay the cabman at once. On hearing this, the magistrate turned to the wife and said, "I suppose you are satisfied if your husband pays? It is another triumph for women. You may both go away."[20] Not all cases of cabmen being collateral damage in marriage disputes were so whimsical.

When forty-six-year-old Agnes Wakefield said she was the divorced wife of a millionaire, she was at least speaking the truth. Her husband had given her an allowance of £750 whilst they were separated but as soon as the *decree nisi* came through the funds were stopped. She was expecting a settlement of £8000 but this was being delayed by her ex-husband. In the meantime, she used a lot of taxicabs. She 'paid' for the cabs by issuing IOU's that could be cashed in at her husband's solicitors. Apparently one, probably the first one, had been. Since then however, none of the IOU's had been honoured. In court, Mrs Wakefield stated that she was practically destitute until her husband released the money the court said was owing to her. She promised that not only would every taxi-driver be paid, but she would also give them a £3 'present' for all the trouble they had been put to. Horace Smith, the Westminster magistrate, released her for a week on her own recognisances but advised her to pay the cabmen in the meantime.[21]

When all the parties returned to court the following week Mrs Wakefield informed the court that her allowance had now been reduced to £30, payable on the first of each month, and from this, she would pay off all the taxi-drivers. The solicitor acting for the taxi-drivers, it was never stated just how many there were, said he had been in contact with Mr Wakefield's solicitors and the allowance was not only voluntary on his behalf, but Mrs Wakefield had borrowed so much against it that there was very little left. Therefore, the taxi-drivers had no option other than to decline the offer made by Mrs Wakefield. This gave the magistrate very few options. "Mr Horace Smith in the case of each driver ordered payment of the amount due, with a shilling fine and costs of attendance added, or 21 days imprisonment in each case, to run concurrently. He refused to allow solicitor's costs. Mrs Wakefield went to prison."[22]

With a taximeter continually showing the fare, it was perhaps, a constant reminder to the hirer that their journey in a motor taxicab would have to be paid for. The novelty of riding in a motorcab, with the added bonus that the meter was the arbiter of any fare disputes and that women no longer travel in a cab in fear of the abuse and intimidation appealed to many. One such woman was an actress, Miss Maud O'Dell, of Eaton Terrace, Belgravia. She had been picked up at her residence at 11am by Frederick Charles Brett, who was described as a "taximeter motor-cab driver". By the time she had finished with Brett, it was quarter to one the following morning. All in all, he travelled 65 miles across London and had waited for her at various locations a total of seven hours. By the time he finished the fourteen-hour marathon, his taximeter had registered £3 11s 8d – and he did not receive a single penny from Miss O'Dell. It was the first recorded bilk of a taxi.

In court, Brett explained that he handed over every penny recorded by the meter and in return he was guaranteed two guineas a week and at the end of each month, he would receive a "bonus" of 25% of the meter reading. O'Dell's counsel tried to show that Brett was a salaried servant of the taxicab company, and it is they who should be summoning the actress. Curtis Bennett, the magistrate ignored that strategy. "The money is due, and must be paid." Brett received the fare plus 15s costs, having spent two days in court.[23]

Penalty for defrauding cabmen

Any person who hires a taxi with intent to avoid payment, is liable, in addition to the fare, to a penalty or imprisonment not exceeding fourteen days.

Or in cab trade parlance – "Doing a runner"

William Inskip gave chase when his passenger ran off, trying to avoid payment in September 1834. The passenger, "an independent gentleman, about four feet high, with a lump on his shoulder," had pointed out a kite flying in the sky as the cab passed through Regent's Park. As Inskip's attention was drawn to it, his diminutive passenger opened the door and ran off. Inskip caught him and the passenger refused to pay the fare, 1s 6d.

"Why don't you pay the fare?" enquired Short, the magistrate.

"I never hired the cab; I was forcibly put into it and carried against my will... Why, I was passing down Oxford Street, when on arriving at a coach stand [Inskip] caught hold of me, saying "Do you want a cab?". "No," said I, "I can walk home." "But you shan't," says the cabman, and, assisted by the waterman, lifted me into the cab, [Inskip] exclaiming as he drove off, "You shall ride, Sir, you shall ride."

"Lord, love your Vorship," interjected Inskip, "I never said no sich thing; the Gentleman got in by himself."

Requiring the judgement of Solomon to settle the dichotomy, both parties were entreated to retire to a side room where after a brief discussion "the defendant made satisfaction to the knight of the whip."[24]

If John Sandham, 6010, knew, in July 1843, why his passenger was getting so many doors closed in his face, he might have terminated the journey at the earliest opportunity. He had driven him to several locations in the Bloomsbury and Holborn areas, before ending up at Wellington Street, Covent Garden, and little did he realise that his passenger was trying to borrow money. In Wellington Street, Sandham asked for his fare, 3s. The passenger replied that he would have 3s 6d if he waited, but still nothing was forthcoming. He was given a scrap of paper "with some sort of scrawl on it" but as Sandham was looking at it, the passenger ran off down Tavistock Street. He ran through the maze of streets, long since demolished following the construction of Kingsway and the Aldwych, before making his way to Chancery Lane. Then across [High] Holborn into Grays Inn Square, up Grays Inn Lane (now Road) and turning right into Liquorpond Street (now Clerkenwell Road) where he was finally caught by Sandham. A large crowd had gathered as the two argued over the payment and on arrival of a policeman, the passenger was taken into custody.

"What are you?" enquired the magistrate, Combe.

"I am an author... of several scientific works... and I am now engaged in a work on the "Nuisances of London", here the prisoner was referring to the nuisances caused by bad drainage and open sewers, every parish had its 'Inspector of Nuisances', but now the arresting officer remarked that perhaps the prisoner should include himself, such was the nuisance he had created. After hearing all the evidence, Coombe remarked that, "Authors who are not able to pay their cab fare ought to walk like other men." The prisoner was told he would have to pay a total of seven shillings, the fare and loss of Sandham's time. The prisoner said he had no means to pay the sum of money and was sent to the House of Corrections for ten days.[25]

Some bilkers fail to appreciate just how understanding a cabman could be. Henry Skeats was one such person. In the summer of 1845 he and four others, after consuming a liberal amount of alcohol, clambered into David Hardment's cab as it sat on a stand in Whitechapel. He took them to Clapton Ponds, but finding the place they wanted was actually in Hackney Wick, he drove them there instead. Once there, the party got out of the cab, it was most likely a four-wheeler coach, and ran off in different directions without having paid the fare. "Skeats ran, Skeats doubled, but close on his heels was cabby in his cab." As he ran, with no doubt, the alcohol taking its effect on him, Hardment closed in on him. Soon he found himself facing the River Lea, with Hardment behind him. With no other option he jumped, but the river was deeper than he anticipated, and faster moving. Eventually Hardment managed to rescue his quarry from his impromptu watery grave. He took him to a nearby ale house and bought him a brandy. Then he took him to his home in Bethnal Green where he was fed and his clothes dried, and still he was bilked.

In court, Skeats was represented by "a dirty dissipated specimen of a tavern waiter" which is probably what he was, as was Skeats. He informed the magistrate that his client instructed him not to deny the fare but for the magistrate to determine how much should be paid. Broughton ordered Skeats to pay the 5s fare as well as 10s in expenses. The money was paid.[26]

There can be problems of a different kind when a cabman chases after a bilker. Whilst one cab driver was chasing after one of his passengers, in 1855, the other two doubled back and stole his cab. The driver caught the man he was chasing after, and even though he could not possibly have been involved in the theft of the cab - it was later recovered safe and sound - the bilker himself was imprisoned for one month with hard labour in the House of Correction. When, in 1867, John Hutson finally caught up with his runner, the man turned and stabbed him in the chest. The blade penetrated the two coats and a waistcoat Hutson was wearing but was stopped by a pocket book. In this instance the sanity of the prisoner was questioned and he was remanded for "inquiries might be made as to his state of mind."[27]

Giving chase to a runner, may not be the appropriate action within the eyes of the law. Benjamin Perridge's passengers had trouble finding exactly where they wanted when he was asked to take a railway clerk and his female companion to the New Kent Road. After driving to several locations, he dropped them off outside the Horsemonger Lane Prison. There then followed an argument about the fare during which the railway clerk took to his heels and ran off. Perridge gave chase and caught him. According to Perrdige, the passenger punched him in the face when he demanded his fare. According to the bilker, he struck Perridge in self-defence as he was grabbed hold of in a rough manner. According to Burcham the magistrate, "You had no right to seize him. If he refused to pay, you should have summoned him." Quite how a cabman is expected to get the name and address from a bilker who runs off was not explained to Perridge. Burcham dismissed the charges, and cautioned the driver as to his future conduct. He was, however, paid his fare.[28]

Some cabmen never seem to learn. On January 2nd 1865, George Jaques was hired by a butcher named Piper and drove him around east London for ten hours. Whilst told to wait for him outside a pub, the butcher climbed over a wall and ran off. Jaques eventually realised that he had been bilked and was not likely to see his money, or the passenger again. Until the following day that is, when, quite by chance, the butcher flagged him down. Piper made some excuses as to why he did not pay Jaques the previous night but added that he had been to his master's yard to enquire of him. Jaques took it all in and drove the butcher around east London, this time for eleven hours – with the same predictable result. It would be another two months before the pair should meet again. Justice finally caught up with the butcher, after he had ignored a summons taken out by Jaques and was arrested on a warrant. Unable to pay, the butcher was sentenced to three weeks in the House of Correction.[29]

Any person who, after hiring a taxi fraudulently endeavours to avoid payment...is liable, in addition to the fare, to a penalty or imprisonment not exceeding fourteen days.

William Southwell's "endeavours to avoid payment" nearly cost a cabman his life, and could have led to a noose around his neck. The night of January 2nd 1852 was a bitterly cold one. Hansom cabdriver, James Harman Crisp, 9079, had been hired by Southwell and had driven him around for several hours before they ended up at Ben Caunt's, a famous pugilist now turned inn keeper. In the pub, Southwell offered a porter, William Joyce (erroneously called William George in several newspapers) to a game of "first slap on the nose" for a pint of beer. Presumably the game involves two people facing each other, with their hands at a predetermined position, and the winner would be the first person quick enough to slap the other person's nose at a given signal. Southwell was not particularly quick and Joyce won his pint of beer. Crisp the cabdriver was then invited to have a go with Southwell. Crisp won but "accidently gave him a rather hard hit", which was not the best thing to do with your fare when you are trying to get paid. William Joyce stated that after, that Southwell was particularly spiteful towards the cabman and that he had given a hint that Crisp would not get his money. Southwell invited Joyce back to his brig, moored on the Thames, for supper. Joyce accepted the offer and informed Crisp that he was likely to be bilked by Southwell, and that he would stick by him to give him support. Having been driven to Cottrell's Wharf in Crisp's cab, the cabman and William Joyce followed Southwell as he climbed over several boats, before reaching his own, the *Petrel*.

On board, Crisp asked once more for his fare. Southwell took up a ham bone and flourished it in the air for a while before hitting Crisp over the head with it, knocking his hat off but causing him no pain. He then picked up a large knife and stabbed a cat that had the misfortune to be in close proximity, "and I believed killed it", stated William Joyce. At that moment the master of the Brig, Benjamin Thaxter, arrived and upon seeing two strangers on his vessel, began to get very irate. William Joyce and Crisp explained themselves and all appeared to be calm, until Crisp once more asked to be paid. Thaxter and Southwell, took up a fighting stance in front of Crisp and William Joyce, who, "fearing some treatment similar to what the cat had received" jumped into a barge moored alongside the *Petrel*. As Crisp clambered down the ladder to join William Joyce, Southwell was heard to shout out, "Go down, you __", and twisted the ladder, propelling Crisp into the freezing waters of the Thames.

To keep out the chill on cold winter nights, a cabman would wear many layers of clothing, up to sixteen such layers was not uncommon. Crisp was wearing a 'great coat' and several layers underneath that, and, as these became saturated, he became heavier and heavier. Three times William Joyce, lying on his stomach and reaching over into the cold water had grabbed hold of Crisp but each time his strength let him down. Realising what was happening, both Thaxter and Southwell, and a cabin boy, jumped down on to the barge to give assistance. It was not far short of high tide and William Joyce was fishing with his hands in a desperate attempt to grab hold of Crisp. Eventually he grabbed hold of his hair and with the assistance of the others, and after a further five minutes, managed to pull him out of the water and onto the barge. "He was in a very exhausted state; in fact, the last stage of existence between life and death."

When it came to the subsequent trial, Southwell stated that at this point that the cabman was drunk, to which William Joyce replied that Crisp was perfectly sober. "So I should think," replied Alderman Humphery at the Guildhall, "or he must have been drowned." The cabin boy was called. He did not see Crisp fall into the river but he could confirm that whilst Southwell did brandish a knife, the cat was very much alive. He believed everyone was drunk. When Captain Thaxter was called to the witness box, he denied that Crisp was in any danger, as he "was sticking in the mud in three feet of water, and did not sink at all." The captain may have been ignorant of the knowledge of a City Alderman. Humphery looked up in an almanac the state of the tides for January 2nd; "High water was at ten o'clock that night, only an hour and a half prior to this affair."

The Alderman informed the captain that the offence was indictable, if not capital, and that he would be released upon his own recognizances to appear, with the cabin boy, at a future date; and that Southwell will be remanded in custody. Crisp then explained to the magistrate that since that night he had been left in a deplorable condition. It had taken six weeks to bring the case to court but in that time he had not worked, having been bedridden since that night. "He was now literally in a starving condition." Taking pity on him, the Alderman awarded him 2s 6d from the poor box.[30]

The case was re-examined the next day in court, presumably at the request of Southwell's defence, who argued that the incident should be settled out of court, and not before a magistrate. Alderman Humphery concurred with the defence that it would be in the best interests of their client to have the matter settled outside, but it would not be in the best interests of justice. Having said that, the Alderman stated that he wished to have William Joyce, who had saved Crisp's life, to be called. He didn't appear, the defence were not expecting him to. This was confirmed by Crisp who said he saw Joyce that very morning, drinking in a pub nearby to the court, with the captain and other friends of the prisoner. This, the captain denied under oath, but the alderman warned him that if he continued in such a manner he would be indicted for the same offence as Southwell.[31]

William Joyce was recalled to the court and informed the alderman that on the date of the last hearing he did indeed meet with the captain and his friends. He had been informed that Crisp had dropped all charges on payment of £5 compensation and that he was paid a sovereign for his trouble. He was plied with several drinks after which he felt he was too drunk to appear in court, hence his non-appearance. On hearing this, the alderman remarked that the captain, on his last appearance, swore that he had not had a drink with the witness, nor done anything to prevent him from attending court. Captain Thaxter was called to the witness box to explain himself.

Thaxter admitted buying drinks for the previous witness, and to giving him £1 for his trouble – despite what he had said at his last appearance. He had not committed perjury as when he took the oath, he was not actually touching the bible. Besides, the sovereign paid to the last witness could not be construed as a bribe on his part as the money came from what was owed in wages to Southwell. Alderman Humphery remarked that such a trick was common enough, but would not be enough to save him from a charge of perjury.[32] It wasn't. Humphery informed Thaxter that he would face charges of perjury and released him on his own recognizances, with suitable sureties. He later discharged the captain and bound him over in the sum of £100 to appear and produce the cabin boy to give evidence at Southwell's trial.[33]

The trial went to the Old Bailey where all the evidence was once again gone into. A policeman testified that the ladder Crisp had climbed down was not properly secured and so would twist under the weight of a person. Nethertheless, the judge had heard enough, Southwell was sentenced to one month with hard labour.[34]

Nearly six years later, Crisp was once more before an Alderman at Guildhall court, only this time he was in the dock. He was charged with being so drunk he was scarcely able to sit on the box of his cab and had nearly ran over a small boy. Crisp explained that he had taken two soldiers who had bought him a couple of drinks but ever since that night he was thrown into the Thames, it appeared that very little alcohol, took a big effect on him. He was given the nominal fine of 5s which he immediately paid.[35]

9 Carriage of Extra Persons, Luggage, etc.

Refusing to carry etc

It is an offence for a taxi driver to refuse to carry a reasonable quantity of luggage.

Just what "quantity of luggage" can be defined as reasonable? That is a question that has plagued the hackney carriage trade for over two hundred years. In 1816, William Cooper, driving hackney coach with plate number 12, was summoned by his passenger for overcharging him. The distance was described as a "short shilling fare" but he also charged an extra shilling for a small portmanteau and it was on this charge that he was found guilty by the Commissioners of Hackney Coaches. What punishment was dealt to him was not recorded, though it could have been a fine of 15s - which seems to have been the fate of the other drivers summoned on that day – but the Commissioners did explain just what a coachman was allowed to charge for. A hackney coachman is "...compelled to carry trifling luggage without additional charge; but they are not compelled to carry weighty luggage or any other that would injure or dirty their coaches or chariots;" So far, so good, but the inclusion and non-definition of "trifling" could lead to disagreements. They continue, "but when they carry other luggage that causes additional trouble, they are justly entitled in a small remuneration, distinct from the legal fare."[1] How much "additional trouble" a piece of luggage can give is again open to interpretation.

When the owner driver of hackney coach 83 was summoned for charging 6d extra for carrying "a few light packages", he informed Rowe the magistrate that it was customary that a 6d charge could be imposed for luggage and had been approved by the Hackney Coach Commission and several other magistrate's courts. Rowe was not convinced, and looking at the legislation remarked that the Act of Parliament made no reference to a charge. The driver agreed it was not within the Act but the practice was pretty standard. Rowe questioned him as to why, when he is obliged to carry four adults without extra charge (as the law then stood in 1823), he feels justified to charge extra for a small piece of luggage with just one person. The driver replied that he would "rather carry four persons than luggage, for his cushions run no risk of being torn by nails." For his 6d overcharge, he was fined 10s with 5s 6d costs.[2]

In 1857 a cab driver sought advice from Beadon after he took a passenger, who had between "one and two tons of luggage four miles for 2s". At the end of the journey the passenger had refused to pay anything extra for the luggage. The cabman wanted to know if he could have legally refused to accept the fare without recrimination. Beadon said the amount of luggage he carried was certainly unreasonable but as he had accepted the fare and loaded the luggage onto his roof, he could not charge for the luggage as there was only one person in the cab, but he certainly could have bargained a price before the hiring actually began. The cabman left the court grumbling that from then on, he would only carry a "reasonable" amount of luggage.[3]

In 1917 the question of a 'reasonable' amount of luggage raised its head once more in two differing actions. In the first case, a driver was summoned for refusing to carry a passenger and £500 in silver, in two bags, more on the basis of the weight of the bags, 1 cwt (112 lbs or 8 stone). The magistrate agreed with the driver, saying that money was not luggage and that special arrangements should be made for its carriage. The summons was dismissed.[4] In the second case, a driver refused to carry two passengers who had two parcels of silk with them, weighing 15lbs, the magistrate, D'Eyncourt interpreted that "a reasonable amount of luggage" had a wider meaning than the term "personal luggage" as used on the railways. The driver in this instance was fined 20s with 6s costs.[5]

If the term "reasonable" was open to conjecture, then what exactly defined "luggage"? In 1853 John Bigg, a fruiterer of Covent Garden Market applied to magistrate Henry at Bow Street for a summons against a cab driver. Bigg explained that for the past few years he had been in the habit of buying a large amount of pineapples from a broker at the Monument and taking them by cab to his premises in Covent Garden.

For this service he would pay the driver 2s, which he felt more than covered the fare according to distance. On Monday 11th of July however, he had hailed a cab and loaded it up with 120 pineapples (some reports say it was 130). All the pineapples went inside the cab, whilst Bigg sat on the box alongside the driver, who was later named as Robert Clark. At the destination, Clark refused to accept the 2s proffered by the fruiterer and demanded 3s instead. Clark then took from his pocket a copy of the 1853 Hackney Carriage Act (the act only came into force on the previous day) and stated that according to the act he could charge 2d for every package, 120 pineapples at 2d each was equal to £1, so he was doing the fruiterer a favour by only demanding a shilling extra to carry all the pineapples. Having never paid more than the two shillings the fruiterer stood his ground but Clark said if he did not pay him, he would take him round to the magistrate's court at Bow Street where he would be found to be entitled to the one pound extra. Reluctantly Bigg paid Clark the extra shilling and the next morning he himself went to the magistrate's court to obtain a summons against the driver for exaction.

After listening to Bigg's story, Henry informed him, "I must tell you that one of the objects of the new act is to provide the public with a better class of hackney carriages, and to have them kept in a cleanly and decent condition. It was never intended that they should be converted into market-carts. It would not be very pleasant, for example, to the next person who engaged the cab in question, after it had been filled with pineapples." Bigg interjected here stating that the smell of pineapples was one of the more agreeable aromas. "But if once the system prevailed," countered Henry, "of sending about merchandise of that kind in cabs, they might soon be employed to convey fish, meat etc."[6] Despite the magistrate's objections to cabs being utilised under these conditions, he allowed the summons to proceed.

A fortnight later, cabman Robert Clark was in the dock in front of magistrate Henry. Clark admitted that he was wrong to suggest he could charge 2d for carrying each of the pineapples, "although they nearly filled the inside of the cab", he still thought charging an extra shilling was not an unreasonable request. Henry informed him that he was wrong in every point of his argument; he was wrong in consenting to do the job in the first place; he was wrong in seeking to charge for them for luggage; he was wrong in demanding more than his fare for the distance; and he was wrong in supposing that he had the power to take the hirer to a magistrate's court for the argument to be settled there – the hirer could force the driver, but the driver had no jurisdiction in forcing the hirer to a court. Henry informed the cabman that it was obvious he used the pineapples as an excuse to extort an extravagant fare from Mr Bigg, and for that he was fined 40s or be committed for a month. Not having access to that sum of money Clark, accepted martyrdom according to some of the press reports, and was sent to prison.[7] Clark was not the only "martyr" to the cab trade to be imprisoned that day by Henry; he also incarcerated Thomas Phillips, whose case was reported on in Chapter 6, for not having the deposit of 5s to have the ground measured.

The backlash over Phillips saw Henry vilified and lampooned by the press and although "The Pineapple Case" excited some public interest, Robert Clark, unlike Thomas Phillips, appears to have served the full term of his prison sentence. To give a better understanding of the different Hackney Carriage Acts then in force, *The Observer* newspaper asked a barrister from Lincolns Inn to explain the current laws regarding cabs for its readers. In the last paragraph the attorney states, "The term luggage according to the true modern doctrine on the subject, comprises clothing and such articles as a traveller usually carries with him for his personal convenience; perhaps a small present, or a book for the journey, might be included in the term. It does not, however, extend to merchandise, or materials bought for the purpose of being manufactured and sold at a profit."[8] Clearly the pineapples were merchandise and although the penalty far outweighed the crime, Henry felt that once Clark accepted the hiring he had to abide by hackney carriage laws.

The 1853 Act had intended that the question of charging for luggage should be simplified – if there were at least two persons inside the cab then any luggage placed on the roof or on the box by the driver, could be charged at 2d an item. In July 1853 Grenville Robert Henry Somerset of Chesham Place, Belgravia, refused to pay the extra 2d demanded by the driver for an item of luggage on the roof as he was the only passenger and therefore exempt from the charge. The un-named cabman obviously seeing that his fare was well-to-do and no doubt part of the aristocracy of the land, with an expensive house in Belgravia, obviously felt that the slight imposition of charging 2d over the top would not be worth the trouble to the passenger. Somerset refused to pay the 2d and insisted that the driver take him to the nearest police court to have the matter settled there. The driver refused to budge, stating (wrongly) that it was not his business to know where the court was or to take him there at all. Somerset remained firmly seated in the cab and said he would wait for a passing policeman. Eventually, under directions from the passenger the driver drove to Westminster Police Court. By now the driver obviously realised he had created a rod for his own back and that the situation was about to get worse for him – the sitting magistrate that day at Westminster was Arnold, whose ambivalence to the plight of a cab driver was worse than his fellow magistrate Henry. The driver tried to claim ignorance of the new law but Arnold was apathetic. For the 2d overcharge the driver was fined twenty shillings or, in default of payment, 14 day's imprisonment. Grenville Robert Henry Somerset of Chesham Place, Belgravia, no doubt went home pleased in doing his public duty that he had acted against the outrageous extortions exacted upon the public by the cabmen of the metropolis.[9]

In a case a few days later, Joseph Shephard, badge 1222, summoned his passenger for non-payment of his fare. Principally the dispute was over waiting time but the case highlights just how hackney carriages were used as carriers. Shephard stated in court that he was called from the stand near Kensington Gate, to pick up at a house there. It was a two-cab job to Paddington Station and after waiting twenty minutes at the pick-up he was loaded up with three persons inside the cab and a quantity of luggage placed on the roof *viz.* "two boxes, two beds, a French bedstead, and the rods, making in the whole six packages." Having unloaded passengers and luggage at Paddington, Shephard was told to wait. As he was not allowed to wait in the yard at the station he was compelled to wait outside. He gave up after 30 minutes and returned to Kensington Gate for his fare. The passenger, who was already home accused Shephard of driving off, presumably with another fare and would only pay him the fare he felt the driver was entitled. Fortunately for Shephard, Beadon the magistrate was well aware that cab drivers could not wait within Paddington Station and he informed the passenger, or rather his representative, who, unusually for the time was a female, that if the driver had waited several hours for the defendant, he would have had to have been paid for his time. The driver did him a favour by only allowing half an hour. The disputed 2s was paid as well as 7s towards Shephard's costs.[10]

The law on charging for luggage was now defined and clearly understood – if there were more than two persons inside the cab, then any luggage placed outside could be charged at 2d per item. That's at least what a cabman believed when he summoned a gentleman who resided in Brixton Road for non-payment of 8d, the charge he made for four items of luggage on the roof. The cabman informed Elliott the magistrate that he had three women in his cab and was therefore entitled to charge for the luggage placed on the roof. The defendant agreed that there were three ladies of his family travelling in the cab but that the luggage, consisting of "a small and empty basket, a small carpet bag, and two boxes each about 15 inches in length" and could easily have been placed inside the cab at no inconvenience to the passengers. The cabman maintained that by the letter of the law he was entitled to charge 2d for each of the four items, Elliott informed him that was not the case. An exception included in the act stated that "when more than two persons shall be carried [...] with more luggage than can be carried inside the carriage, a further sum of 2d for every package carried outside [is chargeable]."[11] Elliott had eliminated another perk of the job. Having loaded three women into his cab the driver was quick to put the small items of luggage on the roof so he could charge an extra 8d. Now it was clear that he could only do this if the inside of the carriage was full – another bone of contention – or that the passenger requested items be placed on the roof of the cab.

If the drivers could be accused of using underhand tactics to wangle a few extra pennies from their passengers, the passenger's themselves were not averse to doing all they could from preventing Cabby obtaining what could be rightfully his. Cab driver Thomas Nathan came unstuck by the new law when he was summoned by his passenger for demanding 2d over his proper fare. The complainant, a gentleman of Bond Street stated that he and his wife and a quantity of luggage were inside the cab, his wife's maid, sat on the box alongside the driver and there was luggage on the roof. Despite the report in the Daily News that Nathan was driving a cab, it had to in fact have been a four-wheeler coach. The driver was offered 2s, being 1s for the distance, 6d for the third person and 6d for the luggage. The driver believed he was entitled to a further 2d as the four pieces of luggage covered the roof. Having looked at the Act, Bingham, the magistrate, agreed it was not very clear but with the wisdom of Solomon declared that both parties were in the wrong: the passenger for having an erroneous understanding of what was meant by "a reasonable amount of luggage" and cabman Nathan for wrongly demanding an extra 2d – the law stated that he could only charge 2d for each package whilst there were more than two persons inside the cab and whilst he carried three persons, a maid was not expected to sit within the carriage along with her mistress. Nathan was advised to take the 6d offered for the luggage but does not appear to have been fined for the overcharge.[12]

John Williams, aka the 'Cabmen's Attorney-General', whom we have met a couple of times already, was one of those cab drivers who, every now and then, like to challenge the interpretation of hackney carriage laws. He was well known to staff at London Bridge, who regarded him as a trouble maker and had just recently ejected him from the station following a dispute. This time, he carried a couple and "a quantity of luggage" to the station but when he was offered his fare he retorted that it was not sufficient and demanded extra for the luggage. If the 'Cabmen's Attorney-General' was at all well versed in the law he would have realised he did not have a legal leg to stand on – there were only two passengers, and if he agreed to carry the extra luggage then he cannot demand a payment for it. A tussle occurred between Williams and a railway porter who was endeavouring to unload the luggage from the cab and place it on the soon-to-be-departing train. Williams grabbed hold of a carpet bag which was wrenched from his grip. He climbed down from his cab and in the ensuing tug of war, the wheel of the cab went over Williams' foot, causing a considerable amount of pain. Williams summoned the railway porter for assault and the passenger for non-payment of the fare.

The assault charge was dealt with first. After Williams gave his side of the story, the magistrate, Gilbert A'Beckett, who was normally sympathetic towards cabmen, said whatever injury he sustained was of his own making, he had no right to prevent the removal of luggage from his cab and therefore the summons was dismissed. Having now lost the 2s cost of summons for that case, Williams now continued with his claim against his passenger for the 6d he demanded for the luggage. Williams' case was that there was a discrepancy between the act of parliament and the Police Commissioners book – the *abstract of law*. "I say we can charge 2d a mile for extra parcels, as well as for extra passengers. [...] The act of parliament gives us authority to charge 2d for every parcel, and I consider that it means 2d a mile for the whole distance the fare may go." In Williams' view, the quantity of luggage he had in and on his cab was not a reasonable amount and thus his interpretation of the law was the correct one. The defence counsel acting for the passenger described Williams' construct as "absurd". If he had not thought that the luggage was a reasonable amount at the start of the journey he could have legally refused to have carried it. The fact that he did carry it without complaint until his arrival at London Bridge shows acceptance of that fact and that the summons should also be dismissed. A'Beckett tended to agree with the defence; he too, was well aware of the finer points in hackney carriage law and the passenger had no case to answer, the summons was dismissed and the 'Cabmen's Attorney-General' tasted yet another defeat.[13]

In 1879, cabman Job Toop summoned his passenger's master for non-payment of the fare. Toop explained that he had been hired by a young boy to convey four large bundles of newspapers from Waterloo Station to a publisher's in the Strand. The price agreed was 1s 6d but when the boy came to pay Toop, he said his master only gave him 1s 4d. Toop sent the boy back up and told him the fare was 1s 6d. The boy came back down soon after, this time with only 1s 2d in his hand. Once more Toop sent him back up. On the third occasion the master came down and now offered Toop just 1s, his legal fare for the distance covered. Toop agreed that distance-wise the fare was only 1s but as the newspaper bundles could not be construed as luggage, he was allowed to name a reasonable charge. The magistrate, Vaughan agreed; "The term 'luggage' was meant by the Act to apply exclusively to articles used by the traveller for his comfort or convenience..." Toop was awarded his 1s 6d fare plus 4s costs.[14]

As stated previously, the public were not averse to carrying as much luggage as they could in or on a cab without making any payment, especially when there were two or less passengers. A point of law arose in 1861 when cabman Elijah Lane was summoned for extortion. He had carried a lady, her nurse maid and a small baby in his cab plus four items of luggage on the roof. Lane demanded the payment for the luggage as he considered there were three persons in his cab and the law states that he could charge accordingly for luggage outside when more than two persons are inside the cab. The complainant stated that the law required that two children under ten can be charged as an adult person (there is more on this debate later in this chapter) and as there was only a small child, who could not be charged for, then the cab driver had no right to charge for the luggage. After studying the relevant act, Dayman the magistrate conceded that the cabman was right, whilst the law stipulated that two children under ten can be charged as one adult person, the clause regarding luggage makes no stipulation as to age and that only the word "person" is used. Elijah Lane therefore made a legal demand and the summons against him was dismissed with costs.[15]

James Western was hired by the hour when he took a passenger to a home where the contents were being sold off. His passenger emerged with a large picture and a bundle of five books, all of which were placed on the roof. Having been engaged for just an hour, the passenger proffered 2s 6d, Western demanded 3s 6d which he said was 2s 6d fare, then as the string holding the books together had (somehow) come undone, he was entitled to charge for the six packages at 2d each. The passenger refused to pay anything and was summoned by Western. The magistrate refused to listen to Western's argument that the *Abstract of Laws* allowed him to charge 2d for every package on the roof and said the proper fare was 2s 10d, allowing for the fare and two packages and the summons was dismissed.[16]

Excess passengers

It is an offence to carry in a taxi persons in excess of the number for which the taxi is licensed.

The phrase "To carry *n* persons" was introduced in the Act of 1831, and has been used ever since. The law was introduced due to the earlier introduction of the cabriolet and chariot. The four-seater chariots were smaller than the traditional hackney coach which could seat four or more; the more nimble cabriolets, such as the Hansom, had room for just two people. This did not stop the public, or the drivers, trying to cram as many as possible into them. The limitation on passenger numbers may have meant the driver may have lost out on any extra charges he could have levied but at least the horse benefitted.

Charges for extra passengers have been an "extra" for the driver ever since the hackney coaches were first licensed in 1654. The Act itself did not specify charges for extra passengers, nor even the rate at which the coaches could charge per mile. The Act did empower the Court of Aldermen to lay down any rules and regulations as they saw fit and one such rule was to charge 6d for each passenger over three.[17]

The un-named driver of a hackney chariot which carried four people from Aldersgate Street to Oxford Street in January 1832 demanded a shilling extra on top of the half-a-crown fare. When he was subsequently summoned to appear at Marlborough Street Court, the magistrate, Conant, informed him that he had an absolute right to refuse to carry more than his licence stated, in this case three, but if he did consent to carry above the stated number then he could not charge for them. Pleading ignorance of the law the driver 'escaped' with a mitigated penalty of 10s plus costs.[18] The magistracy were not prepared to prevent any number of people travelling in a cab, just that the driver should not benefit from it. The public were not to be taken advantage of and they had the full protection of the law. No doubt in many cases cabmen did receive a tip for carrying extra people, probably after informing the passenger that four people in one cab is a lot cheaper than two in two cabs. The effect of the added burden on the horse was rarely considered.

One case which did evoke sympathy for the horse was when George Cocks was charged at Southwark Town Hall of carrying eleven people. There were "five persons inside, one on the box, one sitting on the shaft, one crouched upon the apron, one on each step and the eleventh on the back rail." Police Sergeant M'Craw informed the magistrate that the poor horse could just about keep its equilibrium, "Indeed Sir, it would have made your heart ache to hear the poor horse groan." M'Craw testified that he had seen the party alighting at the King's Arms in the Borough where they all went for a drink. They were inside for a few minutes before telling Cocks to take them on to Billingsgate, where the cabman would be "well paid". It is not stated if Cocks did receive his money but "in consequence of his poverty" the magistrate only fined him 30s.[19] At least in this case the plight of the horse was taken into consideration, but Cocks was fined not for cruelty to the horse but for carrying an excessive number of passengers. Even members of the public had their own interpretation of the law as will be seen by the next case.

In 1835 a cabman took a party of five shoemakers in his cab from somewhere in the West End to an ale house in Coleman Street in the City. The driver, again un-named, waited outside on the cold January day, whilst the five inside were seen to be having a good time drinking gin. After a while, the cabman has entered the pub and asked for his fare, to which he was told that as he carried more than he was allowed to, they would take him before the Lord Mayor and see that he was punished. They were indeed soon before the Lord Mayor, who was sitting in his capacity as chief magistrate of the City of London. It was the cabman who was the prosecutor and one of the shoemakers, Thomas Seeker, was charged with bilking him of his fare. In court the cabman was attracting criticism from both the Lord Mayor and the shoemaker: "What on earth could have induced you to let five great fellows into your cab to fag your poor horse?" asked the Lord Mayor. Before he could answer, Seeker from the dock gave his thoughts on the matter, "Ay, my Lord, there's the thing, as I said – the Society for cruelty to poor hanimals ought to take it up; it's a [damn] shame to come down so heavy upon the loins of a poor beast, and I'm blest if us didn't sweat him like smoke. When we com'd to Holborn Hill you'd a laughed to see the [damn] pucker he was in." With much laughter resounding throughout the court, the driver explained that he was not aware that he was carrying five. When the Lord Mayor, somewhat sarcastically remarked to the cabman, "Well, you certainly are a very nice humane driver", the shoemaker, no doubt with full justification that the driver should be the one on trial added, "Yes, your Worship, these fellows has no more feeling. – It's a pity they an't obleeged to drag their own cabs." The Lord Mayor agreed. "So it is; but I'm afraid you must pay him his fare for all that, my friend. Although he has been unjust to his poor horse, I must not let you be unjust to him; so pull your money out." Again, to much laughter in the courtroom, the crestfallen shoemaker replied, "My Lord, I'm astonished! What, pay this man?" The Lord Mayor confirmed his judgement, and added that he would have to pay the expenses and costs of the cabman as well. "I an't got no money, my Lord, about me" cried the shoemaker, who had obviously not been expecting this turn of events. "Perhaps you'd let me go for it?" The Lord Mayor would not let him leave the court; "You can send for it, my friend; but you'll stay with me until you get it. Gaoler, put this gentleman in the cage; he's a very good man, and a friend to the brute creation; but he must get a little money if he cabs it any more." And so the shoemaker was "locked up amidst the laughter of the crowd".[20]

The Act of 1853 attempted to settle the problem – drivers could be compelled by the hirer to carry up to the number of passengers as marked on the plate – as had always been the case. Hackney coachmen were only allowed to charge 6d for any number over two persons. A coach carrying 3, 4 or 5 persons could only charge the same flat rate of 6d extra. A cab could only carry two persons, a driver would be acting illegally if he carried more than that number, whether or not he charged for them.

It has already been seen how the Act of 1853 had not only provoked the first general strike within the cab trade but the case of cabman Thomas Phillips (Chapter 6) had also seen questions raised in the House of Commons. Thomas Phillips was not the only consequence of the ill-informed act that the members were discussing. Within a fortnight of it being passed, MP's were debating an emergency Bill to correct the errors of their own making which was not without its own problems.

Several members expressed their reluctance to rectify the law whilst the drivers were out on strike. Others argued that the new charge for extra persons, 6d for no matter how many more than two people, was unjust and needed to be rectified as soon as possible as a cabman could not possible earn a living at the present rate.

"Mr GROGAN… As he understood it, [The Hackney Carriage Duties Bill] enacted that if a cab carried more than two persons the owner should be entitled to 6d for every additional person. To that he had no objection (hear, hear); but he did not like the clause which provided that where a person hired a cab licensed to carry two persons he should only have 6d for it [the minimum fare].

Mr LOWE: He may carry more than two.

Mr GROGAN: I always understood he was not to carry more than two.

Mr LOWE: Then, the hon. member is mistaken."[21]

If the law makers did not know the law, what chance the humble cab driver. The law regarding charging for extra passengers was changed in the Hackney Carriage Act (No 2) of 1853. Cabmen could now charge for any number of persons above two. So simple, even peers of the realm should have understood it. Lord Marcus Hill evidently did not. He sent a servant to obtain a cab to take four members of his family and a servant to Divine Service. The driver charged Lord Hill's servant, who rode on the box, 6d for the distance and 1s 6d extra, being 6d for each of the extra persons over two. The servant responded by saying that his lordship would not pay more than a shilling. The driver, William Davis, took the shilling, then took out a summons against Lord Hill. The nobleman stated that earlier that day a different cab had been procured for the same people and on the same journey. That driver asked for, and received, 1s, being, the Lord presumed, 6d for distance and 6d for extra persons. As he had only paid 1s for the one trip, he could not see how the Davis was justified in charging double for the same journey. The magistrate, Arnold, informed him that the cab driver was in his right to charge 2s as the law was very much in his favour, and that he was perhaps fortunate that the first driver was not aware of the change in the law. Lord Hill said he would be happy to settle the matter but after paying the outstanding shilling, and 5s costs, he remarked that William Davis was certainly not so reasonable as the earlier driver.[22] As a servant was sitting alongside Davis, then the carriage could only have been a coach. Presumably the cabman who took the party to Divine Service was also driving a coach but he, like Lord Hill, was unaware that the Act of 1853 now allowed for a extra charge regardless of whether a person was in or on a hackney coach.

Clause XIV of the second Hackney Carriages Act of 1853 states; "Whenever more than two persons shall be conveyed by *any* [my italics] Hackney Carriage drawn by One Horse only, a Sum of Sixpence for each Person above the Number of Two shall be paid for the whole Hiring in addition to the Fare..." Now it was enshrined in law, a cabman could ignore the plate that allowed a maximum number of people in his cab and he could charge accordingly. "Licensed to carry *n* persons" was now a redundant phrase.

In 1854 a cab driver named Gathercole carried eight people in his cab, "three on the roof of the cab, two inside, one on the box, and two on the springs behind". Not only overburdened, but Gathercole drove at speed, in the middle of the night, through the grand central arcade of the Covent Garden building, then, as now, a pedestrian precinct. Gathercole was arrested and his cab was taken to a green yard. Gathercole explained that as his guests were in a hurry, and the roads around Covent Garden were blocked, he decided to drive through the arcade. Fortunately for him it appears that nobody's life and limb were in danger. He was fined £2, which was paid immediately. *The Observer* reported that the whole escapade was as a result of a wager for £5 by Gathercole's passengers. Whether he had to pay the fine out of his winnings however, is not recorded.[23]

There are numerous instances of drivers trying to get as many people into their cab as physically possible for greater reward. When stopped by the police in 1876, George Collins, badge 852, was found to have five women and a small child in his cab, which was a four-wheeler but described in the press as a cab, he also had two men sitting on the roof and a man and boy sharing his seat with him. Rather oddly, given recent magisterial decisions, as two of the children were under ten years of age he was only guilty of carrying nine persons whilst licensed to carry five, for which he was fined 2s 6d plus 2s costs.[24]

Lazy reporting often described a four-wheeled coach or chariot as a two-wheeled, two-seater cab but when John Ulstenson, badge 13386, agreed to carry seven people, his cab was a cab. He picked the group up in Haymarket and two sat inside whilst the five others climbed on the roof. At nearby Cranbourn Street the two seated inside the cab decided to get out and they walked away. Not wishing to take the remaining five any further he asked for his fare which they refused to give him. One of them asked for his ticket and as he was reaching for it he was struck a violent blow from behind. He soon found himself surrounded by the five men who punched and kicked him as he fell to the floor. Eventually he was rescued from the "melee" and one man was arrested. In court the prisoner denied that he had anything to do with the assault and appealed to one of the witnesses, one of the two men who had been inside the cab but had left before the assault took place, that he was trying to rescue the cabman. Tyrwhitt the magistrate said there was little doubt "a most brutal assault had been committed on the cabman" and that the prisoner was one of the guilty attackers. Using magisterial dexterity that was seldom prevalent in others, Tyrwhitt informed the prisoner that unless he could come to a settlement outside court with Ulstenson he would be fined £3 or two month's imprisonment if he failed to pay. After retreating to a side room, the badly bruised Ulstenson returned and informed Tyrwhitt that the prisoner had agreed to pay him 36s to have the charges dropped, and this he was happy to accept.[25]

WS Gilbert, collaborator of the Savoy Operas with Arthur Sullivan, once asked a cabman the largest number of people he had ever carried. "He had carried seventeen at a go once. He was the last cab at Cremorne but the fellow did it for a lark. He had five or six inside, and a lot of them on the roof, one or two on the box, and one or two on the horse. he might have lost his licence, but he made nearly thirty shillings by it."[26]

If the story was true, then that particular driver benefitted from carrying more than he was obviously licensed for. But the question remained, could a cab driver charge for more people than he was actually licensed to carry? The question had all but been settled at Clerkenwell Police

Court in 1873 by magistrate Cooke. Cab driver John Cleney had summoned his passenger for non-payment of a 5s fare. The passenger refused to pay the fare as he argued that being charged 6d extra for the third person in a cab licensed for two was an illegal act. Cooke adjourned the case to look further into it. His judgement sided with the passenger; if a cab was licensed to carry only a certain number of people, then the licensing authority deemed what they thought to be a safe maximum number of people for that cab to hold. If a driver carried more than that number, then he was in breach of his licensing conditions and as such, could not be rewarded, by the extra payment of 6d, to carry an excessive number of passengers. It was a pyrrhic victory for the passenger whom Cooke accused of committing perjury in attempting to demolish the cab driver's complaint. The magistrate accepted the cabman's version of how long he had been kept waiting outside a pub and told the passenger he would have to pay the 5s fare as well as Cleney's 6s 6d costs.[27] Until the seatbelt law simplified the matter, Cooke's interpretation prevailed. Usually.

Ten years later the question arose again, this time at Hammersmith Police Court before magistrate Paget. A cabman named Hall informed the magistrate when he applied for a summons, that he had taken a lady and two others from St John's Wood to Cheniston Gardens, Kensington. At the destination the lady gave Hall 2s 6d, but he said his fare was 3s. The lady took the money back, and instead of giving him 3s she then said, "You'll have nothing," threw her card at him and shut the door in his face." Paget warned the cabman that the passenger was bound to raise the point that his cab "was only constructed to carry two persons". Hall replied that if he drove a four wheeled growler they would have been bound to pay him the extra 6d. Before warning Hall that he could be making himself liable to a penalty for overloading if he persisted with the summons, he acquiesced and allowed one to be made.[28]

Five days later the parties were in court and Hall was represented by barrister William St Aubyn, whose success rate on behalf of several cabdrivers up to this point had been pretty dismal. St. Aubyn opened the proceedings by stating that it was not a question of the amount, but one of principle – the driver had carried three people, he should be allowed to charge for the third person. The lady's husband, W Henry Vignoles, had accepted the summons on behalf of his wife. He argued that payment for a third person when carried in a two-seater cab was entirely optional, although, he hastened to add, he always paid the extra 6d himself. St. Aubyn brought the attention of the court to the ticket that each driver must hand to his passenger, on which it was stated that he was entitled to charge for extra passengers. If a Hansom cab could not carry more than two, then there could not be any extra passengers – if that were so, why was the ruling printed onto the ticket. Despite his reluctance to issue the summons in the first place, Paget came down on the side of the cabman and told Vignoles he would have to pay the disputed fare of 3s plus £1 8s in costs, it seems that although victory by St Aubyn was somewhat rare, it came at a price.[29]

Driver Robert Collins was not as fortunate when, the following year, he tried to charge his passenger, an extra 6d for carrying three people. Collins testified that he dropped the passenger, who was a barrister, and two women off at Clarendon Street, Pimlico and was offered 18d. Collins informed the gentleman that his fare was 2s, he wanted 6d for the third person in his cab. "[The] defendant said he would not give him another farthing, and, calling him a filthy name, struck him a violent blow in the face, knocking him against the cab wheel." This was too much for the prisoner in the dock, "It's an utter falsehood," he shouted out. "Let anyone examine my biceps and see if I am a strong man and capable of doing it. The cabman demanded more than his fare, and was very irritating, I admit that I gave him a slap." Fortunately, a medical examination was not needed, a police constable had witnessed the assault and the bad language from the barrister and fining him 20s or 14 days, D'Eyncourt the magistrate, expressed that as a member of the bar "he should have known better". As for Collins, D'Eyncourt believed that he had brought much of the trouble upon himself by attempting to overcharge, it was obviously his view that a cab licensed for two could not charge for a third person and as such he would not allow any costs to be awarded to the cabman.[30]

The arrival of the taximeter-cab in 1907 brought with it a new set of problems. The taxicabs, particularly the Renaults employed by The

General Motor Cab Company had four seats fitted and a sign inside the taxi proclaiming that for every passenger over the number of two, the driver was entitled to charge 6d extra. This sign was nullified by the plate on the rear of the taxi that the vehicle was only licensed to carry a maximum of two passengers. Peter Kent was possibly the first taxi driver to find himself in court on a charge of carrying excessive passengers. He had four in the back of his taxi and a fifth person riding on the box - the luggage compartment - which for the next fifty years would be door-less. Lawyers for the General Cab Company informed Sir Walter Wilkin sitting at the now defunct City Summons Court, of their grievance of spending a lot of capital on four-seater taxicabs but for some obscure reason, the police would only allow for them to carry two persons. The magistrate had sympathy for their position but it was his belief that at the present time, the police turned a blind eye to any taxi carrying four persons inside the taxicab, but Kent carried one outside and that was why he was stopped. Peter Kent was fined 16s plus costs.[31]

A few days later at the same court, a driver named Goodhall, was summoned for carrying five persons in his taxi, but he had a good excuse; the five adults were French, as such, they were small and he had plenty of room in his taxi. He may have evoked a note of sympathy from the sitting Alderman, he was only fined 5s plus costs.[32]

The following day, taxi-driver William Alfred Bryant was in the nearby Guildhall court and although he admitted to carrying five persons, he had actually issued a summons against one of his passengers. He had picked up the five passengers at Kempton Races and agreed to take them to Fleet Street. As they could not all fit in the back, he allowed one of the men to ride beside him in the luggage area. There were a number of stops on the journey at various public houses and it was after waiting at one of these that Bryant noticed that the passenger who was seated alongside him in the luggage compartment, had raised the flag, thus resetting the meter to zero. With nothing registered on the meter, the passenger's refused to pay him. His claim was for 21 miles at 8d a mile and 6s for waiting, a total of £1.

"But why" asked the clerk of the court, "did you carry a man on the box at all? You know it's illegal."

"We do it in a friendly way because we like to oblige the public. We are only licensed to carry two, and that is all I claim for."

"You are only licensed to drive within the Metropolitan Police district. Is Kempton Park within the area?"

"I cannot say; but no end of public carriages [i.e. London taxis and cabs] ply for hire there."

The defendant at this point stated that he was willing to pay the 14 shillings for the distance, but disputed the waiting time. He argued that the driver was drunk and nearly crashed the taxi at Richmond Bridge, so much so that one of his fellow passenger's got out and presumably caught a train. Bryant denied he was drunk. The clerk noted that under the Act, the sole arbiter of such disputes was the taximeter, but there was no provision for it either not working or having been tampered with. The defendant admitted that they stopped "once or twice" on the journey back, but not as long as the driver was stating. When pressed, he said he was willing to pay two shillings towards the waiting, instead of the six claimed by Bryant. "It is a most unsatisfactory case." Explained the magistrate. "In the first place you [Bryant] had no right to take five people in your cab, and therefore I have not that sympathy I should have had under other circumstances. It was owing to your conduct that it was possible for one of these men to tamper with your taximeter. The defendant admits owing something, and in making an order, I should in the usual way have allowed the cabman 10s for his expenses. But, inasmuch as he broke the law himself, I shall not do so. The order will be for the defendant to pay the 14s fare for distance, 2s for waiting, 4s for the cabman's expenses and 3s for the summons.[33]

In 2003 Mayor Ken Livingstone abolished all charges for carrying extra persons. Despite the extra wear and tear a taxi suffers, five or six people can travel as cheaply as one.

An infant in arms does not count as a person, and two children under 10 years count as one person.

When the author received his badge in 1987, he and the rest of the cab drivers who had just obtained their "rec" – their final chat before embarking as a fully-fledged cab driver - were asked "What is the legal number of people you can carry in a cab?" The question appeared straight forward, the FX4 could seat four people and the newly introduced Metrocab could seat five. In their well-rehearsed routine and with an air of authority, the carriage officer in question informed us that the correct answer was sixteen and twenty respectively. If two children under ten count as one adult and babes in arms do not count at all, then eight or ten children, each carrying a baby, would fall within the bounds of legality and would not infringe on the maximum number of passengers allowed in the cab. That they were wrong there is little doubt, but these were the very people who were guiding the fledgling cab drivers on their new, and presumably lawful, career. If carriage officers (who at the time were all ex-policemen) and the magistrates over the centuries had trouble interpreting the law, there was little hope for the cab driver. There has been much confusion over the "infants in arms", as well as "two children under ten count as one" rules and whilst, as paragraph 55 of the *Abstract*, stated above, maintains the precept, the subsequent paragraph of the *Abstract* then states that the maximum number of passengers allowed in a cab cannot exceed the number of seat belts fitted. So, thanks to the seat belt law, the maximum number of people allowed to travel in a cab is set, as per licence plate.

The charging of children was a vexed question to the cabman of the nineteenth century. There were two points facing the cabmen, could they charge for a baby carried in the arms of a passenger? and could they charge for a small child? Many drivers may not have made the effort to insist on charging a small child, particularly one that was carried or held in the lap throughout a journey. There were some drivers who believed it was their right to charge. One such was an unnamed driver who was brought before magistrate Birnie, in 1816. The complainant argued that he was charged 3s 6d for a 1s 6d fare, for putting in the coach, two adults and four children. The most recent Hackney Coach Act stated that the hackney coaches were only compellable to carry four adults, but gave no definition of what was meant by an 'adult'. The youngest child was three years-old, and whilst the complainant travelled in another coach, he thought it most unlikely the child would have occupied a seat on his own as he was so small. The legal argument then centred around the point that if the children could get into or out of a coach unassisted, they should be chargeable. Clearly, a three-year-old was incapable of such actions. The driver in this case, having charged for the youngest child, was ordered to return the shilling he had charged and ordered to pay the costs.[34]

The phrase "two children count as one adult" was introduced in the second Hackney Carriage Act of 1853. On the face of it, there can be nothing simpler than the phrase "two children count as one adult". Usually, children are smaller than adults, they take up less room and weigh less. Straightforward enough you might think, and no doubt the legislators were of a similar mind. As usual, the cab trade was not consulted and it was not long before the drivers threw the proverbial spanner into the works: If two children count as one adult, what does one child count as?

On December 30th 1853, cab driver Richard Fayler presented himself at Westminster police court to answer the charge of extracting more than his proper fare from his passenger, Captain Allen RN who had been accompanied by his two sons, one of whom was ten, whilst the other was younger. Fayler charged Allen 3s for the journey from the Eastern Counties terminus at Shoreditch (now Shoreditch overground station) to his residence at Warwick Terrace, Pimlico, 6d for one extra passenger and 2d for the luggage. When they arrived at the destination and Fayler made his demand, Allen paid it, though informed the cabman that he would be summoned. With regards to the overcharge, Fayler said he believed that both children were over ten, "If he wasn't", he argued, "he was a very fine child for his age." The magistrate, Arnold, said that such a fact was probably very gratifying to Captain Allen but that did not alter the fact that he charged 6d for a child who was under ten years of age. Fayler responded by saying that as far as he was concerned, a child, even one under ten years of age, was a person, and he had a right to charge 6d for every extra person. "Supposing", he continued, "I had killed this youth by any misconduct of mine, shouldn't I have been tried for manslaughter? so, of course, I've a right to be paid for him. Arnold reminded Fayler that if he was responsible for the death of a "babe in arms" he would be charged with manslaughter, even though there was no question of him being paid to carry a baby in his cab. Arnold found the driver guilty of the overcharge but as it was more to do with misguidance than malice he had only to pay back the 8d overcharge (once it was established that the child could not be counted, there were in effect only two people in the cab so the 2d for luggage could not be charged for either).[35]

Eight months later, in August 1854, John Waller was brought to Westminster Police Court by his passenger, John Scott, to have the same question settled by the magistrate, who by coincidence was once again, Arnold. As with the previous case there were two adults and one child in the cab. The magistrate admitted that the question was a vexed one and sent a policeman around to various courts to try to ascertain the feelings of other magistrates as regards whether a child under ten is a person, and whether the cabman can charge for them. When the officer returned he informed Arnold that a similar case had arisen at Guildhall and the cabman was allowed to charge for the child, but there had been two cases at Bow Street and one at the court they were now within, that the decision went against the driver. One in favour of the cabman charging, two against. Arnold bowed to democracy and informed the driver and his passenger that a charge could not be made for the child. As he himself had trouble interpreting the law he felt it prudent that the cab driver could not be expected to know more than him so no penalty was imposed after what proved in the end to be an overcharge.[36]

Hardwick, the magistrate at Marlborough Street, had no such qualms about dealing with the matter. Cab driver William Crawshaw summoned a Colonel Mitchel for not paying him his full fare, after having demanded 2s and receiving only 1s 6d. He carried four women in the cab and charged 1s for distance, and 6d each for the extra passengers. Colonel Mitchel responded by saying that one of the ladies was his daughter who was under ten years of age. The driver, he continued, had no right to charge for her. Hardwick agreed, he dismissed the summons, which meant that Crawshaw could not recover his 2s outlay in taking it out in the first place, and awarded the Colonel a further 2s for his time in attending court. To add insult to injury, as far as Crawshaw was concerned, the Colonel asked that the two shillings be placed in the poor box.[37] When George Phillips was summoned to appear a few weeks later at the same court and the same magistrate, he pleaded guilty to overcharging by 6d when he carried two adults and a five-year old boy, but pleaded ignorance of the law. Hardwick was not interested. The defendant's "alleged ignorance was quite inexcusable, as there were books of regulations [*The Abstract of Laws*] printed for the use of the drivers and public, and the question as to the right of charge for a child under 10 years of age had been over and over again decided." For the 6d overcharge, Phillips was fined 20s or, in default of payment, fourteen days' imprisonment.[38]

The question continued to be a "ticklish one" as one magistrate put it, and by the end of 1855, Arnold had set aside judgement in two cases and consulted his fellow magistrates again on their opinion as to whether a single child under ten years is a person. Changing his stance completely from the earlier cases, he now pronounced that he himself believed that a cab driver was fully entitled to charge for a child aged ten or under, if there were two adults in the cab. However, on conferring with his fellow magistrates he had been outvoted, "The question was now set at rest, and it must be understood for the future to be the law that a cabman was not entitled to charge for one child as an extra person."[39] The two drivers who had prompted the debate were not punished for what was now decided was an overcharge. They had paid 2s each for a summons against their respective passengers for not paying them the 6d. The matter was now dropped, and the money they had paid for the summons was returned to them. There was now uniformity across the magistracy of London, the cabmen had been warned - charge for a child and you will be fined, or imprisoned. But that did not stop cab driver George Smith.

A month after Arnold felt he had settled the question, he was confronted by another testing cabman. The passenger, Robert Side, a slate manufacturer, had hailed a cab from a stand accompanied with another adult and a child. The cabman, George Smith (another driver who earned the epithet 'Cabman's Attorney-General'), refused to take the child as he would not be paid and this ended up with him appearing before Arnold for his adjudication. Arnold told Smith that by law he is compelled to carry both luggage and children; "I am bound to carry the boxes for nothing if I have only one or two persons in the cab because the law says I am to do so," argued the cabman, "and if a child is put in a box I'll carry it by act of parliament." Arnold then read from the relevant statute that whilst a driver cannot carry more than the number of persons specified on his plate, he is compellable to carry up to that number when so desired by the hirer, and refusal to carry that number will result in a penalty.

Arnold; "How many are you certified to carry?"

Smith; "Five persons. But a child is not a person. It is not a person by your worship's own decision, because if it is a person a cabman has a right to charge for it as an extra, and if he can't charge for it, why then it can't be a person."

Arnold; "It is nonsense to assert that it has been decided that a child is not a person."

Smith; It has been decided that two is a person, and that one isn't. Under your decision a child of under ten years of age don't constitute a person, and, therefore, as it isn't a person, I refuse to carry it."

Arnold: "It was your duty to have taken the child, and if there had been a refusal to pay for it, to have brought the matter before me."

Smith; "It has been decided by you that it was not to be paid for, and I should therefore have carried the child for nothing."[40]

Smith's argument carried little weight with Arnold, after all, the exact question had been decided upon at the last quarterly meeting of magistrates. He conferred with his fellow magistrate, Paynter, and the two agreed that Smith was guilty of a refusing to carry a passenger. Just as their verdict was about to be announced, Smith asked for an adjournment so he could seek legal advice. Having already addressed and decided upon the matter, Arnold was under no pressure to delay the stay of execution, but to his credit, no doubt feeling that the argument put forward by Smith carried some validity, he allowed an adjournment for one week.

There was to be no decision by Arnold. In the following days it had come to his attention that the case was a "got up" case. No offence had taken place, the aim of the defendant and complainant, who knew each other prior to the case, was to test the law, or bring ridicule upon the magistracy as Arnold believed. Arnold was scathing in his attack and he would have no more to do with the "sham dispute" and that the cabman and the supposed passenger were very close to having contempt charges pressed against them. Smith's legal advisor, who evidently was not aware the case was a "put up job" wanted to continue the debate, to have a decision on whether a child under ten is a person or not. It was not a *bona fide* case, there had been no summons. Arnold was in no mood to waste his time discussing the matter any further.[41]

In what was a *bona fide* case of a similar nature that came before the Lord Mayor at the Mansion House a short time later. Though the press reports did not name the driver, just his badge number, 1911, it was almost certainly another put-up case orchestrated by George Smith, who had been summoned for overcharging. The cabman stated that as far as he was concerned he could charge for the six-year old child as there were two adults as well. The Lord Mayor reminded him that he knew full well that he could not charge for a single child, the matter had already been decided. "But two magistrates have decided in favour of my view" said Smith, even the Alderman sitting in court alongside the Lord Mayor, had decided a case in favour of his view. Like Arnold before him, the Lord Mayor was not willing to entertain a debate on the meaning or intention of an act of parliament. In fact, whilst not levelling a charge of contempt at him, he let the driver know that as judge, he would always decide against him. "Whenever you come here, if I am sitting, I shall decide in the contrary direction. I must fine you a shilling for the offence, and you must pay 2s the costs of the summons." The cabman paid the fine and remarked "If Mr Withers [the passenger] wants to ride in my cab again, I shall refuse to take him unless he agrees to pay for the child if he has a grown-up person with him as well." The Lord Mayor warned him that if he did, he would be opening himself up for a summons for refusing a proper fare; "I certainly shall refuse," continued the driver, "and abide by the consequences. We are compelled to carry a bag for nothing, and if Mr Withers wants me to take a child without charging anything for it, he will have to put it into a bag."[42]

Henry Fry was called from a rank in the City of London by a policeman in September, 1857. The officer put two ladies and two small children into the cab and asked Fry what he was to charge to Hoxton. Fry replied that the fare was 1s 6d, which the policeman informed him was 6d more than he was entitled to as the children were both babes in arms and therefore not chargeable. Not wishing to create a stir, the two women left the cab and made their own way home. Fry, having been called off a rank, and losing his position, demanded 6d from the policeman. The policeman, having done no more than oblige the two ladies in getting a cab, and ensuring they was not overcharged, refused to pay the 6d and was subsequently summoned by Fry for that amount. In court, Fry denied that he was guilty of refusing the fare, the two women had got out of the cab on their own accord. The Lord Mayor hearing the case had no option than to order the policeman to pay the 6d for calling Fry off the rank. Fry then complained about his costs, having lost three day's work in attending court to have the matter settled. "I have grave doubt in my own mind," warned the Lord Mayor, "as to whether you did not refuse to take these persons to Hoxton and I cannot allow you anything in the shape of expenses." The policeman paid Fry the outstanding 6d, as well as the 3s costs of the summons but both left the court "neither of them seeming very well satisfied with the magistrate's decision."[43]

In October 1861, Dayman, the magistrate at Wandsworth, presided over a case where the cabman had allegedly made an illegal charge for luggage. The fare consisted of two adults and a baby in arms, the driver argued that whilst he could not charge for the baby, it was a person and if three persons travelled in a cab, then any luggage on the roof was payable at 2d an item. Dayman agreed with the driver's interpretation that a babe in arms was officially a person. It was only a few weeks later that another driver summoned his passenger to court for a very similar case, two adults with a child under ten years of age and five pieces of luggage on the roof. The passenger would not pay the 10d for the parcels and so was summoned by the driver. In Westminster police court the cabman cited the decision by Dayman in allowing a driver to charge for the luggage. Arnold delayed his decision and once again consulted several other magistrates. On returning to court a few days later, he informed all present that he had "given the matter his fullest attention, and had much difficulty in coming to his present conclusion with which he was by no means satisfied." Arnold said he had consulted with Dayman – who had now apparently changed his mind and believed he was now wrong in allowing the cabman to charge for luggage. Arnold also consulted fellow magistrate Paynter, who was of the opinion that a cabman could charge for luggage where the third person was an infant. Once again it was obvious that the magistracy themselves were having difficulty in interpreting the law but it was the cabmen who were being fined as ignorance of the law was no defence. Arnold said he agreed with Paynter and that in the case before him the cabman could charge and that a babe in arms was in fact a person. "If a person under 10 years of age – a boy of 9 – wanted to be driven anywhere, and called a cab, the driver would incur a penalty [for refusal] and therefore it must be fairly argued he would be a "person" and would be liable to the usual fare for his conveyance. The law did not draw any distinction between the child of nine months and nine years."[44] The passenger was ordered to pay the cabman his 10d plus costs.

In December 1861, cabman Thomas Burrows was summoned for charging 6d extra for a child carried in the arms of the mother. His defence when he answered to the charge before D'Eyncourt at the Clerkenwell police court was that the magistrate at Westminster, Arnold, had recently ruled in a case that a child under ten was a person and was therefore chargeable. D'Eyncourt adjourned the case to consult with Arnold and several other magistrates. On resumption, Burrows was told that he was indeed wrong in his assertion of the action of Arnold. That case had centred on whether there was a charge for luggage. If only two persons travelled in the cab, then there was no charge for luggage placed outside the cab. As the two adults in that case had a small child with them, Arnold had decided that in that particular instance, the child was a third person and therefore the luggage was chargeable – therefore there was no charge for carrying a third person, because the child was too young to be a person, but the child was a person when it came to charging for luggage. Fortunately for Burrows, D'Eyncourt did not inflict a fine or add an endorsement to his licence, it had, after all, taken him three weeks to conclude that the cabman was in the wrong. Burrows was ordered to repay the 6d overcharge and the costs of the summons, so it may have felt like a fine in all but name. He would allow a special case for the question to be put before a higher court if the cabmen so wished. Burrows paid the 2s 6d and informed the magistrate that he would consult with others before deciding whether to take the matter any further.[45]

In May 1862, James Norton, an owner driver, was summoned to appear before Tyrwhitt at Marlborough Street police court, charged with demanding and taking more than his legal fare. He carried three adults and a baby and with his fare being less than a mile, he charged 6d for the journey, 6d for the third adult and a further 6d for the baby, and it was for this latter charge that the summons was issued. His defence barrister cited the decision of Arnold the previous November that a babe in arms was in fact a person. Tyrwhitt was aware of Arnold's interpretation but said he did not agree with it, neither, he added, did Mr D'Eyncourt the magistrate at Clerkenwell. Like Arnold, Tyrwhitt adjourned the court for several days to mull over the point and when he did return it was to find Norton guilty of over-charging. A request by the defence team to seek a mandamus from the Queen's Bench was granted by Tyrwhitt.

Arnold did not need the decision of a higher court when, in September 1862, cab driver James Price summoned his passenger, Francis Boileau, for refusing to pay his fare. Price stated that he took two of the defendant's servants, a child in arms and six packages from the Great Northern Railway terminus (King's Cross) to the defendant's home, Chester Street, Belgravia. The defendant and his wife rode in another cab. Outside his home, Boileau gave each of the cabmen half-a-crown which included a 6d tip. The cabman who carried Boileau and his wife was perfectly happy and drove off, James Price however said that his fare was actually 3s, being 2s for the fare and 1s for the six packages he carried on the roof. In court the passenger cited Tyrwhitt's decision in May that a baby in arms is not a person, therefore there were only two persons in the cab and no charge can be made for luggage when only two persons are carried. Arnold countered this, somewhat surprisingly by stating that if Mr Boileau's child was murdered by someone, "he should then think it was a person, and have whoever had killed it apprehended." Boileau was forced to agree but he had only refused to pay the cabman because of Tyrwhitt's decision. Arnold replied that he remembered the case Tyrwhitt was judging on which unlike this one did not involve charging for luggage. The two cases were totally different. Boileau would have to pay the cabman his full fare of 3s plus costs. Arnold actually gave permission to Boileau to seek higher adjudication at the court of Queen's Bench but he declined to do so, merely "wishing to try the question."[46] Mr Boileau could have saved himself a lot of effort had he carried his child in the same carriage as he and his wife. The driver of that cab could not charge for a single child and James Price could not have charged for the luggage as there were not more than two persons in his cab.

The following day cabman James Gundry was before Tyrwhitt at Marlborough Street for taking more than his fare. He had carried one adult and two children and a small box on the roof. The legal fare was 2s but Gundry demanded 2d extra for the luggage as he had "more than 'two' persons" in his cab. As far as Tyrwhitt was concerned "two children under ten counted as one person" and that he should abide by that decision "until set right by the Queen's Bench before which the question was now pending." If two children count as one person, and one other person was in the cab, according to the law there were only "two" persons in the cab and no charge could be made for the luggage. Gundry was fortunate that he was not fined for the exaction, he had only to repay the 2d back to his passenger and pay his costs (usually about 2s).[47]

In April 1863 Tyrwhitt was finally "set right" by the Court of Queen's Bench. They maintained that two children under ten count as one person but that if the third person was a child then the cabman was right in asserting his charge of 6d for the third person. If there were two children and two adults, the two children could not be charged as two separate persons but as one adult. Therefore, for the same distance and with no luggage, two adults with one child, was exactly the same fare as two adults with two children. James Norton the cabman found guilty of overcharging by Tyrwhitt had his conviction quashed. A rare victory for the cab trade.[48] "The Child Question", as the press liked to call it, was finally addressed. The magistrates had a directive from a higher court telling them what the cab drivers had been telling them all along – if two adults were accompanied by a child under ten years of age, whether it be a nine-year old child or a nine-day old baby, that child could be classed as a person and so was chargeable. And so The Child Question had finally been answered and the matter was finally put to rest – but not for long.

When a Mrs Berry, her nurse and her four-month old child travelled in a cab, they were expecting to pay 1s for a ride that was under two miles. The cabman said his fare was 1s 6d and informed her that the extra 6d was for the four-month old child that had sat in the lap for the whole journey. Mrs Berry refused to pay the 6d which she saw as an extortion on the part of the driver. The driver, clearly had a legal right to 1s 6d for the fare and duly summoned Mrs Berry for the outstanding 6d. The Honourable GC Norton, the chief magistrate at Lambeth presided and remarked that, "although it has been decided by the Court of Queen's Bench that an infant must be paid for, the judge who decided the case expressed a doubt, and wished the question to be raised again. He (Mr Norton) should under these circumstances act upon his own conviction, which was that the cabman had no right to charge for an infant; and he should therefore dismiss the summons."[49] The directive from a higher court, informing the magistrates how to act in such a case had lasted a little more than eighteen months. Norton had acted unilaterally and the un-named cabman had not only lost the 6d fare, which according to the law he was entitled to, he lost two days' earnings in attending court as well as the 2s costs of the summons. He was perhaps fortunate that Mrs Berry did not put in a claim for expenses as well. Norton also added that the secretary of an association of cab proprietors was also of the persuasion that a single child could not be charged. Just who this person was and what organisation he represented is not recorded but it is unlikely a cab proprietor would have objected to the possibility of their drivers legally charging more, a system which would ultimately benefit themselves. Despite Norton's unilateral stand, the decision of the Court of Queen's Bench was adhered to.

A few years later a cabman [Benjamin] Hepplethwaite summoned his passenger for non-payment of the 6d charge he made for the small child. The magistrate, Dayman, reiterated the law as it now stood and informed the passenger that the cabman had made a legal demand and he must be paid. The passenger tried to explain that he had never been charged for one child previously, to which Dayman could only respond by saying he had therefore been let off by the cabmen in their generosity.[50]

When the short-lived experiment in free trade, (where drivers could charge what they liked as long as the tariff was displayed on the outside of the cab), was abandoned by the Home Secretary, Austin Bruce, in March 1871, he made several decisions that were, in the main, to the benefit of the cabmen. His most important decision had been the introduction of a hiring fee, which meant that the minimum fare a driver could receive would be 2s for any distance up to two miles. As to the vexed question of a child under ten when accompanied by two adults, Bruce decided that a charge of 3d could be made by the driver. It probably made more sense to the public than it did to the drivers who still saw one child as a person, and a person was chargeable at 6d when more than two were carried.

In 1899, James Dew took Lady Franklin, another lady, a nurse and a small child, as well as a pram and a bath, from Euston Station to Emperor's Gate, South Kensington. Dew said his fare was 3s 4d but Lady Franklin insisted it was only 3s, and she insisted that the cabman could not charge 4d for a child "as two children under ten counted as one adult" though one child did not. Dew actually charged 6d for the child (the rate had increased from 3d to 6d the previous year), the 4d was for the two items placed on the roof. "Mr Lane [the magistrate] remarked that it did not matter how the claim was made up. He explained to Lady Franklin that one child under ten with two persons must be paid for as an adult." She was ordered to pay the 4d as well as costs amounting to 5s 6d. Dew had been expecting more than this but the magistrate believed the cabman had not "behaved quite correctly."[51]

Plowden had to explain the law to another person, who refused to pay for a babe in arms; "The law is that a child under ten can be charged for as one person, and two children, no more. In other words, twins go as cheaply as single babies." The passenger, an officer with the Charity Commission, argued his point further; "I am unable to find anything that warrants a cabman to charge for a baby, nine months old and in arms, as though it were an adult. I admit, that if a child occupies a seat, it should be paid for, but I do not think that applies to an infant in arms. I refused the demand in the public interest." The driver, Robert H Buchanan stated that he had originally charged 3s 6d for the journey but his passenger was only willing to pay 3s. As was the right of the passenger, the whole party drove around to a police station to have the matter settled, but after looking at the book of fares, the inspector told the passenger that the driver's demand was just. The passenger then ordered Buchanan to drive him back to his home, which increased the fare to 4s, Buchanan adding another sixpence on. Needless to say, that the passenger objected to that as well. Plowden did have some sympathy for the passenger; "If a baby occupied a seat, it certainly ought to be charged for as a person; but whether it ceased to be a person when it was carried in arms was a different matter. [I think] it is most unreasonable that a baby should be charged for, it practically took up no room, and did not add appreciably to the burden or weight. [I would] not like to commit [myself] to say that a baby was not a person, and if it was a person [I] suppose it must be charged for under this Act." The passenger then queried the charge for distance in going to and from the police station. In this, the law was much clearer. A passenger had the right to demand to be taken to the nearest police station or police court in matters of dispute, and the driver could not charge any extra for doing so. However, having been told that the cabman's demand was just, by the police inspector, Buchanan was under no obligation to take him any further. In fact, had Buchanan refused to take him home, it would have cost even more. The passenger was told to pay the 1s demand, plus expenses of 8s. "You have made a great fight for the nursery." Plowden informed the passenger as he went to pay the fine.[52]

A Mrs Lubbock was summoned to appear before D'Eyncourt in 1919 for non-payment of 2d. A driver named Kemp said his fare was 8d, plus 6d "war bonus" (6d was added to every fare to compensate drivers for the rising cost of petrol and tyres etc) and 6d for the child that Mrs Lubbock had with her and which was carried in the arms of a nurse. Mrs Lubbock in her defence stated that she had never been asked to pay for a baby carried in arms before in all the cabs that she had travelled in and as far as she was concerned she had no objection to the 8d fare, nor the 6d war bonus and had even added a 4d tip. Kemp had gone to an awful lot of trouble in trying to get an extra 2d out of Mrs Lubbock. It usually took half a day to obtain a summons and the best part of another day in attending court. The driver may have felt he had a cast iron case and that with victory he would be awarded costs, which would amount to a day's income. In this he was to be sadly disappointed. D'Eyncourt said that as far as he was aware, a child in arms was not counted and dismissed the summons. Kemp argued that the magistrate was wrong, that he was allowed to charge for any child. D'Eyncourt added that he thought it was a doubtful point and if the taxi driver wanted to carry it further, he would state a case to go to a higher court if required. Not only was the summons dismissed, but Mrs Lubbock was awarded 10s costs. Chasing after tuppence proved to be very expensive for that particular cab driver.[53] To be fair to Kemp, it may not have been greed that motivated him. He did indeed take the case further, at much more additional expense but at the Divisional Court, two judges ruled that an infant in arms could not be charged for in a taxicab as an additional person.[54]

The matter should have ended there but ten years later the *Daily Mirror* remarked, "Many people will be surprised to learn that even a baby only a few months old is a person when travelling in a taxi." A spokesman for the Cab Proprietor's Council, a society formed from the larger fleets and owner drivers, told a reporter, "The Commissioner's orders are quite definite...the driver is entitled to charge 6d for a child whether it occupies a seat in the cab or not."[55] The debate was not sparked by any particular case, but to the general practice of not adding extras to the meter. Given that Britain, and most of the western world, was in a depression following the Wall Street crash, it would appear that the drivers were struggling to make ends meet, even resorting to demands they could not make – despite what the Commissioner, may or may not have said.

The question of charging for a babe in arms was finally ended in 1933 when the then Home Secretary announced - "The new Order also provides that an infant in arms shall not count as a person for the purpose of calculating the authorized extra charges for more than two persons in a cab. This provision merely expresses what is understood to have been the ordinary interpretation of the law by magistrates in the past."[56]

Passengers on driving box

It is an offence for any person, other than the driver, without the authority of the Licensing Authority, to be carried on the driving box or platform of a taxi.

This clause represents another of the anachronistic tendencies of the governing powers to bring in change. The box was originally the driver's seat on a horse-drawn hackney coach, within which he would carry his provender for the horses and occasionally luggage from the passenger. The last horse-drawn four-wheeler was licensed in 1938 and ever since there has never been a box of that description on a cab and therefore no ruling is necessary. The platform is only slightly less outdated than the box but was around to at least the 1960's. The FX3 taxi cab, a mass-produced model that was the archetype taxi design from which the FX4, Fairway and TX series have spawned, had such a platform. There was no nearside door and any luggage within would be secured by restraining straps. Even when the FX3 was superseded by the FX4, which had a nearside door, these restraining straps still had to be fitted on pain of a stop note being issued and the cab being off the road for several days. The last FX4 rolled off the production line in 1997, still with straps that would never be used, such was the Public Carriage Office's inability to modernise.

Hackney coach drivers were prone to carry a friend with them on the box, without the consent of the fare paying passenger. Sometimes this friend was a fellow hackneyman who just happened to be going in the same direction as the fare. Of course, if at journey's end there was a dispute over the fare then the driver had back-up and the passenger invariably paid the overcharge. The Act of 1831 brought in a clause preventing anyone other than the driver riding on the box without the express permission of the hirer but the practice continued for some time afterward.

There was also a class of people that could sit on the box, not only with the permission of the passenger but under their direct orders, and without the consent of the driver, and who could not even be charged for, - servants. No self-respecting person of the middling class could be expected to travel inside the coach with their servants, they would be suffered to sit on the box next to the driver, in all weathers. There is an irony that the very people who formulate the laws, the members of parliament, all of whom had servants, pass a law that allows them to travel with a servant but without paying for him or her. The driver loses out on his 6d extra, which could certainly add up to a shilling or two at the end of the day which could see him possibly finishing his shift earlier, which in turn would give the horse a rest but all to no avail as the middling and upper classes could save the 6d in the first place.

In 1816 the driver of hackney coach number 957 was summoned for overcharging five men on a journey from Mile End to Newgate Street. One of the passengers stated that they were officials of Christ Church parish and had frequently gone over the same ground for 3s but the driver of 957 charged them 4s. Four of the men travelled inside the coach, whilst the fifth rode on the box alongside the driver. As this fifth man was a beadle of the parish he was therefore classed as a servant and therefore according to the Act, no extra charge should be made. The magistrate disagreed and stated that as an Alderman of the City of London he could designate any of his marshals as servants thus depriving the coachman of what he was entitled to. Reluctantly the passenger acquiesced to the decision of the magistrate but declared his intention of appealing to the commissioners and having legal advice on the subject.[57] A month later at another court, another unnamed driver was not so fortunate. The driver of hackney coach 145 carried five people and the passenger was summoned by the driver for refusing to pay what he had deemed an extortionate demand. Once again four people were inside the coach whilst the fifth, a maid servant, rode alongside the driver on the box. The driver stated that he was entitled to charge for the servant as she was not in livery and therefore could be charged as an ordinary passenger. After having looked through the Act, the magistrate could not see any clause that said a servant had to be in their livery and as such the driver's charge was deemed to be extortionate.[58]

Whilst the magistrate at Queen's Square was right in his interpretation of the law, a tacit acceptance that only liveried servants could travel free on the box seemed to have gained approval from all parties. All parties except the cabman. During the discussion stages of the 1853 Act an amendment was sought that would enshrine in law the right of a servant to travel on the box free of charge. The amendment was dropped after another MP pointed out that the cab horse would never be able to understand the distinction between a man and his servant.

In December 1853 Miss Mary Craigie of Hyde Park Place was summoned by cabman Frederick Rothwell for refusing to pay him his full fare. The journey was less than a mile but Rothwell demanded 1s, 6d for the distance travelled and 6d for the third passenger who sat on the box. Miss Craigie stated that as her servant sat outside with the driver there was no charge applicable, whereas there would have been had the servant ridden inside the cab with her. The magistrate stated that it was no matter where the servant sat, inside or outside, a charge of 6d was still payable. A letter was then handed to Mr Long, the magistrate, from a clerk at Bow Street magistrates court stating that a magistrate there, Jardine, had recently ruled in a similar case that a liveried servant can be carried free of charge. Notwithstanding the uneasiness of coming into direct conflict with a fellow magistrate, Long said he disagreed with Jardine and that Miss Craigie must pay the driver the 6d she owes him as well as the costs of the case.[59] Even though Long, the Marylebone magistrate, had ignored the decision of Jardine, others began to cite the Jardine ruling as actual law and refused to pay for a servant on the box. This prompted Jardine to give a statement to the press stating that he and his fellow magistrate were both agreed on the fact of the law with regards servants on the box and that Long had been right to come down on the side of the driver in the case that was before him. Jardine stated that the confusion arose from a case that had been before him back in July, shortly after the first Hackney Carriage Act was passed of that year. Jardine's interpretation of that Act was that no provision within the legislation allowed the driver to charge for somebody sitting on the box, although the driver could refuse to have somebody there in the first place. Since that case, the second Hackney Carriage Act was passed which changed the law in the cabman's favour and as such, drivers were then allowed to charge for someone sitting next to them on the box.[60]

What was true of a lady's maid-servant was also true of a gentleman's 'tiger'. The tiger was a footboy, regaled in full livery who followed their master around. Many a gentleman had for years transported their tiger around town at the cabman's cost. Now, thanks to the second Act of 1853, as long as there were two people inside the cab, the tiger could be charged for, as many a gentleman found out when they were confronted with a summons.

It was not uncommon at one time for passengers to mount the box and insist on driving themselves. James King, an independent person, who was also described as a "good whip" was one such person. Taking the reins from the driver he attempted to pass an omnibus in Vere Street, Oxford Street in September 1834, only to collide with a cab, plate 696, coming in the opposite direction. The driver of 696, Francis Purse, was thrown from his box to the street where his injuries proved to be serious and he died three hours later. James King compensated Purse's family and paid for the funeral. He was later found guilty of feloniously killing Francis Purse and was sentenced to three month's imprisonment in Newgate.[61]

In 1832 hackney coachman W. Jobbins, with plate number 162, was driving along Chancery Lane when a waggon came out at pace from a side street. Jobbins escaped injury but the small 'lad' that was sitting on the box with him was thrown to the ground where one of the wheels of the waggon rode over his leg, which had to be amputated.[62]

It was bitterly cold and wet in the early hours of the morning of 8th December 1862 when Edward Freeman was driving his four-wheeler along Parliament Street towards Charing Cross. Inside the cab were three persons, alongside him on the box was his own wife and small child. It's possible that Freeman may have been visiting friends and when a fare approached him it was a matter of taking advantage of the circumstances and put his wife and child on the box with him, no doubt with the acquiescence of the passengers. It was a decision he would regret. A Hansom cab, driven at speed by Edward Hope, who was drunk, crashed into Freeman's four-wheeler, overturning it. Freeman, his wife and child were all thrown from the box and the overturned coach landing on both the mother and her daughter. The child lived for a few more hours before dying, Mrs Adams, described by Freeman "as his wife" was in hospital for over a month before she died. At his subsequent trial at the Old Bailey, Hope admitted to having had a drink but felt he was quite capable of driving safely. He alleged that Freeman was at fault. Freeman had overtaken two omnibuses and was on the wrong side of the road. Freeman could not see Hope's Hansom coming towards him from his nearside as Mrs Adams had an umbrella up to protect her from the rain. There was conflicting evidence from both sides but the jury returned a verdict of not guilty against Edward Hope for manslaughter.[63]

Luggage on Roof

It is an offence to carry luggage on the roof of a taxi unless the taxi is fitted for that purpose and is licensed to carry luggage on the roof.

A driver who fell victim to his passenger's whim of overloading a cab was Thomas Dawson. He had been summoned for demanding 8d over his legal fare. The passenger, a servant, stated that two boxes were placed on the cab and that at the destination he proffered 1s 4d as the fare but the driver said his fare was 2s which was paid and formed the basis of the summons. In reply, Dawson stated that he was hailed in the Haymarket and after several minutes was told to drive around to the rear entrance of the Civil Service Stores in Oxenden Street. There, two large boxes weighing 6¼ cwt [over a quarter of a ton], were placed on the roof of his cab, each one requiring the use of four men to place them there. Dawson informed the passenger that he was not compelled to carry merchandise and it was agreed that he would be paid by time and distance. With both parties satisfied they drove off, but not before the passenger clambered onto the box alongside the driver. In the passenger's opinion there was so much weight on the roof that he feared the roof of the cab would cave in, crushing him under civil service apparel. It all seems to have been friendly between the two, they even stopped for 15 minutes at a pub in Halkin Street, which was doubly beneficial to Dawson, he had a beer bought for him and he was being paid the time to drink it. Dawson said his proper fare was 2s 4d, but he was only claiming 2s as "he did not wish to quibble over 4d". He wished he might have done. The sitting magistrate was Arnold and whilst he conceded that Dawson had made out his claim he also believed he had evidently misled the hirer in the first instance – but did not elaborate on what the cabman had been guilty of. The summons against Dawson was dismissed but he was not allowed to claim any costs for his time etc.[64]

A cabman appeared before Alderman Sir William Rose at the beginning of January 1877 charged with refusal. He had been hired to carry a gentleman, two ladies and two boxes from the Great Eastern Terminus to Kensington. The complainant then stated that the cabbie refused to carry the two boxes, for just 2d each. The passenger was not willing to give more than he was legally required and so the cabman refused the fare. The driver said that "the two boxes were as high as a table and so large they covered the roof of his cab" and he did say to the passenger that he was not willing to carry such boxes on his roof for five miles for just 2d. The Alderman agreed with the cabman, the amount of luggage was not reasonable "The Act of Parliament did not contemplate that a cab should be turned into a van." The summons against the driver was dismissed.[65]

William Lewis sued the Great Western Railway for the princely sum of 9d in 1910. He informed the judge that he was engaged by a porter at Paddington Station to take up a lady with a box. Lewis insisted that the box should go on the roof of the taxi as it might damage the interior of the cab. After a heated argument he was told to leave the station by a railway inspector. He now sued the GWR for the 1d yard fee he paid to enter Paddington and for the 8d he had on the meter. The judge heard that that box in question was a light hat box that could not possibly cause any damage to the interior of a taxi. The judge agreed and told Lewis that he had no right to insist on carrying such a box on the roof of his cab. He not only lost the 9d he was claiming for but the cost of taking a claim all the way to the county court.[66]

The dangers of heavy luggage on the roof of a cab were only too real. In

1867, 68-year old Mrs Hilton was riding in a four-wheeler when, putting her head out of the window to give the driver instructions, she inadvertently tipped the cab over, fatally injuring herself. "The inquest jurors remarked upon the frequent and dangerous manner in which cabs were "overloaded" on the top, and passed a "resolution" calling the attention of the police to the fact, with a view to its being prevented as much as possible."[67]

Luggage on the roof may not always have had such fatal consequences, but both cabs and the four-wheelers had their own unique problems. With its large flat roof, the growler, or four-wheeler was ideal for the carrying of bulky items. The driver sat at the front of the coach so his view ahead was not impeded. This meant that security wise, theft of luggage was always a risk. Many drivers would secure the luggage with rope – but many would not and this would create opportunities for the chancer or professional thief to run up behind the coach and steal some luggage. The hansom cab was not built to carry luggage. The driver of a hansom cab sat at the back of the cab. Looking over the roof and the horse. His finely balanced position allowed him to move in and out of the traffic at a pace, but denying a cab driver the ability to carry luggage on the roof was also denying him extra income. In 1879, the *Pall Mall Gazette* was calling for a law to ban hansom cabs from carrying luggage on the roof. It related the case of a young boy knocked over by a rapid moving cab which had a large box on the roof. The box prevented the cabman from seeing his horse and, according to the Gazette, that the pedestrians "seeing the predicament in which he was placed, would prudently get out of his way." The driver in that instance was fined 10s. "Hansom cabs may be seen daily careering through the streets with luggage on their roofs as they convey their fares to or from the railway stations; and it is marvellous that street accidents from this cause are not more frequent."[68]

When Charles Edwards found that a box he was to carry on the roof of his cab was too large, he found himself at loggerheads with the magistrate. Edwards had been called from a stand in February 1883, to pick up at a house in Powis Square, Notting Hill. On arriving there an "American trunk" was brought out from the house and placed upon the roof of his hansom cab. On mounting his seat, Edwards found he had trouble seeing over it, he refused to carry it and the trunk was taken off. A maid servant then informed him that a four-wheeler would be sent for. As he had been called from a stand, Edwards felt he was entitled to his shilling minimum fare, which the passenger refused to pay, so Edwards took out a summons. The passenger, a General Campbell, said it "…was a light lady's box, and there was no difficulty in carrying it." Edwards had said nothing about the weight of the box, just that it "…covered the whole roof of the cab, preventing him from seeing the 'butterfly'" – the brass guiding rail at the front of the roof of a hansom. Edwards said it was not safe to carry such a large box and the magistrate, Shiel, agreed with him, "A driver of a hansom cab should not be asked to carry a parcel of that sort on account of the danger." He told the General that he must pay Edwards the one shilling for calling him off the stand, but then surprisingly he would not allow Edwards any costs, such as the 2s to take out a summons in the first place, and for loss of time. Shiel, who was generally sympathetic to cabmen, would not allow costs because he accused Edwards of being "too fond of litigation." The magistrate had decided that Edwards had been wronged in not being paid his one shilling and the only redress Edwards had was to summon the passenger. Now he was being punished for doing just that. Edwards pressed his claim and Shiel relented somewhat by allowing him the cost of the summons but would not grant anything for loss of time – Edwards, according to Shiel "should have gone away when he found he could not carry the box."[69]

Persons not to be carried without hirer's consent

A taxi driver must not permit any person to be carried in, upon or about the taxi without the express consent of the hirer.

Samuel Pepys was hailed by a coachman who noticed that the diarist was heading in the same direction. When Pepys got into the coach he found that another passenger was inside, and although nothing was said to Pepys himself, when that passenger was set down just past the Old Exchange, he refused to pay the coachman what was his due, namely one shilling, citing the fact that "he carried a stranger with him". The two argued for some time before the coachman accepted that all he was going to receive from the original passenger was no more than 6d. The coachman then argued with Pepys that he was to pay not only the 6d he had lost out on but extra for taking him onto his home. Diplomatically, Pepys records that "with fair words he was willing [to continue the journey]."[70]

Monsieur Achilles Pinto missed his boat to France at Tower Stairs in 1835 and hired William Robins to convey him to Blackwall where it was hoped the boat could be met. On arrival at the docks, Pinto went to give Robins 10s for getting him to the boat on time, even though the actual fare was only 4s. Robins, however, said that his fare was a sovereign (20 shillings). Not wishing to miss the boat for a second time he paid the demand but before he could go any further, Robins then said he would have to pay the other man who sat on the box with him 2s 6d "for showing him the way". Not only had he not given his permission to take up another passenger, he was not even asked. Again, Pinto paid the demand but he had the presence of mind to take the number of the coach, 261, and when he returned to London he reported the imposition. In court Robins said he charged extra as Pinto had promised him a guinea to make the boat but this was vigorously denied by the prosecutor. Robins was fined 40s and ordered to pay back 16s. In order to avoid a month in the House of Correction, Robins had to pay a total of 62s 6d.[71]

With a passenger in his cab, John Wheeler was seen driving at speed down Caledonian Road, with another man beside him, standing on the springs. Both men appeared to be drunk. As the cab entered Pentonville Road it crashed into a four-wheeler cab, badly injuring the horse and causing damage to the cab. Wheeler, badge 11115, denied being drunk, the horse was "fresh" and he had trouble reining it in. He admitted to carrying a stranger but felt there was nothing wrong as it was another cabman who he was giving a lift to in the direction of his home. Unable to pay the 20s fine and 30s damages, Wheeler was sentenced to one month with hard labour in the Clerkenwell House of Correction.[72]

When Johnson Boswell took up a passenger inside Liverpool Street Station in 1893 he was being watched by a railway policeman. On several occasions previously, the policeman had noticed Boswell slowing down to take up another man who rode on the outside. Boswell was stopped before he could leave the station and the policeman asked the lone female passenger if she had consented to another man riding on the four-wheeler. "Certainly not" came the reply, with which Boswell was charged with carrying an unauthorised passenger. There was probably nothing more sinister in Boswell's intentions than trying to let a friend earn a few pennies by helping the passenger with their luggage, which in this case was piled high on the roof. The magistrate read no more into in than that and taking into consideration Boswell's clean licence, fined him the nominal 2s 6d plus costs.[73]

Hirings for Luggage and/or luggage alone

A driver is not compelled to accept a hiring for luggage and/or animals unaccompanied by a passenger, or to carry articles or animals likely to cause damage to the taxi or its fittings.

"When is a cabman, not a cabman?" Was a question posed in the West London police court, after a driver was accused of blatantly overcharging. On August 16th 1899, a gentleman appeared before the magistrate, Mr Plowden, to seek a summons against a cabman for overcharging him. Mr de Gruyther, related how he had engaged a cab to convey some luggage from Paddington Station to Nevern Square, Earl's Court. On reaching the destination the cabman said his fare was 5s, the gentleman said it was only 2s, to which the cabman replied that "5s was the usual charge for any distance, long or short, when no passengers travelled by the cab." The magistrate said he knew of no such charge, De Gruyther added "It is a preposterous one, if it exists." A police inspector who was present informed the court that there was indeed no such charge. Plowden granted the summons.[74]

For all of Plowden's faith in the wrongness of the cabman, his fellow magistrate Mr Lane, was under no illusion as to the situation of the law. "The summons must fail" he informed de Gruyther, "There was no passenger in the cab and... in engaging it for the conveyance of luggage, diverted it from its usual purpose, and therefore the Hackney Carriage Act could not be brought into operation." The cabman, Joseph D Woodman, was within his rights to charge a fair sum for his trouble. His charge was 5s which he asked for without any extortion and which was paid. It was confirmed to de Gruyther that if somebody had travelled with the luggage, then Woodman could only have charged him 1s 6d, as did the other cab driver who carried Mr de Gruyther and his wife. The summons against Woodman was dismissed and he was awarded 5s costs.[75] So, "When is a cabman not a cabman?... when a man places his luggage inside a cab and does not travel by it himself, he transforms the cabman into a carrier..."[76] A few days after the decision of the magistrate was published, "A Lawyer" suggested in correspondence to the *Standard* that anyone faced with a similar predicament in future should pay the cabman what they think was appropriate, and leave it for the cabman to summon him, if he thought fit.[77]

10 Lost Property

Taxi to be searched

Immediately after the termination of the hiring of his taxi the driver must carefully search his taxi to ascertain whether any property has been accidentally left there. If this is not practicable he must at least look inside his taxi for this purpose. In any event he must make a careful search as soon as practicable after the hiring.

It is probably true to say that there has never been a cabman in the history of the trade who has "carefully searched" his vehicle after every hiring. Today a quick glance over the shoulder reveals any items left on or against the seat, but anything left against the driver's partition is hidden from view. A Hansom cab driver could open the hatch which looked down upon the seat but even this did not fulfil the "carefully search" criteria. It was certainly in the interest of the driver to search his vehicle so he could at least claim a reward and, as will be seen in this chapter, some drivers were determined to get their reward by reporting an item as left in their vehicle, rather than returning it direct to the owner.

On January 6th, 1663, Samuel Pepys recorded in his diary: "Thence Mr. Battersby the apothecary, his wife, and I and mine by coach together, and setting him down at his house, he paying his share, my wife and I home, and found all well, only myself somewhat vexed at my wife's neglect in leaving of her scarf, waistcoat, and night-dressings in the coach today that brought us from Westminster, though, I confess, she did give them to me to look after, yet it was her fault not to see that I did take them out of the coach. I believe it might be as good as 25s. loss or thereabouts." The loss was probably permanent. If the coachman was honest and had found the items he may have returned them to Pepys's house in the hope of a reward. Alternatively, the coachman may have been totally unaware of the items left behind and the items taken by the next passenger. The likelihood is that the coachman was fully mindful of the items being left behind and soon disposed of them for a ready profit.

Even if the coachman was honest and, for whatever reason, could not take the items back to Pepys's house, there was nowhere for him to take them as in some form of lost property office. Pepys's only redress was to advertise for the return of the items and offer a reward, but in the days before daily newspapers such methods, of having bills printed, were expensive, probably more so than the value of the lost items.

From 1666, with the arrival of the *London Gazette*, forgetful Londoners had a newspaper with which they could place advertisements offering a reward for the return of lost property. One such advert promised £5 for the return of a large black box containing writings, the coach was driven by "a man of about 50 years' of age, fat, with short black hair [and] a Blew Livery..."[78] Many future editions of the *London Gazette* contained similar adverts, though the items left behind range from the expected - coats, gloves, snuff boxes, to the less obvious; a guitar and, on two occasions, a brace of pistols. In 1829, four hundred sets of human teeth, worth several hundred pounds, were left in a hackney coach. On that occasion, the driver, James Hayden, was charged along with another man, of trying to sell some of them.[79] The rewards offered ranged from a few shillings to £100 for the return of a bag of guineas left in a hackney coach in Pall Mall.[80]

When the Hackney Coach Office was formed in 1687 there was at least a physical location to where the coachmen could take items found, or the owner of the property could go to report a loss. If they had been fortunate to recall the number of the hackney coach, then an officer would be sent to the registered address. If the plate number had not been recorded, then it was all down to the honesty of the driver. There does not appear to be any compellability on the part of the driver to return items left in his coach until the Hackney Coach Act of 1815 which allowed drivers up to four days to hand in any property left in their vehicles to the Hackney Coach Office. Failure to do so could result in a fine of up to £20.

An added incentive for the hackney coachman in handing in property was not only the reward, if claimed, but the item became his if it remained unclaimed after one year. This was reinforced by the Act of 1831, which maintained that a driver could be liable to a fine of £20 if items left behind were not deposited with the Stamp Office, the new controlling authority, within four days. The Act of 1831 also led to the end of limitation on the number of licensed hackney carriages. A greater number of carriages meant an increase in the number of drivers and, as seen in Chapter 1, they were not licensed or badged. By 1835 it is noted that more items were deposited by the drivers restricted by limitation (1200 hackney carriages) than during the period following when there were about 1700 drivers. This was seen as an indication that much of the new intake of drivers had neither the honesty nor the integrity of most of the original 1200. Throughout the years, the number of items handed in by drivers has always been seen as a measure of their honesty.

A story that did not quite ring true, was the excuse offered by Benjamin Hazell in 1858 for failing to hand in lost property. He had picked up a woman and her two daughters from Waterloo Station and dropped them off at Swan and Edgar's, Piccadilly Circus. One of the daughter's, believing that Hazell had been told to wait, left a sable muff inside the cab. When she realised the cab had been discharged they returned to the street and enquired at several nearby stands, without any luck. Fortunately for them, Hazell, an owner driver, usually worked from Waterloo Station where his plate number, destination and time of departure from the station were recorded. With sufficient information, a summons was issued against Hazell for not handing any item left in his cab into the nearest police station within 24 hours (reduced from 4 days in 1853), Hazell denied the charge as he was not aware of any property left in his cab. He maintained that after dropping off at Swan and Edgar's, he hurried back to Waterloo Station in order to put himself in a good position for the two o'clock train. On driving through Kennington he saw an elderly lady waiting for an omnibus and he offered to take her to the corner of York Road for just 6d, which she accepted. She must have found the sable muff and kept it. Blaming the next passenger is an oft heard excuse. There is little doubt that some passengers would be inclined to keep an item they found in a cab but the vast majority hand it over to the driver. Even back in 1858, Hazell's excuse was considered weak. The police even found out that a sable muff had been taken into a pawnshop in Piccadilly that same day but it was refused. The magistrate warned Hazell that "it was no answer to say that he did not look in the cab, as that was neglect, for which he was liable." Hazell was further warned that more enquiries were to be made and that if he failed to attend at a future date if required, a warrant would be issued.[81]

Disposal of property found in taxi

Any person finding any property accidentally left in a taxi must hand it immediately to the taxi driver.

In 1838 two women climbed into a cab in Chelsea and found a gold ring which they handed to the driver. He told them that he knew the ring must belong to his previous passenger who lived in Pelham Crescent. The two sisters were not wholly convinced by the driver and a few days later they went to the address given by him but the occupant there knew nothing about the matter. They then proceeded to the Stamp Office to enquire if the ring had been handed in there. It had not, and not being of the absent-minded type, the women had actually taken note of the badge number and the driver was duly summoned. William Jarman, 6476, told the court that he had been in error thinking the ring belonged to a lady in Pelham Crescent and that as the two ladies were his first passengers of the day, he asked the man who drove his cab on the previous evening, "an odd man" [a licensed driver who covers for drivers when they cannot work] about the ring. It transpired that the ring belonged to a coffee-house keeper in Farringdon Street and Jarman had returned the jewellery to the owner. The prosecuting barrister stated that even if the defendant's story was true, and it did take some believing, it was no answer to the charge in question, that the property was not deposited at the Stamp Office within the then legal timeframe of four days. Jarman asked the magistrate, Bond, for an adjournment, so that he could produce the gentleman in question. This was agreed and a few days later, a coffee-house keeper of Farringdon Street informed the court that the defendant did indeed restore a lost ring to him. The magistrate acknowledged the proven honesty of Jarman but as he had not entirely complied with the law in handing in the property to the Stamp Office, he was ordered to pay the costs of the prosecution without a fine being levied.[82]

A case that arose at Westminster County Court in June 1859 raised the question of just who was responsible for items left in a cab. Mrs Francis Nash informed the court that the previous April she entered a cab with a friend of hers, who happened to be a county magistrate, and found a carpet bag. On the advice of her friend she kept possession of the carpet bag and did not inform the driver about the find. The owner of the bag was a barrister of the Inner Temple and also secretary to the Public Drinking Fountains Association. Most of the documents in the bag referred to the association and the barrister, Wakefield, advertised for the safe return of the bag and contents with a reward of £2. After being in possession of the bag for five days, Mrs Nash took it to the Inner Temple and claimed her reward. Wakefield was not so obliging and Mrs Nash was forced to summons him to the county court in order to receive her reward of £2. In court Wakefield contended that the contents of the bag clearly gave his address and the bag should have been returned to him the following day. He accused Mrs Nash of retaining the bag just to see if a reward was advertised. He also informed the court that the cabman should have been notified. If his number had been taken the driver could be accused of stealing the items of which he knew nothing about. Had the cabman been in possession of the bag and taken it to Scotland Yard, he would have been entitled to a reward of a third of the suggested value. Judge Bayley surprised the court when he stated that items found by a passenger in a stage carriage must be handed to the driver, but there was no mention of cabs or cabmen. He deferred his decision.[83]

Paynter the magistrate, was under no doubt as to the legal path in such circumstances. On Boxing Day, 1859, a cabman sought his advice on property left in his cab by one passenger and claimed by the next. Cutlery and jewels had been found by the woman and despite the cabman telling her that he was legally responsible for the items, she would not give them up unless she was rewarded. Paynter informed the police to go visit the woman, the cabman had stated her address, and if she refused to restore the items to the owner, legal proceedings would be initiated against her.[84] In another case, this time in 1882, 29 year old Louisa Joyce was sentenced to ten days hard labour after being found guilty of retaining two bracelets she found in a cab which she tried to pawn.[85]

A taxi driver finding property left in a taxi or having such property handed to him must deposit it in the state in which it was found by or handed to him at a police station in the Metropolitan Police District or the City of London within 24 hours and truly state particulars of such finding, unless it is sooner claimed by the owner to whom it shall be restored forthwith on satisfactory proof of ownership.

When a "dashing Cyprian" left a "valuable shawl" in a hackney coach from the Haymarket theatre in 1823 she reported her loss to the Hackney Coach Office and advertised it in a newspaper, each to no avail. She then asked a hackney coachman who she regularly employed to see if he could find it. The driver, who would perhaps be better employed in the near future as a detective in the soon-to-be-formed Metropolitan Police, made several enquiries and found that a coachman named George Martin was the man who had taken the fare. Martin was actually being held in custody at the time, though for what crime is not recorded, but he told the amateur detective that the landlady of a public house in Dean Street, Soho, had the shawl which he had pledged with her for 15s. On payment of this sum the landlady gave up the shawl but she denied that it was as security for the shawl. The 15s was a loan to Martin, something she had often done before. At his trial, Martin was threatened with being fined the full £20 for not handing in the shawl but owing to his previous good character and the prosecutrix's adversity to have a heavy punishment bestowed on him, the magistrate took into consideration the several days he had been incarcerated in awaiting trial and dismissed him with a warning as to his future conduct.[86]

In February 1847, McGregor, Secretary of the Board of Trade, hurried out of his cab and into his house at Lowndes Square as it was snowing heavily. He immediately directed his servant to go to the cab and collect the despatch box that was on the seat. Although only seconds had elapsed the cab had gone, and with it the despatch box. Three days later a woman, Lydia Rathwell, enquired of a policeman, directions to Lowndes Square. She volunteered the information that the box she carried under her arm had been left in her husband's cab and she was returning it to its owner. Suspecting all was not quite right, the policeman accompanied her to McGregor's house. The servants identified the box as belonging to Mr McGregor, of that there was little doubt, his name and address were emblazoned upon it. The servants also noted that the lock had been forced and the contents obviously inspected. The policeman then charged

Lydia with theft and took her to the police station. In court it was pointed out that none of the contents were missing and that as only three days had elapsed since the property was lost to its return, no law had yet been broken. Broderip the magistrate was not interested. He knew that a large number of cabmen were prone to drive off quickly so they could deposit the property at Somerset House and claim the reward. Just such a thing had happened to an acquaintance of his, despite the property having his name and address on it, it was taken to Somerset House where a value of 13 shillings was placed on it by the clerks there. On his acquaintance presenting himself at Somerset House, he refused to pay, saying it perpetuated dishonesty in cabmen and allowed them to profit by it. He remanded Lydia in custody.[87]

The next day the same policeman met with Lydia's husband, John Rathwell, in Vauxhall Bridge Road, and charged him with theft of the despatch box, the property of Her Majesty the Queen. He explained to the officer that he was not aware of the box in his cab until the next passenger pointed it out to him. Since then however he had been ill in bed and it was on the Monday that he advised his wife to take the box to the address upon it and that he knew nothing of the lock being forced. He also was remanded but as they had two children, Lydia was released.[88]

Both John and Lydia were charged with theft and stood in the dock at Westminster Police Court. The charges against Lydia appeared to have been dismissed and Burrell the magistrate informed Rathwell that he was liable to a fine of £20 but he will only impose one of £10 upon him. Rathwell's solicitor pleaded with Burrell to mitigate the fine even further as he only earned on average 9s a week. Burrell consented and agreed to reduce the fine to £5, but payable at 10s a week.[89]

The London Hackney Carriage Act of 1853 readdressed the business of handing in lost property. No longer would the driver be allowed to hold on to the property for four days (in the hope of seeing if a reward was advertised in the papers) but it had to be deposited within 24 hours "to the nearest police station". Quite what this means is open to speculation; the nearest police station to where the passenger alighted, which could be the other side of London; the nearest police station to where the cabman lives. Surely the correct phrase should be the "any police station in

London". All property handed in, whether in the Metropolitan Police District, or the City of London, would then be delivered to the Lost Property Office at Scotland Yard where it could be collected.

As a consequence of the reduced amount of time the driver could hold on to the property, failure of the driver to deposit the property with the police within the allotted time made him liable to a fine of £10, reduced from the previous £20. This law remains pretty much in force today; a taxi driver must deposit an item left in his cab with *any* Metropolitan or City of London police station (if they can find one that's open of course) within the predetermined period of 24 hours.

The reward system was also changed in the Act of 1853 with the owner of the property liable to pay any expenses incurred by the driver in depositing the property and "such reasonable sum" as the commissioners saw fit by way of a reward. The cabman lost the opportunity of claiming the property as their own if the owners did not claim it themselves. Under the new act the item would be sold and all monies thus collected would be paid into the Inland revenue after "a reasonable sum was paid to the driver". All in all, it did not bode well for those absent-minded people who relied on cabmen handing in the property. This remained only until the Act of 1869 that allowed cabmen once more to claim any unclaimed items, after a three-month period.

George Doe was the type of cabman who chose not to hand items in. To him it was a perk of the job and any such items left behind he either sold or pawned. In 1858 he was seen to be selling a silk umbrella to a coffee stall keeper in the Harrow Road. A plain clothes policeman just happened to be at the stall and heard Doe boast that he had a lot of items left in his cab and still had many items to sell. After selling the umbrella, Doe drove away in his cab but was soon stopped by the plain clothes officer. On searching Doe's room where he lived, above a stable in a mews in Notting Hill, the policeman found three umbrellas, an almost-new overcoat and several pawnbroker duplicates, including one for a gold watch.[90] The case was adjourned in the hope of finding the owners of the property but, fortunately for Doe, none came forward and all charges against him were dropped for lack of evidence.[91]

365

In 1862, John Gregory, 13627, was questioned about a shawl that had been left in his cab the previous month. Gregory admitted taking the passenger up at Waterloo Station but denied, twenty times, according to the policeman, any knowledge of the shawl, which was valued at 35s. Gregory was made to drive home with the police and on the journey he appears to have panicked and confessed that he had the shawl but hoped he would not get in trouble for it. No doubt the accompanying police sergeant told him it was a bit late in the day for that. At the home he shared with his widowed mother, who was also a cab proprietor, all knowledge of the shawl was denied by her until Gregory told her to come clean. She informed the police sergeant that she would retrieve the shawl but only on the condition that he "would not go with her to get it." The sergeant could not agree to this and eventually Mrs Gregory was forced to walk round to a nearby pawnbroker where the shawl, and another item left in a cab had been pawned for 8s. The charge had actually been brought by The South Western Railway Company at Waterloo rather than the owner of the shawl, the railway company feeling that a prosecution of such a case would act as a deterrent to other cabmen at the station when property was found in their cab. Neither John Gregory or his mother could raise the bail required for their release and they were both locked up.[92] At their subsequent trial a week later, charges against Ann Gregory were dropped but her son pleaded guilty to the theft and was sentenced to six month's hard labour.[93]

Pawnbrokers were the favourite place of cab drivers to cash in on the property left behind in their cabs. It was fortunate for the passengers that the pawnbrokers themselves were usually more honest than the cabmen, or at least their wives. Joseph Hedges found a "valuable carbuncle with rose diamonds" in his cab and sent his wife with it to a pawnshop in Camden High Street. Wanting only 5s for a brooch that was worth more than £100 alerted the pawnbroker who immediately informed the police. Both husband and wife were taken into custody but the charges of theft were dropped until the owner of the carbuncle could be found. Mansfield the magistrate directed the police to charge Hedges instead with not depositing the item in a police station within 24 hours.[94]

George Newman was even more fortunate. Like Mrs Hedges, his wife was arrested at a pawnshop trying to pledge a diamond brooch valued at £105 – she claimed she was only trying to establish its worth. Both Mr and Mrs Newman were charged with the theft but at his subsequent trial Newman stated that when he finished his shift that day, he took out the rug from the cab and the brooch fell out from it. He went home and placed the brooch on the table and, according to him, forgot all about it. When Mrs Newman saw the brooch on the table when she awoke she took it round to a pawnbroker in Kingsland Road. The magistrate, Ellison, informed Newman that he was obliged to take any property left in his cab to a police station with 24 hours. Newman's reply to this was that he did not have time. He had finished work at two-thirty in the morning and gone to bed. The next thing he knew the police were knocking at his door accusing him of theft. As he had been arrested before the full 24 hours had elapsed, the magistrate had no option other than to release the couple, whatever their intentions might have been.[95]

In 1885 Thomas Parslow, aged 23 of Redhill Street, Regent's Park, found a valuable necklace in his Hansom cab. The pendant of the necklace had 15 diamonds along each side with a cluster of diamonds forming a heart at the centre. Later, it was to be stated that the necklace was worth £400. Quite what Parslow intended to do at this point remains unclear. Newspaper reports state that he was going to take the necklace home, but the route he took suggests he was going to return the property directly to its owner, Miss Nellie Addington, of Kent Terrace, Regent's Park. On route he chanced upon another cab driver, Charles John Coghill, outside Baker Street Station. Parslow informed Coghill about the necklace and told him a lady residing in Kent Terrace, had hired him the previous night to go to the Promenade Concerts, then held at the Opera House in Covent Garden. Coghill agreed to accompany Parslow, which suggests that the intention was to return the necklace to Miss Addington and Coghill was to be a witness. They soon came across a third cabman known to them, Edward Swire, who joined them in the endeavour but before they were to hand in the necklace, they all went into the Windsor Castle public house in Park Road for a drink. In the pub, which still survives, Parslow pulled out the necklace and showed it to Coghill and Swire. Parslow then had the idea of going to a shop in the neighbourhood, probably a pawnbroker, where its value could be ascertained. Leaving Parslow and Coghill in the pub, Swire was entrusted with the necklace. When he returned he informed Parslow that "he was a lucky fellow", the necklace was estimated to be worth about £175. Swire then suggested that Parslow would be a fool to take it back to its owner as he might not get anything from them, instead, they should hand it in at a police station where a reward would be guaranteed. This plan of action was agreed, even though the Windsor Castle pub was only a matter of yards from Kent Terrace where the owner of the necklace resided. On their way to the police station, Swire informed Parslow that he could get rid of the necklace and make some money for themselves. They did not go to the police station, instead they went to another pub, the Duke of York, on the corner of Westmoreland Street and Great Marylebone Street (now New Cavendish Street). Swire took the necklace to a second-hand clothier, Benjamin Barnett, who allegedly paid Swire £18 for it. It could have been more as Swire negotiated with the clothier on his own, Coghill had gone and Parslow, the driver who had found the necklace in the first place, waited around the corner.

Coghill met up with the other two cabmen shortly after and all three went to another pub called the Windsor Castle, this one was in Albany Street, where they divided up their booty. Over whisky and cigars, Parslow informed Coghill that his share of the proceeds amounted to the princely sum of 4s 6d, which disappointed Coghill who thought he was entitled to more. He returned the money to Parslow who increased his bounty to half a sovereign – ten shillings.[96]

Earlier that same day Nellie Addington had reported her loss to the police and advertised a reward of £50 for its return. The day after, following "information received", she was confronting Benjamin Barnett, and informed him that she knew he had bought a diamond necklace for £18 the previous day and that she was willing to buy it back and that would be an end to the matter. Barnett denied all knowledge of the necklace and Miss Addington left the shop informing him that she was going straight to the police. When she did arrive back at the shop it was to find it was closed and that there was no sign of Barnett.[97] That the "information received" had come from Coghill there is little doubt. It may have been malice at not getting a fair share of the £18, or fear of being an accomplice to theft that he turned informant. Having been told by Parslow that the passenger had resided in Kent Terrace, less than 20 houses, it would not have been difficult for him to locate her. Parslow, Swire and Barnett were all charged in connection with the theft. The two cabmen pleaded guilty at the Middlesex Sessions, the charge of receiving stolen property against Barnett had been dropped earlier, there being no proof of his complicity. Despite pleading guilty neither Parslow or Swire would divulge who had purchased the necklace, which was never recovered. It was recognised that Parslow had been led astray by Swire, and would have in all probability, handed in the necklace to the police had it not been for Swire's influence. Judge Edlin QC sentenced Swire to a year imprisonment and Parslow to nine months.[98] It was noted by the press at the time that if he had handed in the necklace to the police, Parslow would have been entitled to a reward of 15%, given that the value of the necklace was put at £400, he would have received £60. Instead, he received a share of £18 and nine month's imprisonment.

Today, a cab driver has the option of trying to return the property to its owner firstly, and failing that, they have to deposit the article at a police station, still within the required 24 hours. In 1871, with the parameter that the article has to be taken to the nearest station, cabman George Bennett was surprised to get a summons for doing just that. Chief Inspector Druscovitch of Scotland Yard (who apparently spoke several languages but English was not his best) informed the court that Bennett had picked up the Duchess d'Alb, a visiting French dignitary. She had left a purse in Bennet's cab and later offered a reward of 10s for its return. It was Bennett's understanding of the law that the purse had to be taken to the nearest station, in this case, Cannon Street station, a railway station, and it was there that he deposited it. As the purse was not deposited within a police station within 24 hours, as required by law, the summons was issued. Bennett pleaded with the magistrate, Knox, that he was not aware of having done anything wrong. Fortunately for him Knox could see the funny side of it and believed that Bennet had not acted with any dishonesty and although no fine was imposed he had to pay costs.[99]

Cab driver John Glass was also treated leniently when he failed to hand in an umbrella left in his cab. His excuse was that the passenger was a regular user of the stand and it was only a matter of time before the owner would require his services again. The "matter of time" was seven days when the gentleman returned to the cab rank, saw John Glass and asked for his umbrella which was duly returned to him. Such an arrangement seemed common sense to the cabman, but not to the owner, who reported him but did not wish to press the charges. As there were no previous convictions against Glass he was fined just one shilling with 2s costs.[100]

James Abbott, 8697, did all that was required of him by law after a gentleman left a number of coats in his cab. Abbott was a privileged cabman who worked out of Broad Street Station, he reported the property to his inspector of cabs within the station then took the coats to Bishopsgate police station where they were handed in. So far so good. After returning to work he was met at some point in the day by two police officers, one from the Thames police, the other from the City of London police. Quite what happened next was not reported, it is not even clear if it had anything to do with the coats, but Abbott alleged that "they treated him very badly", *i.e.* beat him up, to such an extent that he claimed he lost a pint of blood "in consequence of their ill-usage". Later, having gone back to work despite losing so much blood, he was questioned by Inspector Butt, also of the Thames police, who was now enquiring about the coats. Having been attacked by the police earlier, Abbott was in no mood to "assist with their enquiries". He told Butt that if he wanted to know anything he should go to the station and enquire there. Butt informed the magistrate that Abbott would not tell him which police station the coats had been deposited in. Such information should have been previously known to Inspector Butt. Presumably the passengers had reported the loss and informed the police of which train station they had arrived in London. The nearest police station to Broad Street is Bishopsgate and it would seem obvious that a cabman would take the coats there during the dead time between jobs. It was also alleged that when Butt asked him for his badge he pulled it out of his pocket and returned it there before Butt could take the number. The magistrate, Alderman Sir Thomas White, was not as forgiving as other magistrates and that Abbott "must be taught that he must not lose his temper when officers were in the execution of their duty came to him on public business." Abbott was fined 10s and costs for abusive language towards Inspector Butt, plus a further fine of 1s and costs for not showing his badge.[101]

Lost property deposited at a police station and not claimed within three months of the last day of the month in which the property reaches the police station may be returned to the driver or sold and an award made to him.

When an unnamed cabman put his cab up for the night after finishing his shift in early October 1887, the horse keeper noticed a pair of binoculars in the cab and handed them to the driver. He in turn deposited them at the Lost Property Office at Scotland Yard. After waiting three months he returned to the office to either claim his award if the binoculars had been collected, or to come away with the glasses themselves. He was to be disappointed. Although he had handed the binoculars to the police, it was the horse keeper who the police handed them over to. The driver now sought advice from D'Eyncourt, the Westminster magistrate, as to what action he should take. The only advice the magistrate could offer, was that if he wanted to take a summons out against the officers at Scotland Yard, for handing the property to somebody who was not entitled to it, he should go to Bow Street police court, as it was in their jurisdiction, not his.[102]

Another unlucky driver was the taxi driver who handed in a "string of graduated pearls, with a diamond and emerald clasp" in September 1923. The necklace, that had an estimated value of £400 remained unclaimed. Just days before the driver could claim it as his own, the police advertised it in the hope of finding the owner. A woman from Chelsea came forward and took ownership of the necklace, just two days before the driver could have claimed it. He would have received a reward but no amount was mentioned by the press and no reason was given why he had to wait six months to claim the clasp, instead of the regulatory three months.[103]

If the property is claimed the driver may be awarded a reasonable sum to be decided by TfL.

In 1836 a very absent-minded banking clerk left behind a carpet bag in a cab which contained bank notes and securities to the value of £100,000 (at least £8,000,000 by today's standards). A rather measly reward of £10 (0.01%) was offered and some officers were despatched with hand bills to the various cab stands. Fortunately for the clerk, the carpet bag was located and two cabmen and a passenger, who first laid his hand on the bag, were each rewarded with £10.[104] Later that same year a driver put his coach onto the stand in Trafalgar Square and sat inside, no doubt to keep warm on the cold December night. There he found a brown paper bag containing "diamonds and other jewellery" to the value of £2000. The four women who hired his coach did not realise their loss for half an hour and had no idea of the coach number, what the driver looked like, or even what colour the coach was. No doubt the rest of the evening was spent contemplating on their loss instead of enjoying the ball. However, when they returned home they found that the hackney coachman had returned the jewels to the house where he had originally picked the ladies up from. No mention was made of any reward.[105] In 1838 a man ran breathlessly into the Stamp Office at Somerset House, reporting that a short time ago he had left a pocket book in a cab containing notes and securities to the value of £23,000. As with such absent-minded people, who naturally have more money than sense, he had no recollection of the plate number nor a description of the cab or driver. Just as he was finishing his statement in rushed another breathless man. This was the driver. He only noticed the pocket book as he was about to pick up another passenger. On examining its contents, he saw their value and drove straight to Somerset House. The gentleman may have been absent minded but he was generous. The driver was rewarded with £200 and a further £100 was donated to the Stamp Office for payment as rewards.[106]

In 1847, cab driver Timothy Sherman, was before Arnold at Worship Street Police Court. His passenger, Mr Nichols, alleged that on July 21st, he hired Sherman to drive him to the Eastern Counties Terminus at Shoreditch and when they arrived, he proffered 2s as being the correct fare. Sherman demanded (the somewhat obligatory) 6d extra but Nichols refused to pay. Sherman grabbed hold of the passenger's collar and a tussle occurred between them. At that moment, Mrs Nichols, who had walked on ahead, returned to say her shawl was still in the cab. On hearing this Sherman let go of his passenger and climbed on the box, driving off as quick as he could. Nichols gave chase and just as he was reaching out to open the cab door, Sherman pulled up sharply, dismounted and "thrust [Nichols] back with great violence". Telling him as he did so that as he had given so much trouble to him, he, [Nichols], could go to the trouble of collecting the shawl from the Lost Property Office at Somerset House. In court, Sherman explained to Arnold that he had an obligation to deposit whatever property left in his cab at Somerset House and that he "had used no more force than was necessary to effect that object." Arnold was unconcerned with this line of defence. To him it was obvious that Sherman had tried to exact more money from his passenger than what he was legally entitled to and that his "object" was nothing more than revenge because he failed in his bid to exact more money. Sherman was fined £3 and in default of payment he was sent to the House of Correction for six weeks.[107]

The *Morning Post* described the "Cabmen's trick," keeping property so they could deposit it and claim the reward, as "an exercise of the ugly ingenuity" that the trade could resort to. The newspaper highlighted the case of a gentleman arriving at Paddington Station where the very "obsequious" cabman, helped unload his luggage and quickly drove off. The passenger noticed straight away that the gun case was missing, and as the planned trip was a shooting party, there was no point in catching the train so he returned to his home. On his way home he was informed by a policeman, who somehow knew that the cabman who had taken him to Paddington was at that moment depositing the gun case at Broad Street in order to claim the reward. The gentleman rushed around to the office and informed the commissioners that he was the victim of a ploy by the cabman and that payment of a reward was nothing more than extortion. The commissioners had some sympathy for the gentleman but the reward system was initiated to prevent the drivers from keeping the property and selling it on elsewhere. If rewards were not paid to the cabmen, then much property would never get restored to its owners. The gentleman did get his guns back but only on the payment of 10s, which was somewhat less than the cabman expected, the commissioners having agreed to reduce the reward in this instance.[108]

It was to be the society wedding of the year, Lord Stavordale was to marry Lady Vane-Tempest-Stewart, daughter of the Earl of Londonderry. On January 20th, 1902, just five days before the big occasion, Lord Stavordale took a cab to his fiancée's home, Londonderry House, on Park Lane (the Metropolitan Hotel now stands on the site). He had with him in the cab a parcel of jewellery, comprising jewels that were not only his own but including ten presents for his intended wife. "Apparently he had no thought but for his bride, for on reaching Londonderry House he hurriedly discharged his cabman and sought Lady Helen, only to remember when he reached her that he had left the priceless parcel of jewellery in the cab."[109]

Francis Howell, 15320, had pulled onto a nearby stand when he noticed the parcel in the back of his cab. Just as he was inspecting it a cab whistle alerted him to a fare. He put the parcel into the nosebag from which the horse had just been feeding from, then hooked it to his dickey seat as he picked up the next fare. And there the bag, containing its mix of worthless straw and priceless jewels, including "an exquisite diamond and turquoise brooch" donated by the King and Queen, and other priceless items from other members of the royal family, hung freely from the side of the cab. For over an hour the bag swung from the dickey and it was not until he finally got home that after telling his wife about the parcel, it was retrieved from the nosebag. Realising how close he had come to losing a fortune, albeit somebody else's, Francis took the jewels to Scotland Yard later that morning.[110] A much relieved Lord Stavordale retrieved them the same day, just four days before his wedding at St Peter's, Eaton Square.

Francis William Howell was the hero of the day and he was due for a large reward, but it was not to be his first reward as a cabman. Seven years previously he had, according to the judge, been instrumental in detaining a 72-year old man, who had stolen a bag from Fenwick's department store. He was commended by the Grand Jury and awarded 10s plus his expenses. There may not appear to be much kudos in detaining a septuagenarian but the man was a habitual criminal and was sentenced to four month's hard labour despite his age.[111]

After Lord Stavordale had reclaimed his jewels there was much speculation in the press as to what reward Howell would be entitled to. The 'priceless' jewels were said to have an estimated value of at least £70,000 and that Howell would be entitled to at least 10% of that figure, others put it at 15%. Several cabmen were more cautious, the reward was set at the discretion of the Commissioner of Police, Sir Edward Henry; others stated that for the reward to have any real value, it would depend on the generosity of Lord Stavordale himself. So how much reward did Francis Howell receive? It is not recorded in the newspapers of the time. After the marriage, the newlyweds in all certainty went on a honeymoon and the bounty to be enjoyed by Howell was forgotten by the press. All that can be said for certain is that it did not change his life. In the census of 1911, he is still listed as a horse cab driver, one of the few of the period still clinging to animal power, whilst many of his colleagues were driving taxicabs.

A taxi driver named Sedgwick possibly fared better than Howell when he found £1000 worth of securities in his taxi in 1916. He handed them into Scotland Yard's Lost Property Office, where they were later claimed by a Russian noble. Sedgwick's initial reward was the statutory £36, based on the sliding scale of awards, but the Russian nobleman invited the taxi driver around to his home where he was treated lavishly. As he left, he was handed an envelope that contained £100, "which enabled him to purchase his own taxicab"[112] – or at least pay a third towards a new one.

The reputation of London's taxi drivers, and the officers at the Lost Property Office were enhanced in America where the efficacy of both made front page news. In the summer of 1927 a Mrs Meyer Rubach left her handbag in a taxi as she hurried to catch the boat train from Waterloo to Southampton. It was only when she arrived home, at Newark, New Jersey, that she could write a letter to Scotland Yard informing them of her loss. She did not know the name, nor badge number of the driver, nor did she notice the plate number either. All she did manage to notice was that the taxi was black. It took nearly a year but Mrs Rubach eventually had her bag returned to her without a single item missing.[113]

Last Word

Many thanks for purchasing this book and I hope you enjoyed it. There is plenty more 'Black Cab Lore' out there. The second volume will not only include the chapters I omitted this time around, but I will also re-visit chapters included in this book with not only tales from yester-year, but more up-to-date stories from contemporary taxi drivers.

If you, whether as a cab driver or a passenger, have a story you think should be included, then please send me an email at

captain.bailey1634@virginmedia.com

This email can also be used to contact me regarding this book.

Be Lucky,

Sean Farrell

Driver's Index

The following is a list of drivers and proprietors whose name appear within the text. Numbers in parenthesis following the names are badge numbers; (od) after a name denotes an owner driver, whilst (p) denotes a proprietor but one who may also be an owner driver.

Index

1 Taxi Drivers Licences & Badges

[1]   May, Trevor *Gondolas & Growlers. The History of the London Horse Cab* p26 Alan Sutton 1995

[2]   *The Standard* 15th August 1828

[3]   *Morning Post* 30th December 1829

[4]   *Morning Post* 5th June 1834

[5]   *The Observer* 29th September 1833

[6]   *The Observer* 15th September 1833

[7]   *The Standard* 14th July 1836

[8]   *Morning Post* 2nd June 1838

[9]   *Morning Chronicle* 18th October 1838

[10] *The Standard* 1st September 1842

[11] *Daily News* 18th February 1850

[12] *Daily News* 7th February 1846

[13] Daily News 4th December 1862

[14] *The Standard* 4th February 1865

[15] *London Cabs and Cabmen's Grievances* by Ex-Cabby Pam 7385 Guildhall Library

[16] *Morning Post* 20th October 1838

[17] *Morning Post* 20th October 1838

[18] *The Standard* 27th October 1838

[19] *Morning Chronicle* 21st April 1841

[20] *Morning Chronicle* 13th August 1841

[21] *Morning Chronicle* 28th December 1842

[22] *Daily News* 27th August 1847

[23] *Morning Post* 11th October 1847

[24] *Morning Chronicle* 24th May 1850

[25] Mayhew, Henry *London Labour and the London Poor.* 1851

[26] *Morning Chronicle* 17th December 1859

[27] *Morning Chronicle* 26th September 1860

[28] *The Standard* 8th March 1880

[29] *Daily Express* 18th February 1903

[30] *The Standard* 28th July 1891

[31] *The Standard* 13th April 1894

[32] *Morning Post* 18th March 1874

[33] *Daily News* 30th September 1867

[34] *London Hackney Carriage Act* 1843 para. 10

[35] *Morning Post* 4th October 1862

[36] *Morning Post* 30th August 1876

[37] *Morning Post* 4th August 1852

[38] *Reynolds Newspaper* 16th June 1878

[39] *The Standard* 2nd November 1878

[40] *The York Herald* 16th February 1875

[41] *The York Herald* 13th April 1875

[42] *Pall Mall Gazette* 15th April 1895

[43] *Daily Mirror* 1st December 1916

[44] Pepys, Samuel *Diary* February 6th 1668. Ed Henry B Wheatley. G Bell & Sons 1962

[45] *The Times* 10th October 1838

[46] *The Standard* 23rd August 1845

[47] *Morning Chronicle* 23rd July 1853

[48] Warren, Philip *The History of the Knowledge of London* p7 London Publishing Company 2003

[49] May, Trevor *Op cit.* p99

[50] May, Trevor *Op cit.* p85

[51] Charley, W T *A Handy Book of the Law of London Cabs and Omnibuses* p56 London 1867

[52] *Daily News* 25th November 1897

[53] *Hansard House of Commons Debate* 09 March 1915 vol 70 cc1269-70W1270W

[54] Ex-Cabby *London Cabs and Cabmen's Grievances* p5 Guildhall Library pam 7385

[55] *Morning Post* 11th June 1888

[56] *Daily News* 26th July 1890

[57] Gordon, W J. *The Horse World of London* p43-44 J A Allen, London 1893

[58] Daily Mirror 16th May 1906

[59] *Action* 3rd September 1938

[60] May, Trevor *Op cit.* p99

[61] *Daily Express* 11th June 1910

[62] *Daily Mirror* 6th June 1904

[63] *The Times* 2nd April 1907

[64] *Old Bailey Proceedings Online* (www.oldbaileyonline.org, version 8.0, 16 October 2018), December 1910, trial of ELLERINGTON, Henry (64, chauffeur) (t19101206-30).

[65] *Old Bailey Proceedings Online* (www.oldbaileyonline.org, version 8.0, 16 October 2018), March 1910, trial of VARDY, George William (57, motor-driver) (t19100308-22).

[66] *The Standard* 30th September 1896

[67] *Morning Post* 1st October 1896

[68] *Daily Mirror* 3rd May 1911

[69] *Daily Express* 29th April 1915

[70] *Daily Express* 20th May 1915

[71] *Daily Express* 13th February 1917

[72] *The Times* 14th February 1917

[73] *The Times* 14th February 1917

[74] *Daily Mirror* 2nd September 1908

[75] Armstrong, Anthony. *Taxi!* Hodder & Staunton. London 1930

[76] *Daily Mirror* 14th February 1917

[77] *The Times* 15th February 1917

[78] *The Times* 16th March 1917

[79] *Daily Express* 19th May 1917

[80] Lucinda Gosling *Great War Britain: The First World War at Home.* The History Press. 2015

[81] *The Times* 24th October 1917

[82] Warren, Philip *The History of the Knowledge of London* pp37-38

[83] ibid p38

[84] *The Times* 9th July 1919

[85] *The Times* 10th July 1919

[86] Levinson, Maurice *Taxi!* p63

[87] Geake, Walter *What Next?* P191

[88] Ibid p42

[89] Warren, Philip *The History of the Knowledge of London* p63 London Publishing Company 2003

[90] *The Spokesman Review* 22nd April 1967

[91] *The Standard* 5th April 1894

[92] *Morning Post* 7th September 1810

[93] *Morning Chronicle* 10th January 1817

[94] May, Trevor *Op cit.* p35

[95] *The Observer* 26th May 1833

[96] *The Observer* 29th June 1834

[97] *Daily News* 30th March 1849

[98] Moore, Henry Charles *Omnibuses and Cabs – Their Origin and History* p261 London 1902

[99] *Morning Post* 28th March 1878

[100] Author's own research, unpublished

[101] *The Standard* 11th September 1888

[102] Author's own research, unpublished

[103] *Morning Post* 2nd September 1893

[104] *The Spectator* 16th September 1893

[105] *Call Sign* December 2008 p3

[106] *The Times* 28th November 1912

[107] *Daily Mirror* 9th January 1913

[108] Honeycombe, Gordon *The Murders of the Black Museum 1870-1970* p217. Arrow. 1982

[109] *ibid*

[110] *The Times* 27th July 1911

[111] Warren, Philip *The History of the Knowledge of London* pp31-32

[112] *Ibid* p33

[113] Maxwell Stamp, The Hon A. *Report of the Departmental Committee on the London Taxi Trade*. Para. 8.42 London 1970

[114] Fisher, Alan *Call Sign* January 2009 p38

[115] Fisher, Alan *Call Sign* September 2011 page 5

[116] *The Standard* 15th August 1862

[117] *The Standard* 31st March 1875

[118] Levinson, Maurice *Taxi!* p61

[119] *Morning Chronicle* 18th October 1838

[120] *Lloyds Weekly Newspaper* 29th December 1844

[121] *Daily News* 15th August 1846

[122] *The Standard* 17th September 1846

[123] *The Standard* 17th September 1846

[124] *The Era* 27th September 1846

[125] *The Observer* 21st January 1849

[126] *Morning Chronicle* 4th September 1848

[127] *The Era* 6th February 1848

[128] *The Standard* 7th September 1858

[129] *Morning Chronicle* 2nd February 1857

[130] *Morning Post* 3rd May 1858

[131] *Reynolds Newspaper* 30th June 1861

[132] *Morning Post* 29th November 1858

[133] *Daily News* 29th November 1859

[134] *Daily News* 27th February 1877

[135] *Old Bailey Proceedings Online* (www.oldbaileyonline.org, version 8.0, 16 October 2018), July 1888, trial of THOMAS POSGATE (48) (t18880730-726).

[136] *The Standard* 27th September 1886

[137] *Morning Post* 23rd August 1888

[138] *The Standard* 21st February 1893

[139] *Morning Post* 15th September 1890

[140] *Pall Mall Gazette* 18th September 1890

[141] Garwood, John *A Million People City* p181

http://www.victorianlondon.org/publications4/peopled.htm

[142] *Morning Post* 17th June 1844

[143] *Morning Chronicle* 25th September 1855

[144] *Morning Post* 11th November 1845

[145] *The Observer* 13th November 1853

[146] *The Standard* 24th April 1865

[147] *The Observer* 7th January 1866

[148] *The Times* 4th January 1922

[149] *Morning Post* 2nd November 1839

[150] *Morning Post* 6th November 1839

[151] *Morning Chronicle* 17th March 1856

[152] *The Standard* 7th January 1858

[153] *Daily News* 21st January 1867

[154] *Morning Post* 26th September 1892

2 Taxi Licences, Plates, Notices and Marks

1 *Morning Post* 18th April 1844

2 *Morning Post* 22nd September 1817

3 *The Observer* 23rd March 1823

4 *Morning Post* 20th December 1832

5 *Morning Post* 9th March 1832

6 *Morning Chronicle* 18th March 1833

7 *Morning Post* 18th September 1850

8 *Morning Chronicle* 17th September 1850

9 *Morning Post* 4th January 1853

10 *Daily News* 24th April 1854

11 *Morning Post* 18th March 1869

12 *Pall Mall Gazette* 27th March 1867

13 Munro, Bill *London Taxis A Full History* p212 Earlswood Press, 2011

3 Plying for Hire

1 *The Observer* 6th March 1836

2 *The Observer* 19th August 1838

3 *Old Bailey Proceedings Online* (www.oldbaileyonline.org, version 8.0, 16 October 2018), November 1856, trial of GEORGE COLE GEORGE BROWN (t18561124-58).

4 *Morning Post* 25th December 1838

5 *Morning Post* 16th April 1851

6 *Morning Post* 20th August 1849

7 *Morning Post* 30th November 1849

8 *The Standard* 14th October 1851

9 *Daily News* 31st July 1851

10 *Morning Chronicle* 5th March 1857

[11] *Daily News* 10th July 1858

[12] Charley, WT. p81 *Op Cit.*

[13] *The Standard* 18th August 1897

[14] *The Times* 2nd December 1948

[15] *The Standard* 4th September 1895

[16] *Morning Post* 28th November 1853

[17] *The Times* 4th January 1922

[18] *The Standard* 3rd July 1862

[19] *Morning Post* 1st November 1862

[20] *The Times* 11th April 1919

[21] *Daily Mirror* 5th August 1965

4 Offences Relating to the Conduct of Drivers

[1] *The Times* 23rd December 1926

[2] *Daily News* 25th November 1897

[3] *Morning Post* 22nd December 1857

[4] *Morning Chronicle* 26th April 1861

[5] *Morning Chronicle* 8th July 1861

[6] *The Era* 19th July 1863

[7] *The Observer* 25th October 1863

[8] *The Standard* 1st January 1870

[9] *Morning Post* 29th January 1870

[10] *Reynold's Newspaper* 27th February 1870

[11] *The Observer* 7th January 1872

[12] *Daily News* 1st September 1876

[13] *The Standard* 3rd February 1899

[14] *The Standard* 4th February 1899

15 *Daily News* 27th February 1899

16 *The Standard* 4th March 1899

17 *The Standard* 25th March 1899

18 *Morning Post* 31st May 1899

19 *Daily Express* 26th September 1903

20 *Daily Express* 28th September 1903

21 *The Times* 2nd May 1911

22 *The Times* 16th February 1934

23 Hodge, Herbert *Cab Sir?* p233

24 *Daily Mirror* 1st December 1959

25 *The Times* 4th February 1960

26 *The Times* 24th March 1960

27 *The Standard* 22nd September 1871

28 *The Standard* 26th September 1871

29 Peacham, Henry *Coach & Sedan, Pleasantly Disputing for Place Precedence*, p38 London 1636

30 Pepys, Samuel *Diary*. June 13th 1663 *Op Cit.*

31 *Morning Post* 15th March 1832

32 *Morning Post* 18th August 1837

33 *Morning Post* 30th August 1837

34 *Morning Post* 22nd August 1870

35 *The Standard* 31st July 1874

36 *Morning Post* 7th August 1874

37 *Pall Mall Gazette* 12th June 1876

38 *Morning Post* 2nd April 1874

39 Charley, W.T. p115 *Op Cit.*

40 *Morning Post* 31st December 1828

41 *The Observer* 14th October 1838

42 *Morning Post* 31st October 1838

43 *The Times* 9th November 1838

44 *The Standard* 30th September 1853

45 *Daily News* 4th February 1854

46 May, Trevor *Op Cit* p8

47 *The Observer* 7th October 1855

48 *The Standard* 14th April 1858

49 *The Observer* 17th November 1861

50 *Daily News* 16th July 1879

51 *Pall Mall Gazette* 24th September 1879

52 *Daily News* 27th December 1879

53 *The Standard* 5th November 1889

54 *The Standard* 12th July 1890

55 *Morning Post* 9th January 1896

56 *Lloyds Weekly* 7th November 1880

57 *The Standard* 11th September 1897

58 *The Times* 2nd March 1904

59 *The Times* 21st July 1908

60 *The Times* 19th October 1908

61 *The Standard* 11th September 1857

62 *Morning Post* 22nd April 1865

63 *Pall Mall Gazette* 30th November 1876

64 *Morning Post* 24th February 1882

65 *Morning Post* 22nd August 1878

66 *Reynold's Newspaper* 19th April 1896

67 *The Standard* 30th December 1895

68 *Daily News* 15th September 1900

[69] *The Times* 17th June 1914

[70] *Daily Mirror* 22nd May 1917

[71] *Daily Mirror* 21st August 1919

[72] *Daily News* 17th February 1855

[73] *Daily News* 14th July 1851

[74] *Morning Chronicle* 3rd March 1853

[75] *Daily News* 18th July 1853

[76] *The Observer* 10th August 1856

[77] *Daily News* 13th August 1856

[78] *The Standard* 18th August 1856

[79] *The Standard* 17th August 1895

[80] *Daily Express* 9th October 1901

[81] *Daily Express* 9th October 1901

[82] *The Times* 27th November 1902

[83] *Morning Post* 27th February 1854

[84] *Reynolds Newspaper* 21st September 1890

[85] *The Standard* 10th February 1866

[86] *Daily News* 14th January 1880

5 Taxi Ranks

[1] Birch, Clive *Carr and Carman* 38-39 Baron Books 1999

[2] *'Plays and players'*, Analytical index to the series of records known as the *Remembrancia*: 1579-1664 (1878), pp. 350-357 http://www.british-history.ac.uk/report.aspx?compid=59965

[3] *Calendar of State Papers Domestic 1634-35* Ed by John Bruce. p8 London 1866

[4] *Calendar of State Papers Domestic 1634-35* Ed by John Bruce. London 1866

[5] *Calendar of State Papers Domestic 1636* Ed by John Bruce. P35 London 1866

[6] *'Middlesex Sessions Rolls: 1648'*, *Middlesex county records: Volume 3: 1625-67* (1888), pp. 102-105.

http://www.british-history.ac.uk/report.aspx?compid=66040&strquery=hackney

[7] *Morning Post* 8th November 1826

[8] *Morning Chronicle* 7th March 1832

[9] *Morning Chronicle* 8th March 1832

[10] *Morning Chronicle* 13th March 1832

[11] *The Observer* 7th July 1839

[12] *Morning Chronicle* 21st November 1839

[13] *Morning Post* 29th December 1835

[14] *The Observer* 27th January 1845

[15] *Morning Post* 16th November 1846

[16] *Daily News* 18th December 1846

[17] *The Era* 3rd April 1853

[18] *Lloyds Weekly Newspaper* 3rd April 1853

[19] *The Observer* 7th Feb 1875

[20] *Morning Post* 24th February 1875

[21] *Morning Post* 28th July 1875

[22] *Daily News* 2nd October 1875

[23] *Morning Chronicle* 2nd January 1854

[24] *Morning Chronicle* 16th January 1854

[25] *Daily News* 8th March 1854

[26] Beauchamp, Henry *The Interesting Adventures of a Hackney Coach as Related by the Coachman* p6   London 1813

[27] *The Observer* 24th September 1837

[28] *Morning Post* 1st March 1843

[29] *The Observer* 10th February 1839

[30] *Morning Post* 21st March 1879

6 Fares

1   Walford, Edward *Old & New London* Vol. 3 p333 Cassell & Co London 1897

2   *Calendar of State Papers Domestic* 1634 Ed by John Bruce. London 1866

3   Warren, Philip, *The History of the Cab Trade* p26 Taxi Trade Promotions. London. 1995

4   Warren, Philip, *The History of the Cab Trade ibid*

5   *Diary of Samuel Pepys* 21st April 1667 *Op Cit.*

6   Diary of Samuel Pepys 11th May 1667 *Op Cit.*

7   *Old Bailey Proceedings Online* (www.oldbaileyonline.org, version 8.0, 16 October 2018), July 1680, trial of Mr. Doughty Mr. Hambleton (t16800707-8).

8   *Old Bailey Proceedings Online* (www.oldbaileyonline.org, version 8.0, 16 October 2018), June 1714, trial of C-- G-- (t17140630-42).

9   *Daily Universal Register* [The Times] 22nd August 1786

10 Warren, Philip, *The History of the Cab Trade* p92 *Op Cit*

11 *Morning Post* 23rd May 1828

12 *The Times* 27th October 1824

13 *Morning Post* 2nd April 1829

14 *Morning Chronicle* 3rd June 1829

15 *Morning Post* 16th February 1831

16 *Morning Post* 15th December 1831

17 *Morning Chronicle* 5th January 1832

18 *Morning Chronicle* 19th January 1832

19 *Morning Post* 19th January 1832

20 *The Standard* 6th August 1838

21 *The Standard* 22nd October 1838

22 *The Charter* 25th August 1839

23 *Morning Post* 9th October 1839

24 *Morning Post* 10th October 1839

25 *Morning Chronicle* 16th October 1839

26   *Morning Post* 11th January 1872

27   *The Standard* 19th May 1851

28   *The Standard* 7th July 1851

29   *Dictionary of National Biography*, Henry Shrapnel

30   *The Times* 30th January 1852

31   Shrapnel, Captain N. Scrope, *Stradametric Survey of London*, Wm Grigg, London 1852

32   *Daily News* 6th September 1852

33   *The Standard* 25th October 1852

34   *The Times* 19th September 1853

35   *The Observer* 30th May 1853

36   *Daily News* 20th July 1853

37   *Daily News* 22nd July 1853

38   *Daily News* 22nd July 1853

39   *Daily News* 23rd July 1853

40   *Reynolds Newspaper* 24th July 1853

41   *Daily News* 25th July 1853

42   *Daily News, Morning Post* et al 25th July 1853

43   *The Standard* 30th July 1853

44   *Morning Post* 19th August 1853

45   *Daily News* 26th July 1853

46   *Morning Chronicle & Morning Post* 7th February 1854

47   *The Observer* 12th February 1854

48   *Morning Chronicle* 24th February 1854

49   *Morning Chronicle* 16th August 1854

50   *The Standard* 21st August 1854

51   *Morning Post* 4th August 1854

52   *The Standard* 5th August 1854

[53] *Morning Post* 8th August 1854

[54] *Morning Post* 10th August 1854

[55] *The Times* 6th October 1824

[56] *The Observer* 26th September 1858

[57] Cussans, J E. http://www.welwyn.org.uk/aythis/aythis.htm

[58] *ibid*

[59] *The Observer* 20th November 1870

[60] *The Observer* 15th January 1871

[61] *The Observer* 22nd & 29th October 1871

[62] *The Sheffield and Rotherham Independent* 24th November 1871

[63] J.E. Cussans *Op cit.*

[64] *Morning Post* 13th May 1872

[65] *Leeds Mercury* 1st February 1873

[66] *Lloyds Weekly* 16th November 1873

[67] *Manchester Guardian* 16th September 1874

[68] *Lloyds Weekly Newspaper* 26th September 1874

[69] *The Observer* 27th September 1874

[70] *The Observer* 4th October 1874

[71] *Pall Mall Gazette* 16th October 1874

[72] *Manchester Guardian* 10th October 1874

[73] *The Morning Post* 12th October 1874

[74] *Lloyds Weekly Newspaper* 11th October 1874

[75] *Pall Mall Gazette* 16th October 1874

[76] *The Observer* 22nd November 1874

[77] *Punch* March 6th 1875 p106

[78] *Morning Post* 28th January 1875

[79] *Daily News* 6th February 1875

80 *The Standard* 9th June 1875

81 *Western Mail* 12th June 1875

82 *Daily News* 30th September 1875

83 *Daily News* 16th October 1875

84 *Daily News* 4th January 1875

85 *Lloyds Weekly Newspaper* 31st October 1875

86 *The Standard* 6th November 1875

87 *Liverpool Mercury* 19th January 1881

88 *The Straits Times* 22nd January 1883

89 *Reynolds Newspaper* 28th November 1886

90 *Pall Mall Gazette* 10th May 1890

91 *The Universal Register* 11th October 1786

92 *Morning Post* 3rd August 1814

93 *Morning Chronicle* 1st September 1814

94 *Morning Post* 3rd September 1814

95 *Morning Chronicle* 16th September 1814

96 *Morning Post* 9th September 1814

97 *The Examiner* 18th September 1814

98 *Morning Post* 24th September 1814

99 Simpson, GK. *Henry Fielding Justice Observed* p17. Vision & Barnes & Noble 1985

100 *Morning Post* 24th September 1814

101 *Morning Post* 4th October 1814

102 *Morning Post* 8th October 1814

103 *Morning Post* 21st October 1814

104 *Daily News* 18th July 1853

105 *Daily News* 20th August 1853

106 *The Standard* 2nd September 1853

[107] *Morning Chronicle* 3rd September 1853

[108] *Daily News* 6th October 1853

[109] *The Observer* 10th October 1853

[110] *Morning Post* 21st September 1853

[111] *The Observer* 1st January 1854

[112] *The Observer* 8th January 1854

[113] *Morning Post* 3rd January 1854

[114] *Morning Chronicle* 18th March 1856

[115] *The Standard* 6th February 1855

[116] *Daily News* 4th August 1871

[117] *Morning Chronicle* 12th September 1856

[118] *Daily News* 2nd February 1876

[119] *Daily News* 30th January 1879

7 Taximeters

[1] Evelyn, John, *The Diary of John Evelyn* Vol. 1 p324 Everyman Library, London 1966

[2] *Letter to The Representatives of London, Westminster, and Southwark on the Subject of Hackney Coach Fares by Distance and a Proposed Method of Preventing Imposition on the Public.* J W Lee. London 1828

[3] *Caledonian Mercury* 4th February 1847

[4] *The Era* 30th May 1847

[5] *Morning Post* 6th December 1851

[6] *Daily News* 25th August 1852

[7] *Morning Post* 1st September 1856

[8] *The Observer* 3rd October 1858

[9] *Birmingham Daily Post* 15th December 1864

[10] *Morning Post* 18th November 1896

[11] *Lloyds Weekly Newspaper* 19th March 1899

[12] *The Standard* 17th April 1899

[13] *The Standard* 16th June 1899

[14] *London Gazette* 31st August 1900. Issue 27225, page 5418

[15] Munro, Bill *London Taxis A Full History* pp 16-18. Earlswood Press 2011

[16] *Daily Mirror* 27th December 1933

[17] *Daily Mirror* 24th July 1905

[18] *Daily Mirror* 13th March 1906

[19] *The Times* 23rd January 1907

[20] *The Times* 12th February 1907

[21] *The Times* 22nd February 1907

[22] *Daily Mirror* 25th March 1907

[23] *Daily Mirror* 28th June 1907

[24] *The Times* 1st July 1907

[25] *The Times* 2nd July 1907

[26] *The Times* 29th October 1907

[27] May, Trevor *Op cit.* pp v & 166

[28] *Daily Mirror* 17th March 1908

[29] *The Times* 19th November 1909

[30] *The Times* 23rd November 1909

[31] *The Times* 6th February 1911

[32] *The Times* 2nd March 1911

[33] *Old Bailey Proceedings Online* (www.oldbaileyonline.org, version 8.0, 16 October 2018), December 1910, trial of ELLERINGTON, Henry (64, chauffeur) (t19101206-30).

[34] *The Times* 10th June 1911

[35] *Old Bailey Proceedings Online* (www.oldbaileyonline.org, version 8.0, 16 October 2018), February 1911, trial of HUNTER, Henry John (44, motor-driver) (t19110228-19).

[36] *The Times* 26th June 1909

[37] *The Times* 17th & 19th July 1909

[38] *The Times* 6th November 1911

[39] *Daily Mirror* 25th September 1908

[40] *The Times* 6th April 1910

[41] *Commercial Motor* 28th April 1910

[42] *The Times* 31st May 1910

[43] *The Times* 21st June 1910

[44] *The Times* 25th October 1911

[45] *The Times* 2nd November 1911

[46] *Daily Mirror* 3rd November 1911

[47] *The Times* 6th November 1911

[48] *The Times* 8th November 1911

[49] *The Times* 9th November 1911

[50] *The Times* 10th November 1911

[51] *The Times* 12th January 1912

[52] *The Times* 1st April 1912

8 Bilking

[1] *Old Bailey Proceedings Online* (www.oldbaileyonline.org, version 8.0, 16 October 2018), September 1732, trial of William Flemming (t17320906-67).

[2] *Reynolds Newspaper* 12th August 1855

[3] *The Standard* 2nd June 1858

[4] *Morning Post* 13th April 1860

[5] *Morning Chronicle* 3rd March 1860

[6] *The Examiner* 21st April 1849

[7] *Morning Post* 24th April 1849

[8] *Daily News* 25th April 1849

[9] *Morning Post* 17th December 1849

10 *Morning Chronicle* 8th July 1823

11 *Morning Post* 18th November 1842

12 *Daily News* 13th October 1851

13 *Dictionary of National Biography* and Welch, Charles *The History of the Cutlers Company of London,* Volume II London 1923

14 *The Standard* 15th October 1851

15 *Morning Chronicle* 30th October 1839

16 *Daily News* 28th October 1886

17 *Morning Post* 10th January 1831

18 *Daily News* 4th December 1884

19 *Morning Post* 8th December 1884

20 *The Standard* 10th October 1900

21 *The Times* 25th December 1909

22 *The Times* 10th January 1910

23 *The Times* 4th May 1907

24 *Morning Post* 3rd October 1834

25 *Lloyds Weekly Newspaper* 23rd July 1843

26 *Lloyds Weekly Newspaper* 1st June 1845

27 *The Observer* 31st March 1867

28 *The Observer* 19th January 1862

29 *Morning Post* 7th March 1865

30 *Morning Chronicle* 13th February 1852

31 *The Standard* 14th February 1852

32 *The Standard* 19th February 1852

33 *Morning Post* 23rd February 1852

34 *Morning Chronicle* 26th February 1852

35 *The Standard* 13th November 1857

9 Carriage of Extra Person, Luggage Etc

1   *The Observer* 21st January 1816

2   *The Observer* 31st August 1823

3   *Morning Post* 27th January 1857

4   *The Times* 30th June 1917

5   *Daily Express* 24th October 1917

6   *The Observer* 17th July 1853

7   *Daily News* 20th July 1853

8   *The Observer* 17th July 1853

9   *The Observer* 24th July 1853

10   *The Standard* 29th July 1853

11   *Daily News* 20th October 1853

12   *Daily News* 20th June 1854

13   *The Standard* 23rd September 1854

14   *Daily News* 30th April 1879

15   *Lloyds Weekly Newspaper* 5th May 1861

16   *The Standard* 1st October 1877

17   Warren, Philip *The History of the Cab Trade* p26 *Op. Cit.*

18   *Morning Post* 30th January 1832

19   *The Observer* 10th November 1833

20   *Morning Chronicle* 27th January 1835

21   *Morning Chronicle* 29th July 1853

22   *Daily News* 29th November 1853

23   *The Observer* 30th July 1854

24   *The Standard* 14th April 1876

25   *Morning Post* 10th August 1863

26 Gilbert, WS *London Characters & the Humerous Side of London Life*, 1870 [Public domain]
   http://www.angelfire.com/ks/landzastanza/london.html

27 *Daily News* 31st December 1873

28 *Morning Post* 8th October 1883

29 *Morning Post* 13th October 1883

30 *The Standard* 14th July 1884

31 *Daily Mirror* 24th August 1907

32 *Daily Mirror* 31st August 1907

33 *The Times* 31st August 1907

34 *Morning Post* 5th February 1816

35 *Morning Post* 31st December 1853

36 *The Observer* 6th August 1854

37 *Daily News* 30th October 1854

38 *Morning Post* 24th November 1854

39 *Morning Chronicle* 17th December 1855

40 *Daily News* 30th January 1856

41 *Daily News* 6th February 1856

42 *Daily News* 23rd August 1856

43 *Daily News* 7th September 1857

44 *Daily News* 7th November 1861

45 *Daily News* 4th January 1862

46 *Daily News* 18th September 1862

47 *Morning Post* 19th September 1862

48 *The Observer* 27th April 1863

49 *The Observer* 25th December 1864

50 *Daily News* 12th September 1867

51 *Reynold's Newspaper* 15th January 1899

52 *The Standard* 12th April 1900

53 *The Times* 22nd May 1919

54   *The Times* 22nd October 1919

55   *Daily Mirror* 24th August 1929

56   *The Times* 20th July 1933

57   *The Observer* 7th July 1816

58   *The Observer* 25th August 1816

59   *The Observer* 11th December 1853

60   *Daily News* 14th December 1853

61   *The Observer* 14th September 1834

62   *The Observer* 16th December 1832

63   *Morning Post* 8th January 1863

64   *Morning Post* 17th February 1870

65   *Pall Mall Gazette* 8th January 1877

66   *Daily Mirror* 12th July 1910

67   *The Observer* 13th October 1867

68   *Pall Mall Gazette* 16th June 1879

69   *The Standard* 6th March 1883

70   *Diary of Samuel Pepys* February 6th 1663 *Op Cit.*

71   *The Observer* 4th October 1835

72   *Morning Post* 7th September 1870

73   *Morning Post* 23rd August 1893

74   *The Standard* 17th August 1899

75   *The Standard* 25th August 1899

76   *The Graphic* 2nd September 1899

77   *The Standard* 28th August 1899

10 Lost Property

[78] *The London Gazette*, 523, 17th November 1670

[79] *The Observer* 8th June 1829

[80] *The London Gazette* 25th September 1684

[81] *The Observer* 31st January 1858

[82] *Morning Post* 16th April 1846

[83] *Daily News* 22nd June 1859

[84] *Daily News* 27th December 1859

[85] *Daily News* 24th May 1882

[86] *Morning Post* 2nd October 1823

[87] *The Observer* 14th February 1847

[88] *Morning Post* 11th February 1847

[89] *Morning Chronicle* 12th March 1847

[90] *Morning Post* 26th July 1858

[91] *Morning Chronicle* 2nd August 1858

[92] *Daily News* 6th January 1862

[93] *The Observer* 12th January 1862

[94] *The Standard* 8th July 1867

[95] *The Observer* 26th July 1868

[96] *Morning Post* 24th September 1885

[97] *Morning Post* 9th September 1885

[98] *The Standard* 7th October 1885

[99] *Morning Post* 18th May 1871

[100] *Morning Post* 12th July 1873

[101] *The Standard* 14th August 1875

[102] *Daily News* 10th January 1888

[103] *The Times* 27th & 29th February 1924

[104] *The Observer* 4th December 1836

[105] *Morning Post* 27th December 1836

[106] *The Observer* 16th September 1836

[107] *Daily News* 6th August 1847

[108] *Morning Post* 1st November 1850

[109] *Daily Express* 23rd January 1902

[110] *Daily Express* 24th January 1902

[111] *Morning Post* 3rd September 1895

[112] *Daily Mirror* 14th April 1916

[113] *Daily Mirror* 9th April 1928

25230906R00248

Printed in Great Britain
by Amazon